A WOMAN'S
PLACE

A WOMAN'S
PLACE

WOMEN WRITING NEW MEXICO

Maureen E. Reed

University of New Mexico Press
Albuquerque

11 10 09 08 07 06 05   1 2 3 4 5 6 7

Library of Congress Cataloging-in-Publication Data

Reed, Maureen E., 1972–
  A woman's place : women writing New Mexico / Maureen E. Reed.
    p. cm.
  Includes bibliographical references.
  ISBN 0-8263-3346-X (pbk. : alk. paper)
   1. American literature—New Mexico—History and criticism. 2. American
literature—Women authors—History and criticism. 3. Authors, American—
Homes and haunts—New Mexico. 4. Women—New Mexico—Intellectual
life. 5. Women authors, American—Biography. 6. Women and literature—
New Mexico. 7. New Mexico—Intellectual life. 8. New Mexico—In litera-
ture. 9. Home in literature. I. Title.
  PS283.N6R44 2005
  813'.6—dc22
                                    2004023664

Cover Art: Pablita Velarde, *Communicating with the Full Moon*, 1962.
Courtesy of Mr. and Mrs. B.W. Miller. Copyright Pablita Velarde.

 Book design and composition by Damien Shay

Body type is Sabon 10/12
Display are OPTI Civet, Brush 455 and Trade Gothic

CONTENTS

ILLUSTRATIONS

ACKNOWLEDGMENTS

When biographers come to write the life of a woman—and this phenomenon has, of course, occurred with much greater frequency since the advent of contemporary feminism, let us say since the late 1960s—they have had to struggle with the inevitable conflict between the destiny of being unambiguously a woman and the woman subject's palpable desire, or fate, to be something else. Except when writing about queens, biographers of women have not, therefore, been at ease with their subjects—and even with queens, like Elizabeth I of England, there has been a tendency to see them as somewhat abnormal, monstrous. It is no wonder that biographers have largely ignored women as subjects.

> —Carolyn Heilbrun, *Writing a Woman's Life*, 1988

*W*riting a generation after Heilbrun, it is no longer possible to claim that biographers ignore women. Biographers, along with literary critics and historians in general, have developed ways of researching and writing about women's lives that recognize and illuminate the distinct circumstances that shape them. Moreover, these scholars have made it possible to see that, despite the ongoing desire of many driven women to "be something else," womanhood can also be powerful. In this book, I chronicle the lives of six New Mexican women writers in order to show how they used to their advantage the traditional notion that "a woman's place is in the home." By presenting their work as advocacy of such tradition, these women encouraged their readers to expand their conceptions of home to include the larger community, and they advocated a distinctive role in this larger community's affairs for Hispanic and American Indian women. On the other hand, the very conception of tradition these women relied on to secure their place also limited their ability to fulfill themselves.

Thus, even though a woman's place on the biography shelf is no longer in question, Heilbrun's arguments about women's conflicts of identity still ring true. In this book, I call such conflict "homesickness": I see it as the distance women have endured from the lives and homes they know are possible. I am grateful to scholars whose work on gender and ethnicity has enabled me to identify this distance and to attempt to illustrate it. Their efforts laid the foundation for this work of women's biography.

While the work of scholars like Heilbrun convinced me that this book needed to be written, it took the encouragement of others to persuade me to write it. I am deeply grateful to Desley Deacon, who served as my dissertation advisor at the University of Texas at Austin. She introduced me to Mary Austin and Mabel Dodge Luhan, and when I grew fascinated with why they sought homes in New Mexico, she helped me transform that interest into this book. Through her expertise in biography and modernism, as well as her continual demonstration of the importance of following curiosity where it leads, Desley inspired me to keep working. Laura Furman, who served on my dissertation committee, reminded me of the particular role creativity could play in writing life stories that could not be explained through analysis alone. I am also indebted to the other members of my committee: William Goetzmann, Jeffrey Meikle, and David Montejano, each of whom

◪ ACKNOWLEDGMENTS ◪

granted this project expertise in the diverse areas of American cultural history it draws from, while also encouraging me to forge my own path.

In the years since Heilbrun noted the lack of women's biography, many organizations have come to the aid of those who seek to write this much-needed form of history. This book has also benefited from grantors that recognize this necessity. At the University of Texas at Austin, a thematic fellowship in migration from the Graduate School (1998–99), a dissertation fellowship from Women's Studies (1999), and a Robert M. Crunden Memorial Research Award from the Department of American Studies (2000) all allowed me to pursue the diverse—and sometimes obscure—sources that lie at the heart of this project. An Andrew W. Mellon Foundation fellowship for one month of residency (August 1999) at the Huntington Library also aided me in my research. In 2002 and 2003, Minnesota State University Moorhead granted me Faculty Development funds with which to complete my research, secure illustrations, and create an index. I am honored that these benefactors shared my belief in the ability of research on New Mexican women's lives to contribute to a greater understanding of American culture.

Thanks to this funding, I was able to visit and correspond with many archives, and I am grateful for the assistance of those who took time to help me track down facets of these women's lives. I would especially like to thank Daphne S. O. Arnaiz-DeLeon at the New Mexico State Archives, Diane Block at the Palace of the Governors Photo Archives, Dennis Dailey at the New Mexico State University Library, Julie Frey at the Rye Historical Society, Sue Hodson at the Huntington Library, Tomas Jaehn at the Angélico Chávez History Library, Justin Parks at University of New Mexico Press, Gary Roybal at Bandelier National Monument, Deb Slaney at the Albuquerque Museum, Ted Sturm at the Indian Pueblo Cultural Center, and Patricia Willis at the Beinecke Library. Thanks also to Andy Deschenie, the librarian at the Tohaali' (Toadlena) Community School, who could not show me "papers" but did give me something even better: a personal tour of a place that Kay Bennett once called home.

When more formal paths of research failed, I gained much from the

☖ ACKNOWLEDGMENTS ☖

willingness of many people to speak with me about their experiences, as relatives and friends, with the women whose stories I tell here. Thanks to Andy Bennett, Martin Link, Rosa Montoya, Esther Branch Sánchez, Bonnie Shirley, J. Paul Taylor, and Mabel Yazzie; your stories made it possible to preserve the work of these women for future readers. Additionally, I am grateful for the assistance of Jane Miller, Jerry Miller, and Margarete Tindel, who ensured that Pablita Velarde's art would be part of this work.

Many colleagues and friends also played a part in making this book possible. I learned much from the research advice offered by Sally Hyer, Merrihelen Ponce, Marcella Ruch, and Lois Palken Rudnick, each of whom knew something I could only learn from them. Leilah Danielson, Kelly Willis Mendiola, and Jolly Corley, who joined me in writing groups in Austin and Moorhead, helped my commitment to this project to remain creative. In Moorhead, I learned much from sharing these southwestern women's stories with a midwestern audience; thanks to the MSUM American Studies and Women's Studies programs for providing me with a home to finish this work. I am particularly grateful to MSUM colleagues Christopher Corley, Peter Quigley, and Helen Sheumaker, who asked just the right questions and demonstrated how intellectualism can thrive even when day-to-day university tasks seem close to crowding it out. Thanks also to Carolyn Thomas de la Peña, who has offered me unfailing optimism and the insightful power of, in her words, an "American Studies mind" since our first day of graduate school. Carolyn continues to cheer me on from afar: her friendship exemplifies the power of collaboration.

I must also note my gratitude to the women whose struggles with "homesickness" serve as the subject of this book. I could not have found a more inspiring group of women to research than Mary Austin, Kay Bennett, Fabiola Cabeza de Baca, Cleofas Jaramillo, Mabel Dodge Luhan, and Pablita Velarde. I especially appreciate Pablita Velarde's willingness to speak with me about her life when she has already told the story so many times before. I hope that I have told it in a way that is pleasingly different.

▨ ACKNOWLEDGMENTS ▨

Because telling the stories of these women often required telling about their unhappy family experiences, I am very thankful for the continuing support my own family offered during this project. Though the generous words of encouragement offered by my parents, in-laws, siblings, siblings-in-law, aunts, uncles, and cousins have meant a great deal to me, I have been even more heartened by what they did not say: they never asked me if I was done yet, thus illustrating both their respect for the project and their lasting faith in my ability to complete it. My parents, James Reed and Nancy Huesmann Reed, are responsible for introducing me to New Mexico through family camping trips. Ensuring that our vacations were learning experiences is just one of many ways they made it impossible for me to fail when it came time to complete this book.

Finally, I offer thanks to my husband, Patrick Walsh, and to my son, Eamon Reed Walsh. Patrick, you are my best friend and my most encouraging reader; Eamon, you are the reason I keep writing. You give me a place that I am content to call my home; I dedicate this work to both of you.

INTRODUCTION
Homesickness

A certain kind of homesickness thrives in New Mexico. It is not a missing of home so much as a gnawing feeling that the home that is supposed to be there doesn't quite exist. It is a longing for the home promised by the state's motto, "The Land of Enchantment;" a home praised by travel books that describe the state as a harmonious host to Indian, Hispanic, and Anglo cultures; a home promoted by galleries selling Spanish colonial carvings, Indian pottery, and abstract paintings by Anglo Bohemians near the Santa Fe plaza. This ideal home possesses vibrant multiculturalism, a rich artistic heritage, and a prideful sense of history: according to this vision of the state, three cultures coexist peacefully in an environment of stark natural beauty.

Visitors to New Mexico often come because they want to see this home for themselves. But when they venture beyond the plazas and the galleries and the ceremonial dances, they may find themselves frustrated by traffic, saddened by poverty, dismayed by graffiti, lawsuits, and other evidence of contentious ethnic relationships. Where are the timeless traditions they yearned for back in New York, Los Angeles, or Dallas? Where is the home they felt such kinship with when they read

1

Fig. 1: Jewelry and Craft Market at the Palace of the Governors, Santa Fe. Courtesy of the New Mexico Department of Tourism.

magazine articles about the wonders of the Southwest? What happened to America's most beautiful multicultural place?

This homesickness could be dismissed as nostalgia, an all too predictable effect of a tourism industry fueled by unrealistic expectations. It is indeed related to the sort of fading idealism tourists experience anytime they visit a place about which they have heard much before arriving. But it is not only visitors who experience this particular sort of New Mexican homesickness. Residents also live with blatant contradictions between "The Land of Enchantment" and the reality of here and now.

This is a state where semi trucks, RVs, and SUVs speed past

✵ Homesickness ✵

Pueblo and Spanish villages predating the Mayflower, where the Los Alamos laboratory ushered in the atomic age not far from ancient cliff dwellings, where oil pumps work ceaselessly on land once granted to ranchers by Spanish kings, and where ski slopes fill with the wealthy while nearby others suffer some of the most abject poverty in the U.S.[1] This is a state where military conquests have more than once deprived people of their ability to feed (let alone govern) themselves, where fights over land remain unresolved decades after they began, and where citizens wage daily battles about whether the economic benefits of tourism and extractive industries are worth the costs they inflict on cultural integrity. This is a state where the idea of a tri-cultural heritage dominates even as it shuts out those residents who don't fit, including African and Asian Americans. Newcomers from Latin America and other parts of the United States may also have little sense of connection to a vision grounded so thoroughly in a tradition-bound past, especially when they encounter so many everyday discrepancies between the state's proclaimed multicultural heritage and its historical and economic realities. Their home is not what it claims to be. Like visitors who see past the glossy image put forth for tourists, New Mexicans can become homesick, even if they do not leave home.

This contradiction between image and reality is not a new development. Homesick New Mexicans have been wrestling with difficult questions about the identity of the state since even before it became a state in 1912. Can a place be modern and traditional at the same time? Can people honor a community's diverse heritage even as they also attempt to come together as a unified, modern society? And, more critically, is it always in the best interest of people to keep traditions "unchanged"? New Mexicans are not alone in attempting to answer these questions. Across the globe, but particularly in America, people have heralded the concept of "multiculturalism" as an ideal with the potential to resolve this dilemma. The concept is simple: multicultural ideals seek to build a society that draws strength from diversity instead of attempting to deny it, that honors multiple past traditions instead of trying to erase them, that imagines its citizenry without confines of race or religion instead of valuing only certain kinds of people.[2]

As with many ideals, multiculturalism's appeal can be strong enough to prevent those drawn to it from noting its full implications. The gap between the New Mexico promised by travelers' guidebooks and the New Mexico experienced by visitors and inhabitants testifies to potential shortcomings of multiculturalism; the particular experiences of women living in New Mexico also illustrate shortfalls in this doctrine. As they have in other places with strong multicultural traditions, New Mexican women have played a distinct role in keeping ties to multiple heritages intact. As perceived keepers of homes, they have passed down recipes, preserved folklore, and maintained customs. While such activities do not necessarily require that women lead traditional lives, women in New Mexico have experienced their own distinct form of homesickness in that they are perceived as needing to act traditionally in order to contribute to the state's multicultural mission.

If one were to believe the photos of women that grace the pages of tourism publications, one might suspect that all women of color in New Mexico are women bound by the past, whether they are taking part in dances, selling jewelry, or preparing and serving chile. Thus, New Mexico's maintenance of its multicultural image employs a sleight of hand that erases the distinction between pride in cultural heritage and strict confinement within it. If a culture remains intact, this logic assumes, then it has done so because of the conservative work of its homemakers. For many New Mexican women, being "homesick" means experiencing not only a gap between the home promised by guidebooks and the home they live in, but also a profound misunderstanding about the role they play in this home.

In order to understand *why* New Mexico continues boosting itself as an "enchanting" home, with "traditional" homekeepers, it is important to acknowledge the distinct history of the state within the context of United States history. The state's American Indian populations, as well as the continuous presence of Hispanic settlements since

fig. 2: *Hispanic Folklore Dancer.* Photograph by Lois Frank.
Courtesy of the Santa Fe Convention and Visitors Bureau.

the seventeenth century, do make the state stand out in terms of population, migration, and conquest patterns. In comparison to the eastern United States, the delayed rate at which New Mexico industrialized encouraged Anglos who settled in or visited the state to romanticize these preexisting cultures even as they themselves increasingly altered the patterns of living in the state. Readers who are new to New Mexican history will likely be struck in the narrative that follows by how "different" New Mexico is from other American states. But the stories that lie ahead also show how important it is to remember that the aura of "difference" associated with New Mexico's vibrant multiculturalism often masks the very modern forces of ethnic and economic conquest that have been at work there.

Anglo "pioneers" to New Mexico did, in fact, have cultural experiences that distinguish them from other groups of westering Americans. The state had been already "settled" several times: by a nonmigratory Pueblo population dating as far back as 2000 B.C., Spanish and Mexican migration that began in the sixteenth century, and the arrival of Navajo and Apache peoples in roughly the same period. When New Mexico became a state in 1912, nearly 60 percent of the population classified itself as "Hispano." This New Mexican term of choice (used somewhat interchangeably in this work with "Hispanic" and "nuevomexicano") referred to people of Spanish or Mexican descent who were lifelong residents of the state, just as their parents, grandparents, and often their great-grandparents had been before them. It served to differentiate this group of residents from Anglo and Mexican immigrants, as well as from American Indians.[3] In fact, Hispanos remained the largest ethnic group in New Mexico until the 1940s.[4] According to more recent data regarding ethnicity, from the U.S. Census 2000, non-Hispanic "Whites" or "Anglos" now make up the largest perceived ethnic group in New Mexico, at just under 45 percent of New Mexico's population, while individuals identifying as Hispanic make up a little over 42 percent. American Indians make up 9.5 percent.[5]

But, again, it was not until the late nineteenth and early twentieth centuries that Anglos made up a sizable portion of New Mexico's population. For Indian and Hispanic residents of New Mexico, the Anglo immigrants who came at this time may have seemed to differ little from the entrepreneurs and land-seekers who began arriving in the state even before the United States took control of the territory with the 1848 Treaty of Guadalupe Hidalgo. Yet the arrival of twentieth-century Anglo immigrants coincided with the beginning of a significant change in the philosophy of cultural relations in New Mexico. Through a complex process of nostalgia, romanticism, and primitivism, as well as a genuine desire for cultural preservation and future cultural understanding, this generation seized upon New Mexico's cultural diversity as an appealing, if not the most appealing, reason for Americans to visit and relocate to the state.

But why has this ideal remained only an ideal in New Mexico? Why do people end up feeling homesick for a home that doesn't really exist—and why are women perceived as guardians for this mythical home? As someone who has never called the state home, and as someone who has felt homesick for the New Mexico I was promised by books, I am the first to say that the fault is not with the place or the cultures, but with the boosters and visitors who have done the imagining. My many visits to New Mexico and my research about it began in a spirit of awe and hopeful idealism: I sought that perfect multicultural home, if not to live in, then to admire. While my fascination with the state has continued, my idealism has been tempered by a growing realization that my multicultural imaginings were flawed.

This book is an attempt to trace that flaw, and to bring about a greater awareness of it, through the life stories of six New Mexican women. While the multicultural dilemmas described above are hardly confined to women's experiences, the history of women's roles does offer one useful way of understanding how and why Americans have longed in vain for a New Mexican multicultural home that does not, and perhaps cannot, exist. In the United States, as elsewhere, women have served our ideals of cultural tradition, both in the labor they do to maintain traditions and in our symbolic vocabulary. In New Mexico, as the stories that follow reveal, women undertook extensive work as "cultural activists," documenting and popularizing diverse traditions. The six women whose stories I tell here stand out because of the sheer amount of labor they did: among other activities, they painted pictures, organized fiestas, collected recipes, exhibited crafts, and took public stands for tradition in newspaper and magazine interviews. But most of all, they left behind a rich source for historical inquiry, because they all wrote books about their personal efforts to sustain New Mexico as an ideal multicultural home. As I point out in each chapter, other scholars have analyzed many of these writings, and their work collectively demonstrates the complexities and contradictions of how the term culture has been used in New Mexico. This book benefits from such work, but it differs in using a biographical approach rather than one that is theoretical, historical, literary, or anthropological. The life stories of these six women, both complemented and contradicted by their published work, collectively present a tale that sheds light on cultural dynamics in New Mexico, but the six stories are also fascinating in and of themselves.

Together, they present a record of activism and publishing that spans the twentieth century. Mary Austin (1868–1934) settled in New Mexico after a long career as a novelist and an activist. Her autobiography *Earth Horizon*, published in 1932, describes how she became a fierce advocate for the preservation of American Indian and Hispanic artistic and literary forms. Mabel Dodge Luhan (1879–1962), whose books *Edge of Taos Desert* and *Winter in Taos* shared an Anglo woman's discovery of New Mexico with a national audience in the mid-1930s, campaigned for American Indian rights and culture during a crucial period of reform. Cleofas Jaramillo (1878–1956), a contemporary of both Austin and Luhan, founded Santa Fe's La Sociedad

❧ Homesickness ❧

Folklórica, a Hispanic women's cultural preservation group, and led the group in planning events for the city's annual Fiesta. She shared her life experiences as a native New Mexican with English-speaking audiences in *Romance of a Little Village Girl*, published in 1955. A generation later, her distant cousin Fabiola Cabeza de Baca (1894–1991), a home economist, served as the first long-term Spanish-speaking female employee of the New Mexico Agricultural Extension Service, as a national officer of the civic group LULAC (the League of United Latin American Citizens), and as president of the New Mexico Folklore Society. She published a memoir of her youth on a ranch in eastern New Mexico, *We Fed Them Cactus*, in 1954. Kay Bennett (1920?–1997), a Navajo singer and political activist who became the first woman to run for the Navajo Nation's highest office in 1986, published a memoir of her childhood, *Kaibah: Recollection of a Navajo Girlhood*, in 1965. Finally, Pablita Velarde (born 1918), a celebrated painter from Santa Clara Pueblo and an activist for cultural preservation, published a collection of Santa Clara stories from her childhood, *Old Father Storyteller*, in 1960.[6]

These six women found their work was successful because it was work that people wanted and expected women to perform. A deeply rooted American ideology concerning the important role women play in maintaining cultural heritage in a democratic and pluralist nation made it possible for them to speak out, even when, especially for women of color, their desire to do so might have seemed otherwise threatening. Voicing concerns for culture in the language of "home" seemed a particularly American and traditional thing for these women to do. In 1947, U.S. Secretary of Agriculture Clinton P. Anderson voiced this philosophy when he affirmed the work of home demonstration agents, including Cabeza de Baca, by reminding them that

> American womanhood has long enjoyed a freedom and
> respect accorded to women in no other part of the
> world. As in every other phase of democratic life, this

position of esteem carries with it some definite responsibilities. It is in the home that the pattern of the culture
of a people is established. The cradle of democracy is a
nation's home and families.[7]

Anderson's statement presents a distinct challenge: though he does not
name the threat directly, women's need to preserve traditional values of
home, family, and heritage presumably arose from dangers posed by
industrializing forces outside the home. In New Mexico, however, the
forces of industrialization also presented economic opportunities.

The work of Austin, Luhan, Jaramillo, Cabeza de Baca, Bennett, and
Velarde shows how New Mexicans approached this dilemma. Women,
the reasoning seems to have gone, could save New Mexican traditions
while men did what they could to bring "progress" to the state and take
advantage of it. But dividing the labor this way, even symbolically, posed
problems and contradictions, because the roles men and women played
were not that simple or unchanging. As the United States changed tech-
nologically and economically in the twentieth century, Americans turned
to the real and imagined work of women when they feared traditions
would be lost. But at the same time, those technological and economic
changes fueled a dramatic transition in women's lives: until the twentieth
century, the vast majority of American women did not vote or work outside the home for pay. Politically, economically, and culturally, the story
of American women in the twentieth century is a story of ever-increasing
autonomy, autonomy that often contradicted the traditional roles
Americans simultaneously looked to women to maintain.

As the following stories reveal, Anglo women like Luhan and
Austin arrived in New Mexico early in the twentieth century as
beneficiaries of these new roles for women. Both were active in the first-
wave feminist movement and would not have given up willingly the
rights they had fought for. And yet they felt ambivalent about leaving
tradition completely behind, especially when they saw the rich and
diverse traditions of New Mexico. This ambivalence and their position

of relative privilege led them to envision the ideal New Mexican multicultural home as a place where communities maintained traditions through the work of women of color.

Jaramillo, Cabeza de Baca, Bennett, and Velarde rhetorically supported that ideal in their writings and other work. They found that audiences listened when they spoke in the language of tradition. But their lived experiences—especially the stories about their lives they left untold—testify to the growing need for a revised ideal of multiculturalism, one that considers culture as a product of change, blending and borrowing, rather than a matter of strict tradition. Austin and Luhan also omitted stories, particularly those about their personal experiences of disillusionment that, if spoken, would have contradicted their account of New Mexico as a model multicultural home. The four other women found that this account had become so powerful that to speak against it would have deprived them of an audience altogether. Rather, they had to craft public personae as "traditional" women—and live privately with knowing that their lives did not meet such expectations. Their work advanced cultural understanding in the state, but it also resulted in their own experiences with New Mexican homesickness.

Together, the lives of these six women offer a rich and complex view of the contradiction lying at the heart of New Mexican multiculturalism. Women in the twentieth century, their stories show, have been caught between the ideal of tradition and the realities of change and conflict; they have experienced New Mexican homesickness in a particularly personal way, and the untold stories of their lives need to be collectively acknowledged by those seeking to understand such homesickness today. Other biographers and historians have studied these six lives individually, but no one has yet considered them collectively.[8] Perhaps this is because New Mexican cultural history still tends to be written along the lines of three supposedly distinct ethnic traditions.

Telling these stories together, however, illustrates how homesickness is a common sentiment among New Mexicans, even though their ethnic perspective may lead them to experience it differently. Such is the case when we review excerpts from poems by two of these women. In

1928, Austin described the Southwest, in a poem she originally titled "Homesickness," as an exotic, but almost unattainable, place where authentic traditions thrived. "Very far there," she longingly wrote,

> The great barrel cactus
> Is swelling with the summer rains.
> Leaning always a little toward the sun,
> Clockwise its shadow goes,
> While the young men gather bisnaga blossoms
> For their maidens to fasten in their hair
> They are singing.... Would I were there now....[9]

In an undated but roughly contemporary poem, Cleofas Jaramillo described her home in more intimate and sentimental terms. "I love old houses with vines running over / Set in a riot of roses and clover," she wrote, in sloping handwriting, on the back of a photo of her country home in the village of El Rito. She continued:

> Set in a wonder of old trees
> Dreaming of far dim memories.
> I love the old windows like old eyes
> That seem to look into paradise
> I love old houses that speak to us
> Out of their ruinous glory....[10]

The styles of verse are dramatically different: one employs romanticism to describe exotic locales while the other longs nostalgically for the good old days. One poet is a newcomer filled with the anticipation of discovery; the other clings to places that have long been part of her family's history. Yet both writers saw New Mexico as an ideal home.

Homesickness

Readers of these poems, whether they approach New Mexican culture as curious tourists or as rooted inhabitants, likely agree with both Austin and Jaramillo that New Mexico is a place for which it is worth being homesick. Because of its inspiring place in the imagination of residents and tourists alike, New Mexico deserves a richer vision of what multicultural homes are all about than the one afforded by our current flawed ideals of tradition and multiculturalism. Telling the stories of Austin, Luhan, Jaramillo, Cabeza de Baca, Bennett, and Velarde alongside one another may not offer a cure to the homesickness we experience when we realize that an ideal multicultural home, one rooted firmly both in tradition and in modernity, cannot easily exist. And yet these stories may ultimately offer a better way to imagine the diverse and changing place that Americans call home.

CHAPTER ONE
In Pursuit of a Home
Mabel Dodge Luhan, Mary Austin, and the Appeal of Tradition

In October 1927, the Daughters of the American Revolution (DAR) called a meeting in Santa Fe to discuss the organization's proposal to place a "Madonna of the Trail" statue in the city. The DAR was engaged in an effort to mark pioneer trails in the United States with statues designed by sculptor August Leimbach. Across the country, the image of a stern, sunbonneted woman with a baby in her arms and a child at her feet would hopefully inspire Americans to remember how their pioneer foremothers had crossed wilderness to pursue a better life and to spread American values. The proposed statue in Santa Fe would mark the end of the Santa Fe Trail, which had opened in 1821 and expanded American commerce to New Mexico, a region then in the midst of a transition from Spanish to Mexican sovereignty. After the United States seized New Mexico in 1848, Anglo migrants in search of land and wealth followed the trail in greater numbers. Hoping to commemorate this process of conquest and expansion in New Mexico's capital city, representatives of the DAR approached Santa Fe's Chamber of Commerce in 1927 with the offer of the ten-thousand-dollar statue.

❧ CHAPTER ONE ❧

DAR representatives seemed certain that their generous offer would find a warm reception, but they soon learned otherwise. Author Mary Austin, who attended the meeting upon invitation, adamantly voiced opposition to the statue. As a local literary celebrity and activist, she held considerable power in Santa Fe's cultural community, and she did not hesitate to use it. According to J. D. De Huff, secretary of the Santa Fe Chamber of Commerce, who published an account of the meeting in the *Santa Fe New Mexican*, "Mrs. Austin made a few remarks, the tenor of which was that the so-called Pioneer Woman monument did not represent the real pioneers of this region at all, that the real pioneers were Spanish people and that they had not been consulted and were not represented at all."[1]

Because she felt this newspaper account portrayed her as impolite, Austin responded by writing her own article. "As a descendant of a long line of Pioneer Mothers myself," she explained, "I felt that the monument did not represent them truly.... Moreover, I meant all that I have been reported as saying, that the Pioneers of New Mexico are not the Pioneers of the DAR."[2] During the whole controversy, this was the closest anyone came to mentioning in print that, in fact, most New Mexican women would not have been allowed to join the DAR; the membership requirements of the organization effectively excluded women of color.[3]

Austin got her wish. The committee decided to place the monument in Albuquerque instead.[4] (It stands today in McClellan Park, near downtown.) Though Austin may have referred only to the statue's lack of representation of Hispanics in her speech before the committee, her opposition likely had a more complex rationale. She believed women had created and could sustain the diverse ethnic climate of New Mexico; such ideas went directly against the DAR's proposed image of a "pioneer mother" who symbolized only Anglo cultural dominance. Moreover, she believed "traditional" American Indian and Hispanic cultures offered modern Anglo Americans powerful alternatives for the conceptions of femininity afforded by a modernized, industrialized America.

Fig. 3: Dedication of the Madonna of the Trail Statue in Albuquerque, 1930. Courtesy of the Albuquerque Museum Photoarchives, Brooks Collection, 1978.152.54.

Austin shared these beliefs with a woman who had played a role in drawing her to New Mexico, celebrity writer and arts patron Mabel Dodge Luhan. Luhan had arrived in New Mexico in 1917 in pursuit of what she called "Change" with a capital "C." Like Austin, Luhan spoke out publicly for American Indian cultural and political causes, but she preferred the role of muse to that of activist. The two women had met in New York, and Austin's move to New Mexico in 1925 deepened their friendship. Like many authors, artists, and activists of the day, including Ansel Adams, John Collier, D. H. Lawrence, Georgia O'Keeffe, and Jean Toomer, Austin stayed at

Luhan's home near Taos during her first visits to New Mexico. Here Luhan used her role as hostess to influence people engaged in the aesthetic and political causes she held dear: accordingly, her support for cultural causes was often intensely personal.

Her approach to political issues took its most notable form in her marriage to Antonio (Tony) Lujan, a native of Taos Pueblo. While many dimensions of this marriage, which lasted from 1923 until Luhan's death in 1962, remain private, Luhan did choose to discuss some aspects of her marriage publicly. Soon after their wedding, Luhan replaced the "j" in the couple's last name with an "h" to accommodate non-Spanish speakers. This gesture alone serves as a loaded symbol of Luhan's forceful style and her continuing desire to use her personal life as a means of educating an Anglo audience about the possibility of cultural reform through personal action. She later described her marriage at length in two autobiographical volumes, as well as in interviews reprinted in newspapers across the United States.

Austin and Luhan both publicly embraced images as "border crossers" who drew strength from multiple cultural traditions.[5] In this respect, they are representative figures of an important age in American cultural history. They provide illustrations of how Americans moved from what we now see as late nineteenth-century cultural ideals to those we now call "modern." While both women began their lives in an intellectual climate that arranged cultures according to a hierarchical system of value, up from the "primitive" to the "civilized," both ultimately participated in a thought process that valorized "authentic" and "primitive" cultural experiences as a way of reinvigorating American culture. In particular, the "living primitivism" offered by the American Indian and Hispanic cultures of the U.S. Southwest offered Luhan and Austin inspiring ideas about womanhood and modernity. Both women used their public writing about their personal lives as a form of activism, one in which they shared their border-crossing experiences in New Mexico with national audiences. As illustrated by Austin's opposition to the ethnocentric DAR statue, they encouraged Americans to live out the ideals of cultural relativism advocated by

On Pursuit of a Home

Franz Boas, Elsie Clews Parsons, and other modernist anthropologists, bringing Americans closer to a doctrine of cultural relations that Americans began to call multiculturalism after the 1960s.[6]

Because of their foresight, the stories of Luhan and Austin, and their settlement in New Mexico, are fairly well known. In the past thirty years, writers have published two biographies of each woman.[7] Since Luhan and Austin are more familiar to Americans, especially to non-New Mexican audiences, than the women I consider in later chapters, I have combined and condensed their stories here; their common experiences and shared place in the intellectual history of the United States make this possible.

But the women share another feature—one that is somewhat disturbing. The ideas they developed about the Southwest, ideas they expressed in numerous writings, did not always match up to the truth of human experience there. Whether they were describing their own supposed happiness in New Mexico or trying to share what they had learned about Hispanic and American Indian culture, Luhan and Austin both ultimately romanticized cultural relations in the Southwest. Comparing what they wrote to what they actually experienced suggests that their desire to see New Mexico in an ideal light, as a home for progressive women such as themselves, led them to distort or to remain willfully oblivious to the truth when it came to describing that home for others. They wanted to will into existence a multicultural society in which border-crossing modern women could have the best of all worlds: the power of tradition combined with the status of modern-day rights and roles. But both women, as we shall see, had to distort the facts of their own and others' lives in New Mexico in order to create this ideal home.

This distortion may have been caused by the ultimate inability of Luhan and Austin to step outside their position of Anglo privilege. For despite their desire to transcend borders, the ideal New Mexican woman they imagined was not the Hispanic woman cited in Austin's statue protest, nor was she the American Indian woman invoked by both writers' calls for cultural appreciation. Rather, she was clearly an Anglo woman who shared the ethnicity, values, and goals of Luhan and

19

Austin: a new and improved "pioneer woman" who shared the DAR's ethnic perspective, if not its ethnocentrism. Literary historian Elizabeth Ammons has described Luhan and Austin's generation of women writers as one that "floated between a past they wished to leave (sometimes ambivalently, sometimes defiantly) and a future they had not yet gained."[8] They would paradoxically attempt to gain a future in which women like themselves found liberation through exploration of the traditions of people of color. By implication, this vision was as exclusionary as the DAR membership policy: it confined women of color to the "authentic," static, and ultimately unrealistic roles of the past.

As later chapters will reveal, Hispanic and American Indian women also came to be "border crossers" who used cross-cultural encounters to increase women's power and advocate diverse cultural traditions. And yet they could not always embrace such roles publicly, as Luhan and Austin did. In order to explain why, this chapter sets out to examine what stories the Anglo women left untold. The stories of why they went to New Mexico and what they did and did not choose to share about their experiences there reveal how they ultimately neglected to appreciate why Hispanic and American Indian women had to cross cultural borders instead of remaining "traditional." Furthermore, in their insistence on such traditionalism, Luhan and Austin ultimately restricted their own ability to live up to the border-crossing ideals of cultural relativism they brought to New Mexico. This gap between the ideal they imagined and the realities of their own and others' lives allows me to tell a new story about these well-known women, one that explains the flawed and ongoing perception of New Mexico as a place steeped in unchanging tradition.

Mabel Dodge Luhan and the Creation of the Taos Ideal

The story of many twentieth-century Anglo New Mexican "expatriates" begins with Mabel Dodge Luhan. Driven by a sense of cultural mission, she used her home, her money, and her know-how to allow other artists and writers to undergo the same dramatic conversion she had experienced upon her arrival in the state. For Luhan, the opportunity to undergo such a "Change" had occurred in 1917, when she moved to Taos from her home in Greenwich Village, New York. Initially she came to the Southwest because her husband at the time, Russian-émigré painter Maurice Sterne, was staying in the area on a painting trip. When he urged her to join him, he appealed to her desire to get involved in a compelling public cause by calling her attention to the campaign for land rights and cultural appreciation for American Indians in the state.

Luhan had, in fact, been searching New York for a reform movement she could dominate. Her interests had ranged from modern art to birth control to labor strife. But in New Mexico, Sterne saw a need for reform work and an opportunity for Luhan to make a splash. "Do you want an object in life?" he wrote. "Save the Indians, their art-culture—reveal it to the world!"[9] Though she initially intended only a short vacation, Luhan underwent a permanent transformation upon her arrival in New Mexico. "My life broke in two right then," she wrote of that first journey to the Southwest, "and I entered into the second half, a new world that replaced all the ways I had known with others, more strange and terrible and sweet than any I had ever been able to imagine."[10]

Understanding what made the "second half" of Luhan's life so dramatically different from the first means understanding her perception of all that led up to that moment. She reenacted this journey in the record of her life that she wrote and published in the 1920s and 1930s. Luhan began her memoirs, inspired by Marcel Proust's *Remembrance of Things Past*, in 1924, soon after the departure of D. H. Lawrence from New Mexico ended her attempts to gain control over his life and writing. Her psychoanalyst, A. A. Brill, suggested that writing for herself could be cathartic because it would allow her to deal with her memories and influences in a creative way. The project soon took on an epic scope: Luhan ultimately published four thick volumes—*Background* (1933), *European Experiences* (1935), *Movers and Shakers* (1936), and *Edge of Taos Desert: An Escape to Reality* (1937)—under the collective title *Intimate Memories*. Luhan did not initially intend to publish the memoirs; instead, she circulated them among friends in the late 1920s. The positive feedback she received, some from literary notables like Willa Cather, convinced her that her story would make a powerful statement about modernity for American audiences.[11]

The memoirs narrate her life from its earliest days until her first year in Taos and present these experiences as her search for the perfect home. As Luhan's biographer Lois Palken Rudnick has aptly noted, she crafted her life story as a "conversion narrative." Like the life stories of Puritan writers, *Intimate Memories* shows a journey from "imperfection to perfection, where new beginnings are often associated with new frontiers."[12] Of course, Rudnick continues, in contrast to captivity narratives like Mary Rowlandson's 1682 narrative of her experiences during King Philip's War, Luhan's story features American Indians as heroic figures.[13] Anglo Americans, on the other hand, are the "barbarians" who need redemptive homes like the one Luhan found in Taos.

The "barbarism" Luhan escaped from includes her aristocratic but unhappy upbringing, her three unsuccessful marriages prior to her union with Tony, and her dissatisfaction with the model of femininity offered by the industrialized nation in which she lived. Born in 1879, Luhan grew up in Buffalo, New York, as the only child in a family made wealthy through the banking achievements of her grandfathers. In *Background*, she recorded her parents' unhappy marriage and the hostile home it created. As a young woman, Luhan desired something more than the elite educational and social opportunities afforded by her class. Yet she also learned to take advantage of those opportunities to create the kind of world she wanted. When she "came out" at age eighteen, she planned her debutante party around the theme of a courtly event at a "Baronial Hall" in Renaissance Europe, hoping to astound her guests with her ambitious intellectual plan. But she watched with mounting dismay as her party followed the path of convention. Luhan's memoir intimates a fascinated disgust with the piles of roses and violets that came to her that day, documenting her dutiful but inwardly seething acceptance of the party's dance and courtship rituals.[14]

fig. 4: Mabel Ganson, age eighteen, in "Coming-Out" Dress. Courtesy of the Yale Collection of American Literature, Beinecke Rare Book and Manuscript Library, Yale University.

◪ CHAPTER ONE ◪

Luhan's life continued to operate as the tug-of-war between conventional privilege and desperate innovation that she experienced at her debutante ball. At twenty-one, she married Karl Evans, a wealthy young man whose chief appeal (to the competitive young Mabel) was that he was engaged to someone else when she met him. She bore her first and only child, John Evans, in 1902, reflecting later that she enjoyed the "reciprocity" she experienced during her pregnancy but felt alienated from her child as soon as he was born. Her marriage soon grew dissatisfying, and Luhan began an affair with her married doctor. When Karl Evans died unexpectedly in a hunting accident and Luhan's affair became a matter of scandal, her mother responded in the true spirit of American industrial aristocracy: she sent her widowed daughter and grandson abroad, in search of refinement and renewal.

Luhan did not find the home she craved in Europe, though she did begin a process of cultural experimentation culminating in her eventual attraction to New Mexico. On her ship voyage east, she met her second husband, Edwin Dodge, a wealthy Boston native trained in architecture in Paris. This marriage did not bring her any more happiness than her first. But she did initiate a project with Dodge that brought her fleeting fulfillment, foreshadowing her later efforts in cultural preservation. In 1905, the couple bought a Renaissance villa near Florence and restored it to its former grandeur by decorating it in epicurean style. To celebrate the project's completion, Luhan hosted a feast that succeeded "dramatically," in contrast to her debutante ball. But she soon found that even creating her own household did not give her the satisfaction she craved.[15] Her medieval-style chamber, for example, featured a silken ladder descending from a trap door above to her bed below. Her hopes for the ladder did not pan out, at least not with her husband. "This silken ladder was for haste," Luhan wrote in *European Experiences*, "lover's haste. But Edwin never hastened down it except once to see if it would work, and it did, perfectly."[16] The house and the guests it attracted, several of whom became Luhan's lovers, absorbed the romantic desires she had channeled fruitlessly into her marriage. She entertained fellow American expatriate Gertrude Stein and Italian actress Eleanora Duse in between conducting affairs with Italian nobles, her chauffeur, and her son's American tutor. She also battled with depression, suicide attempts, and a sense of boredom with the life she had created.

Her recounting of her life before New Mexico clearly invites critiques of her narcissism and idleness. But she also describes her frank self-awareness of the desires resulting in this hedonistic existence. "I began to buy things," she recalled. "With love unsatisfied, some people turn to food, others to drink, still others will add pearls to pearls, turning frantically here and there to satisfy the basic craving."[17] The economic status that gave Luhan the leisure to have and seek satisfaction for such a craving failed to give her the power to achieve it, and she did not know how to remake herself. But she did know she needed to try something else. Amid the demise of her marriage and the onset of the conflicts leading to World War I, she returned reluctantly to the United States in 1912. "I felt nowhere—suspended 'between two worlds,'" she recalled. At the sight of the Statue of Liberty from the deck of their ship, she clutched her ten-year-old son in what she acknowledged as a rare maternal moment. "Remember, it is *ugly* in America," she told him. "We have left everything worth while behind us. America is all machinery and money-making and factories—it is ugly, ugly, ugly!"[18]

Luhan ultimately found a home in New Mexico that defied her impressions of American "ugliness," but for the time being, she stayed in New York, among the Greenwich Village radicals who launched reform movements against the excesses of modernity during the 1910s. While her life in Italy had been a conservative retreat into romance and materialism, the life she made for herself in New York channeled her economic power into efforts at social upheaval. She divorced Dodge, established a "salon" for reformers and artists in her Fifth Avenue brownstone, and sought out new ways to realize her identity. She helped plan and publicize the 1913 Armory Show, the introduction of modern art to mainstream U.S. audiences. She entertained and befriended muckrakers like Hutchins Hapgood and Lincoln Steffens, and more militant reform activists like Emma

CHAPTER ONE

Goldman and Big Bill Haywood. When Haywood told her of his desire to create awareness of laborers' plight during a 1913 silk workers strike in Paterson, New Jersey, she suggested that he stage the events of the strike to a mass audience; this "pageant" remains a well-known milestone in the labor movement.

Despite these political activities, her quest for the spiritual fulfillment she claimed to eventually find in New Mexico used romance as its primary vehicle. Through taking on the production of the Paterson Strike Pageant, she met and fell in love with an aspiring young journalist named John Reed, who gained fame and notoriety as an advocate of Communism. The two began an affair in which Luhan attempted to test out the ideas about "free love" and "New Womanhood" she had encountered in the writings of Margaret Sanger and during her participation in the feminist group Heterodoxy. While their passionate romance engaged Luhan momentarily, she found herself feeling vulnerable and used when Reed's attentions drifted elsewhere.[19] Her attraction eventually fizzled, but it was not long before she had become infatuated with Sterne—and engaged in a bitter tug-of-war for his affections and the direction of his career as an artist. She confessed easily in her memoirs that one of her chief sources of attraction to him was her desire to transform him from a painter into a sculptor. She saw herself as one of many women who unsuccessfully adhered to men in order to "change" them. "That is the way I was thinking and planning then," she wrote, "and that is the way many women do, and will go on doing until they learn better. (Forgive me, all you women!)"[20]

Before she arrived in New Mexico, her fruitless search for the perfect romance coincided with her similarly difficult quest for perfect spirituality. Her recurring interests in theories of mind and body healing ranged from Christian Science, to psychoanalysis, to varying forms of meditative practices. In fact, for a short period of time between August 1917 and February 1918, she wrote a syndicated column in which she shared advice and her ideas about psychology with a mainstream audience.[21] For Luhan, ultimately unable to find satisfaction in villa renovations, reform movements, or romantic relationships, the next best thing seemed to be taking charge of other people's lives. She increasingly found, through her relations with Reed and Sterne, that trying to act as a "muse" to creative men gave her a sensation of control she could not achieve in her own life.[22] She was fed up with a life in which she wanted no master except herself but found no effective material tool, radical measure, or "mind cure" to achieve such actualization. Nevertheless, in 1917, she again entered an institution that had not served her well in the past: she married Sterne. Almost immediately, in a fit of dissatisfaction with his interest in other women, she sent him off on a painting trip to the West.

When she took the train from New York to New Mexico to join him, in 1917, she sought a release from her overwhelming romantic and spiritual frustrations. And by her own account, she found it. In *Edge of Taos Desert*, the climactic volume of her memoirs, she wrote of the profound sense of difference she experienced during even her first moments in New Mexico. "Santa Fe was the strangest American town I had ever seen," she confessed. "The first Indians I had ever seen, except at the circus, were there in the plaza that first morning." In her description of the people she saw that day, Luhan compared them to what she had known in Europe and New York. "They had black, glossy hair, worn in a Dutch cut," she wrote, "with brilliant, folded silk fillets tied around their bangs. With their straight features, medieval-looking blouses and all the rest, they were just like Maxfield Parrish illustrations."[23]

What Luhan saw in Santa Fe thrilled her with its "difference" even as it seemed strangely familiar. She soon met other "expatriate" artists and writers who had established themselves there, but she eschewed this community in search of even greater escape. Against Sterne's wishes, she planned a visit to the town of Taos. The Pueblo and the old Spanish village with the same name nearby had already become a home to a group of Anglo painters. But the town's relatively remote location, a rugged seventy-five miles from Santa Fe, made it less appealing as a destination for casual visitors. Determined to see

Fig. 5: Mabel Dodge Luhan and Antonio Lujan, Taos, New Mexico, 1924.
Courtesy of The Huntington Library, San Marino, CA.

it for herself despite the long day's drive, she commandeered a car and took in the impressive mountainous scenery on her way north. They arrived after dark, and Luhan was instantly captivated. "Taos took me that dark winter night and has held me ever since," she asserted in her memoir. "I am glad I capitulated in the dark, blindly but full of faith. It was a real conversion, and something accepted on trust—recognized as home."²⁴

She had at last found her place. Within a day of arriving, she rented a house in Taos with the intention of staying for a long time. Within a few months, she met Tony, whose face she claimed to have seen before, in a dream she had had in New York.[25] And within six months, boosted by his encouragement, she had purchased land in Taos on which to build her own house. Tony supervised its gradual construction, crafting a home that combined Pueblo architecture with her desire to create a center of cultural and intellectual activity. Before she had even been in Taos for a year, she began to invite guests to visit her and to take part in the world she had discovered at the "edge of Taos desert." What she saw and felt convinced her that this was a place worth sharing. In her relationship with Tony, begun before Sterne left Taos, Luhan, now entering her forties, believed she had found liberation: "Here in Taos I was awake to a new experience of sex and love," she wrote, "more mature and more civilized than any I had known before."[26]

The experience gave her a new mission of prophecy, one she realized through the publication of her memoirs, especially *Edge of Taos Desert*. "If I who was nobody for so long, a zombie wandering empty upon the earth, could come to life, who cannot?" she asked. In print, her missionary zeal ascribed to her Taos experience all that could cure the societal and personal woes that had beset her in previous existences:

> It is for those desperate and frightened people I am trying
> to write now as it was for them I wrote before.
> Revelations of the hidden distortions, the cripple under
> the veils of civilization, the mind breaking under its
> strain, and the heart atrophying in its insulation—those
> were the intimate memories of my life until I came to
> Taos where I was offered and accepted a spiritual therapy
> that was cleansing, one that provided a difficult and
> painful method of curing me of my epoch and that finally
> rewarded me with a sense of reality.[27]

Among the Taoseños—or at least with Tony—Luhan claimed, she had at last found herself. She crafted a narrative of this homecoming experience to share with other Americans, hoping that they, too, would acknowledge their need for a new center of existence, one richer in cultural experience. She shared what she actually found in Taos only selectively, but she did not restrict herself when it came to recounting the forces that had driven her toward her new home.

Mary Austin and the Long Road West

Austin's pre-New Mexican life resembled Luhan's in that her previous homes had offered her only frustratingly narrow patterns of living and made her yearn for a better way. She came to assume, after so much negative experience, that she knew the better way and others did not know enough to follow it. Thus, she did not portray her arrival in New Mexico in the dramatic tones of "conversion" used by Luhan. Rather, Austin's life story, as she told it, conveys her belief that she knew what was best all along, and New Mexico conveniently allowed her to fulfill herself according to her cultural, environmental, and spiritual ideals.

In 1929, when Houghton Mifflin paid her a twenty-five-hundred-dollar advance to write her autobiography, she began a narrative showing why and how New Mexico provided her with such a home.[28] Three years later, she published *Earth Horizon: Autobiography* to a warm critical reception.[29] In fact, the book arguably became the most successful of the more than thirty she wrote during her lifetime. The Literary Guild adopted it as a recommended selection for readers, which boosted the book's sales even during this Depression year. Written partially as a third-person narrative (in the style already adopted by Henry Adams for his own intellectual autobiography), the book recounts Austin's lifelong attempt to achieve the promise of the "earth horizon," an image from the "Rain Song of the Sia."

On Pursuit of a Home

Presumably derived from a chant she had recorded at Zia Pueblo in New Mexico, Austin used the symbol to express her desire to have her spiritual experiences come together like the "incalculable blue ring of sky meeting earth."[30]

The scope of these experiences and the wide range of literary and political notables they brought her into contact with impressed readers and reviewers.[31] Publicity materials for *Earth Horizon* listed the names of celebrities mentioned within the pages as well as rave reviews from leading intellectuals of the day.[32] Austin knew when she began to write her autobiography that her reputation preceded her—but not in the ways she preferred. In 1922, after a National Arts Club Dinner in New York honored Austin and her work, she wrote about her realization of the limitations of her fame to a friend who had not been able to attend. "I got home to reflect," she confessed, "that no one who spoke revealed any intimate acquaintance with my books, that two of the speakers seemed to be uncertain just what books I had written...." Her correspondent, naturalist Daniel T. MacDougal, was a confidant, and she revealed her worst fears about her literary reputation with a higher-than-usual degree of vulnerability: "What's the use of being praised as a good mother," she asked, "by people who can't even remember the names of your children?"[33] Readers' greater interest in her life story than in her books attests to her ability to use her persona to generate attention for controversial issues of gender, race, and culture. She thrived on being a contrary voice and cultivated an image of herself as a mystic, a genius, and a sage that only served to fuel fascination: her dramatic third-person presentation of herself in *Earth Horizon* shows this process in action.

But in her early years, Austin's desire to stand out only made her life difficult. As she described in *Earth Horizon*, she was born in 1868 in Carlinville, Illinois, to a family that prided itself on its upstanding Midwestern values and tended to look down upon any deviance from tradition. Her father, George Hunter, a Civil War veteran and lawyer who had pulled himself up by his bootstraps after his immigration from England as a young man, encouraged his daughter's literary efforts. But

Austin's mother, Susanna Graham Hunter, a strict Methodist, rebuffed Austin's imaginative temperament as well as her efforts to win her mother's affection and support. Austin's father died after a long illness when she was only ten years old, leaving her without a mentor.

In the years that followed, she vigorously pursued her education and her desire to be a writer, but she did not have a home that supported her efforts. Upon graduation from high school, she attended the State Normal School with the intention of becoming a teacher. After enduring only a semester of a rigid curriculum and poor facilities, Austin, never in strong health, returned home in 1886 due to what she later termed a "breakdown." Her mother submitted her to the watchful eye of the family doctor, who apparently felt that Austin's "condition...might have something to do with the natural incapacity of the female mind for intellectual achievement."[34]

She did not give up so easily. After recuperating, she attended a local liberal arts college, pursued studies in science, and planned her career as a writer. Despite the lack of familial support, one of her mother's church-related activities did provide her with a socially acceptable model of self-assertion: the role of the temperance woman. Susanna Hunter led Carlinville women in this "feminine" venture to right society's wrongs, and through her and other temperance leaders Austin learned much about the potential for women in the public sphere. Indeed, she wrote in *Earth Horizon* that Frances Willard, leader of the Women's Christian Temperance Union (WCTU) from 1879 to 1898, had a "more informing" influence on Austin's life than "almost any other of that time."[35] By speaking "in the key of her audience," Austin wrote, Willard was able to transform women's femininity into women's social power. She "swept [women] into suffrage" by convincing them that only through voting could women improve society.[36] Thus, during this formative period, Austin found she could tie her education and her career goals to the "feminine" ideals for increased social power for women advocated by Willard.

In the meantime, she still had to contend with the unequal balance of power within her family, a struggle for self-actualization that dominated her account of her life before she came to the Southwest. Her mother increasingly let Austin's older brother control the household. Thus, the family left Illinois a few weeks after her graduation in the spring of 1888 to travel west to California, where her brother believed he would have better opportunities as a homesteader. The journey opened her eyes to a new landscape and to the new wonders of cities like San Francisco and Los Angeles. The change dramatically affected her in ways she could not easily overcome. In a letter Susanna Hunter sent from Pasadena to Carlinville in the fall of 1888, she wrote happily of finding a church that proved that "Methodism is the same at home or abroad." As for her daughter Mary, the trip had "almost killed her" and she was still recovering from the "nervous prostration" that had come from "going to school a little too long."[37] Perhaps Austin simply longed for school, a feeling that could only have intensified when the family finally settled in a remote area of the San Joaquin Valley near Fort Tejon, a hundred miles north of Los Angeles and a rough thirty miles of desert from Bakersfield. Austin suffered from physical, environmental, and intellectual malnutrition in a country that "failed to explain itself," a desert lacking all she had previously considered sustenance: plentiful water, cultivated food, and books.[38]

She would write dramatically about how she found a way to live in this desert by slowly casting off her family. She escaped initially by accepting a teaching job at a dairy farm, and then, more drastically, through a wedding. At first, she felt optimistic about her marriage to Stafford Wallace Austin, a man she met through teaching. He had ambitious plans: he intended to raise money to irrigate land in the Owens Valley, an area on the eastern slope of the Sierra Nevada in central California, and then to establish vineyards in partnership with his brother.

As Austin put it in *Earth Horizon*, "nothing in Mary's married life turned out as she expected it." Wallace's irrigation plans failed, leaving them economically devastated.[39] He expressed support for her writing but was actually bewildered by her literary ambitions.[40] Both eventually had to teach to support the family, even after Austin gave birth to their only child, Ruth, in 1892. Ruth had severe developmental disabilities, which

Fig. 6: Mary Austin and Stafford Wallace Austin, Wedding Portrait, 1891.
Courtesy of The Huntington Library, San Marino, CA.

Susanna Hunter pronounced as a "judgment" on her daughter. Austin came to blame her husband for her daughter's condition, claiming he had not shared information about a "taint" marking his family history.[41] The home she made with her husband had failed. Moreover, she found herself ostracized by the Anglo community: her career as a teacher, her entrusting of Ruth to the care of others, her unconventional literary interests and her

34

disregard for social distinctions alienated her from the homesteaders and miners in the area. As she wrote in her autobiography, controversies ensued when she gave a cake to a Chinese "wash boy," and local women called on her "to ask what I meant by taking part in Indian dances." She was "read out" by the local Methodist church after she taught liberal interpretations of the Bible during an adult Sunday School class.[42]

During this devastating period, she began to cultivate a sense of home in the physical and cultural environments that had initially overwhelmed her but would eventually save her. She familiarized herself with the Owens Valley landscape and with the Paiute and Hispanic peoples who made their homes there alongside the Anglo homesteaders. The empathy she professed for the non-Anglo cultures of the West made her even more unusual to the people who knew her in the 1890s, but it would impress the audiences who read *Earth Horizon* in 1932. In particular, she came to believe that her idiosyncratic views of religion and pantheistic views of spirituality and creativity forged a kinship between her and the American Indian people she came to know. In Paiute culture, Austin discovered a way of thinking about life and art that her Methodist upbringing and conventional education in the Midwest had never provided. She came to believe she could "borrow" a philosophy of creation from the Paiutes. In *Earth Horizon*, she wrote movingly about this process:

> The Paiutes were basket-makers; the finest of their sort. What Mary drew from them was their naked craft, the subtle sympathies of a twig and root and bark; she consorted with them; she laid herself open to the influences of the wild, the thing done, accomplished. She entered into their lives, the life of the campody [settlement], the strange secret life of the tribe, the struggle of Whiteness with Darkness, the struggle of the individual soul with the Friend-of-the-Soul-of-Man. She learned what it meant; how to prevail; how to measure her strength against it. Learning that, she learned to write.[43]

Austin's sense of "immersion" may seem naïve or paternalistic today, especially in its emphasis on supposedly essential cultural traits. But the sincerity of her devotion to these ideals remains compelling. As Ammons has written, Austin's "interest in Indians was for the most part a genuine attempt to participate in the values of a culture she believed more life-supporting than the one into which she was born."[44]

This sense of cultural connection, one that eventually pulled Austin to New Mexico, had its roots in her intense personal experiences with American Indians. At a moving moment in *Earth Horizon*, she describes how a Paiute woman journeyed to see her when she heard Ruth was suffering. "Because Mary's child was not talking as early as it should, [she] came all the way to Lone Pine to bring her dried mead-owlarks' tongues, which make the speech nimble and quick. It was in experiences such as this that Mary began genuinely to know Indians."[45] Austin's affinity for this woman and her culture carried heavy emotional weight, especially given the disapproving reception her own family had granted her daughter's problems. Soon after, an incident prompted her to expand her interest in American Indian culture to a concern for their welfare. A group of Anglo men brutally raped two girls who attended a school for Indian children in Bishop, an Owens Valley town. The girls, traumatized and ashamed, committed suicide by eating a poisonous plant, but the rapists escaped punishment, an injustice Austin protested amid the silence of the larger Anglo community.[46]

Around 1900, fueled by her experiences in the Southwest, she began to write professionally, gradually making contact with the literary communities of San Francisco and Los Angeles. Supported by literary notables like Charles Lummis, a southwestern popularizer and the editor of *Out West* magazine, she found she could share her experiences with the growing numbers of Anglo Americans who were interested in learning more about this "exotic" region. In 1903, she published a collection of lyrical essays about the landscapes and people of the Owens Valley, *The Land of Little Rain*, to wide critical acclaim. The book's serialization in *Atlantic Monthly* brought her a degree of financial success. In one of the book's essays, Austin wrote of a Paiute woman who "made baskets for love and sold them for money." "Every Indian woman is an artist," she broadly asserted, no doubt pleased that her own first major artistic effort seemed to bring her both love and money.[47] Her Paiute models, as essentialized as they were in her imagination, served her well.

With money of her own, she placed her daughter in an institution, a painful decision she came to see as a necessary step in her gradual journey toward self-fulfillment in New Mexico.[48] In 1907, Wallace Austin officially charged Mary Austin with "desertion" and initiated their divorce, but their marriage had truthfully ended long before then.[49] By that time, Mary lived in the Monterey Bay town of Carmel, where she built a small house in the developing writer's colony. At last, she believed, she was creating her own true home. She attracted attention through her penchant for dressing up in Indian costume and for writing in a "wickiup," a treehouse she named using the Paiute word for shelter. She continued writing fiction and sought literary camaraderie among other Carmel residents, including poet George Sterling, who entertained his friend Jack London. She also met muckraker Lincoln Steffens, who visited Carmel in 1907 and later lived there permanently. To her dismay, she learned that the "unconventional" lifestyle of these men did not break with traditional ideas of womanhood, or, at least, traditional ideas about how to treat women. She felt excluded by the male literary bonding—and in a few years' time believed herself to be the victim of romantic exploitation by Steffens.[50]

These experiences deepened her confidence in modern feminism and increased her commitment to finding a more hospitable community. She came to believe that the model of women's rights utilized by the nineteenth-century temperance movement, in which women relied on ideas about feminine moral superiority to achieve power within existing roles, had outlasted its efficacy. Sensing that ideas about women's roles in marriage, sexuality, and labor needed to change if women were to gain power, Austin turned to women like Susan B. Anthony, Anna

Howard Shaw, Charlotte Perkins Gilman, and Jane Addams, who—as Austin saw it—resisted using "charm as a means of establishing a personal advantage." Frances Willard, their predecessor, had "almost achieved...the re-making of society from the Hearth as the Sacred Middle." But her new role models had gone further, and "hazarded...a remaking of the pattern in which the Hearth itself should be reformed, should itself be made to revolve about a Middle whose true name was as yet undiscerned, but as the lodestone of their compass daily felt."[51]

This new method of "homebuilding" became her mission. In coming to rely on "charm" for their power, she implied, women had fallen away from the powerful role they had held in preindustrial economies—like that, she implied, of her pioneer foremothers, or of the basket-making Paiutes she knew in Owens Valley. Austin wanted women to capitalize on their "hearth" instincts and extend their intellectual and management skills into the public sphere. She believed that doing so would allow women to not only improve their status, but also improve society in general. In a pamphlet she cowrote in 1914 to advocate women's suffrage, she argued that such a blend of past and present strengths could benefit all of society: "The men of the states [who vote for suffrage] are...yielding instinctively to what is the modern, no less than the primitive, necessity of all communities: the free opportunity for women to do their special work, to use their mothering, their conserving powers for the good of the home, the town, the state."[52]

She relied on these themes often in her writing in the 1910s and 1920s, when she temporarily left the Southwest for Europe and New York. She went to Europe in pursuit of a spiritual cure for a tumor on her breast. Encouraged by the health she achieved there, she produced an outpouring of fiction and nonfiction and settled in New York to be close to the literary "scene." This work dealt extensively with feminist issues and her increasing advocacy of cultural relativism, especially in her writings about American Indians.[53] But contemporary critics received much of this work poorly. One of her books, *A Woman of Genius* (1912), told the story of an actress from a small town in Illinois who leaves a stale marriage to pursue goals of fame and fortune. Since the book clearly emerged from her own life experiences, she must have felt doubly devastated when it received little attention. Austin later claimed in *Earth Horizon* that the publisher "dropped the book" after an executive's wife decided the heroine's actions were "immoral." Austin found that her more rhapsodic works depicting an exotic Southwest, such as the collection of stories she called *Lost Borders* (1909) or her American Indian play *The Arrow-Maker* (1911), received more positive attention. Her lack of complete success only made her more convinced that Anglo Americans should learn from other cultures, as she herself had done with the Paiutes when forming her ideas about the potential of the "hearth."[54]

Her disappointment with California's rapid development and increasing population convinced her it was no longer a place to find cultural inspiration. In 1918 she traveled for the first time to a place she believed could provide that inspiration: New Mexico. According to *Earth Horizon*, she had planned to visit Mexico that summer, but she stopped in New Mexico because the raging flu epidemic made further travel unadvisable. She went to stay with Mabel and Tony Luhan in Taos and soon found herself not only a visitor but also an expert. The Carnegie Foundation commissioned her to conduct a study of the Hispanic population of Taos, and thus began Austin's work in New Mexico.[55]

Before long, she chose to make the state her permanent home. "I settled in my mind that I would write the closing years of my life into the history of Santa Fe," she explained in *Earth Horizon*. "I could be useful here; and I felt I could get back a consideration from the public that would in a measure make up for the loss of certified ladyhood."[56] In a magazine piece published in 1932, she described her choice of home as "deliberate," drawn from the influences of the mountain and desert landscape as well as the "element of aboriginal society" she felt was her "proper medium." While she cited American Indian culture as the most "intriguing" element, she added that the "folk culture" of Spanish-speaking New Mexicans as well as the "people of the first rank of creative and intellectual achievement"—that is, other Anglo expatriates—had also drawn her to this area.[57] Indeed, her enthusiasm for Santa Fe led her to make two contradictory claims about the city's

Fig. 7: Mary Austin, Arizona, 1923. Courtesy of The Huntington Library, San Marino, CA.

potential in 1931. Speaking to a group of New Mexican educators, she reportedly claimed the Southwest would be home to the development of the "next great English-speaking culture," and there would also arise "a polyglot language" suited to Santa Fe's cultural heritages and proximity to the Mexican border.[58]

She poured her life savings into the building of a Pueblo-style home in Santa Fe that she named *Casa Querida*. In 1925, she settled into her "beloved" home. She had "not been entirely happy" in her life, she wrote in *Earth Horizon*, but in New Mexico she found the wholeness she had been seeking:

> At the core of our Amerindian life we are consummated
> in the dash and color of collectivity. It is not that we
> work upon the Cosmos, but it works in us. I suffer
> because I achieve so little in this relation, and rejoice that
> I have felt so much. As much as I am able, I celebrate the
> Earth Horizon.[59]

With this closing, she invited her Anglo readers to look beyond the confines of their ancestry and to feel, as she had felt, the moving pull of other ways of living. Like Luhan, she had built herself the new sort of home she had been searching for all her life, and she invited others to do the same.

New Homes, New Dilemmas

If we ended Luhan's and Austin's stories with their "arrivals" in New Mexico, as they did in their autobiographies, we would be left with the sense that multicultural New Mexico turned their lives around and enabled them to show others how to do the same. Both *Edge of Taos Desert* and *Earth Horizon* argue passionately for change. Luhan used a conversion narrative to lure her readers, while Austin shared her journey from alienation to eventual fulfillment to show her audience the "better way." By revealing their life experiences, they translated some of the core messages of cultural modernism—the ideals of cultural relativism, the quest for authentic experience, and the appeal of the "primitive"—into narratives of personal experience that American readers could easily understand and identify with. Both autobiographies drew national literary attention when they were published, and they continue to find empathetic readers today.

Both Luhan and Austin found channels other than writing to express their commitment to the ideal New Mexican homes described in their autobiographies. In 1922, for example, both women participated in the efforts of the American Indian Defense Association to counteract federal legislation known as the Bursum Bill, which threatened to remove lands of disputed ownership from Pueblo control. Additionally, both women assumed patronage roles in the preservation and cultivation of folk art traditions in the state.

But historical records of these well-intended efforts ultimately tell another story about Austin and Luhan in New Mexico, one that neither of them acknowledged in their autobiographies. Though each described her arrival there as the end of a quest, they were not entirely open-minded when they undertook their campaigns for cultural relativism. They had come to the state, after all, with certain needs. Luhan sought a community where she could at last place herself in relation to others. Austin wanted to tap into other cultures and to develop an artistic vision that seemed impossible elsewhere. Luhan wanted to lose herself, while Austin wanted to find herself. Hispanic and American Indian cultures in New Mexico gave them new sources of inspiration for these missions, but only when they fulfilled these specific purposes. As Tey Diana Rebolledo has written, Luhan and Austin, among "others who helped create the mystique of New Mexican culture during the period were, in effect, appropriating the culture they found so fascinating."[60]

◪ On Pursuit of a Home ◪

They looked to these cultures with deeply engrained convictions about how each tradition could best contribute to the multicultural mix they envisioned, and they opposed policies addressing present-day needs of and changes in these communities. While this work would prove disheartening to people of color, it also ultimately limited the ability of Luhan and Austin to be truthful about their lives.

Their campaign against the Bursum Bill begins to illustrate this process, showing how they each dismissed alternative views on how best to guard cultural traditions in the state. The controversy emerged in 1922, when a U.S. senator from New Mexico, Holm Olaf Bursum, proposed that the state resolve long-standing landownership disputes between Pueblos and other claimants by granting land titles to any non-Pueblo owners whose titles dated back to at least 1902.[61] Though Bursum intended his bill to resolve disputes between Pueblos and individuals (many of them Hispanic) who both claimed title to the land, he and other lawmakers soon found themselves targets of disapproval from several different groups of protestors.

The nineteen New Mexico Pueblos, who stood to lose substantial portions of land, joined together in an All-Pueblo Council effort to campaign against the bill. Tony Lujan played an active role in this protest. The General Federation of Women's Clubs, in one of the century's most interesting political alliances, joined the Pueblos in their efforts. Stella Atwood, the organization's "Indian Welfare Committee" chair, recruited John Collier, a former settlement-house worker (and later the commissioner of Indian affairs under the Roosevelt administration), to campaign against the bill on their behalf. Under his direction, thousands of clubwomen from across the nation wrote informed letters of protest to their representatives in Washington. Collier had, in fact, first experienced life at the Pueblos as a visitor to Luhan's home in Taos. And it was Luhan, Austin, and their literary and artistic comrades who made up the third wing of the attack on the Bursum Bill: as intellectuals, they took up their pens and wrote passionate pieces in defense of Indian rights and culture. Thanks to these multilayered efforts, the bill was soundly defeated.

⬙ CHAPTER ONE ⬙

In the behind-the-scenes work that went into this heavily orchestrat-ed fight, Luhan and Austin revealed both their strengths and limitations as cultural visionaries. Luhan threw herself into the project with a passion she usually reserved for romantic affairs: this was the work she had come to New Mexico to do. The protest against the bill was a political effort, but for Luhan it carried deep cultural connotations. During the campaign, she wrote to Austin about her goals: "I am having 500 Pamphlet copies made for distributing. . . . So little has been written or said during our pub-licity wave that is of any permanent value for the *real* thing that interests us—i.e., the preservation of the Indian culture."[62] Luhan felt encouraged by the public's response, which she referred to as a "latent sympathy" that had been "awakened." "The country almost has seemed to *go Indian*," Luhan exclaimed to Austin in a subsequent letter, professing her certainty that "we want *as a nation* to value the Indian as we value our selves. . . . Please get busy and write—write. Keep the indian [*sic*] *in* the public eye and soon he will be an integral part of the public welfare."[63]

Austin, who was back in New York at this time, promised Luhan her full participation: "You can count on me," she wrote, "for all that I am able to do."[64] In 1923, she made a speech about the bill before the National Popular Government League in Washington, D.C. Sliding between the political goals of the campaign and the cultural goals artic-ulated by Luhan, she argued the United States not only needed to honor its treaty obligations to the Pueblos, but also to recognize Pueblo cul-ture as a model. "Every year," she explained to her listeners, many of whom were women, "increasing thousands of us have come to know the Indian and realize that he has a contribution to make to our culture that we cannot throw away." In a passage showing the influence of Frances Willard in its presumption that women wanted to make their society a better "home" for all, Austin challenged her audience:

> Wouldn't you like to know how these co-operative
> commonwealths managed to avoid prostitution?
> Wouldn't you like to know how they manage that

there are no mothers of dependent children working their hearts and lives out in the struggle to keep the family together? Wouldn't you like to especially know how they manage to raise the plane of crowd activity until it is their highest and not their lowest state, as it is with us? But how shall we learn if we permit the present political policy to be carried out?

Austin encouraged her listeners to remember the duties of suffrage: "Now that American women have assumed the rights and obligations of voters," she told them, they had a service to perform on behalf of American Indians.[65] Her remarks imply that women are white and Indians are Indians, leaving one to assume that Indian women were better off preserving traditional life than becoming modern, active participants in the political process.

While the speech clearly reflects Austin's good intentions, it shows how these intentions contributed to the ultimately static version of New Mexican culture that she and Luhan offered Americans. Like their autobiographical writing, Austin and Luhan's struggle against the Bursum Bill formed part of their larger strategy to increase American recognition of cultural diversity. And like their autobiographical writing, the rhetoric they espoused against the bill illustrated a tendency to essentialize and romanticize American Indian culture. This romanticism was a means to a noble end: the preservation of American Indian land rights. Still, other stories about Austin and Luhan's public work illustrate the extent to which they consciously crafted idealized portraits of culture in New Mexico rather than deal with the actual complexities and tensions of cultural coexistence, thus sustaining the flawed conception of New Mexico as a haven for timeless tradition that continues today.

For example, Luhan's relationship to Tony, portrayed so romantically in her writing, actually generated controversy, playing a particularly divisive role in the Bursum Bill campaign. At this time, Mabel and Tony lived together openly at her house in Taos but had not yet married. In fact, Tony was still married to his wife from Taos Pueblo, Candelaria. Austin felt her friend's adulterous relationship with a Pueblo man would be a radical impediment to the more moderate reforms they were pursuing and a threat to the coalition they had built. In April 1923, Austin wrote to Luhan that recent "inquiries" had confirmed that "while there is no danger of any action against you, there is a determined effort to push you into newspaper publicity. The remedy for that is as I told you, to go away and be married quietly where there are no newspapers, and stay away for two or three weeks."[66]

While Austin and Luhan's activist friends may have been most concerned about perceptions of adultery, they were also likely aware that many Americans opposed interracial marriages, especially those that disrupted both racial and gender hierarchies by uniting white women and men of color. Interracial marriages had long been a part of the social fabric in New Mexico, but in neighboring Arizona, the state's Supreme Court upheld a law banning marriage between Anglos and American Indians only two years before Mabel and Tony wed.[67] Mabel and Tony's marriage violated deeply ingrained codes of behavior.[68]

Despite the bravado Luhan eventually displayed regarding her relationship in her writings, she did in fact experience deep conflicts over what to do about her relationship with Tony. She knew it posed larger problems than the "scapegoating" issue feared by Austin: already it had distanced Tony from Taos Pueblo.[69] She shared many of her fears and hesitancies in letters and journal entries she sent to her friend Alice Corbin Henderson, a poet living in Santa Fe. As Luhan confided to Henderson, marriage would force them to confront their cultural differences more directly than they had in the past.[70] She feared marriage would sever Tony from the Pueblo and lead her mother to discontinue the one-thousand-dollar allowance she sent each month. But she feared losing Tony more than these consequences, and apparently he felt the same way. With the help of allies in Taos and a thirty-five-dollar monthly payment to Candelaria, Mabel and Tony arranged for Tony's divorce and their own wedding license.[71] On April 17, 1923, as Luhan confided in a letter to Henderson, they were married in a hasty ceremony, at the home of a local clergyman.[72]

Contrary to the sense of contentment Luhan used to describe her relationship with Tony in her published writings, her correspondence with Henderson and Austin attests to the nervousness she actually experienced in awaiting the response to her marriage. Luhan wrote to Austin a few days after the wedding to assuage her friend's fears about the publicity consequences of getting married locally. "Tony and I were married this week and everybody has been very pleased about it here," she asserted, with a tinge of overconfidence. "Also, Tony and I are happier and feel very good about it. So that's all right."[73] Austin congratulated her friends, but with reservations: "I am sure you will feel better satisfied with your life now that it is four square with the world in which we happen to be living," she wrote. "I was sorry you didn't go away and avoid the newspaper publicity, I hope it won't make any difference with your family, it won't, of course, with your friends."[74] The conflict between the women was clear if not fully articulated: Austin believed Luhan's decisions had set her at odds with mainstream America, making reforms on behalf of American Indians more difficult, while Luhan felt compelled to follow her heart. For Luhan, political reforms had taken a temporary backseat to personal and cultural ones. Neither woman, however, elaborated on their differing approaches to reform in their published work; to acknowledge such tension might have called into question the potential achievement of a peaceful multicultural home.

In fact, the tensions between Luhan and Austin did not dissipate easily, but rose to the surface again in later years, when a crisis in Austin's life led her to lash out at Mabel's relationship with Tony Lujan. Failing to disclose bitter personal incidents may not reveal conscious distortion of the truth, but the facts of this particular disagreement do at least testify to the discrepancy between the vision of multicultural harmony that the women popularized and the actual tension of cultural relations in New Mexico. In the mid-1920s, Austin accused Luhan of diminishing her in the eyes of Austin's niece, whom Austin had tried unsuccessfully to adopt following the deaths of her parents. Austin responded to this perceived breach in Luhan's loyalty by proclaiming that her own faith in Luhan, especially with regard to Tony, had far exceeded that of others. "I have never mentioned this to you before, because I did respect your relations with him," she explained, "but you make it necessary that I should explicitly tell you that [he is] a joke—a good natured and occasionally ribald joke, but still a joke—to most of the people who come to your house." Austin also chastised Luhan for once preventing her husband from keeping an engagement to participate in a performance of Indian music she had arranged for a radio show. She accused Mabel of putting Tony in a position where Austin had "no choice" but to blame his unreliability on his race, the only excuse, she claimed, that the audience would accept. "I gave you and Tony a chance to play a respected part," Austin chided, trying to lay the blame for her derogatory remark onto her friends.[75] For her part, Luhan later wrote a posthumous piece about her friend in which she claimed that Austin had humiliated Tony during their appearance before a New York audience. After giving a lecture about "Indian Life" (while wearing a "shawl over her head" and holding "two bunches of flowers in her hands"), Austin ordered Tony to sing the Corn Dance song, an embarrassment from which, Luhan claimed, Tony never recovered.[76] Such personal disputes and acts of cultural insensitivity hardly expose Austin and Luhan as failed seekers of cultural reform, but they do begin to tell stories the women left out of their autobiographies.

Mary Austin's Frustrations

The tone of certainty characterizing Austin's autobiography ran counter to the insecurities and arrogance plaguing her personal life. For this reason, the pursuit of cultural relativism that she undertook in Santa Fe (and congratulated herself on in *Earth Horizon*) did not bring her the self-satisfaction she craved. Her spite toward Mabel and Tony Luhan, revealed in the incidents described above, may have emerged from jealousy of their happiness. In one letter to Luhan, apparently written while Tony was away, Austin wrote grumpily, "Yes, I can understand how lonely you are without Tony. I have been lonely for many years, and don't look forward to being anything else for the rest of my life, but one never gets used to it."[77]

Collectively, Austin's outbursts toward Luhan reflect just one facet of her frustrated desire to "belong" to a home like the one she expressed hope for in *Earth Horizon*. To live without the emotional benefits Mabel received from her relationship with Tony was one thing, but to find herself an isolated member of her larger community posed greater dilemmas. Again, Austin did not hesitate to express contrary opinions, but her autobiography did not deal at length with the ultimate difficulties she faced in creating the home she longed for. Despite her publicly professed hope for Santa Fe's promise of acceptance, she privately continued to find herself experiencing misunderstanding, often because she refused to practice the cultural tolerance she preached.

The DAR statue controversy is but one example of many instances where Austin felt certain she knew better than her Santa Fe neighbors about how to preserve multiple cultural heritages in New Mexico. In 1926, she offered vocal opposition to an effort by the Southwestern Federation of Women's Clubs (likely boasting membership that had participated in the campaign against the Bursum Bill) to establish a "Chautauqua" event in Santa Fe. The program promised to bring thousands of Anglo visitors to New Mexico—but, in Austin's opinion, such tourism threatened the traditions that attracted visitors in the first place. By her reasoning, the Chautauqua would kill cultural traditions through connoisseurship, making them something to be "learned" rather than the defining features of living communities.[78] Austin and others who sided with her won the debate. But she no doubt also alienated the very people who most needed the education in diversity that Santa Fe could offer. In this respect, her actual experiences in Santa Fe had a less successful outcome in winning hearts and minds to cultural relativism than *Earth Horizon* had promised. In some ways, she wanted to keep Santa Fe to herself.[79]

She pursued her work in preserving American Indian and Hispanic cultures with a passion for "authenticity" that led her to exclude others, including American Indians and Hispanics, from her work. In 1927 she participated in the founding of the Spanish Colonial Arts Society, and in 1929 she undertook a study of Spanish folklore in New Mexico. But she resisted the assistance of Arthur Leon Campa, an aspiring University of New Mexico folklorist now regarded as one of the founding intellectuals of Chicano Studies.[80] She even went so far as to state in a letter to the university that she might accept his work as a translator but not as a collaborator.[81] Her Spanish skills were apparently quite weak, making her reluctance to bring Campa's work into her own project all the more striking.[82] Only after it became clear that Campa had the support of both university officials and Bronson Cutting, local arts patron and U.S. senator, did Austin consent to the collaboration. She continued the project with Campa, but she never lost the tone of an "expert" speaking to a supposed novice, even advising him on how best to pursue the studies he eventually undertook at Columbia University.

Similarly, in the field of Spanish colonial arts, Austin believed that only she knew best when it came to preserving them, thus limiting the possibility of realizing the multicultural ideal she supposedly espoused. While recuperating from an illness, she perceived the need for an active campaign to preserve this style of craftsmanship, and, as she put it in *Earth Horizon*, she "got up from [her] bed and set the Spanish colonial arts in motion." She also wrote proudly in her autobiography of the efforts made by her and other artists to rescue Santa Fe's annual Fiesta from the hands of tourism promoters and instead to "persuad[e] the natives and finally the rest of the community" that the event "should be Spanish." (As the efforts of Cleofas Jaramillo, detailed in Chapter 2, exposed in later years, this did not mean "Spanish" people could expect full participation in planning this event.) She further prided herself on finding the money, through a private anonymous donor at Yale, to preserve the *santuario* at Chimayo, "an excellent example of an old private chapel, with painted reredos and altar and decorations."[83]

Austin's efforts, as she so boldly put it, to recover and rebuild the "shattered culture" of New Mexico, earned her the commendation of Anglo peers and Hispanic and American Indian beneficiaries even as it frustrated the Chamber of Commerce forces she pitted herself against.[84] When I interviewed the niece of Jaramillo, Rosa Montoya, she was eager to point out how highly her aunt had thought of Austin (especially in contrast to Luhan, whom Montoya, who grew up in Taos, remembered first as a woman infamous for her adulterous acts).[85] Austin worked at preserving Spanish traditions in New Mexico as devotedly as she had campaigned for American Indian culture since her Owens Valley days.

But for both cultures, her efforts carried a tone of paternalism and a lack of consideration for representatives of "shattered" cultures' own plans for renewal and advancement. For example, she argued that the Spanish American Normal School started by Jaramillo's husband in 1909, as well as another state-sponsored training school in San José, should prepare children for craft production, not for teaching skills. In a letter to the president of the University of New Mexico, she explained her belief that the "racial temperament" of Hispanic New Mexicans was suited for "creative craftsmanship" rather than a curriculum designed for "Nordic temperaments." (She did not explain, exactly, which kind of curriculum suited this group.) Thus, Austin saw the proper role of such schools as that of preparing young Hispanics to make a "gift" to the state's culture, failing to consider whether a craft-oriented education would, in fact, help them to balance success in a changing economy with preservation of cultural identity.[86] Again, Austin's active campaign for multiculturalism did not appear to be as "open" to cultural influences as *Earth Horizon* led readers to believe.

She expressed her ideas about the potential for Hispanic culture in New Mexico more publicly in a magazine article prepared for *The Survey*'s 1931 issue devoted to the topic of Mexicans in the United States. In "Mexicans and New Mexico," Austin described "native

Fig. 8:
Mary Austin in High
Comb and Shawl, 1932.
Photograph by Arnold
Genthe. Courtesy of the
Library of Congress,
Prints and Photographs
Division, LC-G412-T-
6085-002.

New Mexicans" (by which she meant Hispanic New Mexicans) as a
distinct cultural group and praised the traditions of "socio-political
inheritance of communistic living," or "group-mindedness," supposedly offered by Spanish and Mexican colonialism to the state. In other
words, she set up this culture, as she had often done before with
American Indian cultures, as an "alternative" to U.S. capitalism, one
that should be preserved without changes. "If we demand that
[Mexican immigrants] become average installment-plan, subrotarian
middle-class Americans," she challenged her readers, "in the course of
time they will become as good at that as our other remotely alien

immigrants. But why ask it?"[87] She encouraged her readers, many of whom likely viewed Hispanics as backward or lazy, to have faith in the contribution of Hispanic folk traditions to the cultural health of the state. Her motives were idealistic, but her vision ultimately argued against expanding American systems of wealth and capital to Hispanics, thus shutting them off from benefiting from the economic changes that had already endangered and changed their culture.

Earth Horizon did not document this aspect of her multicultural strategy, only what she had learned about the value of the "authentic" cultures she had found in the Southwest. Her preference for preserving cultural traditions rather than creating economic opportunities took place at the expense of Hispanic and American Indian New Mexicans, as the stories of Jaramillo, Fabiola Cabeza de Baca, Kay Bennett, and Pablita Velarde will further reveal.

Mabel Dodge Luhan's Retreat

Where Austin's views show the limitations of her multicultural ideals in the public sphere, Luhan lived with the limitations such a vision could put on private life. Her relationship with Tony continued to prove susceptible to the cultural barriers that she proclaimed it had transcended in *Edge of Taos Desert*. The Luhans had a tumultuous marriage that included her pursuit of the affections of D. H. Lawrence and Tony's continued involvement with his ex-wife and other women. As Luhan's biographer Lois Palken Rudnick has noted, Tony underwent changes during his years with Mabel that "were not in keeping with the pristine image of him she always created for public consumption." He had a passion for modern clothes and cars that conformed neither to rules for living at the conservative Taos Pueblo nor to Mabel's vision of the "primitive" life she had discovered there.[88] Nor did Mabel adapt to this world according to the vision she proclaimed in *Edge of Taos Desert*.

She remained for the most part a New York society woman who had moved to Taos rather than a woman who had integrated herself into the village or the Pueblo.

In fact, Luhan's first book about New Mexico, *Lorenzo in Taos*, an exploration of her relationship with D. H. Lawrence, included a poem that remarked "What incomprehensible aloneness for the white woman / Who crosses over into the Indian heart!," thus indicating the gulf that had continued between her and Tony.[89] Similarly, *Winter in Taos*, also published before *Edge of Taos Desert*, also makes allusions to her sense of distance from the Pueblo traditions that had drawn her to New Mexico, thus contradicting her account of "conversion" in the later book. *Winter in Taos* describes the events of one winter day in Taos, during which Luhan rhapsodizes about the natural world and how it manifests seasonal changes at Taos, all the while staying at her home and waiting for Tony to return from his daily errands. Rudnick has interpreted this text as a "utopian domestic novel" in which Luhan "integrates Pueblo and Anglo traditions" in her examination of the seasons. This allowed her, Rudnick asserts, to give "her Anglo readers the chance to enter imaginatively into a new Eden that has been regained by the interracial partnership of a restored Adam and Eve."[90]

But as Rudnick recognizes, the "Adam and Eve" in *Winter in Taos* bear unbalanced powers of influence. Luhan's ideas about seasonal changes and the natural world, as expressed in this text, had been influenced by Tony, and she presents them as ideas she has borrowed and incorporated into her own worldview. But she seems to have believed such interchange should only be a one-way process. She expresses an implicit disapproval for Pueblo adaptation of Anglo traditions, as when she stands by her decision to eat whole wheat bread prepared in the traditional Pueblo manner, while many residents of Taos Pueblo preferred the bread more easily available at the market. "The Indians are, by some kind of predilection, and by the destiny that has been determined for them by the influence of the Indian Bureau Schools, headed for Progress," Luhan complained to her readers, "a mechanical civilization and an undermined racial stock, while some of us white people are said to be regressing to an earlier mode of life instead of conforming to our present-day environment."[91] Her awareness of these conflicting views about the proper direction of American Indian culture is striking, but she leaves readers wondering how such conflicts can be reconciled with the utopian vision of cultural coexistence she offers elsewhere. She also seems to dismiss American Indian desires for economic progress as the outcome of shortsighted U.S. government policy, rather than seriously exploring why some American Indians, like her husband, desired some forms of cultural change.

A few years after publishing *Winter in Taos*, Luhan would publish *Edge of Taos Desert*, a book that implied she had broken with all the confines of Anglo tradition, but *Winter in Taos* carries more conservative messages about womanhood. In the earlier book, she portrays herself as a housewife who finds she has "something left over in me from my grandmother" and turns her attention to preserving and baking (or paying her Mexican housekeeper to perform these tasks).[92] Similarly, the drive of the book's narrative is her day-long wait for Tony to return home, reflecting her dependence on her husband. Thus, while *Winter in Taos* bears the exotic setting of a multicultural environment, it ultimately conveys fairly traditional ideas about culture and gender and the comforts of the "old ways," ideas she obscured in *Edge of Taos Desert*. In her analysis of Luhan's search for sexual innovation and fulfillment, historian Ellen Kay Trimberger has written that Mabel and Tony's marriage "was perhaps not so different from the union of the separate spheres characteristic of the mid-nineteenth-century American bourgeoisie."[93] Furthermore, historian Margaret Jacobs has concluded that Luhan saw her interracial marriage as a means for an "Indian man [to] save his white wife and her decaying society."[94] Through Tony's Indian masculinity, Mabel may have hoped to recapture the traditional femininity she ascribed to women of color.

Still, her ultimate uncertainty about the possibility of doing so became evident when she confessed to a friend that she did not truly support marriages between Anglos and American Indians, even though she actively pursued making public statements to the contrary. In 1933, she wrote to John Collier of a lecture on "the Mestizo" she had recently heard, and she shared her own thoughts on the subject with her old friend, who had recently been appointed by President Roosevelt as commissioner of Indian affairs. "Although I married an Indian," Luhan mused, "I did not do so when we were both young (and I don't believe in this for others). I cannot bring myself to change from my previous hope that the indian [sic] culture may be saved, as it cannot be if he becomes absorbed into the Mexican or the white races, though I must admit I do not yet see the solution for the growing indian [sic] generations."[95] Only a year before, she had in fact made great public relations efforts to describe her marriage in newspaper interviews as a model for others imitate: "I believe other marriages will follow mine," she had indicated to one reporter, "that the races may amalgamate and the Indians will be the ones that will save our race."[96] Thus, Luhan had chosen a public stance on her marriage that reflected her progressive views about the potential for multicultural environments. But this private correspondence suggests she did not necessarily recommend intermarriage as a route for cultural preservation. Neither, does it seem, could she favorably imagine a place in even a multicultural society for people with more than one ethnic background. Apparently she believed her marriage was a symbol of cultural interaction and appreciation rather than a model for action. This was the vision of her marriage that she wrote into *Edge of Taos Desert*, a book which contradicted her earlier writing by implying that her marriage made it possible for her to "escape to reality" through the vehicle of an invigorating, "traditional," and interracial marriage.

In another version of reality, Luhan's marriage and life in Taos often put her directly at odds with the norms of the Pueblo as well as the Hispanic residents of the area. Her role in ending Tony's marriage to Candelaria effectively alienated her from many people living at Taos Pueblo, and her status as a divorced and adulterous woman hardly ingratiated her with the Hispanic (and Catholic) members of the community. Moreover, she took stands on land issues that further

Fig. 9: Mabel Dodge Luhan with Indian Friends in Taos. Courtesy of the Yale Collection of American Literature, Beinecke Rare Book and Manuscript Library, Yale University.

distanced her from the townspeople, such as when, in 1935, she initiated a lawsuit against the village because she opposed its incorporation and the accompanying widening of streets.[97] Hispanics served as the civic leaders of Taos during Luhan's time there: as ethnologist John Bodine wrote of the Taos community in 1968, "Anglos relished their enclaved minority status in this 'foreign' community and were quite willing to allow the local inhabitants to run the petty affairs of government."[98] But when Luhan and others began to believe that the 1934 incorporation of the village threatened, as her lawyer put it in one letter, the "unique condition" of the village, they took a stand against the development sponsored by the town leaders.[99] Apparently the matter ended when the state interceded to draw clearer demarcations between land belonging to the village and land belonging to Luhan.

"Control over land and water," writes anthropologist Sylvia Rodríguez, "remains the primary bone of contention in the relations among Indian, Hispano, and Anglo populations in northern New Mexico."[100] Luhan's public, utopian vision of Taos did not highlight such tensions, but it likely exacerbated them. As Austin did in her efforts to popularize and preserve a tri-ethnic idyll, Luhan reduced Hispanics and American Indians in New Mexico to premodern "types" who needed to play a certain part to fulfill that ideal. And in the case of Taos, Luhan's ideal held a particularly harsh vision for Hispanics, who were excluded from many of the benefits of cultural esteem and tourism that residents of Taos Pueblo received in the wake of Luhan's arrival. "The Spanish find themselves victims of a system which demands attitudes of accommodation," wrote John Bodine of the Taos community, "in decided contrast to their personal goals of achievement, but which has so far offered them no real avenue of escape. They are trapped." Austin's point about the need to prevent Hispanics from becoming "average installment-plan, subrotarian middle-class Americans" and Luhan's interference in Taos's attempt to develop itself economically show how this trap emerged not just from the economic forces of conquest predating their arrival in New Mexico. Rather, Austin and Luhan's one-sided ideal of cultural "purity" served as an idealistic but ultimately restrictive and essentialist form of cultural conquest.

This conquest, unsurprisingly, did not play out for Hispanics and American Indians in the same way. Luhan, described by Rodríguez as the woman who really "inaugurated the campaign to make Taos famous," did so according to a hierarchical vision of culture that placed the "purity" of Pueblo culture at the top. A wistful longing for the "Spanish" culture that had held reign in New Mexico before the arrival of Anglo conquerors (and, it was implied, recent immigrants from Mexico) ran only a distant second in this paradigm. Both Austin and Luhan also maintained a commonly held distinction between

"Spanish" and "Mexican" that I will discuss at further length in telling Jaramillo's story. What bears stating here is that this distinction emerged from Anglos' perception of a change in the status of Hispanic culture over time, a supposed decline from "Spanish" regality to "Mexican" poverty, rather than from an actual difference in the ethnic roots of Hispanic New Mexicans.

Luhan included descriptions of Hispanic culture in the Taos area in *Edge of Taos Desert*, but they read almost like an afterthought. "The Mexicans in Taos Valley seemed a sad lot to me when I first came," she reflected, moving on to remind her readers of the history of Spanish conquest in New Mexico. She speculated that feelings of "hatred and fear of the white American conqueror" among "Mexicans" had combined with "a half-contemptuous, half-envious regard for the Indians who have kept themselves to themselves through everything from the Spanish conquest and on through the American conquest." She did not hesitate to share her negative first impression of Hispanic New Mexicans: "Dreary feelings seemed to me to rule them and sap their vitality and their hope."[101]

Her assertions here exemplify the narrow cultural vision that she, Austin, and other Anglos imposed on all people of color in New Mexico. In her estimation, cultures were most valuable when they were most "pure," doing everything they could to function as if conquest had not occurred. This traditionalist approach clearly privileged American Indians over Hispanic and mestizo cultures, and it could be politically effective, as seen in the case of the Bursum Bill. The campaign to defeat that legislation won overwhelming support among Anglos because it fulfilled their ideals of preserving ancient traditions: as Rodríguez writes, it is "no mere coincidence that while an Anglo lobby stepped forth to advocate the Indian land cause, none did so for the Hispano."[102] One historian has argued that Hispano subsistence farmers in northern New Mexico lost 80 percent of their lands between 1846 and 1912.[103] Still, Hispanics' attempts to reclaim land they had lost wrongfully did not draw the general attention of Anglos until the late 1960s. As the stories of Jaramillo and Cabeza de Baca reveal,

Hispanics in New Mexico considered the rectification of this dispossession a priority for cultural activism long before it became a matter of the Anglo vision of "multiculturalism."

The Appeal of Tradition

Austin and Luhan did not see dispossession and poverty as issues that needed or could receive immediate correction; undoubtedly they prioritized the preservation of culture over the reversal of economic conquest in which they felt they had played little part. While the Bursum Bill campaign was one notable exception, they primarily concerned themselves with cultural, rather than economic issues: even when that campaign pursued land rights, cultural preservation provided the rationale for doing so. Driven to New Mexico by the dilemmas they had faced as women in more industrialized regions of the United States, they turned to women in American Indian and Hispanic cultures for inspiration and sought ways to prevent those cultures from changing. Historian Margaret Jacobs has called this movement "antimodern feminism," pointing out in particular that Austin, Luhan, and others were eager to seize on an image of American Indian women as embodiments of "a natural and healthy sexuality." Controversies in the 1920s over the rights of the Pueblos to stage dances that some moral reformers considered lascivious drew heartfelt passion from these antimodern feminists. They sought ways not only to preserve this form of cultural expression but also to support other efforts, such as arts and crafts, that, as Jacobs puts it, might help "Pueblo women to retain their premodern role in the home."[104]

Austin and Luhan both defined themselves as "modern" women, which makes these efforts at preserving premodern roles for women a little puzzling. Yet both had come to feel that "modern" life had left Anglo women worse off in terms of cultural power than they had been in the premodern world. Luhan tried to reaccess this power of sexual difference in her life through the role of romantic muse and as a wife to a "truly masculine" Indian man. For her part, Austin tried to blend Frances Willard's power of the "hearth" into her own less traditional pursuits. Neither advocated that American women move back to preindustrial models of womanhood: they had gained too much in their own lives from the twentieth-century possibilities for American women—education, employment opportunities, activism skills, sexual identities, and a certain amount of liberated individualism—to suggest moving backward. But in New Mexican Hispanic and American Indian cultures, in which they felt women still benefited from the power of the home, they perceived a way in which they could simultaneously argue for modern American feminism *and* traditional models of womanhood. This is difficult to see by reading their memoirs alone, but by comparing these memoirs to the actions and statements they left out of their memoirs, and reading them within the context of U.S. women's history, we can see a certain logic to their method.

Austin and Luhan crafted a new approach to resolving what was actually an old feminist dilemma. In the nineteenth-century industrializing United States, the era from which Austin and Luhan had both sought distance, women had accessed power through the "separate spheres" model of difference. They maintained power in the domestic sphere, where they cultivated communalism through nurturing their children, while men relied on the model of individualism and maintained political and social power in the public sphere. The late nineteenth-century "Woman's Movement" drew steam from arguing that woman (with a universal "a") should extend her domestic virtues further into the public sphere. Through causes like abolitionism, temperance, and suffrage, women sought to extend the definition of "home" to encompass a broader sphere of influence. With the passage of the Nineteenth Amendment in 1920, women gained suffrage but lost some of their power to advocate social change through the voice of "difference."

This shift from arguing for greater power for feminine virtue to negotiating the terrain of civil equality posed rhetorical difficulties for

Fig. 10: Woman at Hearth. Photograph from Mabel Dodge Luhan's Collection. Courtesy of the Yale Collection of American Literature, Beinecke Rare Book and Manuscript Library, Yale University.

women's movements after 1920. Austin and Luhan, who took part in the women's movement both before and after this shift, did not want for causes to advocate, but they did lack a rallying cry that united women as much as suffrage had. This crisis of a directing philosophy did not stall gains in women's power, particularly in terms of the increased number of married women who began to work outside the home during World War II. But it did make it impossible for a widespread women's movement to emerge until the 1960s, when second-wave feminism at last attempted to embrace the different approaches and perspectives from which women could argue for power.[105]

❦ On Pursuit of a Home ❦

In the 1910s, 1920s, and 1930s, Luhan and Austin attempted an earlier solution to this problem by rhetorically displacing the power of "difference" onto women of color while embracing the modern role of "equality" for themselves. Comparing their rhetorical strategy and the realities of their and others' experiences in New Mexico suggests they desired a greater break from nineteenth-century ideas of gender and race than they were actually able to achieve. Just as it continues to do for some today, New Mexico seemed to promise Luhan and Austin a multicultural "utopia," one particularly suited for their project of reimagining women's roles in the public sphere. But their actual experiences in New Mexico fell short of perfection, as revealed when Luhan discovered that her husband, like many other Pueblo Indians, actually desired change, as well as when Austin found herself isolated by her conviction that she knew better than the people she wanted most to help. Moreover, Austin and Luhan clearly attributed "truths" to Hispanic and American Indian cultures that emerged from their own ideal visions of those cultures, rather than from the realities faced by Hispanic and American Indian people.

Thus, Luhan and Austin begin to tell us a new story about the history of cultural relativism. They faced dilemmas inherent to what has come to be called multiculturalism when they failed to recognize that cultures that coexist ultimately change as a result. For Anglos of their generation, this "coexistence" seemed a treasure worth preserving with all of its elements intact. But they did not acknowledge that processes of conquest, in which Anglos had the firm upper hand, had already taken place, and that they, in fact, were acting out those processes themselves. When they maintained clear-cut expectations for what a culture should be, and how it should best contribute to the good of a multicultural society, they ultimately rendered such cultures into less powerful, if not powerless, contributors to the "blend" they sought. And when they implicitly expected that Hispanic and American Indian women should decline to take advantage of the advances in the U.S. women's movement that had allowed Austin and Luhan to move away themselves from "traditional" roles, they only made this dilemma worse. They split "traditional" and "progressive" womanhood along ethnic lines, failing to envision a way for women in New Mexico to be on an equal footing with one another. The sentiments behind the ideal home they promised readers actually perpetuated, even intensified, the inequitable distribution of economic and social power.

It would not have been impossible for Austin and Luhan to suggest an alternative model of New Mexican multiculturalism, one in which Anglo cultural values did not remain dominant and Hispanic and American Indian traits were not confined to static traditions. Had they been more interested in advocating such a model, they would have found a ready source for ideas in the anthropological theories of Elsie Clews Parsons, a prominent modernist anthropologist who made Pueblo cultures in New Mexico the subject of some of her most groundbreaking work. A good friend of Luhan's, Parsons did fieldwork in New Mexico in the 1910s and 1920s, focusing on how centuries of Hispanic and then Anglo presence in the region had changed Pueblo culture. She attributed the strength of Pueblo culture to its ability to change and adapt, and reported her findings to the American Folklore Society as part of her presidential address in 1920: "Were there less mobility or elasticity [in Pueblo culture], given such an encroaching culture as that of proselytizing Spain or of the United Sates, industrializing, and intolerant of social dissimilarity, rigidity of pattern would mean cultural downfall and annihilation."[106] Parsons also found extensive cultural variations from one Pueblo to another to be exemplary of this culture's ability to change without losing core values. Based on her findings, she developed an influential theory of cultural adaptation. Cultures like the Pueblos, she argued in *Pueblo Indian Religion*, finally published in 1939, do not simply either stay the same or die out: they are always undergoing processes of change, borrowing from other cultures especially when doing so will help to strengthen cultural identity.[107]

Clearly, Luhan and Austin were aware of this emerging theory of "cultural borrowing," and clearly they saw it in action in New Mexico. Why, then, did they choose to focus their public portrayals of New Mexico on "timelessness" and "traditionalism"? Perhaps the idea of

Fig. 11: Elsie Clews Parsons in the Southwest, 1920. Courtesy of the Rye Historical Society.

antimodern Hispanic and American Indian cultures appealed to Anglo romanticism and the desire for escape from the modern world in the 1910s, 1920s, and 1930s as much as it does to some Anglos today—in fact, contemporary visitors to Taos can indulge in such perceptions while staying at Mabel Dodge Luhan's house, now an upscale bed and breakfast. For despite the all-too-modern evidence of New Mexico's technological and economic state of existence, Anglo visitors and residents of the state continue to be pulled in by the vision of New Mexico outlined in this book's introduction, as a place that is not only different from the rest of America, but is so by virtue of its supposed timelessness.

Still, Luhan and Austin should have known better—and perhaps they did. Their public embracing of New Mexico as a premodern place, where premodern roles for women provided a traditional source of strength and a necessary complement to the progressive roles attained by Anglo women, seems to have been a strategic decision that recognized this rhetoric as the most direct way to capture Anglo audiences' attention and support. Describing New Mexican cultural change in its full complexity, as Parsons attempted in her anthropological theories, may have been more realistic and more beneficial for the economic status of the state's American Indian and Hispanic residents. But relying on more stereotypical Anglo ideas about tradition and women of color granted them a more immediate and more interested audience.

In this respect, Austin's and Luhan's projection of "traditional" feminine power onto Hispanic and American Indian women produced a valuable lesson for Jaramillo, Cabeza de Baca, Bennett, and Velarde. When these women undertook their own writing and activism, in the years to come, they used Luhan and Austin's rhetoric, rather than Parson's theories, to advocate cultural preservation. As the stories to come show, they found that conventional ideas about tradition carried the most power, even when they did not match up to their actual experiences and economic needs as women of color. Moreover, the idea of women as spokespeople for individual cultural traditions, rather than of the blended and borrowed culture they actually inhabited, continued to provide an expedient means of gaining an audience. While no one woman could perfectly occupy the pedestal of New Mexican womanhood left vacant by the "Pioneer Mother," different women could put on the costumes of traditional New Mexican women in ways that appeased the Anglo-driven desire to preserve "true" cultural traditions and bring about respect for them. Even while publicly emphasizing attributes that filled out such costumes, these Hispanic and American Indian women would privately use their skills as modern, multicultural women to act in ways that advanced their own visions of cultural relations.

Comparing what the women of color wrote while in costume to what they did while outside the public eye, as we have done for Austin and Luhan here, offers contemporary readers a way to understand the dilemmas of multiculturalism in greater depth. This admirable model of cultural relations, we shall see, promises equality and tolerance even as it covers up inequities, and it ultimately places a burden of "traditionalism" onto the backs of women citizens of color. It is my hope that the stories that follow will encourage Americans to more realistically and more equitably embrace the cultural differences that made New Mexico so appealing to Austin and Luhan in the first place.

CHAPTER TWO
Clinging to Tradition
Cleofas Jaramillo and the Transformed Home

*N*o group of New Mexicans found its sense of cultural identity more radically challenged by the gradual forces of Anglo conquest than the elite, or *rico*, class, descendants of the Hispanos who dominated New Mexican affairs at the time of war between the United States and Mexico (1846–48). But this transformation did not occur overnight. The prestige of this class continued even after the Treaty of Guadalupe Hidalgo in 1848 placed New Mexico under U.S. control. As in California, Anglo immigrants to the territory found that working one's way into these existing channels of social power, especially through intermarriage, proved an expedient means of establishing one-self.[1] The higher density of the Hispanic population in New Mexico, combined with intimate ties between Hispanics and American Indians, allowed New Mexican ricos to maintain cultural power in New Mexico that outlasted the ability of Hispanics to do so in California. The absence of a transformative demographic event, such as Anglo immigration to California during the Gold Rush, also made New Mexico's changes in population more subtle and complex. In New Mexico, the decline of Hispanic power took place at a slow, insidious pace as the gradual effects of economic conquest and land dispossession took hold.

While the New Mexican Hispanic elite of the early and mid-twentieth century refused to concede power altogether to the forces of Anglo conquest, they found they needed to define and assert themselves in new, Americanized ways. "Hispanos" became "Spanish Americans," at least when they spoke in English: as the stories in this chapter reveal, they rallied to declare their support for U.S. troops during the 1898 Spanish American War; they socialized with the new Anglo elite of politicians, merchants, and lawyers made rich through land settlements; and they increasingly participated in cultural preservation efforts similar to those initiated by Austin and Luhan. They sent their sons to elite American universities and their daughters to the same convent schools their mothers and grandmothers had gone to, but increasingly educated them in English rather than Spanish.

Cleofas Jaramillo (1878–1956) was one such daughter. She ultimately became a leader in this generation's effort to cultivate awareness of and pride in the Spanish past among all New Mexicans. For audiences of today, this work is most vivid in her book *Romance of a Little Village Girl*, published the year before her death. This series of narratives combines her life story with her accounts of the history and customs of Hispanic New Mexico. In the book's preface, she explained how she wanted to share an otherwise unknown "quiet romance." "Under the apparent deadness of our New Mexico villages," she confided, "there runs a romantic current invisible to the stranger and understood only by their inhabitants." Her preface promises a tale about a sheltering home: an account of "girlhood years that were enriched with comfort and love, innocent of any wickedness, sheltered from all care and grief" and of how "cupid found its way" into this "verdant little nook."[2]

And yet the book ultimately delivers quite a different kind of story. The events described in Jaramillo's autobiography include the loss of two infants, the fatal illness suffered by her husband, the economic devastation endured by her family, the rape and murder of her only

Fig. 12:
Cleofas Jaramillo in
Traditional Dress for
Santa Fe Fiesta. Courtesy
of the Museum of New
Mexico, Neg. No. 9919.

surviving child, and the economic and cultural onslaught waged
against the Hispanic traditions and ideals with which she had grown
up. Moreover, *Romance* hints that her life experiences forced her to
question her most fundamental ideas about tradition, race, and
women. In one devastating instance, when Santa Fe authorities condemned an African American man to death for alleged crimes against
her daughter, she found herself caught in the middle of a painful dispute about race—one she ultimately evaded through silence. Despite
this loss and conflict, she closed her book optimistically, with a

description of her success in starting a Santa Fe folklore society, reviving Spanish traditions, and writing several books documenting these traditions and expressing her nostalgia for them.

Like Austin and Luhan, Jaramillo's books romanticized Hispanic life in the Southwest. But unlike her Anglo literary predecessors, her portrayal of "traditional" New Mexico was fueled by a realistic and deeply personal sense of all that Anglo conquest ultimately cost Hispanics. Her life story shows how women in this generation participated in the efforts of the rico class to cultivate for itself a sense of "Spanish" identity that resisted Anglo stereotypes even as it recognized and profited from them, to cling to the past even when they were so inalterably changed by the present. She capitalized on the romantic view of cultural preservation offered by Luhan and Austin because she found it afforded people like her esteem; as a high-class "Spanish" woman, she was just as reluctant to let go of the privileges of her ethnicity as Luhan and Austin were.

Still, Jaramillo faced a more daunting task. Her writing openly described her quest to preserve Spanish identity as a process of self-defense: economic conquest cost her family its land and wealth, and personal tragedies robbed her of her status as a traditional wife and mother. Still, she proclaimed she had emerged from these tragedies as a champion of tradition. But as I will show here, she chose not to openly reveal the extent to which she had been changed, even modernized, by the events of her life. As a young woman, she embraced some aspects of Americanization, in the spirit of Elsie Clews Parson's theory of cultural borrowing, but as she grew older, she was forced to reckon with changes she did not desire, both in her own status and in that of her culture. Like Austin and Luhan, she ended up homesick for the place she tried to idealize in her writings.

The contradictions between the "romance" promised by Jaramillo's autobiography's title and the tragedy expressed within its pages testify to this homesickness. One literary critic, Genaro Padilla, has attributed her memoir's lack of clear resolution to the difficulties any writer would face in saying exactly what she wanted to in a climate of ethnic hostility and willful erasure. Rather, like other Hispanic writers, she found herself considering "lies, secrets, and silence" as the only conceivable responses to conquest.[3] Her clinging to tradition became one such sort of lie, a way of attempting to adjust to a modern world that would have disempowered her otherwise. Her story, told here against the backdrop of the history of race relations in the state, helps to explain why Americans have continually imagined New Mexico as a place that is unchangingly traditional, even when New Mexicans' lives have actually included both difficult and empowering forms of cultural change.

"Of Spanish Descent"

Jaramillo's privileged young life began in 1878, when she was born to one of the richest families of the state's Hispanic elite. When she later published an account of the ceremonial customs of late nineteenth-century Hispanic New Mexico, she wrote that "the arrival of a new baby was always announced to the relatives and friends by word sent by a messenger saying: 'Mr. and Mrs. So and So announce *que ya tienen un criado, o criada mas a quien mandar*—that you have one more servant at your command.'"[4] If Jaramillo's parents, Martina Lucero Martínez and Julián Antonio Martínez, sent such a message when she was born, it was a purely symbolic gesture: as a daughter of the Martínez family, Jaramillo's "servitude" was characterized by social bonds and standards, especially those for women, but not by hard labor. Understanding these social codes requires a general understanding of the Spanish and Mexican pioneer experience in New Mexico, and its social, religious, cultural, and political foundations and legacies.

When the Spanish entered the region they named New Mexico, they brought a hierarchical but somewhat mutable system of racial identity, with innumerable categories of identity derived from contact between Spaniards and the native populations of Central America.

⬛ CHAPTER TWO ⬛

Historian Juan Gómez-Quiñones and others have demonstrated that the majority of the pioneers who began making their way north from New Spain to New Mexico at the end of the sixteenth century were *mestizos*—the descendents of both Spaniards and the natives of interior Mexico.[5] In fact, of the one thousand or so colonists who settled in Santa Fe by the late seventeenth century, three-fourths were mestizos. A slightly larger number of settlers lived in more dispersed communities by this time, close to the Indian pueblos, which were inhabited by sixty to ninety thousand Pueblo Indians.[6] In 1680, a mestizo named Popé from San Juan Pueblo led a revolt that drove Spanish authority from the region for a time, but by 1693, Governor Diego de Vargas had reestablished colonial New Mexico. Along the lines of the rest of New Spain, these eighteenth-century settlements developed a mestizo and increasingly national character that distanced citizens from Spanish authority and identity.

In the years leading up to 1821, when Mexico achieved its independence from Spain, citizens of colonial New Mexico mostly experienced the events at a distance. But nuevomexicanos definitely engaged in the ideological debates and effects of independence, even if, like citizens in all of Mexico, they had not reached a clear consensus about its desirability and meaning. Through the experience of revolution and the development of Mexico as a consciously mestizo nation, nineteenth-century nuevomexicanos grappled with what it meant to be mestizo both practically and ideologically. Moreover, nuevomexicano interactions with the native inhabitants of New Mexico, primarily the Pueblo tribes, added yet another element of difference to the Mexican system of race and caste.

I emphasize the importance of mestizo identity in the historical development of New Mexico because Jaramillo's narrative of her family's pioneering in New Mexico during this period determinedly ignored this identity. Mestizo qualities did not suit her conception of what it meant to be a Hispanic New Mexican. Jaramillo quite determinedly saw and wrote about herself as "Spanish." To those New Mexicans who today identify as *mestizo/a*, *mexicano/a*, or *chicano/a*, and to those who doubt that any New Mexican family could have maintained a "blood line" as "pure" as Jaramillo claims, her Spanish identity, regardless of its origins, may seem a myth perpetuated by racist prejudice. Nevertheless, to Jaramillo, this identity was very real.

She included elements of her family's history in New Mexico, which began in the early nineteenth century, in *Romance of a Little Village Girl* as well as in the folklore collection *Shadows of the Past/Sombras del Pasado*, published in 1941. In both books, she emphasized the fortitude and faith of the early Spanish settlers in the region. She wrote that her paternal great-grandfather, Don José Manuel Martínez, himself a descendant of the settlers who participated in the reconquest of New Mexico after the 1680 Pueblo Revolt, attempted a settlement in the "wilderness" near Abiquiu in the early nineteenth century. He came to believe that extensive Indian resistance, in the form of raiding, and poor land hindered his progress there, so he petitioned the Mexican government for new land in 1832. He received the title to Tierra Amarilla, described by Jaramillo as "three hundred thousand acres [of] the richest grant in timber, water, and pasture in northern New Mexico."[7] Her grandfather, Don José's son, "inherit[ed] the spirit of colonization from [his] ancestors," and struck out on his own to buy and settle a portion of the Arroyo Hondo Grant in Taos County.[8] This man, Don Vincente Martínez, built a seventeen-room house for his family, as well as a private chapel where they could express "thanksgiving for the safe delivery of the family on several occasions from the attacks of the Indians, who once in a while raided the village."[9] She characterized her grandfather as a leader who came "to help, by means of bloody battle and peaceful law, to bring 'civilization' to 'wilderness'—another family, in short, to help adapt the old customs of Spain to a new land, adding something to the heritage of the Spanish *conquistadores* who came before them."[10]

The story of her maternal grandparents' family, also included in her writings, echoes this theme of heritage-based pride. Jesús María Lucero, Jaramillo's maternal grandfather, met her grandmother on a trade journey from northern New Mexico to Mexico. While in

Chihuahua, Lucero fell in love with a young girl with a "fair face, large blue eyes, and ebony curls" and asked her to be his wife. Jaramillo emphasized her grandmother's "fair" features so readers would see her as the author herself did: as a European pioneer, and not a mestiza. Her grandfather, she wrote, brought his new wife north through "wild and uncivilized land" to Taos County. Jaramillo reported that her maternal grandmother earned a name for herself in New Mexican history: "she has maintained the reputation and fame," she boasted, "of being the most beautiful and charming woman of Spanish descent who came to New Mexico in those early days."[11]

"Of Spanish descent." This phrase became a key aspect of Jaramillo's conception of both her family's past and her own upbringing. Her insistence on this phrase emerged from her investment in what "Spanish" identity had come to mean in the twentieth century. In fact, despite Jaramillo's presentation of her family's heritage as a continuous line back to the conquistadores, historians have shown that the distinction of "Spanish" identity became most powerful in New Mexico *after* the 1846 Anglo conquest of what is today the U.S. Southwest. After this conquest, historian Juan Gómez-Quiñones argues, "a portion of the elite, seeking Anglo acceptance, adopted the euphemistic identity of 'Spanish.' Particularly in but not limited to New Mexico, some individuals among the native-born eventually followed the example of the elite and used the term *Spanish* to designate themselves in their dealings with Anglos."[12] He explains this as a result of the pressures of "Americanization": Jaramillo saw it as a way to distinguish herself both from Americans and other New Mexicans.

Her ability to do so depended on the hierarchical racial system of Spanish colonialism. As historian Ramón Gutiérrez has documented, after the 1750s New Mexican officials increasingly used legal categories of "color," ostensibly depending on a person's parents, to distinguish between New Mexican citizens in court documents, census records, and birth and marriage records.[13] These categories also depended upon subjective assessment. As Gutiérrez explains, "Sometimes a person's racial classification was the result of a personal declaration, at other times it was the subjective assessment of, say, a census taker."[14] While skin color undoubtedly played an important part in determining this classification, other factors had a decisive impact. To be "Spanish" was not only to be "fair" like Jaramillo's grandmother, but also to be a person of reason and honor, the child of a legitimate marriage, and perhaps most importantly, to *not* be a slave. Thus people became "Spanish" when influence (and, perhaps, color) permitted them to do so.[15] Despite flexibility for individuals, the categories remained in place, distinguishing the aristocratic elite from workers and slaves, both through physical associations of color and social associations of wealth and landwnership. While Mexican independence in 1821 had ostensibly laid the groundwork for equality between all Mexican citizens, regardless of racial classification, the legacy of these categories continued.

With the U.S. conquest culminating in the Treaty of Guadalupe Hidalgo, these already established classifications took on new connotations, and thus a renewed intensity. In 1846, General Stephen Kearny proclaimed to the citizens of Santa Fe that they were "no longer Mexican subjects," but had instead "become American citizens."[16] American immigrants to the region, however, not only resisted perceiving nuevomexicanos as citizens, but also persisted in seeing all nuevomexicanos as "Mexicans"—an English term which nuevomexicanos rightfully perceived as having derogatory and racist connotations among Anglos. This was particularly insulting to elite nuevomexicano families such as the one Cleofas Jaramillo was born into because, as historian David C. Gutiérrez puts it, such families already "consider[ed] themselves to be of inherently higher status than the Mexican working masses by virtue of their class standing and their *calidad* and their sense of *limpieza de sangre* (that is, their social 'quality' based on their supposed 'pure' European blood)."[17] According to Gutiérrez and other historians, American immigrants to the region both before and after the conquest were able to establish familial and economic bonds with this elite class because the two groups possessed a common European heritage.[18] But as both Anglo and Mexican immigration to New Mexico increased, calling oneself Spanish became less effective as a strategy for maintaining prestige and more of a symbolic gesture of distinction, an attempt by Spanish-speaking New Mexicans to step away from the derogatory English label of "Mexican." In the early twentieth century, Anglos like Mary Austin ensured the success of this gesture by participating in a celebratory revival of a "pure Spanish" past.

In this respect, calling oneself "Spanish" in English, as Jaramillo would do all of her life, became a defense mechanism. A survey conducted in the mid-1950s by folklorist Arthur L. Campa (the scholar that Mary Austin had hesitated to work with) showed how Spanish-speaking New Mexicans used the term selectively, and the pattern of their selections reveals their motives. He found that his bilingual subjects, when asked "what term they used to designate a person who spoke Spanish and was a native of New Mexico," "invariably" answered "Spanish American" when asked in English, even though they answered "*mexicano*" when asked in Spanish. They elaborated with "*mexicano de México*" when they wanted to emphasize that someone had been born in the other country.[19] Such responses indicate that nuevomexicanos whose families had been in the U.S. Southwest for generations felt they needed to present themselves to Anglos as distinctive from more recent Mexican immigrants, especially since doing so affected Anglo conceptions of whether or not the person in question was "White."

Fading Fortunes

Jaramillo likely did not have to make these kinds of highly charged choices about what to call herself in English until she left the village she grew up in, which may account for her persistence in presenting it as a romantic place, untouched by the outside world. In Arroyo Hondo, her family maintained its elite position well into the late nineteenth century. In *Romance*, she described her parents as hardworking but decidedly aristocratic. Her father's "chief industries were sheep raising, farming and mercantile," but she added that he also had time for "hospitality, religion and even politics."[20] Her mother not only "did her share of the work, raising her large family of five boys and two girls," tending to the family-owned store if necessary, but also "kept three, and sometimes more, servants busy." Jaramillo took care to characterize the relationship between her parents and their servants as a bond of mutual, though clearly hierarchical, devotion. *Shadows of the Past* describes the servants' work as difficult but adds that "nevertheless, the *peones* worked happily, taking great interest in doing their best for the *patron*, whom they held in great esteem and respect."[21] In a passage in *Romance* that is laden with her sense of class privilege, she explained that compensation for the servants was "not material, but rather the kind that is felt in the soul...the satisfaction of doing their duty well."[22]

Not surprisingly, given remarks like these, Jaramillo felt compelled to explain how this Eden had passed by the time she published her books in the 1940s and 1950s. She described the decline as a gradual process unleashed after U.S. conquest in 1846. "Adventurers, trappers, wise-eyed gamblers, and towering gold seekers" all came to New Mexico, she wrote, with increasingly devastating results for the state's Hispanic residents. But in Jaramillo's account of the history that followed, mining near Taos did not devastate the existing culture as much as the liquor and gambling the miners brought with them. These elements, she claimed, along with the "energetic race" of Anglo entrepreneurs who came to the area, were what destroyed traditional Spanish values. Moreover, she seemed somehow to hold those values responsible for their decline. "The Spanish Dons," she wrote in *Romance*, "could not prevent their leisurely sons from patronizing these gambling places and squandering fortunes." Though they tried to educate their sons by sending them to schools in the eastern United States, the boys came back "still playing the part of the fine gentlemen they had been brought up to be. They would not take to work."[23] Thus, Jaramillo's story goes, families lost their fortunes. Her explanation echoes Anglo stereotypes of "laziness" among Mexicans first perpetuated in the nineteenth-century drive for "Manifest Destiny."[24]

❧ CHAPTER TWO ❧

But Jaramillo's condemnation of "American" vices in this passage hints at other messages about whom she blamed, exactly, for Hispanic decline. Though it does so subtly, her narrative also hints at her growing realization of how the lure of Anglo culture masked the process of conquest that had hurt her family's class status. "The first year I came to Santa Fe," she wrote of her arrival in the city for high school, "modern, two-story brick houses were very rare. The Catron mansion on Grant and the Stabb one on Palace Avenue were such curiosities to us girls that we used to take walks just to see these homes with their nice green lawns and trees enclosed with wrought-iron fences instead of the high adobe walls, which selfishly hide the beauty of the grounds." The irony implicit in Jaramillo's report of youthful admiration for the Catron home is that, as an adult, she also told her readers that Thomas Benton Catron managed to take ownership of the Tierra Amarilla Grant away from her grandfather's heirs. "One of the heirs sold, it is said," Jaramillo divulged cautiously, as if repeating a rumor rather than claiming to know the truth, "only his share to Mr. Catron, but turned over to him the deed for the whole grant. Mr. Catron made a great profit by selling the whole grant to an Eastern company, and the many heirs each received a small amount."[25]

Jaramillo's suspicion of Catron's methods coincides with a general belief, cited by historian Roxanne Dunbar Ortíz, that he and other land speculators acted illegally. In fact, Ortíz asserts, "the speculators acted within U.S. and territorial law in their dealings.... They invented a process of acquiring land grants which simply evaded the law."[26] Increased economic pressures led grant holders to sell their interests one by one until speculators held the title to everything. Additionally, because the U.S. system favored individual ownership of land as a commodity while the Spanish system had depended on using land for subsistence purposes, common lands once used as communal bases of production now immediately fell into the "public domain" held by the U.S. government. Thus, even lands that had not once belonged to a specific grant holder were taken by a government regulating them in unprecedented ways—in this respect, the experience of Hispanics under U.S.

rule resembled the situation faced by American Indians since the arrival of the Spanish. Nuevomexicanos who did hold grant titles and sought to defend their claims had to turn to lawyers like Catron, and in the process, they had to pay for their services, usually through land, their only source of wealth. Indeed, as a result of many transactions like the one involving Tierra Amarilla, Mr. Catron, who was a central figure of a powerful political alliance known as the "Santa Fe Ring," became one of the wealthiest men in New Mexico.[27]

Arriving in Santa Fe first made Jaramillo aware of men like Catron. Further removed from the "little village" of Arroyo Hondo than she had ever been before, she must have begun to see the emerging inequities between Anglo and non-Anglo citizens of New Mexico. She had already attended the Loretto Convent School at Taos for five years, a place where Anglo nuns had required her to speak only English.[28] But as a student in Taos, she had studied among other "descendants of prominent pioneer families."[29] When, at age fifteen, she went on to her five years at the Loretto Academy in Santa Fe she found herself one of only two Spanish girls in her class. While she wrote that she soon felt "perfectly at home," she decided after a few years that she had been "neglecting [her] beloved language" and that she wanted to study Spanish. She told the academy prefect about her desire for lessons; the "amused" nun replied by asking "And who is going to teach it to you?"[30] Another nun was soon recruited, but the message was clear: to those who ran the school, Spanish was not crucial to the education of a young woman, even in New Mexico.

Despite her frustration with the convent's English-only emphasis, Jaramillo enjoyed school enough to consider turning down a proposal of marriage in order to pursue her education further. At this moment in her life, she came perhaps the closest she ever did to completely breaking with her family's expectations of traditionalism. In retrospect, she wrote, "I wanted a year at one of those fine colleges I saw advertised in my *Home Journal* magazine."[31] Instead, she married the young man who courted her during her last two years at the academy. From her parents' perspective, marriage was the logical fulfillment of her education. According to *Romance*, when Jaramillo's mother learned her daughter was considering rejecting her suitor's proposal, she responded pointedly: "Do as you like but you will never find another boy like Venceslao."[32]

Young Cleofas had to agree this was so; Venceslao Jaramillo was a man of great promise. She met him at a relative's wedding in Abiquiu in 1895, when she was sixteen years old, and by the next summer, he had asked her father's permission to begin corresponding with her. As one of Cleofas's second cousins, Venceslao belonged to an assuredly good family.[33] He had attended Regis College, a Catholic school in Denver, and was already, as a young man, involved in territorial politics.[34] Soon after they first met, when he was only twenty years old, he was elected as the territorial legislature representative from Rio Arriba County. He had sustained a political attack against his tenure in this position—Democrats attempted to unseat the young Republican when they found out he was below the age requirement (twenty-one years) for voting and holding office. After he served out this term, from 1897 to 1900, the Republican governor of the territory, Miguel A. Otero, appointed him to be a member of his personal staff. In addition to all of these accomplishments, he was the only son of a family that possessed considerable interests in land and business.

In *Romance*, Cleofas revealed that her doubts about marriage had less to do with Venceslao than they did with a vague sense that marriage at such a young age did not correspond to the values to which her education had exposed her. In both her autobiography and in the surviving letters he wrote to her during their courtship, Venceslao comes across as a loving and earnest person, who clearly held much admiration for his "dearest Cleofitas," the name by which he often called her.[35] "This genteel young man," she wrote, "had become my ideal suitor and had changed my mind from my becoming a nun or remaining an old spinster."[36] Little in her home life or convent education had prepared her to think about becoming anything other than a wife or a nun. In short, there was no acceptable way for her to explain, either to her fiancé or her parents, her desire both to go to college and

Fig. 13: Cleofas and Venceslao Jaramillo, Wedding Portrait from Honeymoon Trip, 1898. Photograph by Schumacher. Courtesy of the Museum of New Mexico, Neg. No. 67224.

get married. She halfheartedly attempted to reject his proposal—a ring sent through the mail soon after her high school graduation—by sending it back with a card that simply said "too big." But she perhaps sensed that Venceslao also wanted to have a "modern" marriage and did not view her strictly as an old-fashioned Spanish woman. When he corresponded with her, he wrote not in the language of their ancestors' courtships, but in English. Thus, when he sent a letter saying he would have the ring made smaller, Cleofas began to consider that her "Romeo," as she called him, might meet another woman if she asked him to wait a year. Her written memory of her decision is abruptly concise: "When the ring came back, I kept it."[37] Her decision cemented her ties to the "Spanish" past she took pride in, even as it also increased her dependence on a system in decline.

A House in Ruins

The Jaramillos' marriage began with great promise, but the stories Cleofas told about it in later years reveal that she came to see the couple's joint effort at "Americanization" as a failed attempt to stave off the forces of personal and economic tragedy that were conspiring against them. While her experiences as a wife and mother did in fact change her into a more independent woman than her own mother had been, the disappointments she faced led her to gradually espouse a nostalgic preference for a more traditional life.

Her remembrances of her wedding day provide insight into this pattern of thought. She described the wedding, which took place on July 27, 1898, in detail in *Romance*. Initially, she explained, she had hoped for a traditional nuevomexicano wedding, like the ones she attended as a girl and a young woman, and would later describe when she published folklore. Such weddings included masses at church and feasts and dances sponsored by the groom's parents but in the bride's parents' home. But Venceslao's desire to accommodate and please all of his political acquaintances, including Governor Otero, led the couple to arrange a reception in a Taos hotel instead. Rather than adhere to the traditional customs Cleofas later attempted to preserve, they planned a wedding in tune with the latest American trends.[38]

She would later recall being very concerned about getting everything just right: "I had been studying about the Denver weddings in the *Post* that my brother received, and now I wrote notes to four young girls at Taos asking them to be my bridesmaids."[39] Bridesmaids were not part of traditional nuevomexicano weddings, but she followed the *Post*'s model in this and other areas. Together with Venceslao, she sent out finely printed invitations (in Spanish, but according to the American custom of listing her father instead of both her parents as the hosts), ordered new clothes for her entire family, rented fine dishes, ordered two kinds of cake, heaps of flowers and crates of wine, and hired a chef from Pueblo, Colorado, to prepare food.[40] For the best man and matron of honor, the couple chose people who were equally suitable for the Hispanic tradition of *padrinos*, an esteemed couple who act as "parents" to the couple for the wedding. By stepping into these roles, T. D. Burns, a prominent merchant and politician, and his wife Josefa Gallegos Burns, daughter of an elite nuevomexicano family, lent the wedding an even richer aura.[41] Moreover, "Mr. and Mrs. T. D. Burns" linked Hispanic and Anglo traditions through their interethnic marriage.

But nothing in Jaramillo's wedding quite turned out as planned—instead, the story of the event became a cautionary tale, for readers of her autobiography, on the dangers of being "fashionable" rather than "traditional." On the night before the wedding, the Taos Plaza filled with people awaiting the arrival of the governor, but due to a railroad problem, he did not arrive until the next day. This was only the beginning of the couple's troubles: though the ceremony went smoothly, the hotel reception was marred by a series of problems. There was not enough seating for all the guests to eat at once, and the servants, inexperienced at attending to so many people in such a high style, simply neglected to serve one dinner course, wine, or cake. When the chef heard that some guests were still waiting for food, he left the kitchen in frustration. And as the dancing began, one of Cleofas's uncles reported to Venceslao that the carriage drivers waiting outside were rapidly becoming intoxicated from the wedding wine, which they and others had furtively stolen from the hotel cellar. "What a mess of a wedding we had," Cleofas remembered remarking to her new husband the next morning, to which he defensively replied, "Forget it. Everybody had a good time."[42]

While their marriage was certainly more successful than their wedding, their failed attempt to have a reception that lived up to the standards of American fashion serves as just one illustration of the larger conflicts they experienced as Hispanics living in this particular time and place. Venceslao's political experiences indicate that he endured these conflicts in his career as well as in his social life: he ended up being caught between his optimism for the "American system" and his loyalty to his people. In Jaramillo's remembrances of her husband's political attitudes, she pointed out that he was "very patriotic," as illustrated when, soon after the couple moved into their new home, he hung the United States flag out for the Fourth of July.[43] To her, such patriotism for the United States was consistent with his desire to "protect his people" by entering politics as a young man. At that time, she later explained, "race issues between the two races began kindling," and her husband "saw no other remedy but to enter politics" in pursuit of the "continuance of the harmonious relations, and political tolerance and respect."[44]

But "political tolerance and respect" for Hispanics on the part of Anglos had really been a problem in New Mexico ever since Anglo traders began making their way along the Santa Fe Trail, and Venceslao Jaramillo thus faced an entirely uphill battle. As early as the 1870s, Roxanne Dunbar Ortíz has written, Thomas Benton Catron and other members of the Santa Fe Ring had been able to use U.S. and territorial law to their advantage in acquiring major portions of the land that once belonged to Hispanic families. Ortíz has shown how other factors producing this decline of the Hispanic elite included the economic changes brought by the arrival of the railroad in 1879, the accompanying jump in livestock raising and investment by foreign capital, and the difficult adjustment to a cash and credit economy by villagers who had little means of developing economic resources at the same time that they were losing land.[45]

Two anecdotes about the career of Catron illustrate how much the status of the Hispanic elite changed during the era of Jaramillo's youth and marriage. When Catron journeyed the Santa Fe Trail to New Mexico in 1866, he, in the words of historian Howard Lamar, "doggedly memorized a Spanish grammar on the trail and deliberately lived with a Spanish-speaking family for a few months after his arrival, until he was fluent in the language."[46] Forty-five years later, his attitude had changed markedly. In 1910, when a convention convened to draft a constitution as part of New Mexico's statehood process, Catron hushed an interpreter as he translated the opening prayer (given by an English-speaking priest) into Spanish. Catron reportedly hissed, "Shut up, you fool; the Almighty understands English." Jaramillo retold this revealing story, which she heard at a reunion of convention delegates, in her autobiography.[47]

While identifying oneself as "Spanish" had once allowed elite nuevomexicanos to declare an alliance with Anglos based on European heritage, Catron's comments reveal that such alliances became more symbolic, and less powerful, by the early twentieth century. By that time Anglos had established enough of an economic foothold to render ties with the Spanish elite unnecessary. For politicians like Venceslao Jaramillo, increased accommodation to American values became necessary. For example, the territorial governor for whom he worked, Miguel Otero, sustained his political position and his popularity by appeasing both Hispanic and Anglo interests. Howard Lamar has written that Otero was able to do so because he "felt equally at home in both cultures."[48] Indeed, Otero was born in St. Louis, educated in the U.S. Northeast, and, as one source puts it, "he married a girl from Minnesota in an Episcopal ceremony."[49] Still, Otero, the Jaramillos, and other elite Hispanic New Mexicans found themselves under scrutiny during this period by some members of the Anglo community, both in New Mexico and on a national level. In 1898, the United States went to war with Spain amid a storm of anti-Spanish propaganda unleashed in the press. Cleofas Jaramillo's autobiography hardly touches on this painful topic, except to note that a few men who later served with the famous "Rough Riders" regiment were among those who defended young Venceslao when the opponents challenged his tenure in political office.[50] In fact, the idea to raise a group of volunteers from the Southwest for the war came from Governor Otero, in a move Juan Gómez-Quiñones has called Otero's "most striking initiative."[51] While the complexity of identity reflected by Otero's actions is indeed striking to historians of today, during Otero's era it led to a degree of precariousness in New Mexican politics and power relations. The rico position depended on a network of alliances and a fading degree of wealth that both ultimately proved to be less than solid.

For the Jaramillos, the erosion of these sources of power was deceptively slow and thus all the more painful, for in the meantime, Venceslao maintained a strong position. In 1903, he reentered politics for a two-year term as a territorial senator for Rio Arriba County. He served as the treasurer of this county in 1905 and 1913.[52] He also became a delegate for the territory's constitutional convention in 1910.[53] During his tenure as senator, he was actively involved in the founding of a new state institution, the Spanish American Normal School, in El Rito, his hometown. Cleofas came to see this school as a "monument to his memory."[54] Though it later became, at the urging of well-meaning activists like Mary Austin, a vocational school for Spanish-speaking youth (where, Austin hoped, training in the "manual arts" would "enable the young people to avail themselves of their native genius"), the plans Venceslao and others initially made for the school used a different strategy.[55] These politicians saw this establishment as a way to address educational inequalities, to prepare bilingual teachers, and to preserve Hispanic political power and culture.[56]

While the Jaramillos traveled a good deal through the United

States and Mexico in the early years of their marriage, they soon settled down in El Rito, where they attempted to celebrate Venceslao's accomplishments. Around 1900, they finished building what Cleofas described as an "elaborate" house, one with a design symbolizing their cultural roots and their fashionable aspirations. The home combined the symmetrical floor plan of the New Mexican "Folk Territorial" style with elegant features, such as a dramatic staircase and balcony, drawn from the "Queen Anne" style that had originated in England and become popular in the United States during the late years of the nineteenth century.[57] They held a large housewarming party, an event Cleofas recalled warmly in *Romance*. Venceslao, who did not dance well, apparently "had great fun calling out the figures in the newly-introduced square dance, the lancers, in a loud voice." Cleofas saw the "mix-ups" and movement of this dance as "a pleasant change from the quiet, dignified Spanish dances."[58]

Despite such social successes, a pair of tragedies eventually marred Cleofas's attempts at the role of wife and mother for which her convent school education had prepared her. She did not bear any children until 1908, ten years into her marriage, and she and Venceslao approached the event with great excitement and concern. Just as they had wanted all that was "best" for their wedding, they wanted the best in modern care for their child. As the time approached, they went to a Denver hospital for the birth, where, as Cleofas recalled, Venceslao "engaged the most noted obstetrical specialist." The baby boy's birth went smoothly, but five days later he was dead, the victim of a cold and a failed attempt at a surgical procedure. Cleofas's written memory of the event was poignantly short: "The baby specialist called in circumcised the baby as a cure. He cut a blood vessel and the baby bled to death."[59] What makes the event even more tragic to readers of *Romance*, as literary critic Tey Diana Rebolledo has pointed out, is that Jaramillo also recounts how a *curandera* who lived nearby in El Rito told her about a simple cure for a cold when the Jaramillos came home. Anglo "expertise" had failed her. Jaramillo believed their attempt to be "modern" cost their son his life; this event contributed to her mounting suspicion of

Anglo cultural values.[60] A year later, she gave birth to a daughter. At age fifteen months, the baby became sick with cholera. Jaramillo kept prayerful vigil by her crib for "eighteen days and nights." But the baby died, and Jaramillo found that her "house seemed so empty."[61]

The next fall, when Venceslao first served in the state senate, Cleofas must have felt relieved to escape the bad memories of El Rito by moving to Santa Fe while the legislature was in session. But she did not feel altogether comfortable there, either. Just as nothing in her life had equipped her to be able to tell her family and her fiancé that she wanted to go to college, her childhood among a family of seven children and her genteel education had offered her little preparation in the way of wifehood without motherhood. Politics had not yet succeeded in fulfilling her, either. Though her time in Santa Fe as Venceslao's wife required her to be in the public eye and to call on other politicians' wives, she later recalled that she "preferred . . . to stay quietly at home." She attributed her shyness to her secluded years among girls at the convent and her lack of familiarity with English. Her reasoning here seems strangely apologetic, given that she had spoken English throughout her education and even corresponded with her husband in the language. "I very much enjoyed meeting intelligent people," she wrote, but

> not having enough practice in speaking their language
> fluently, nor being yet schooled in their social ways, I was
> afraid to make a mistake, and rather profited by my quiet
> observation; although I felt I was giving people the
> impression of being stupid, and many times felt
> dissatisfied with myself because I was not a smarter
> woman, more able to help my husband more intelligently
> to carry on his social and political ambitions.

Perhaps her discomfort arose less from the language than from the shifts in political power that made her husband's position all the more precarious. As a result of her sense of inferiority in this particular public sphere, she later recalled, she tried to play her roles at home assiduously, doing everything she could to make their home "attractive and comfortable."[62]

For a short time, she was able to play the part of wife and mother she had hoped for; in 1913, while she and her husband were living in Santa Fe, she gave birth to her third child, a healthy girl named Angelina. Not long after this, however, Venceslao's health began to decline. Cleofas's memoirs do not specify his ailment, but she mentions that he had radium treatments, and one historian has concluded that he developed tuberculosis.[63] He sought out the best medical care, making two trips to the Battle Creek Sanitarium run by the famous Dr. John Harvey Kellogg, and one to the Johns Hopkins University Hospital in Baltimore. The family also built a winter home in Santa Fe where he could spend his winters more comfortably than the "country home" in El Rito.

In Cleofas's recollection, Venceslao seems to have been convinced, for a time, that he could beat his illness. He had always been a lavish spender, and facing death did not, at first, make him less generous with his family and friends. But as he grew more ill, Cleofas could "guess his inner torments" about finances, despite his attempt at "diguis[ing] all with apparent cheerfulness."[64] All around the couple were signs of economic decline for the people who had once been the elite of New Mexico. By this time, Cleofas's father had sold his store in Arroyo Hondo. While he had been able to settle comfortably in Santa Fe, many families had not fared so well.

In *Romance*, Jaramillo described the moment in the 1910s when the extent of decline became painfully clear to her. She had taken a trip to Taos with her friend Ruth Laughlin Barker, the Anglo author of *Caballeros*, a nostalgic portrait of Spanish culture in New Mexico.[65] Jaramillo suggested stopping at one of the nearby "big attractive homes" that she remembered from her school days at Taos. But when they drove up to see the "fine Gonzales home," she found it had deteriorated to the point that she did not recognize it. "The whitewashed porch with the blue railing was gone," she recalled, "and the whole house was in ruins. Juanita, whom her mother always had kept so well-dressed at school, came to the door with torn hose and shabby shoes." In an attempt to allow Juanita Gonzales to show Barker some of the family treasures that merited her pride in the region's past, Jaramillo asked Gonzales to bring out some of her mother's silver. When Juanita brought out "a silver set with an exquisite design and silver grape bunches on the lids," Barker offered to buy it. Jaramillo was shocked when Gonzales accepted fifteen dollars rather than the already low price she had first suggested, thirty-five dollars. When she privately asked Gonzales why she had done so, she responded simply that she "needed the money to fix the house." Jaramillo summed up the incident bluntly and powerfully: "This is how our rich Spanish families have been stripped of their most precious belongings."[66]

The fact that her Anglo friend was the agent of this transaction only made it worse. Friendly bonds between Anglos and the fading Hispanic elite made that process of decline assume a guise of normalcy. As historian Charles Montgomery has argued, Spanish revival efforts undertaken by Anglos like Barker and Hispanos like Jaramillo "seemed to elevate the status of Spanish-speaking society" but actually "helped to naturalize the material inequality of Anglos and Hispanos."[67] Moments like Jaramillo's visit to Juanita Gonzales, however, exposed the process as devastating. And moments like these were happening more and more frequently for the Jaramillos. As Venceslao's illness progressed, he became increasingly anxious about a ranch in Chama (a town near the northern border of New Mexico) that he had borrowed heavily to buy and now was unable to sell. When he had bought the ranch, Cleofas remembered, she had questioned why, and he had, perhaps bitterly, answered, "Because we Mexicans can only make money with sheep, and land is getting scarce."[68] Now, it seemed, they could not even make money that way.

Despite all these hints, Cleofas had little knowledge of the extent of the problems that were in store for her after her husband's death in a Denver hospital in December 1920. Looking back at the painful moment, she wrote that she regretted that her "exterior reserve" had kept her from showing how much she loved him while he was on his deathbed, but nevertheless, she described a moment of profound intimacy. "As the cord of his life broke," she wrote in *Romance*, "I felt something rush into my hand. Was this undescribable thing something of my husband's spirit that passed into me, through my hand? Was this what gave me the courage and strength needed?"[69] Even at the point in her life at which she was first fully responsible for herself as an individual, she felt herself depending on her husband's memory: she found that it might be all she had to depend on. The settling of her husband's estate revealed that she and her daughter faced serious financial troubles. A bank seized the little money she had in her own name for payment of one of her husband's debts. Though her father and some of her husband's friends tried to help her negotiate the tangle of debt, other former friends of her husband's were among those who made claims for money. Suddenly, she was very much alone. The "traditional" world had collapsed around her, and the economic realities of the modern one loomed menacingly.

Race on Trial

Eventually, the experience of her husband's death and the debt that followed would lead Jaramillo to embrace a romantic view of life before Anglo conquest. But in the meantime, she focused on using the skills she had cultivated through her modern education to deal with the immediate crises she faced. As coexecutor of her husband's estate (with her father), she found she had a sudden and desperate need for the limited studies in business she had pursued in high school.[70] Her record of her attempts to salvage anything from her husband's estate is an account of grim but calm determination. She invited farmers in the area to buy (at prices calculated to beat local merchants) a load of farm equipment her husband had ordered just before his death, and she sold some of her own belongings and her daughter's nursery furniture. She moved temporarily to Denver, with young Angelina in tow, to take over the management of an apartment building her husband had bought and stayed her ground when a relative claimed Venceslao had promised the building to her. Initially she believed she would be able to earn money from the building, but she had to sell it a few years later when a crack appeared in the foundation. She could not afford to fix it, and the market had begun to become depressed. She and Angelina moved back to Santa Fe, where they lived near her family.

Self-preservation, it seems, kept her going, especially since she increasingly felt there was a "danger of being alone" for a woman in her situation. This feeling intensified after an experience at her relatively isolated home in El Rito, where she went occasionally to attend to business. A man who came to inquire about purchasing the Chama ranch entered her house without her permission and persisted in asking her if he could rent a room. Jaramillo described him as a "heavy-set, red-haired cattleman" who seemed to be surveying the area to see if anyone else was around. He stepped outside for a minute, and at the same time, Angelina ran onto the porch. Jaramillo pulled her daughter inside the house and locked the door. Clearly, Jaramillo, a tiny woman, felt not only physically threatened by this man, but frightened and insulted by his failure to treat her and her home with proper respect.[71]

Her attempt to sell the ranch was an uphill battle in the days leading up to the Depression and an experience that ultimately advanced her antipathy toward calculated Anglo efforts to take over Hispanic landholdings. Just when she had nearly secured a buyer, the mortgage holder, a man whom Venceslao had helped get started in business, foreclosed. She did not mention his name in her memoir, but archival records of the District Court of Rio Arriba County include a 1927 decree that the ranch once owned by Venceslao would be ceded to Edward Sargent, a Republican National Committee representative for New Mexico from Chama.[72] When Jaramillo's bank folded, as many did during this time, and she lost the money she had made from selling some of her husband's properties, the ruin seemed complete. She remembered this event with bitterness: "My last thread of hope in saving a home for my daughter broke, after nine years of hard work trying to save something."[73]

She returned to the protection of her family. Though her father had also lost a good deal of money from bank closures, she was able to depend upon some help from him, as well as the meager profits from what little remained of her husband's property. She was not able to live fashionably, but she was able to send her daughter to private schools, including the Loretto Academy in Santa Fe, where she herself had been educated. At this time, they were living in a home she had been given by her father. Though it was once a separate structure, it stands today as part of a monumental stucco building across from the Santa Fe First Presbyterian Church, at Griffin and McKenzie streets, just a few blocks from the Santa Fe Plaza.

By all accounts, including her own, Jaramillo raised her daughter very strictly. Having ultimately been failed by Americanization, she was reluctant to adopt the American style of the day when it came to her daughter's upbringing, especially given the increasingly relaxed codes of behavior for young women. Looking back on her daughter's teenage years, however, Jaramillo chided herself for being old-fashioned: "My mistake was, I see, that in trying to keep her free from gossip and innocent of worldly knowledge, I had failed to see that she was living in a different age, when girls were not so submissive as in my time. Perhaps I was too much against the modern codes, and fashion fads."[74] Her niece, Rosa Montoya, remembers her aunt's strictness well because she stayed with her during the year that she and Angelina were in eighth grade at Loretto. She believes that part of "Tía Cleofas's" reluctance to let Angelina try out the latest fashions stemmed from financial considerations. "Angeline [Rosa called her cousin by this Anglicized version of her name] couldn't have what all the rest had," Rosa explains, "which was all right with her. She didn't really mind."[75]

But Jaramillo did. She may have missed the aura of gentility even more than the money. When she and her daughter fought about

Fig. 14:
Angelina Jaramillo,
1931. Courtesy of the
Museum of New Mexico,
Neg. No. 173525.

Angelina's desire to correspond with a young man she had met one summer in El Rito, Angelina protested that her mother disliked the boy only because he was poor, but Jaramillo confessed that the divorce of the boy's parents was what really gave her a "doubtful opinion." "In my opinion," she wrote in her autobiography, "character, education and refinement have always counted more than money."[76] She wanted to raise her daughter to be educated and refined in the manner of the old "Spanish" families, even when it came to the strict gender roles that she herself had resisted, but doing so without money proved to be a challenge. In the eyes of Santa Fe society, she must have thought, her remaining status as Mrs. Venceslao Jaramillo, "tradition-al" daughter of the elite Martínez family and wife of the political leader, depended on her ability to raise her daughter well. In her auto-biography, she notes the "swell" of pride she felt at a party when she saw Mrs. Miguel Otero leading Angelina through the crowd to meet her husband, the former governor under whom Venceslao had served.[77] "Angie," now a bright, energetic, and pretty young woman, was, in some ways, all her mother had.

Angie's murder, then, was more than just devastating to Jaramillo; it was a brutal experience that forced her, once again, to drastically change her conception of herself and the world in which she lived. It robbed Jaramillo of her traditional role of mother even as the publici-ty and trial that followed illustrated all too starkly the benefits that her traditional "Spanish" identity could afford her. These events also encouraged her to undertake a traditionalist, defensive, and ultimately racist approach to promoting public awareness of Hispanic culture, for they would illustrate that to do otherwise was to risk losing the only remaining stature that the ricos of Santa Fe possessed.

On the night of Sunday, November 15, 1931, an intruder entered eighteen-year-old Angelina's room through a window facing the street, gagged her, raped her, and then stabbed her through the temple with a small sharp knife. She died instantly. Her mother woke up soon after-ward, when a light turned on in another room reflected on a mirror over her dresser. She rushed to her daughter's room, and saw "standing by Angie's bed the broad shoulders of a man in a black and white shirt." She screamed and the man grabbed her by the throat—she then passed out, either from fear or from being hit over the head. "I was spared the terrible fright of seeing his face," she explained, "which like those black and white stripes, would have been impressed upon my mind, making me shudder every time I see a dark face."[78]

Jaramillo's memoir's reference to a "dark face" is ambiguous. But the headlines from the *Santa Fe New Mexican* are all too clear. The man convicted of Angelina's rape and murder, Thomas Johnson, was African American. He was arrested in Albuquerque not long after the attack, after a series of discoveries by the Santa Fe sheriff, Jesús Baca. Baca drove to a garage that stayed open all night to get gas, so he could begin a search for suspects. But the garage was closed when he got there, and when the sheriff called the owner to come and open it, they found the night attendant, Oscar Churchill, badly beaten and unconscious inside. Someone had also stolen a car and cash. Because Churchill had recently had an argument with Johnson, a former garage employee, the sheriff tracked Johnson down in Albuquerque, where he was arrested and questioned. He confessed to the beating of Churchill but adamantly denied having anything to do with the murder of Angelina Jaramillo. The sheriff maintained, however, that Albuquerque police found a small knife in Johnson's possession when they arrested him. To these officials, this evidence and Johnson's existing criminal record (he had been released from a prison in New Mexico the previous July and had also served time in Ohio, Michigan, and Kansas, each time, it seems, for theft), seemed to cinch the case.

Doubts about his guilt have lingered since the day of the murder, culminating in the recent publication of Ralph Melnick's *Justice Betrayed: A Double Murder in Old Santa Fe*, which maintains Johnson's innocence.[79] But in the immediate aftermath of the crime, some Santa Feans needed to know nothing but Johnson's race before they condemned him and all residents of African American descent and threatened him with lynching. The *Santa Fe New Mexican* reported the next day that, on the way back to Santa Fe from Albuquerque, Johnson and an escort of armed deputies sped past a crowd gathered on the road. Another "crowd was gathered outside the prison gates," though the paper also obliquely noted that "there was no demonstration."[80]

The newspaper, for its part, ran an editorial (on only the day after the murder) entitled "A Lesson." It proclaimed Johnson's guilt and concluded that all "negroes" posed a threat to the town. "Santa Fe for the first time has gone through the indescribably sickening shock of having the Negro Crime committed at her own doors," the editorial began, likely alluding to the "Scottsboro Boys" case that had begun attracting national attention eight months earlier. The writer, apparently newspaper editor E. Dana Johnson, advocated the "barring in future of negroes" and the "deporting of discharged convicts" from Santa Fe. The "black and white problem," he argued, could be avoided through vigilance. "Santa Fe has had always a few respected and often much beloved colored citizens," he acknowledged. "But for 300 years we have escaped this particular social problem." He believed it was both possible and necessary to keep African Americans out of Santa Fe: "They do not belong here, they bring a racial conflict even more intense than elsewhere, we do not need them economically."[81] Santa Fe's way of life seemed to be at risk: the newspaper responded with a vicious attack upon an "alien" group of people.

While the editor's blatant attempt to incite racial hatred attracted condemnation, voices of reason had little effect on perceptions of the case. The *Albuquerque Journal* asserted that the *New Mexican*'s editor had given "unwise advice" and had unfairly condemned "the entire negro race."[82] As a conciliatory gesture, the *New Mexican* published a letter signed only by "An Old Subscriber" a few days after running "A Lesson." It "respectfully protest[ed]" that the suspicion of Johnson did "not justify an implied indictment of the negro race," and went on to ask, "and really, Mr. Editor, has not Santa Fe advanced too far to talk about 'barring' or 'deporting' as matters of public policy?" The writer alluded here to the dangers such attitudes posed to Santa Fe's reputation as a cultural meeting place, a history lauded by artists, writers, and intellectuals who had recently moved to the Southwest—and the Anglo tourists following them. "Guilt is personal, not racial," the writer continued, finishing by holding the newspaper up to its own apparent standards: "It seems to me that the *Santa Fe New Mexican* has made too consistent a fight against racial intolerance to permit itself to be carried away by momentary horror into a position which in more sober moods it would find difficult to sustain."[83]

According to Melnick, the prominent appearance of this letter in the newspaper it attacked is explained by the fact that it was actually penned by the newspaper's owner, U.S. Senator Bronson Cutting.[84] Cutting had worked with Mary Austin and other Anglo modernists on progressive causes, advocating cultural understanding between Hispanics and Anglos. But he also had cultivated support for his political stature among conservative ricos, like the Jaramillos, who identified as "White," and so his measured response to the case stopped short of an outright attack on racial hierarchy. Moreover, he did allow the newspaper's coverage to continue in a lurid and racially biased tone.

Another aspect of this sensationalism included the paper's description of Angelina and her "old Spanish family." A front-page article noted that "her beauty was of the type that is characteristic of the Spanish people.... She was of the 'petite' type, with large, brown, expressive eyes, a wealth of raven black hair and a sunny smile. She had a delightful disposition and the most charming manners." The site of the murder was "one of the old houses of Santa Fe, charming in its Spanish design." According to this coverage, the Jaramillos had declined from their position as "at one time one of the richest Spanish families in northern New Mexico" as a result of the "bank disasters which occurred after the World war throughout the southwest."[85]

A beautiful member of a "charming" and "old" race, this news coverage collectively implied, had been viciously killed by a man of a race that "did not belong" in Santa Fe: headlines and articles in the *New Mexican*'s coverage repeatedly referred to Johnson as "a Negro," as if that identity could explain the horror of the crime. In sensational coverage like this, Jaramillo and other ricos could easily see that what status they had left after Anglo conquest depended upon their supposedly pure European heritage and their fading tradition of wealth; had they embraced mestizo culture or, more realistically, vocally criticized the unfair dynamics of Anglo land takeovers, they would have found themselves confronting racial hatred like that directed at Johnson. Jaramillo, who had begun to resent Anglo conquest and pursue modern strategies of survival in the months following her husband's death, undoubtedly perceived that justice for her daughter's case depended on her appearing as "traditional" and demure as possible.

Still, she seems to have made a conscious effort to avoid making or encouraging racialized judgments of the case. Aside from her reference to a "dark face" in a book published twenty-three years later, she remained silent in public about the racial identity of her daughter's assailant. She may have been reluctant to publicize the suspect's race for fear of damage to her own family's reputation, but she may also have been hesitant to portray Angelina's murder as a racial conflict, given her own experience with anti-"Mexican" racism. From her autobiographical writings, it is clear she believed that, in addition to bank failures, racism had contributed to her family's decline from prominence. She wrote that her husband entered politics because "race issues between the two races began kindling," referring to the 1890s, well before the advent of the "racial conflict" of "black and white" cited by the editorial of the *New Mexican*.[86] Jaramillo had seen Anglo ideas about the "Mexican" race take their toll. Anglo teachers had discouraged her from studying Spanish; her friend could buy Spanish family heirlooms for fifteen dollars; her family had lost their land through a legal but unjust transaction. She knew what it meant to be judged, even persecuted, on account of one's "race."

Perhaps one reason she was glad to have been "spared" the sight of the murderer's face was that it meant that she could be silent on this matter. During the trial, a sensational and crowded event held in a special court session less than a month after Angelina's murder, she testified she did not know what the murderer looked like. "A man's life was at stake," she wrote in *Romance*; "I could not lie. Some people thought I could have said that I had seen his face."[87] She resisted making such an accusation. In fact, when Johnson's court-appointed attorney, J. H. Crist, appealed the conviction to the New Mexico Supreme Court, his brief, according to the *New Mexican*, mentioned that "one of the inexplicable things about the case...was that the girl's mother was not asked whether the man she testified she saw at the foot of the girl's bed was white or black."[88]

Jaramillo apparently believed Johnson was guilty, but she was not willing either to account for his guilt by referring to his racial identity or to advocate stepping outside the law for his prosecution. She later noted that "our testimonies of not having seen his face encouraged the criminal to deny his guilt and to carry on his fight for freedom." In light of this, she pointed out, "men friends of my father's came and offered to do whatever he said, but my father was a peaceful man and told them to let the law take care of the case."[89] Here she refers to the threats of lynching that marred the trial. The Ku Klux Klan apparently never established a strong foothold in New Mexico, as it did in other western states during the 1920s, a fact that one historian attributes to the high percentage of Roman Catholics in the state.[90] But unadulterated racism toward African Americans led to a prejudicial and apparently unfair trial. The presiding judge was none other than District Judge Miguel A. Otero, Junior, the son of the governor whom Venceslao had worked for, and whom the Jaramillos had taken such pride in inviting to their wedding. His stance on the case could hardly have been completely objective.

The details and aftermath of the trial illustrate the extensive prejudice in which Jaramillo found herself enmeshed. Evidence presented against Johnson did not sway him from his plea of innocence. The list of "clues" included the knife, bloodstains, fingerprints, eyewitness sightings of the accused near the scene of the crime around the time of the murder, and ostensible traces of lipstick, reportedly matching a dark shade that Angie wore, under his fingernails. Crist charged that this evidence was skewed by prejudice, while prosecutors maintained the "scientific" evidence was incontrovertible. The jury, composed almost entirely of Spanish-surnamed men, found Johnson guilty and sentenced him to death. The conviction sustained two appeals. Crist met with Governor Arthur Seligman in the days leading up to Johnson's execution, reportedly "not as the negro's appointed counsel, but 'as a citizen and a man,'" and asked Seligman to grant Johnson a stay so that leads on new evidence could be pursued.[91] The governor's papers include several letters about Johnson's case: one maintained that "to keep men alive like him is a great injustice to our taxpayers," but the rest of the letters and telegrams on file, many from African Americans, hold appeals to Seligman to pardon Johnson.[92] In addition to letters from concerned citizens, the governor received a telegram from Mabel Dodge Luhan, who wrote that "FRIENDS [she didn't specify whom]

HAVE ASKED ME TELEGRAPH YOU PLEASE COMMUTE SEN-
TENCE TOM JOHNSON IN VIEW OF NEW EVIDENCE STRONG-
LY IN FAVOR HIS INNOCENCE." Walter White, then secretary of
the National Association for the Advancement of Colored People
(NAACP), also sent a telegram, urging the governor to allow for more
time because of new evidence and concerns for Johnson's sanity.[93]

Despite numerous references to "new" evidence, no record of exactly what it was seems to exist. Jaramillo's niece Rosa indicated to me, as
she did to Ralph Melnick, that some people suspected that a man married to Jaramillo's sister Mae, Bob Smith, may have been involved in the
crime: he left his wife and New Mexico soon afterward.[94] An article
about the history of executions in New Mexico published in the *New
Mexican* in 1979 indicates only that "some contemporary observers
believe authorities put Johnson's fingerprints on the vase after he had
been arrested."[95] Another article relates that stories told about the crime
in Santa Fe suggest that Smith "confessed to the crime and asked for forgiveness" just before he died.[96] Melnick's recent book attempts to make
a stronger case against Smith, implying that Cleofas's family participated in covering up his guilt so as not to add disgrace to tragedy, but no
concrete evidence exists to tie Smith to the crime.

In any case, the dominant view of the case among Santa Feans of
the day was that Johnson was guilty as charged. A sensationalized article about the case, "The Clue of the Lipstick: An Enigma of New
Mexico," appeared in a popular crime magazine, *Master Detective*, in
1935, bringing the murder and the methods used to convict Johnson to
the attention of a national audience. Though it called the case an "enigma," the article made no mention of evidence in Johnson's favor and
emphasized instead both Johnson's race and the "bitter" sentiment
against him.[97] Jaramillo remained convinced of Johnson's guilt; she
briefly recounted her daughter's murder in her autobiography, she told
her readers, "not for the curious, but to let the truth be known and dispel suspicion on some other person," perhaps her sister's former husband.[98] Whether Johnson was the murderer remains uncertain, but it is
unfortunately certain that on July 21, 1933, he became the first man to

be executed by electric chair in New Mexico. A crowd of seventy witnesses, including Jaramillo's brother Ben, witnessed this killing.[99]

Jaramillo confronted racism head-on during the trial and found herself the unhappy winner when Johnson was convicted. The newspaper's portrayal of her family as righteous due to its "Spanish," and therefore "White," heritage undoubtedly inspired her to cling only further to this identity in the aftermath of losing her daughter. She had tried and failed to protect her against the threats of contemporary life, willfully forgetting the fact that she herself, as a younger woman, had found the opportunities of modern-day life, such as education and travel, appealing. Angelina's death ultimately pushed her toward the work in folklore that became her vocation. It provided an escape into a past in which, as the newspapers had recently publicized, her family had been rich and safe. Though her work in folklore would actually require that she use the modern-day skills of public relations she had learned through her education and as a witness to the arguments unleashed by her daughter's death, retreating into traditionalism became a way to protect herself and her culture from further onslaught. She stepped into the "traditional woman" role Austin and Luhan had outlined for Spanish and American Indian women in their campaign for cultural preservation because this role provided the only way she could conceive of preserving the small amount of privilege left available to her.[100]

Returning to the Past

Jaramillo cited several motivations for the beginning of her career as a writer and folklorist: the urging of Angelina, during her lifetime, that she should write down her stories; her sister Mae's suggestion that she should write down their own mother's stories; and perhaps most significantly, her sense that Spanish folklore work was already being done in Santa Fe, but not always being done correctly. Her niece Rosa asserts her aunt's belief that many writers, especially those who only visited the Southwest temporarily, recorded Spanish history and folklore inaccurately. "She figured that she would set them straight," Rosa explains. "She wanted to get things the way they should have been."[101] She sought to ensure the existence of written records and public celebrations of Spanish customs in New Mexico.

Undertaking this mission, however, required that she cultivate new sources of personal strength. She had to overcome her reservations not only about placing herself in the public eye, but also about doing so in a language she maintained she felt uncomfortable with; doing so for the cause of "tradition" eased this process. She began both *Shadows of the Past* and *Romance of a Little Village Girl* with apologies for her supposedly limited command of English. Her niece sees her decision to write in English as a matter of necessity: "Because everything was in English by that time.... Everybody was learning English, reading English, so everything was turning, so it had to be that way. It just turned."[102] But Jaramillo, who had demanded Spanish lessons as a high school student, probably disagreed that she *had* to express herself in English. What she may have believed necessary, however, was writing in English in order to reach the generation starting with her daughter's and the otherwise misinformed English-speaking audience. On the one hand, she drew inspiration from artists and writers whom she felt were doing a good job at publicizing New Mexican native culture: she wrote in *Romance* that such work was "contagious" in Santa Fe, and that she had "caught the fever from our famous 'cinco pintores' and author Mary Austin."[103] But, on the other hand, Jaramillo was driven by a desire to correct impressions that did not match up, in her view, to the quality of Austin's. Every time she read a sensationalistic account of Penitentes in New Mexican villages, or a bordering-on-lurid description of a beguiling "Spanish señorita," she must have gritted her teeth and vowed to keep writing, even in a discomforting language. Due to these experiences, English became a nontraditional tool with which she could advocate tradition.

One such moment happened around March 1935, after she had begun writing but before she had published any of her work. A friend who

CHAPTER TWO

knew of Jaramillo's interest in recording traditional New Mexican recipes recommended that she look at the latest issue of *Holland's* magazine to see a feature titled "Intriguing Mexican Dishes." This magazine, subtitled *The Magazine of the South*, and marketed as the "most valuable and enjoyable magazine to *southern homes*," regularly included features about towns in Texas and New Mexico as well as in the Deep South.[104] The recipe feature promised to help its readers "to appreciate New Mexico's genuine native cooking and the romance of its simple peasant life."[105] Jaramillo saw these recipes as blatantly inauthentic. Moreover, the article's portrayal of a "Mexican-American housewife" fretting over chile peppers was offensive to her, as it portrayed this character, in supposed "genuine" dialect, complete with "translation," as backward and dogmatic: "I got no use for thees kind of chile. . . . Ees no gude! Ees very bad for the e-stomark. . . . Those e-skeens on the chile, they ees only gude for thoos burros (donkeys). I got no use for thet ground chile een the e-store."[106]

This was too much to bear. She tactfully recorded her response, directed at the supposed "authenticity" of the recipe, in *Romance*: "In giving the recipe for making tortillas it read, 'Mix bread flour with water, add salt.' How nice and light these must be without yeast or shortening! And still these smart Americans make money with their writing, and we who know the correct way sit back and listen."[107]

In frustration, she turned to another article in that issue of *Holland's*, one on the "Natchez Pilgrimage" in Mississippi. The magazine promoted the event as a week-long revival of the "quaint" and "picturesque" antebellum South: "During this week all Natchez reenacts its romantic past, and hospitality and chivalry become magic passwords. Pretty maids with bobbing curls and mittened hands are escorted hither and thither by youths in tight trousers [and] long coats."[108] Jaramillo had a flash of inspiration:

> This sounds so much like our Santa Fe Fiesta ought to be,
> I thought. Our mansions have crumbled back to the earth
> from which they sprung. Nevertheless, if we were to

ransack our mothers' old trunks, I would find some fine old-fashioned silk gowns and jewels. So far we have been seeing mostly what Americans have arranged.[109]

She began to consider what Natchez and Santa Fe might have in common. In the early 1900s, Santa Fe community leaders had revived the city's eighteenth-century custom of Fiesta, an event commemorating the Spanish reconquest of New Mexico by Don Diego de Vargas in September 1692 (after the Pueblo Revolt), amid what Chris Wilson, a historian of Santa Fe, calls a "national craze for historical pageants."[110] As Jaramillo's remarks hint, Anglos fueled the revival of Fiesta; perhaps the most prominent sponsor during this time was Edgar Hewett, the head of both the School of American Research and the Museum of New Mexico. Jaramillo believed Fiesta events could be patterned after those in Natchez if Hispanic women took charge of celebrating their foremothers' culture.

And yet the parallels to Natchez were not as strong as she construed them to be. Southern women in Natchez dressed up to celebrate the wealth and prestige their families once had at the expense of enslaved African Americans, notably absent from the Natchez festivities. ("With man power decimated, wealth swept away, and slaves free," the article describes Natchez history, in its only mention of African Americans, "it was all many families could do to cling to their ancestral estates."[111]) While this wealth may have faded, their relative class and social power had not.

As Jaramillo recognized, Hispano participation in Santa Fe's Fiesta was a romantic gesture rather than an assertion of power. The Anglos who brought about the revival of Fiesta honored a past and a people whom they and their ancestors had, in fact, taken part in dispossessing.[112] While Hewett's Fiesta included "processions, performances, and Indian dances" depicting all of New Mexico's cultural groups, the audience for these events was increasingly Anglo tourists rather than the descendants of Santa Fe's earliest inhabitants. Wilson writes that

⚅ CHAPTER TWO ⚅

organizers began to fence off areas of the plaza so that admission could be charged, and "by 1924 paid performances of Pueblo dances, Hispanic folk plays, and historical romances written by members of the art colony also catered to tourists in the Palace [of the Governors] courtyard, Saint Francis auditorium, and Santa Fe's two new movie theatres."[113] Beginning in 1924, events began with the burning of what Jaramillo called a "Spanish effigy of gloom," a giant figure named Zozobra created in fact by the Anglo artist Will Shuster. While Jaramillo believed Zozobra helped to make the event "a genuine Spanish fiesta," she and others saw limitations in an event that honored Spanish history but left out Hispanics. Shuster wrote, in 1958, that "Zozobra belongs to ALL the people," but he acknowledged that even after thirty-four years the figure was only *almost* traditional."[114] When Jaramillo contemplated Fiesta in 1934, she wanted to make things *really* traditional. She believed that a strategic adoption of technique from the Natchez festival could allow "Spanish" New Mexicans to reclaim the celebration of their history.

From the Natchez event, she borrowed a woman-centered strategy and a sense of the event being the province of the "elite." After reading the *Holland's* articles, she stayed up late planning. In the morning she called five women "from the elite of the Spanish families of the city" to invite them to tea. She revealed her "plan, which was to arouse more interest in taking part in the fiesta in greater numbers." She proposed that she and her five friends each invite several other women to join them. All would then take part in Fiesta's church procession "wearing old-fashioned gowns."[115]

Though Jaramillo initially proposed organizing a group of male and female dancers to take part in the festivity, she dropped that plan when she found she could not recruit enough men to take part. Similarly, she changed her initial plans to serve a barbecue supper to the daintier form of a "Spanish chocolate merienda," a tea event in which she and her friends "all wore old-fashioned gowns or silk shawls while serving." She declared her first year of Fiesta activities to be a success. Inspired, she and her friends expanded the merienda to include an "old fashioned style show" in which the women modeled their female ances-tors' gowns and shawls. They did the same on floats entered into Fiesta's historical parade. Moreover, she organized the group into a folklore society, La Sociedad Folklórica.[116]

Jaramillo's efforts would not challenge romantic Anglo views of the Hispanic past, but they would challenge the ownership of that past. Her Fiesta plan's emphasis on an elegant past illustrates what Charles Montgomery has called a "civil" language of symbolic heritage: Hispanics in Fiesta "played themselves, or rather the image of the Spanish colonial" for an audience that continued to see them as a "peo-ple of the past."[117] Still, by taking charge of an organization, she implicitly challenged the idea that Hispanos, especially Hispano women, were tradition-bound.

Nevertheless, the goals and structure of La Sociedad Folklórica reveal Jaramillo's strictly traditionalist view of which aspects of the "Spanish past" she wanted to preserve. She came up with the idea for a folklore society because Texas folklorist J. Frank Dobie, knowing of her interest and knowledge of Hispanic folklore, had invited her to join the Texas Folklore Society, and she believed New Mexico should have its own.[118] While the Texas Folklore Society, which began in 1910, set out to record "all forms of Texas folklore," Jaramillo limited the scope of her organization to preserving only aspects of the state's Hispanic cultural history.[119] She determined "the society should be composed of only thirty members, all of whom must be of Spanish descent, and that the meetings must be conducted in the Spanish language, with the aim of preserving our language, customs, and traditions."[120] Furthermore, it would be the domain of women.

The organization, still active in Santa Fe, became an institutional reflection of what she had discovered through her experiences with Anglo conquest and the publicity unleashed by her daughter's trial: the most expedient way to cultivate respect for Hispanic culture was to focus public attention on the "romance" of the Spanish elite. One of the first floats that La Sociedad Folklórica presented in the Fiesta parade featured "three brides, attired in beautiful old-style wedding

Fig. 15: La Sociedad Folklórica's Ten-Year Anniversary, La Fonda Hotel, Santa Fe, June 1945. (Cleofas Jaramillo is third from the right, and her distant cousin, Fabiola Cabeza de Baca, is second from the left.) Courtesy of the Museum of New Mexico, Neg. No. 9928.

gowns, their little train bearers wearing hooped skirts and long curls. On the floor sat an Indian maid drawing long strings of pearls and gold chains out of a large jewel box, 'las donas,' the gift brought to the bride by the bridegroom."[121] As a child, Jaramillo recalled in her books, she herself had served as a "little train bearer."

But most nuevomexicanos of the nineteenth century probably had not experienced such lavish celebrations—except, perhaps, from the perspective of an "Indian maid." La Sociedad Folklórica, proclaimed a preface to a 1988 publication by the organization, set out to preserve the "customs and the traditions of the Hispanic culture planted here by the Colonists and the conquerors of centuries past."[122] The goal was noble, especially given that Anglo conquest had done much to make such customs disappear. Perhaps the determination of this twentieth-century group to resurrect only "Spanish" traditions, at the expense of explicit attention to mestizo elements of New Mexico's past, was, after all, ultimately part of the lasting legacy of Anglo domination—just as describing oneself as "Spanish" became an adjustive effort by the nuevomexicano elite in the nineteenth century. And perhaps it also served as a way for the group to preserve a class hierarchy that had existed before Anglo conquest. Either way, La Sociedad Folklórica's advocacy of Hispanic tradition embraced a vision of the past more akin to the "romance" Jaramillo associated with her childhood than to the difficult events she and other Hispanics actually lived through. This class-biased vision of the Hispanic past did not directly confront Anglo stereotypes about Hispanic culture, but it did allow ricos like Jaramillo to use the guise of patronage to take possession of the cultural preservation work initiated by Luhan and Austin and to preserve a sense of class privilege.

Jaramillo's Writings and the Capture of Tradition

Just as the folklore society's public displays did not call explicit attention to changes in nuevomexicanos' lives since the idyllic era the Fiesta events ostensibly represented, Jaramillo wrote books that emphasized her desire to preserve tradition and mourned the passing of time with nostalgia. Nevertheless, her books unwittingly also show the willful cultural negotiations that she and other nuevomexicanos made with Anglo customs in the late nineteenth century. Read in progression, they illustrate the changing identity of a woman who faced an overwhelming degree of cultural change and embraced tradition as an act of cultural self-defense.

Her first two books, both published in 1939, represent recuperative efforts with regard to Hispanic culture, attempts by Jaramillo to recover material that might otherwise be lost. And yet they both also suggest recovery is not as easy as it may seem: just writing things down as they are remembered may not, in the end, preserve knowledge for contemporary people. *The Genuine New Mexico Tasty Recipes/Potajes sabrosas*, published by Santa Fe's Seton Village Press, seems to be a direct response to the *Holland's* article that Jaramillo saw in 1935. It pulls together recipes for foods Jaramillo ate while growing up, using ingredients native to New Mexico and traditional preparation methods. Her tiny introduction to the collection of "Spanish recipes" promises "only those used in New Mexico for centuries are given, excepting one or two Old Mexico recipes."[123] As Genaro Padilla has written, the fact that Jaramillo incorporates into her cookbook a few remembrances of occasions on which certain foods were eaten suggests she wanted her readers to know they needed to understand nuevomexicano culture in order to understand nuevomexicano food: "Hence," Padilla suggests, "Anglo-Americans can follow the recipe and still not eat Nuevomexicano cooking."[124] In a similar vein, Anne Goldman has demonstrated how Jaramillo's insistence on her cookbooks' "genuine articles" indicates her desire to get at the authentic and to critique those who offer false recipes, and Rebolledo has noted the implication that only "lived experience" produces authenticity.[125]

Yet none of these critics call attention to the simple fact that Jaramillo's cookbook does not list amounts of ingredients; as her niece Rosa pointed out to me, "That wasn't too good. People knew what the items were, but they couldn't follow them because they didn't know how much to put in of each thing."[126] Supplying measurement amounts wouldn't even have been enough, as Padilla and Goldman suggest. While Jaramillo may have been suggesting that "true" Spanish American women should know exactly how much of each ingredient to use, her reluctance to be specific may also suggest her belief that there was no one correct way to make these recipes. Her mother may have made them differently than she did. Cooks had to figure out the "genuine" for themselves, by experimenting with the recipes in the book; that process of trial and error was what made the recipes "genuine." Thus, even while claiming to be writing the book as an act of encoding tradition, Jaramillo inadvertently demonstrated how cultural traditions need adaptation and experimentation to survive, just as she herself had needed modern skills in English and publishing to undertake her work.

Similarly, the other book she published in 1939 promised to preserve Spanish fairy tales but actually updated them for contemporary readers. *Cuentos del Hogar/ Spanish Fairy Stories*, published by the Citizen Press of El Campo, Texas, collected stories she remembered hearing from her mother. The table of contents lists the stories with both Spanish and English titles; many of them are moralistic tales about the rewards of being good. The preface explains her desire to ensure the stories' survival, especially since they had been part of Spanish folklore for centuries, as indicated by the ones titled "El Arabs y El Magol/The Arab and the Magician" and "El Cantaro/The Little Moor." Nevertheless, she made two significant changes. First, stories originally spoken aloud in Spanish were written down in English; she explained that "we modern mothers no longer have the time nor the patience to sit down and tell our children these lovely stories," implying that "modern" women spoke English. The other most significant change was her substitution of the character of the fairy godmother for her mother's choice of savior: "María Santísma."[127] This choice shows her desire to have the stories read by Protestant Anglos, or by Hispanic children influenced by the culture of Protestant Anglos. Perhaps she had found the term easier to use when retelling the stories to Angelina, who grew up among English speakers in Denver and Santa Fe, distant from the village upbringing of her mother.

In her first two books, then, Jaramillo combined a preservationist's desire for "authenticity" with her practical concerns about making the recipes and stories interpretable by reader's own standards. In both cases, embracing tradition made her publications authentic enough to be of interest to Anglos, but what actually made it possible for her to preserve such traditions were her skills in adaptation.

When writing her later two books, she had more trouble resolving these two conflicting impulses. She discovered that writing *Shadows of the Past*, her book on New Mexican folklore, was a particularly "difficult task": she "had the material, but like a builder without experience, did not know how to put it together."[128] She had perhaps been inspired in this attempt by her work with the Fiesta, as well as her brother Reyes's work as a folklorist with the Federal Writer's Project.[129] She hoped to publish a book about the customs of nuevomexicano life that she both remembered and heard about from others, and, as her niece put it, to set the record straight.[130] She sought help from Mary Austin; in April 1934, in the one existing letter between the two women, she wrote the author to thank her for offering to recommend the manuscript to Alfred A. Knopf. She announced she had finished the book and asked Austin to now send her endorsement to the publisher.[131] Jaramillo trusted the backing of the renowned Austin would grant her manuscript the attention it deserved. An editor at Knopf, however, disagreed. In a June 1934 letter, he thanked Austin for the "wealth of material" she had sent their way but asserted that the manuscript required "a good deal of editing to make it an interesting and readable book."[132] Austin saved both letters, perhaps intending to offer Jaramillo further help with her manuscript. But Austin's always-weak health took another downward turn, and she passed away two months later. When Jaramillo sent her manuscript to university presses (she did not name which ones) instead, they returned it, months later, declining to publish it. "One professor said," Jaramillo remembered, that "he was writing a book. Would I permit him to use two or three of my stories in his book? I then understood. All they wanted was to read my manuscript and get ideas from it."[133]

Jaramillo continued her publication efforts alone. Since she wanted to maintain control of her memories and those of her family, rather than simply allowing them to be absorbed into a large body of material for the benefit of the newly established academic field of folklore, she had *Shadows of the Past* published by a small and local private press. This choice allowed her to maintain the book's personal and idyllic focus on the past. The book describes long happy days of both work and play, characterized by cyclical customs of ritual and seasons. Compared to her life upon leaving her home village, Arroyo Hondo seemed ideal: "In those days," she writes, "nature supplied all the simple wants of the people."[134]

At the end of the book, she finally reveals what destroyed this way of life. In the book's second-to-last chapter, a brief essay titled "Old

❧ Clinging to Tradition ❧

Customs Vanish," she writes of Kearny's conquest of New Mexico, political changes, and the ways in which "the young generation, finding the strangers' customs new and attractive, began to adopt them and to forget their own." *Shadows*, then, serves as a chronicle of a lost way of life; it is a story that begins and ends in the past. "The land of *Poco Tiempo*," she concluded this chapter, employing Charles Lummis's romantic phrase for the Southwest, "has become the land of haste and hurry."[135] The final chapter of the book collected the bits and pieces of folklore from the old days that did not fit elsewhere, as if she wanted to finish the book with the vanishing of the old ways but ultimately could not end on such a depressing note.

Perhaps another reason her narrative backtracks is that she knew the decline of nuevomexicano customs was not as simple as she had tried to make it out to be. Indeed, her own experiences had shown her that some nuevomexicano customs lasted long after Kearny's days in Santa Fe, and that young people like herself and Venceslao had begun their adult lives believing it was possible to combine old and new. Her own negotiations between tradition and modernity—her education, her wedding, the birth of her first child, her raising of her daughter, her work with La Sociedad Folklórica—had met with success as well as disappointments. The disappointments had been bitter enough to make her ponder long and hard about what accounted for them, and more often than not, the loss of the old ways (and the old wealth) at the hands of Anglos seemed to be to blame.

Yet she realized her life and those of others went on in important ways after 1846, ways that revealed both the integrity of the culture being lost and the tenacity of the people who were losing it. She publicly pointed to "tradition" as the authority for her work in the public eye. Privately, however, she seems to have come to an understanding not unlike Elsie Clews Parsons's theory of cultural borrowing: incorporating tools from Anglo culture, such as her business education, the English language, and the authority of a "woman's club" like La Sociedad Folklórica, made it possible for her to command respect for the elite, Spanish, and "traditional" identity with which she felt most comfortable.

So it was, perhaps, that when she sat down to write the expanded version of her autobiography, *Romance of a Little Village Girl*, she took a different, more complex, approach to writing the story of Hispanic culture in the Southwest than she had for *Shadows of the Past*. Published fourteen years later, in 1955, by the Naylor Company, a more prominent regional publisher than those who had published her previous books, *Romance* is Jaramillo's most comprehensive book. It is an invaluable source because it neither leaves out any major periods of her life, nor does it back away from the issues most personal to her: her relationship with her husband, her emotions upon his death and that of her daughter, and her motivations for beginning her work in folklore. In fact, her work provides a much more accessible and open account of its author's life than writings by Fabiola Cabeza de Baca, Kay Bennett, and Pablita Velarde do.

Yet she began the book, like *Shadows of the Past*, with an apology: "I feel an appalling shortage of words, not being a writer, and writing in a language almost foreign to me. May I offer an apology for my want of continued expression in some parts of the story."[136] She *was* a writer, and English was hardly "foreign" to her. The "continued expression" she was striving for more likely was missing due to her life story, not her writing abilities, because in many ways, her life does not make a "good story." Partially because it uses English to contradict some of the myths about conquest spread by Anglos, her story falls strictly neither into the category of romance, promised by its title, nor tragedy, as implied by its contents. Something important is missing: not an event, not an emotion, but rather, a sense of resolution. Her story, as presented in *Romance*, is profoundly divided between who she thought she was in the past and who she thought she was as she wrote.

Perhaps this is most pronounced in her sense of herself as a woman. Near the beginning of the book, she describes traditional women's roles in nuevomexicano culture as idyllic:

> Everyone was happy in those days. . . . People's lives radiated between church and home. Mothers stayed home

taking care of their children, satisfied to live on their
husbands' earnings. They were not buying new clothes all
the time nor visiting beauty shops. No one was ever late
for church, although some of them lived two and three
miles distant and rode in slow wagons or even walked.
How nice it would be if people now would live thus![137]

This is the same woman whose autobiography also describes how hard
it was to suppress her desire to put off her marriage and go to college,
the same woman who was ultimately so disappointed in her efforts to
be an ideal "modern" wife and mother. Thus, her approach to women's
traditionalism was more complicated than this passage implied.

It was not until the end of her life, after all, that she settled on a
clear sense of purpose, a public career devoted to folklore. When
describing events that honored this work, she wrote that "I will always
treasure these incidents as the happiest and most cherished in these latter years of my life."[138] But her niece Rosa maintains that her aunt
probably would have neither started the folklore society nor published
her books were it not for the deaths of her husband and daughter. She
believes her aunt ultimately saw herself as a traditional woman and saw
her work as supportive of tradition. She also points out that the structure of La Sociedad Folklórica, which met during the day on weekdays,
was not intended to accommodate working women.[139]

Clearly, Jaramillo saw herself as traditional and ideal women's
roles as traditional. But that did not prevent her from experiencing
"happy" and "cherished" moments as a woman in the public sphere,
taking a stand on public culture in Santa Fe. Like other "clubwomen"
of her generation, she maintained a precarious balance between "traditional" ideals for women and what could be termed feminist goals for
women's active direction of and participation in the public sphere.[140]
Her contradictory statements on what made her happy as a woman
reveal just how precarious this balance was, and how unresolved these
issues remained for her and other women during her own lifetime.

❧ CHAPTER TWO ❧

Her stance on racial issues also remained unresolved. On the one hand, she clung to her sense of herself as part of a "Spanish elite," failing to acknowledge mestizo elements of nuevomexicano culture and touching on "Indians" in her folklore work only when she mentioned "maids" and "peasants" in passing. And yet her lifetime had shown her what a relative position that "Spanish" identity really was—though it set her above mestizos, it ultimately separated her from the Anglos the Spanish label had originally sought a bond with. When the "red-haired cattleman" made an intrusion into her house at El Rito, and when her husband's former friend took over his ranch, she realized that her "Spanish" identity did not always do much to protect her from greed and disrespect. Witnessing the antiblack sentiments unleashed by Thomas Johnson's trial showed her just how relative and powerful ideas of whiteness could be. In what may be the most notable omission of her memoir, a clear identification of Johnson's race, she indicated either a growing ambivalence about using race as a standard of judgment or a reluctance, as a "white" woman, to associate herself explicitly with issues of "color." Either way, she implied the presence of racial issues that New Mexican writers following in her footsteps have pursued in more depth.

Writing books in English about a life that had been characterized by conflict with all that language represented to her was a difficult and painful enterprise. Moreover, the life that she led as an adult in post-Anglo-conquest New Mexico was in many ways a disappointment to her, a far cry from the world she imagined as a girl in Arroyo Hondo. Understandably and admirably, she avoided completely capitulating to the "modern" world she found. And yet she did not find herself unchanged by it, nor uninspired. She could write and publish books in English, and she could attempt to resolve the tension between herself and the "new order" by using English to critique that order. Finally, she found she could ultimately turn to tradition for comfort, even as she had to adopt nontraditional means—organizing a Hispanic folklore society, writing in English, politicking with the Fiesta organizers—to do so.

Clinging to tradition ultimately became her way of adjusting to the future, and yet to view her as a tradition-bound woman denies the complexity of this process. Her life—which ended, peacefully, at age seventy-eight, in 1956—was actually a continual process of adjustment and negotiation. She used a traditionalist approach to take advantage of the rhetoric of cultural preservation established by people like Austin and Luhan and to preserve her own sense of racial and economic privilege; she "borrowed" aspects of Anglo culture so she could better cope with those forced upon her. Like the adoption of the English term *Spanish* during Anglo conquest, her efforts ultimately served as defense mechanisms in a climate of disenfranchisement.

The extent of Jaramillo's efforts to portray herself and her culture as traditional actually attests to the rapid rate of cultural change occurring in New Mexico during her generation and continuing today. Thus, it is not surprising that her life illustrates a pattern of action undertaken by women of color in the years to come. It remained for the generation that followed hers to more assertively counter restrictive ideas about the "traditional" roles women of color should play in sustaining New Mexico's multicultural environment, even as they also recognized, like Jaramillo, tradition's potential as a powerful tool for change.

CHAPTER 3
Making Homes in a Changing Land
Fabiola Cabeza de Baca and the Double-Edged Present

*T*he Hispanic generation that followed Cleofas Jaramillo's came of age with a new set of expectations for life in New Mexico. Having grown up fully aware of the impact of economic decline that Jaramillo only realized later in life, leaders of this next generation of nuevomexicanos saw that a romantic approach to their past cultural heritage limited opportunities for social change in the present. They increasingly devoted themselves to advocating civic equality for Hispanos through organizations such as the League of United Latin American Citizens (LULAC) and through pursuit of economic and educational reforms. Hispanic leaders of the mid-twentieth century carried on the work of the earlier "elite" generation, but they adopted middle-class American approaches to social reform. They applied the philosophy of the Progressive movement in U.S. political culture to efforts to improve the lives of Hispanic New Mexicans who struggled to preserve their homes in the ever-widening wake of economic conquest; this work became even more pressing when World War II and the defense projects it brought to New Mexico heightened both the rate of Anglo immigration to the state and Hispanics' sense of civic inequality. While they did not extensively press for retribution for the land dealings that had dispossessed Hispanic New Mexicans in the years following 1848, their increasing awareness of this injustice and the impediment it presented to civic and economic equality paved the way for yet another generation of activists.

Like their female compatriots in the Progressive movement at large, New Mexican women involved in this early and mid-twentieth-century movement for Hispanic equality found an opportunity to bring the strength of traditional female roles as nurturers into the wider realm of the public sphere. And yet, as Jaramillo had found a generation before, their identity as Hispanic women posed a complicated set of expectations for their proper contribution. Emphasizing their "traditionalism" increased respect for their voice in social affairs—this was also true for Anglo Progressive women such as Jane Addams. What differed for Hispanic women in New Mexico, as the story of Fabiola Cabeza de Baca (1894–1991) illustrates, was the degree to which their voice as cultural activists depended on presenting themselves as traditional *Hispanic* women—as representatives of a "pure" cultural tradition, according to the framework set forth by Austin's and Luhan's generation of romantic multicultural activists.[1]

Critics who have analyzed Cabeza de Baca's two major literary efforts have faulted her for relying so heavily on this rhetoric of tradition. *The Good Life: New Mexico Traditions and Food* (1949), a composite account of the folkways and food customs of a traditional New Mexican village, and *We Fed Them Cactus* (1954), an autobiographical history of the Llano Estacado, the ranching area where she grew up, both present romantic accounts of the Hispanic past.[2] Cabeza de Baca also became deeply involved in traditionalist preservation efforts like Austin's Spanish Colonial Arts Society and Jaramillo's La Sociedad Folklórica.

But she undertook such efforts in preservation after a long career as a home extension agent, work that required her to inform clients about the benefits of making changes in the way they managed their homes. Writings she published prior to *The Good Life* and *We Fed Them Cactus* included two Spanish-language bulletins she composed in the 1930s for the New Mexico Agricultural Extension Service (NMAES)—one on canning, one on the preparation of meals—that taught New Mexican homemakers how to bring "modern efficiency" and nutrition to their households.[3] Thus, when Cabeza de Baca turned to writing romanticized accounts of Hispanic tradition later in life, she did so only after devoting many years of her career to a Progressive approach to cultural change.

In fact, a contradictory approach to questions of cultural tradition characterizes her entire life story. Unlike Jaramillo, a woman who always approached the present and future tentatively, Cabeza de Baca defied conventions frequently. But, like Jaramillo, she found benefits in embracing convention in print. Consider, for example, that despite her career in home economics, she apparently did not like to cook.[4] Nevertheless, in 1939, she published the first widely distributed New Mexican cookbook, *Historic Cookery*. Its emphasis on accuracy and the science of nutrition stands in stark contrast to the informal recipes published by Jaramillo, but like her predecessor's cookbook, it boosted the traditional life of New Mexican women. The quality of the recipes caught the attention of New Mexico Governor Thomas Mabry, who held office in the late 1940s. He believed this guide to tri-cultural cooking would make an excellent public relations tool, and according to one newspaper report, he sent copies to the governors of every other U.S. state, "along with a sack of the pinto beans so necessary for carrying out its recipes."[5]

Through such experiences, Cabeza de Baca came to realize that changes New Mexicans considered in social policy were often offset by a deep conservatism when it came to cultural ideals, especially about gender. The state agency she worked for as a home economist helped rural Hispanics and American Indians use technology to improve their lives, but it also reinforced strict gender roles. When she participated in efforts of LULAC to advocate social equality, she found herself relegated to an auxiliary role, despite the leadership skills she had cultivated during her career. Embracing a feminine voice became an empowering way to reckon with such obstacles. Thus, even though her experiences with cultural change and inequality would lead her to publish books that implicitly criticize static notions of culture and femininity, the voice with which she did so is often romantic, accommodating, and traditionalist.

But more than any other woman in this study, her life story and writings also reveal an increasing willingness to speak openly about the complex processes of cultural change. Reviewing her life and her writing in tandem shows how she came to defy the ideology that bound women to tradition, even as she made strategic use of its capacity for boosting the developing discourse of multiculturalism. Critically conscious of the role that the past could play in the present and highly motivated to find a usable Hispanic past, she sought a balance between tradition and change for others as well as for herself. Living in this double-edged present, looking simultaneously forward and backward in time, led her to conceal aspects of her private life that others could consider nontraditional, but the transformations she lived through also made her eager to share observations about cultural change.

Thus, while Austin and Luhan's rhetoric of tradition may better describe the voice Cabeza de Baca often used, Elsie Clews Parsons's theory of cultural borrowing better explains the strategies she developed to affirm Hispanic cultural identity. Examining her work as a teacher, a home economist, an activist, and a writer shows how she derived power from expectations of traditionalism even as she increasingly defied them. Ultimately, she would advocate a vision of New Mexico as a changing multicultural home, a vision that directly challenges Austin and Luhan's rhetoric of tradition.

Roots in the Colonial Past

Like Jaramillo, her distant cousin, Cabeza de Baca belonged to a family that felt distinguished by its roots in New Mexico's Spanish Colonial past.[6] The Cabeza de Baca name linked her to one of the first Spaniards in what is now the U.S. Southwest, Alvar Núñez Cabeza de Vaca, who explored present-day New Mexico in the early 1530s.[7] She wrote proudly of her paternal great-grandfather, Don Luis María Cabeza de Baca, and of his title to the Las Vegas Grandes land grant, given to him by the Mexican government in 1823.[8] She was also related, on both her mother's and her father's sides, to the prominent Delgado family.[9] These deep roots in New Mexico, combined with her family's high class status, led her, like Jaramillo and many others, to identify explicitly as "Spanish" or "Hispano."

Cabeza de Baca's family instilled, even demanded, a strong sense of pride in this Spanish heritage and its accompanying duties. She was born in 1894 on her grandparents' ranch in La Liendre, the New Mexican ranching town where her parents had also built their own home.[10] When she was four, her mother died. She and her siblings stayed at the ranch where her father and his parents raised them. Her grandparents inculcated her with a sense of the value of education and the importance of giving to the poor, as she remembered many years later, when asked about her most vivid memories of her young childhood on the ranch. She recalled listening to her grandfather—who had been educated in Durango, Mexico, and spoke Spanish, English, French, and Latin—reading *Don Quixote* aloud in front of the fire while her grandmother did needlework. She also described Sundays spent in the village of La Liendre while her grandmother visited the poor and the sick, dispensing care and gifts.[11]

Even from a young age, however, Cabeza de Baca rebelled against what her family considered appropriate behavior standards for a "Spanish lady." Her grandparents built a house in Las Vegas, a booming railroad town less than twenty miles north of the family ranch, when their grandchildren were old enough to go to school. Cabeza de Baca attended Las Vegas's Loretto Academy, the girls' convent school similar to the ones in Taos and Santa Fe that Jaramillo attended, and at which her own mother had been a student. But during her first year, she was reportedly expelled for slapping a nun.[12] Luckily, she was able to attend a public school run by New Mexico Normal, the teachers' college in Las Vegas that became New Mexico Highlands University in 1941. She learned to speak English within her first year of school. In 1906, when she was only twelve years old, her family sent her to Spain for a year-long educational trip; she visited Spain again as a college student. In 1913, as part of her graduation from high school, she earned a teaching certificate that qualified her to teach elementary school. Despite her degree, her father discouraged her from taking a job when it was offered to her a few years later.[13]

Perhaps he did so because her education, funded by her family for the purpose of bringing her up properly, took her in a different direction than her grandparents and father had expected. While her time as a young woman surrounded by prominent relatives in Las Vegas and by high culture in Spain led her to pursue an interest in documenting her family's history and Spanish traditions in New Mexico, her teenage years also included many nontraditional experiences. During the school year, she lived with her grandparents in their large house on Las Vegas's Hot Springs Boulevard, in a neighborhood called "Old Town." She remembered Las Vegas, historically a trading center, as a place that was exciting because of its diversity. Families living nearby, she remembered, included African Americans, Jews, Germans, "plain Americans," and Hispanics. "There was no discrimination as to color or race," she claimed. "We all played together as one big family."[14] (Perhaps this sense of harmony in Old Town had something to do with the wealth these families shared due to ranching, trade, and the railroad, as well as the fact that some rich Anglo families who came in with the railroad, and proved to be less tolerant, established a separate town of Las Vegas across the Gallinas stream.) According to Cabeza de Baca, only four Spanish-speaking students went to her high school.[15] Her father did not allow her to go to dances, she remembered, but her time in school certainly involved other steps away from the customs of her grandparents' ranch.

Even at home, Cabeza de Baca lived a life that was quite different from her grandmother's and mother's. After she was twelve years old, she spent summers at the Spear Bar Ranch near Newkirk, New Mexico, where her grandfather, father, and uncles had moved their operations.

At Spear Bar, about one hundred miles from Las Vegas, she did not take pleasure in her grandmother's pastime of needlework, but loved the time she spent among the men who worked there. If her "fastidious" grandmother had known how "carefree" the housekeeping was on the ranch, she later wrote, "she would never have permitted my summer vacationing on the rancho."[16] As in Las Vegas, Cabeza de Baca's time on the ranch brought her into contact with non-Hispanic people and customs, especially those of the waves of Anglo homesteaders who settled nearby. Despite her father's reluctance to associate with these families, they frequently invited her and her brother to picnics and dances. "If today I can fry chicken, make sour milk biscuits and cornbread," she wrote of the homesteaders in *We Fed Them Cactus*, "I owe it to the friends of my youth on the llano."[17]

Cabeza de Baca's experiences on the Llano Estacado ranch also included a good deal of time outside, wandering her family's land, often alone, by foot and by horseback. "True to my aristocratic rearing," she recalled, "I had to lead a ladylike life and should not resemble that of our uncouth neighbors whose women were able to do men's work." By this logic, her family gave her a "gentle pony" to ride instead of "broncos," but still her father allowed her to help during branding time.[18] Such summers always ended too quickly. "Before I realized," she later recollected, "I had to go back to school and leave the land I loved."[19]

From what she wrote in her memoir and revealed in interviews later in life, Cabeza de Baca seems to have always known that her grandparents' way of life was passing. Her writing would express nostalgia for the "hacienda life," but she knew it had begun to disappear long before her time. The customs she saw on her family's ranch, the stories she heard around the hearth, the fragmented local history of Spanish colonialism she read—all were remnants of an earlier era. Her admiration of this heritage did not preclude her growing awareness of the consequences of "Americanization" and its deep effects on her own identity. In an unpublished manuscript about the descendants of Spanish colonists in the twentieth century, she emphasized this awareness by identifying herself as a person of dual heritage. "Although I am of the People and of Spanish ancestry," she explained, "my background is a mixture of Spanish and American cultures."[20] She recognized the extent to which ideas about strict ethnic identities did not reflect actual New Mexican cultural experience.

She also recognized, however, that such ideas about ethnicity could have powerful effects, as they did for Hispanics who faced racism and economic decline in the early twentieth century. Land grant controversies, like the one that plagued Jaramillo's immediate family, also directly had impact on Cabeza de Baca. Her family, once owners of the Las Vegas Grandes Grant, ceded that land in the mid-nineteenth century to the citizens of Las Vegas in exchange for five parcels of land known as Baca Location Number One, Baca Location Number Two, and so on. By the first years of the twentieth century, Anglo American merchants and lawyers, the same people who had built a new, incorporated city of Las Vegas, had managed to seize the Las Vegas Grandes Grant through legal wrangling. The new Land Board parceled pieces out to those who could purchase them and initiated a doomed irrigation project intended to benefit Anglo farmers.[21] Meanwhile, the Cabeza de Baca family's defense of their title to the Baca Location ranches apparently forced them to sell off some portions in order to pay lawyers to save others.[22]

In addition to leaving her with a grim awareness of the declining power of Hispanics, Cabeza de Baca's youth allowed her to see how the matriarchal authority exerted by her grandmother was not necessarily a powerful path for a woman of the twentieth century. Her education and exposure to newer models of femininity offered her different options. In the late 1890s, Jaramillo had not known how to explain to her family that she wanted to put off marriage until after attending a women's college. Cabeza de Baca, who was seventeen years younger than Jaramillo, came of age a generation later, when citizens of New Mexico and elsewhere paid more attention to the rights and education of women.[23] She also had the advantage of living close enough to a college, New Mexico Normal, where she could pursue a teaching degree while living at home.

The content of Cabeza de Baca's education did not directly challenge her family's views of feminine roles, as one anecdote reveals. In a speech she later gave to home economics students, she described a cooking class she took as a senior at New Mexico Normal High School in which students competed to serve the best meal at lowest cost to four people. Cabeza de Baca won second place in the contest after serving "roast beef, mashed potatoes, creamed peas, and snow pudding" to four "guinea pigs" from the Board of Regents of New Mexico Normal.[24] While fairly conventional, this coursework, as well as the college classes she took in pedagogy and language, demonstrated possibilities for professional women in the fields of education and home economics. By combining her grandmother's drive for service to the community with the skills she was acquiring through education, she crafted her own position of female authority. Like young Progressive social workers and clubwomen around the country, she extended the rhetoric of feminine power in the home to a larger sphere.[25] Through teaching, and later through extension work, she found a way to meet the Hispanic New Mexican community's need for social services that went beyond the informality of noblesse oblige. Her two younger sisters, Guadalupe and Virginia, as well as two of her female cousins, also became schoolteachers, testifying to the appeal of this option for young Hispanic women of similar educational and social status during this era.[26]

A One-Room Schoolhouse

Cabeza de Baca took her first teaching job in 1916. This work was in a one-room schoolhouse located in a rural part of Guadalupe County, six miles from her family's ranch, and nearly a day's journey from the closest sizable town, Montoya. Away from academics and progressive city schools, she began to learn more about the needs of the diverse rural population and the distinct role an educated woman could play in addressing them.

In her memoir, she wrote that she took this job soon after becoming aware of how "the children around us had from five to seven

Fig. 16: Fabiola Cabeza de Baca at a Country School, c. 1920s. Courtesy of the Center for Southwest Research, University Libraries, University of New Mexico, No. 000-603-0002.

months of school and...many of the teachers in the county did not have even an eighth grade education." In light of her family's privileges, this inequity seemed unfair. Her father opposed her acceptance of the job, however, because he feared his daughter would have trouble maneuvering the class boundary between herself and her students. She convinced him to let her sign the contract after "a great deal of pleading" but he made her promise to stay the full seven months. He worried that exposure to the conditions of the school might drive her away.[27]

Cabeza de Baca's time teaching in this Guadalupe County school was, in fact, very challenging. The school board divided over her appointment because one member felt the job should go to one of his relatives; thus, she began her work with less than full support. Because her family's ranch was too far from the school for her to live at home, she had to board with a family living near the school, and the bare surroundings of the room she stayed in made her especially homesick. The harsh conditions of the schoolhouse, the lack of funds available for improvements and supplies, and the demands of a student body diverse in age and ethnicity also made her work quite difficult. Cabeza de Baca and the children cleaned the school thoroughly as their first task together and coped accordingly when one of the school directors told her father no "privy" was necessary because "there were plenty of junipers around the schoolhouse."[28] She managed to teach with a cracked oilcloth blackboard, an unsanitary drinking water bucket with a common cup, and outdated books. She brought magazines from home, ordered inexpensive reprints of "classics" whenever possible, and improvised a phonics chart from her school notes. Admittedly, she had more resources at her disposal than many county teachers. Her salary was seventy dollars a month, but since it was paid in county bonds for which the county currently had no cash equivalent, she lived at her father's expense and saved the bonds for later years. Despite his initial disapproval, her father also did what he could to help her with supplies. "Having been trained in a teachers' Normal School," Cabeza de Baca explained in her memoir, "I had high ideals, and Papá's pocketbook was the victim."[29]

She eventually found that the diversity of her students made her job much more interesting. "It was a mixed school," she recalled, with "the children of the homesteaders, the children of parents of Spanish extraction and children with Indian blood but of Spanish tongue." This environment, Cabeza de Baca implied in her memoir, allowed the students to learn more. The bilingual readers, although "out-of-date" by the county superintendent's standards, did allow Spanish-speaking students to learn English, and vice versa. During singing lessons, the "Spanish" children taught the others folk songs and the Anglo children taught "cowboy ballads and hillbilly songs." Cabeza de Baca recognized that her ability to teach about local history was limited by the textbooks' focus on American colonial history, as well as her own education's emphasis on this perspective. "One sentence or perhaps a paragraph," she recalled with bitterness, "told about the Indians and the Spaniards in the Southwest." Her students, however, supplemented this curriculum with experience, thus dramatically widening her perspective as a teacher. "I learned the customs, food habits, religions, languages, and folkways of different national groups," Cabeza de Baca proclaimed in *We Fed Them Cactus*. "They were all simple, wholesome people living from the soil. . . . My education was from books; theirs came the hard way. It was superior to mine."[30] Still, the people of the area treated her with a good deal of respect, on a ranking, she later recalled, with the priest who visited the area. For example, her position as a schoolteacher permitted her to successfully encourage full community participation in the 1916 gubernatorial election, even though she and other women did not get to vote for the winning candidate: her uncle, Ezequiel Cabeza de Baca.[31]

Cabeza de Baca memorialized this first year of teaching in *We Fed Them Cactus* when she published the memoir in 1954. She spent more than ten years of her life as a teacher, but only this first year received such attention in her writings. Perhaps her later move into extension work, which also required that she bring a "modern" curriculum to a diverse rural audience, accounts for this distinct emphasis on the "country school" year. But for the decade after her year of teaching in Guadalupe County, her work actually took place in less rural settings. She taught at a school in Santa Rosa, as well as at the school for Spanish-speaking youth that Vencesleo Jaramillo helped to start in El Rita. In 1921, after several years of hard work and summer study, she earned her Bachelor's degree from New Mexico Normal, with a major in pedagogy and a minor in Romance languages.[32] After graduation, she took another yearlong trip to Spain, where she enrolled at El Centro de Estudios Históricos and conducted genealogical research.[33] When she returned to New Mexico, she began teaching again at El Rito.

She wrote and said little about personal matters at any period of her life, and her years as a university student and teacher were no exception. In *We Fed Them Cactus*, she mentions in passing a "young man to whom [she] was betrothed," but she does not provide any further details.[34] Had she married as a young woman, her life probably would have followed the domestic patterns of Jaramillo's. Instead, she continued to educate herself and to teach even though she could have returned to the ranch her father and brother now worked. Her time at

El Rito, a school with Progressive goals for "Spanish-American" youth, indicates that her choices may also have been influenced by a sense of mission for the future of her community. This was what had driven her uncle, to whom she was close, into politics.[35]

Cabeza de Baca's portrait of her own family's economic decline also helps to explain why she felt it was important to seek her way in the world. The title of her memoir, *We Fed Them Cactus*, refers to her family's experiences during the severe drought of 1918. Their ranchland was so devastated that most of the cattle had to be sent by train to a relative's ranch in northeastern New Mexico. Because her father had reduced his staff, Cabeza de Baca helped with the roundup, performing "real work" on horseback for the first time in her life. The most poignant passage of *We Fed Them Cactus* describes how she and her father wept as railroad cars hauled away the cattle. Cows that could not stand the trip were left on the ranch, but all the family had to feed them was cactus with its spines burnt off. She and her sisters, "on vacation," as she put it, from school, did work around the home and ranch they "had never dreamed [they] could do."[36] Her father had to sell the ranch, and though he bought a smaller parcel of land, the droughts of early 1930s "Dust Bowl" infamy reduced his herds completely. She ended her memoir with a tribute to her father's ordeals—and an implied promise to redeem him from his loss. "Each generation must profit by the trials and errors of those before them," she wrote of later efforts to farm and graze on the Llano Estacado, "otherwise everything would perish."[37]

A Demand for Home Economists

Cabeza de Baca's effort to learn from her father's generation included the transition she made during her late twenties, when she returned to school to pursue a degree in home economics. Entering this field in 1927, at a key moment in its history, helped her to develop a complex view toward cultural tradition and change even as the field's reliance on traditional ideas of gender would limit her ability to voice that view. In this respect, understanding her career as a home economist is a crucial part of understanding the guarded voice she would develop as a writer.

Initially, she returned to college only so that she could learn enough about home economics to teach the subject to younger students. In a speech she apparently gave to home economics majors at New Mexico State University in the 1960s, she explained how she actually began teaching courses in the subject at El Rito before she had a degree in the field; her four years of domestic science classes in high school made her the most qualified staff member to introduce the curriculum. "I struggled through the year" of teaching the new course, she recalled, "and that summer I attended Highlands University where I took courses in clothing, foods, and chemistry. These courses aroused my interest in that field." She moved to Las Cruces in 1927 to attend New Mexico State, paid her way by teaching Spanish courses, and completed her degree in 1929.[38] The state's director of extension work, W. L. Elser, happened to take one of her language courses. Eager to hire a Spanish-speaking woman who could carry the mission of the Extension Service to areas and populations not previously served, he convinced her to turn down teaching job offers and to accept instead a position as a home demonstration extension agent.[39]

The beginning of her career as a professional home economist coincided with a demand for the profession in New Mexico brought on by both political and economic factors. Concerned by droughts like those that devastated Cabeza de Baca's family's ranch, state and federal policymakers had begun to channel concerns for New Mexican rural populations into Progressive era models for social reform. The field of home economics had come into being around the turn of the century, an era cited by historian Dolores Hayden as one in which "women pioneered the use of applied natural science and social science to analyze the problems of urban life."[40] While home economics pioneers such as Ellen Swallow Richards and Charlotte Perkins

Fig. 17: Fabiola Cabeza de Baca (top stair, far left) with Home Economics Students
in El Rito, c. 1928. Courtesy of the Center for Southwest Research,
University Libraries, University of New Mexico, Neg. No. 000-603-0014.

Gilman focused on urban efforts such as community kitchens, settlement houses, and cooperative living, rural reformers during the same
era sought to improve home conditions in what they perceived as more
wholesome agricultural settings.

A diverse set of concerns that historians have come to call the
"Country Life Movement" (because of the Country Life Commission
appointed by President Theodore Roosevelt in 1908) resulted in an
increased devotion of federal funds and attention to the needs of rural
Americans. Progressive reformers came to apply the same logic to country living that they did to city government, believing that increased
efficiency and training by experts could improve agricultural life and

thus encourage Americans who lived on farms to stay there. The Smith-Lever Act, passed by Congress in 1914, responded to these concerns by providing federal funds for state efforts to educate farmers through agricultural and home extension agents. Additionally, the Smith-Hughes Act, passed in 1917, provided funds expressly for vocational education in agriculture and home economics. The increased demand for agricultural production brought on by World War I intensified the perceived needs for these programs.[41]

While historians have concluded that high ideals, continued industrialization, drought, and above all, the Great Depression prohibited success for the Country Life Movement in general, the particular challenges of the state of New Mexico made the work there exceptionally difficult. In New Mexico, the Smith-Lever Act did not prove effective because of the state's distinctive demographic features. While Country Life reformers' fears were realized when the 1920 census revealed that more Americans lived in urban areas than in rural areas, New Mexico's population remained 82 percent rural that year. Thus, the goal in this state was not to keep a dwindling number of citizens on farms, but to help improve the lives of people already deeply entrenched in a declining agricultural economy. Moreover, 60 percent of the state's population was Hispanic, and almost one-half of the state's total population, including the majority of rural women in the state, spoke only Spanish.[42] Almost none of New Mexico's agricultural and extension agents during the program's early years, however, spoke Spanish.[43]

Soon after Cabeza de Baca began her home extension career, the inflated sense of prosperity brought on by World War I gave way to the devastation of the state's agricultural economy caused by the combined impact of the Depression and ecological hardship in the early 1930s. This decline made the particular needs of New Mexican rural women even more starkly apparent. The women who worked for the NMAES as home extension agents were supposed to carry "modern" home economics to rural women by organizing lessons in nutrition, food preservation, food preparation, and home technology use. Given the state's ethnic diversity and its Spanish-speaking near-majority, historian

Sandra Schackel has written, "crossing the cultural boundary proved to be one of the greatest challenges facing the extension agents in New Mexico."[44] To a large extent, however, the NMAES ignored this cultural challenge. Historian Joan M. Jensen has documented this pattern of exclusion, noting that NMAES officials recognized their inability to serve most of the state's rural people but persisted in believing there was no easy way to solve the problem of the need for "qualified" women to hold the jobs.[45] From 1914, when the extension program began, to 1917, only English-speaking women held the state's lone position as home demonstration agent. The war-induced creation of more positions resulted in the hiring of a few Spanish-speaking women, but in the decades that followed, Cabeza de Baca was the only Hispanic home demonstration agent employed for a significant length of time. In fact, the commissioners of Rio Arriba County, where she worked, raised money for the position with the explicit requirement that the agent must be Hispanic.[46]

When she accepted her position as home demonstration agent for Santa Fe and Rio Arriba counties in 1929, she held the highest possible credentials. But her courses may not have prepared her to contend with the conflict between the pressures for "modernization" exerted by the NMAES and the centuries of tradition that guided her clients. Teaching her clients about canning, for example, meant challenging long-established patterns of food preservation in the Hispanic and Pueblo villages to which she had been assigned. Advocating changes in food cultivation and preparation also meant indirectly advocating changes in gender roles. The Smith-Lever Act reforms offered a "separate spheres" model of male and female roles that emerged from Anglo cities in the eastern United States, one that did not correspond to the seasonal patterns of work rural life in New Mexico actually required and benefited from. While male agricultural extension agents trained farm men and boys to raise livestock and crops more efficiently, the NMAES directed home extension agents to instruct farm girls and women in cooking, sewing, and poultry raising—and not the more active labor in food production that New Mexican farm women had traditionally performed. These women were rightfully suspicious of the ability of such lessons to help them address extensive economic crisis.

This sentiment, combined with previous experiences with female missionaries and state social workers who viewed Hispanics and American Indians condescendingly, made the population Cabeza de Baca served understandably suspicious of her intentions. It is also likely that they initially considered her social background an obstacle; indeed, she considered herself different from the villagers she worked with, by virtue of her class, her education, and her position. She was able, as she remarked in a matter-of-fact fashion later in life, to hire someone to help her with the housework she trained other women to do.[47]

Despite such barriers, her dedication to her clients soon impressed them. Her work days as an extension agent began when she left her home in Santa Fe "no later than six o'clock in the morning" and ended when she came "home as late as midnight at times." On these long days, she toured the rough roads and unbridged arroyos of her assigned counties in the car her father had bought her and taught her to drive. She had not been interested in driving before, but this skill was required for her work with rural clients.[48] She was determined to undertake her work: sharing information about nutrition, cooking, and crafts, and organizing women's and 4-H (Head, Heart, Hands, and Health) clubs for young people.[49]

Perhaps even more impressively, from her clients' perspective, she did not simply impose NMAES standards, but rather worked with people to determine how they could combine tradition and progress to improve their lives, often disputing ideas they had encountered elsewhere. A story about her early career that she later shared with readers of the *Journal of Home Economics* shows one such moment of successful negotiation. When a family invited her to supper, she was surprised to be served "fried potatoes with canned corned beef and white bread" while the family ate "beans and chili with whole-wheat tortillas, cheese and other milk dishes." When she asked "why they had not served her the food they ate, they replied, 'We thought you didn't like the kind of food we poor people eat.'"[50] She not only had to work to convince this family and others that she shared their tastes, but also that the food they ate was, in fact, more nutritious than what they served her. This situation provided her with an opportunity to use her modern skills to show why a traditional way of life could be preferable.

At the same time, she did encourage the use of some modern technologies, such as canning. She knew Hispanics had adopted the drying methods they currently used from Pueblo culture and that using sunshine to dry meat and vegetables had proved to be a good method for food preservation in the New Mexican climate. But canning, she believed, was an "easier way" for New Mexicans to continue eating the same nutritious foods.[51] Perhaps she believed that the time canning saved was worth some costs to culinary traditions if it made it easier for people to continue eating foods that had sustained them in the past.

Thus, her touring car and the information she carried made it possible for Cabeza de Baca to become a living agent of Parsons's "cultural borrowing" theory, offering the people she worked with empowering resources—some of which encouraged them to change their ways, and some of which affirmed their current cultural practices. She taught them to can foods and to organize Progressive-style crafts clubs, but she also emphasized that the way of life that their grandparents had practiced, complete with tortillas and beans, was healthy and desirable. Historian Virginia Scharff has noted that, as a folklorist, Cabeza de Baca "took evident delight in seeing the ways in which modern New Mexicans used new means to preserve old practices."[52] In her work as a home economist, she made such adaptation possible.

In later years, she blatantly resisted interviewers' attempts to characterize the people she worked with as reluctant to embrace change. Anglo social workers who had also worked with Hispanic and Pueblo villagers had cited such reluctance, but she asserted in one interview about her extension work that she "never encountered any problems."[53] In another interview, she responded to a question about whether Anglos, Indians, or Hispanics were easiest to work with by challenging such assumptions of ethnic difference: "If [people] want to learn," she explained patiently, "they are not hard to reach."[54] Despite this optimism, she likely did face difficulties in her work, especially because of the stark disparities between the goals of the program she worked for and the actual needs of the people. In a community marked by increased economic difficulties, one wonders if Cabeza de Baca always felt lessons in cookery or efforts to preserve traditional recipes could help.

In this respect, her work was probably hampered less by indifference among her clients than by the conflicted sense of purpose among the administrators who sent her to them. While Cabeza de Baca expressed such reservations neither in agency reports nor in later memoirs and interviews, historians who have studied the NMAES in the context of other New Deal–era reforms in New Mexico have criticized the agency's attempts. Suzanne Forrest characterizes the policies of the era as a "Janus-faced" attempt to "modernize" Hispanic villagers even as it maintained an essentialist and romantic belief in the sustainability of preindustrial village life.[55] Similarly, Sarah Deutsch's study of the rise and fall of a Hispanic regional community along the Colorado–New Mexico border argues that extension agents and other New Deal social service workers, both Anglo and Hispanic, "were missionaries by other names." Such women "saw themselves," Deutsch argues, "as organizers and advocates of the women they taught and as inculcators of proper gender roles and values": government intrusion into a community that had previously been able to sustain itself through adaptation, even at the hands of seemingly innocuous extension agents, achieved the "ultimate Anglo conquest."[56]

Deutsch holds that Cabeza de Baca contributed to this conquest because she was "virtually indistinguishable" from her Anglo counterparts in efforts to "render the villages closer to the romantic vision they wanted Hispanic culture to fulfill."[57] Cabeza de Baca's writings did, in fact, romanticize the life she experienced growing up near Las Vegas and working in northern New Mexico villages; she would call this "the good life" in one of her later books. Some scholars see this romanticization as evidence of her acceptance of Anglo cultural domination. The

extension bulletins she published in Spanish, literary scholar Anne
Goldman has noted, defer to stereotypes when they emphasize the need
for rural people to "progress" and to achieve "propriety." This writing,
Goldman continues, "reflects the compromising—as well as compro-
mised—role their author occupied by working on behalf of a government agency as eager to assume ignorance, incivility, and inability on
the part of its Hispano residents as it was willing to trumpet the advantages of eastern farming and housekeeping methods."[58]

While these interpretations accurately apply to many NMAES
texts, they do not fully describe Cabeza de Baca's work. They criticize
her both for believing in cultural tradition and for advocating
progress, without recognizing the significance of the fact that she did
both. Jensen's analysis of Cabeza de Baca's annual reports cites multiple examples of her ability to effectively blend these two impulses,
such as helping women to obtain and repair sewing machines even as
she also encouraged them to use the technology to create *colchas*, or
quilts, in traditional styles. Similarly, while the NMAES bulletin that
Cabeza de Baca wrote on preparing meals emphasizes the "proper"
methods for setting a table and using utensils, it also includes recipes
for chile con carne, enchiladas, tamales, chiles rellenos, and "arroz a
la española." "Este boletín no es para enseñar todo lo que hay que
saber sobre los alimentos (This bulletin is not intended to teach all
there is to know about food)," Cabeza de Baca's *Los Alimentos y su
Preparacion* begins.[59] Rather, the bulletin supplemented NMAES
clients' existing knowledge with information about nutrition and
preparation. Cabeza de Baca, Jensen concludes, "began with what
people wanted most and then introduced other programs as they saw
their relevance to their survival and prosperity."[60]

Cabeza de Baca's extension work was a determined effort to help
American Indian and Hispanic New Mexicans move forward into the
future while drawing from cultural strengths they had cultivated in the
past. Deutsch recognizes this distinctive approach to romantic preservation when she acknowledges that Cabeza de Baca "fostered
Hispanic crafts and legitimized Hispanic recipes" during her time with

the NMAES.[61] She recognized that traditions did not have to be "useful" or "romantic" in order to be maintained; respecting traditions because they were traditions was reason enough. She shared this message with other home economists:

> The public worker must be sympathetic with people she
> works with regardless of their background or extraction;
> she must respect their customs, their habits and beliefs;
> and foremost she must know that though individuals may
> differ, people are people in any language, race, or creed.[62]

Cabeza de Baca offered rural New Mexicans a way to assert tradition even as they also sought change.

In this respect, her sense of mission toward rural New Mexicans differed from that of Austin and Luhan, who both feared technology could destroy the attributes of American Indian and Hispanic cultures they most admired. They felt certain they knew better methods for cultural preservation than the introduction of products like sewing machines. It is worth recalling that Austin published one article critiquing attempts to extend consumerism to Hispanic New Mexicans: why encourage them, she asked rhetorically, "to become average installment plan Americans, socially and intellectually inferior to standardized Anglo labor, when they can be highly individualized artist-craftsmen?" Clearly, Austin assumed it was for her and other intellectual Anglos to decide the fate of this group of "immigrants" and how "to make the most sympathetic, and therefore the happiest, and so the most effective, use of them."[63] Cabeza de Baca, who had grown up in an environment not far removed from the small Hispanic villages that others wanted to preserve, and who reportedly learned Tewa during her work at Pueblo villages, had a different approach: ask the people what they want, and use the system and your knowledge to help them achieve it.[64]

Her ethnicity ensured her success as an extension agent. But her success also hints at what may have made some other aspects of her life decidedly more difficult. Her education, her relative wealth, and her family's position all distanced her from the women with whom she worked. She faced the difficult task of serving as an intermediary between the Anglo cultural imperatives represented by her government employer and the traditional Hispanic values with which she had been raised. Her Hispanic identity distanced her both from the NMAES and the emerging Anglo intellectual elite of New Mexico. In a letter to the *Santa Fe New Mexican* published in 1932, Austin recognized the contributions of "Miss Fabiola Cabeza de Baca" and others to the Spanish Colonial Arts Society; Cabeza de Baca's name was the only one with a Spanish surname on the list.[65] She crossed such boundaries often, but it could not have been easy to do so alone.

Developments in her personal life made her sense her distance from her origins even more acutely. In January 1932, a brief notice in the *New Mexico Extension News*, a newsletter for NMAES workers, offered "best wishes and congratulations to Miss Fabiola C. de Baca and Mr. Carlos Gilbert, who announce their marriage as taking place April 20, 1931."[66] Carlos Gilbert was Hispanic, but the fact that his previous marriage had ended in divorce ran counter to Cabeza de Baca's staunchly Catholic upbringing. She delayed announcing the controversial marriage to her employer and others, and her family, especially her father, found it upsetting.[67] Gilbert had a successful career as an insurance agent when they married and he later held positions as an elected school board official and within the state's branch of LULAC. Despite this social standing, his previous marriage made him an unacceptable son-in-law.

According to Cabeza de Baca's niece, Esther Branch Sánchez, the couple eloped to Mexico to marry, and upon their return, Cabeza de Baca's father never allowed Gilbert into his home.[68] Sánchez described Gilbert as a man with whom Cabeza de Baca was deeply in love, despite his dominating tendencies and the fact that his divorce required that they be married outside the church.[69] They traveled extensively together, often for LULAC events, and Cabeza de Baca apparently helped her husband to improve his speaking skills and thus his success as a salesman. The marriage ended in separation about ten years later, by 1941, at which time she probably suffered from remembering that her father considered the marriage a mistake. Gilbert, who remarried soon after, was permanently memorialized in Santa Fe when officials named a new elementary school after him in 1942.[70] His prominence as a local figure and the potentially scandalous beginning and end of their marriage may have contributed to Cabeza de Baca's decision to avoid referring to their marriage in her writing or in interviews.

She may also have avoided public mention of her marriage because her career path so clearly contradicted expectations of both Hispanic and Anglo married women during the 1930s. Even before her divorce she broke with convention, simply by remaining in the workforce. While the *New Mexico Extension News* often announced the retirement of a home extension worker whose marriage had been announced only a few weeks before, Cabeza de Baca continued her work. Others may have seen home economics work as a prelude to the domestic responsibilities of marriage; she clearly viewed her work, as devoted as it was to domestic ideals, as a career, one that she apparently chose not to interrupt, not even for children. Gilbert's two children from a previous marriage may have led them to decide against becoming parents together, or perhaps she did not want to or could not become pregnant.[71] Serious health problems may also have contributed to this decision. Not long after her marriage, in December 1932, a train struck the car in which she was riding.[72] She fought for two years to save her right leg, injured in the crash, but eventually she asked doctors to amputate it.

She remarked in a 1977 interview that "I have an artificial limb, and it has not been a handicap, and I don't think a disability either!"[73] The accident did in fact provide her with an opportunity to take her work as a home economist in new directions. She spent time during her recuperation authoring the NMAES bulletins on canning and meal preparation. This work apparently gave her the courage to return to extension work soon after her recovery, once again dismissing others' expectations of the proper thing to do. With the aid of a driver hired for her by the NMAES, Cabeza de Baca continued her career.

Though her work branched out in new directions in the 1930s and 1940s, it did maintain a consistent focus on traditional domestic issues, which allowed her to affirm Hispanic identity in a nonthreatening way. During these decades, Cabeza de Baca (who apparently did not, it is worth emphasizing again here, like to cook) published recipes in a home economics column in the Spanish-language Santa Fe newspaper, *El Nuevo Mexicano*; eventually she also hosted a weekly bilingual program on homemaking for the Santa Fe radio station KVSF.[74] In 1939, she wrote *Historic Cookery*, a NMAES English-language publication that included recipes she described as "typically New Mexican," because they emerged not from a static past but from processes of cultural change and interaction.[75] The book, which was republished several times, went on to be distributed in the tens of thousands.[76] "The recipes in *Historic Cookery*," she explained to her English-speaking readers, "are a product of the past and present—an amalgamation of Indian, Spanish, Mexican, and American."[77] Dishes ranging from red and green chile con carne to sponge cake show these multiple origins in action. It was this cookbook that Governor Mabry shared with other U.S. governors in order to popularize the state; Cabeza de Baca had become famous by crafting a nonthreatening testament to living multiculturalism in New Mexico.

Erasing LULAC, Embracing Reform

Such recognition undoubtedly encouraged Cabeza de Baca to continue her work; it also probably affirmed her decision to remain anchored in the field of domestic science and other existing channels of moderate reform. She worked with a wide range of voluntary service organizations, including the Girl Scouts, the Red Cross, and Jaramillo's La Sociedad Folklórica. In interviews she conducted later, she spoke fondly of her involvement in all of these groups.[78] She left one organization, however, out of her reminiscences: LULAC, the twentieth century's most prominent civil rights advocacy group for Hispanics in the United

CHAPTER THREE

States.[79] She correctly assumed that her work as a home economist would carry more weight if she did not openly present herself as a divorced woman who did not like to cook; perhaps she also felt Governor Mabry would not be as eager to share the recipes of someone who believed Hispanics suffered from unfair treatment. While her exact reasons for distancing herself from LULAC in later years remain unclear, this possible implication calls for contemplation, as it helps to explain the traditionalist path she would choose when she later turned to historical writing. Her time with LULAC reinforced her awareness of the fact that women were more likely to be heard when they served as nostalgic voices for cultural pride, rather than as more confrontational activists.

Her work with the organization did, however, begin optimistically, perhaps because she felt it offered a way to voice the concerns about the civic and economic status of Hispanics she had developed as a home extension agent but could not voice in that capacity. She, her husband, and their friends played leadership roles in LULAC, beginning in the late 1930s. Gilbert served as the state organizer for New Mexico from 1937 to 1938 under the national LULAC presidency of fellow New Mexican Filemón T. Martínez. During that same term, Cabeza de Baca (listed on records as "Mrs. Carlos Gilbert") served as a trustee for the national organization and as the president of the Santa Fe Ladies Council for a local chapter of the group. During November 1938, a special tour of Texas LULAC chapters by Martínez, his wife Antioneta Delgado de Martínez, Gilbert, and Cabeza de Baca took her away from her work in New Mexico for at least a few weeks.[80] In 1939, she served as director of Junior LULACs for the region of New Mexico. In other words, she committed much time and energy to this organization, perhaps recognizing the major role it would play in establishing civil rights as an organized cause for Hispanics.

LULAC had begun in Corpus Christi, Texas, in 1929, after leaders of several Texas Mexican American civic organizations came together to form a new union of interests. A generation of middle-class Mexican Americans, many of them veterans of World War I, had grown increasingly dissatisfied with the systematic denial of civic equality for U.S. citizens of Mexican descent in the U.S. Southwest, injustice only intensified by the hostile reactions of Anglo Americans to the dramatic rise in immigration of Mexicans to the United States during the 1910s and 1920s. As historian David Montejano has noted, this era saw a sharp upsurge in violent acts against Mexican nationals and Mexican Americans by Anglos, as well as escalating discriminatory practices in education and politics, especially in South Texas.[81] LULAC banded together local organizations to call attention to this widespread discrimination.

LULAC organizers controversially restricted membership to United States citizens. They hoped an alliance based on patriotism and civic duty (as well as an emphasis on their "European" or "White" heritage) could maneuver the channels of power successfully and achieve positive social change for all "Latin Americans." LULAC conducted voter registration drives, funded legal efforts to oppose segregation in schools and other public facilities, and held meetings that began with the Pledge of Allegiance. In an "Aims and Purposes" statement the organization reprinted throughout the 1940s in the *LULAC News*, LULAC leaders stated the primary goal of the group succinctly: "to develop within the members of our race the best, purest and most perfect type of a true and loyal citizen of the United States of America."[82] Though the "LULAC Code" reminded members to "be proud of your origin and maintain it immaculate," and to "respect your glorious past and help to defend the rights of your people," LULAC members of this era prioritized a display of loyalty to U.S. citizenship and its accompanying institutions.[83]

LULAC emerged so strongly during this era, historian Mario T. García has written, because of a group of social and intellectual leaders he and others have termed the "Mexican American Generation." These leaders came of age, much like Cabeza de Baca, during the years of the Progressive reforms of the New Deal and were further motivated to "patriotic idealism" during the World War II era.[84] Like Cabeza de Baca, they possessed economic and social power that made them less than representative of all American residents of Mexican descent.[85] By virtue of her birthplace and her education, not to mention her job, Cabeza de Baca lived as an "American" and thus identified with the accommodation-oriented goals of LULAC. Like Jaramillo before her, Cabeza de Baca described herself as "Spanish American" rather than Mexican, emphasizing her ancestors' long history in what became the United States as well as her European heritage. She probably would have felt, as recent LULAC leaders have asserted, that pressuring the U.S. Bureau of the Census to change the racial categorization of residents of Mexican descent from "Mexican" to "White" in the 1940 census was one of the organization's earliest major successes.[86]

LULAC's efforts to combat discrimination and segregation emerged from an elitist perspective, but LULAC also quite explicitly critiqued racist and romanticized views of all persons of Mexican descent, regardless of their citizenship status. This aspect of LULAC, argues García, makes it valuable to the historian concerned with identity in a multicultural society. Members of LULAC "sought to synthesize their experience based on their relationship to their Mexican roots, their Mexican-American reality, and their search for an American future," and in this respect, their "search for America" encompassed a search for a new sort of American identity.[87] Using the same language of democracy embodied in the U.S. Constitution, LULAC called for the extension of the full rights of citizenship to Mexican Americans while relegating Mexican American culture to a more private sphere.

The controversial role played by LULAC intensifies the need to understand why Cabeza de Baca distanced herself from the organization in later years. A 1946 report on the "Activities of Santa Fe Ladies Council No. 18" noted that Cabeza de Baca, "a charter member and one of the most outstanding...of the group," had only recently returned to meetings "after a leave of absence due to pressing business in connection with her work."[88] While a busy career may explain her need to withdraw from the organization, it does not explain her decision to omit it from her later recollections. The end of her marriage to Gilbert, with whom she directly shared involvement with LULAC, may have predisposed her to do so. Discussing her involvement in the Girl Scouts or the Red Cross may have been more appealing, as she was involved in them independently. In fact, on a certificate of appreciation the Red Cross issued her in 1946 for her work during World War II, Cabeza de Baca quite determinedly scratched out the "Carlos" in "Mrs. Carlos Gilbert" and wrote "Fabiola" above it.[89]

But her refusal to let her marriage and divorce interfere with her other work makes this explanation seem inadequate, hinting instead that her turn away from LULAC may have been a result of the way in which the organization treated her and other women. Never one to make conventionally feminine decisions, Cabeza de Baca may have resented the organization's prioritizing of male leadership.[90] She would not have been the only LULAC member who felt this way: the anonymous writer of an editorial in the March 1938 *LULAC News* criticized members of the organization who harbored a "cowardly and unfair," not to mention "narrow-minded," sentiment against women's influence. It further warned against apparent plans by these parties to propose legislation barring the direct influence of "Ladies' Auxiliary" groups at LULAC's next convention.[91] Cabeza de Baca's roles in the national organization and in a Ladies' Auxiliary at the local level indicate the potential for women in LULAC that she and others saw at one time. Historian Cynthia Orozco writes that, especially in comparison to women's LULAC groups in Texas, New Mexican women participated in joint endeavors with men; still, these groups fostered "gender-typed" behaviors when they initiated separate efforts like girls' and boys' groups for youth.[92] This coincided with the "feminine" work that Cabeza de Baca did as a home extension agent, but within LULAC circles she may have felt more confined by her status as Gilbert's (ex) wife. The fact that she later received so much recognition as a home economist and writer—and not as a LULAC member—supports this conclusion.

Another, perhaps the simplest, explanation for Cabeza de Baca's lack of reference to LULAC in later years may be that no interviewers appear to have asked her about her involvement. LULAC, one historian has shown, changed directions in the 1960s when it became an organization driven less by local membership than by corporate and governmental sponsorship at the federal level. Some members lost interest in the group because the goal of civic equality seemed to have been achieved; others found its message insufficiently critical of U.S. policies, especially in comparison to principles offered by the emerging leadership of the Chicano movement.[93] This change in LULAC's standing manifests itself in the writing done about Cabeza de Baca after the 1960s. Oral historians who approached Cabeza de Baca for interviews in the 1970s and 1980s took much interest in her NMAES work and her writing but asked her next to nothing about her political attitudes or activities.[94] Similarly, those who wrote profiles of her for New Mexico newspapers apparently did not ask about the organization, either because they were not aware of it or because it did not seem as potentially interesting (and as seemingly apolitical) as groups like La Sociedad Folklórica.

In fact, LULAC's politics never carried as much weight in New Mexico as they did in other parts of the Southwest: gradually realizing this may also have led Cabeza de Baca to separate herself from the group and turn instead to "preservation" work. LULAC did attract a New Mexico membership not long after its emergence in Texas, but the causes LULAC has earned a national reputation for—civil rights and the end of segregation—did not seem as pressing in a state that had long-established Hispanic cultural patterns and institutions. New Mexico also had an elite Hispanic class that, despite its economic decline, maintained powerful positions in local and state politics. Compared to Texas, the rise in Mexican immigration that contributed to the growth of LULAC had a different, though hardly negligible, effect in a state that espoused a myth of romantic "tri-culturalism" and pride in a Hispanic past. This pride may have made LULAC's emphasis on "Mexican-American" identity less respectable among New Mexican Hispanic elites, another potential explanation for Cabeza de Baca's reticence regarding her involvement in the organization.[95]

This New Mexican pride in the Spanish cultural heritage actually led to divisions over LULAC's emphasis, at that time, on "Americanism." One notable Hispanic woman leader in New Mexico, Concha Ortíz y Pino de Kleven, resigned from LULAC because of its "English only" emphasis. As a New Mexico congresswoman from 1937 to 1942, she advocated bilingual education for the state's

Hispanic children as a way to preserve New Mexican cultural identity, which set her at odds with LULAC leaders like Filemón Martínez, who opposed public education in Spanish.[96] Cabeza de Baca, it is worth recalling, wrote favorably of her experiences with bilingual education; perhaps this issue also factored into her eventual distance from LULAC.

One of the most famous presidents of LULAC during this era, the intellectual and educator George I. Sánchez, was New Mexican. His contributions to the organization help to illustrate both why Cabeza de Baca was drawn to the organization and why she eventually turned elsewhere for fulfillment as an activist. Sánchez came from a Spanish-Mexican Albuquerque family, taught at New Mexico schools, and rose to prominence as the author of *Forgotten People*. This study, first published in 1940, called attention to structural inequalities in northern New Mexico. In an edition of the book he published in 1967, after he had become an education professor at the University of Texas, Sánchez recalled that his optimism in the 1930s and 1940s grew from a particularly American form of idealism. "The New Deal of Franklin Delano Roosevelt raised our hopes," Sánchez explained, and then called for renewed efforts to extend a policy that would help New Mexicans to lift themselves "by their bootstraps" rather than continuing to "[take] away our boots!"[97] Sánchez, who served as LULAC president from 1941 to 1942, wanted the federal government to help New Mexican communities guard against discriminatory measures more subtle than school segregation, such as substandard funding for education and health and the continuing assault against Hispanic titles to land grants. His position, argues García, was that "Mexican Americans needed to undergo a type of 'modernization' that would equip them to compete with other Americans at all levels: economic, political, and cultural." Like Cabeza de Baca, he favored cultural progress for Hispanic New Mexicans, and thus went against the romantic views of "timeless" Hispanic villages advocated by Austin, Luhan, and other Anglo activists.

Despite these apparent similarities, Cabeza de Baca's choice to deemphasize, if not erase, her LULAC membership hints that she felt that her work could be more effective if she took it outside the channels of political activism, especially since the group seemed dismissive toward women. This choice would be validated by the scant attention that historians of the organization have paid to women's contributions when they consider the leadership that fueled LULAC's growth in New Mexico. García prefaces his consideration of Sánchez and two other "Mexican-American generation" intellectuals (Carlos E. Castañeda and Arthur L. Campa) by emphasizing the institutional role that this "triumvirate" of university professors played in dominating Mexican American thought of the era. While he acknowledges that fiction writers—he lists "Cleo" Jaramillo as one—played a "marginal" role in the process of creating the "Mexican-American mind," García does not consider that a woman whose sex took her outside the dominant channels of power may offer another, significantly contrasting, perspective on this process.[98]

Cabeza de Baca, whose work with rural Hispanic and American Indian women demanded that she offer "modernizing" strategies for homemaking even as it taught her about the staying power of cultural tradition, held such a perspective. LULAC espoused pride in cultural heritage, but it ultimately prioritized U.S. civic rights and obligations and male leadership in a very public sphere. Her work within homes may have led her to think more carefully about the role of women in private spheres. As "guardians of tradition," women could play a role that complemented the work LULAC members were attempting in the realm of civic action. Achieving cultural pluralism, Cabeza de Baca might have suspected, required more than civic equality in politics and education: it required preservation, appreciation, and strengthening of independent cultural traditions that emerged from homes like the ones in which she worked.

During her time with LULAC, Cabeza de Baca wrote an article for the *LULAC News* that, interpreted with an eye to her other writings, explains the incentive for this realization to come. Writing under the name of "Mrs. Carlos Gilbert," she published a piece titled "New Mexicans in Texas" that chronicled the ambassadorial visit she and her husband made to Texas with LULAC president Filemón T. Martínez and his wife, Antioneta. Recounting their initial fear at entering a state where "No Mexicans allowed" signs might be prominent, she hinted at the elite position she and many other LULAC members shared in regard to other Mexican Americans. "Mrs. Martínez said," she recalled of their arrival in West Texas, "'the name Gilbert and our fair skins may get us through.' We got past Lubbock without meeting [other LULAC members] for our protection."

The rest of the article chronicled the devoted attention they received in several Texas cities but did not mention any direct efforts LULAC was making to counteract the prejudices cited above, other than through muted references to meetings with public officials. Rather, it seems that "Mrs. Gilbert" and "Mrs. Martínez" were often asked to wait while the men went into "private conference." Cabeza de Baca only mentions personal interests when she recalls enjoying the flower exhibits at the fairgrounds in Harlingen, which she visited because gardening "happened to be her hobby."[99] For a woman who trained others in growing, preserving, and cooking sustainable and nutritious garden crops, the remark is a strange one, and perhaps a testament to the limited voice women had in LULAC affairs and publications. Recall that during the same year she published this self-deprecating feature, she wrote the very popular *Historic Cookery*, complete with an introduction about cultural interaction in New Mexico. When the end of her marriage required that she act and speak without being tied to the authority of her husband, she produced a body of written work that differs markedly from the *LULAC News* piece and that exceeded the scope of *Historic Cookery*. This work made its own significant, distinctly feminine, contribution to the Mexican American intellectual tradition.

Writing in New Directions

Authoring two bulletins for the NMAES left Cabeza de Baca with a lasting belief in the power of the written word as a form of social action; she remarked with satisfaction in an article she published about her work as an extension agent that "next to her prayer books, the rural Spanish-speaking woman treasures these two booklets."[100] *Historic Cookery* also received wide acclaim, and thanks to the governor, national attention.

At first glance, the writing she began in the 1940s seems to be an attempt to repeat the success of this domestic writing. She published her first literary piece, a portrait of Christmas in a Hispano village titled "Noche Buena for Doña Antonia," in a 1945 issue of the *New Mexico Extension News*, among updates on extension workers, 4-H contest winners, and agricultural methods.[101] This issue also features a photo of "Mrs. Fabiola Gilbert, Santa Fe County, president of the Home Demonstration Agents' Association," standing alongside the man who currently served as the president of the County Agents' Association.[102] "Noche Buena" thus initially seems to be a tribute to the "country life" that home extension agents paradoxically sought to strengthen by altering.

Closer reading of the piece, however, reveals that it departs significantly from the modernizing philosophy of the NMAES, offering instead a portrait of a village in which tradition thrives without interference. Cabeza de Baca's decision to publish this piece in a home economics publication nevertheless is not surprising, when one considers that this field and her standing within it offered her the sort of leadership role that LULAC had denied women. Women in home economics were charged with a noble mission well into the late twentieth century. Even as late as 1964, the *New Mexico Extension News* cheered on extension workers by publishing this tribute:

> Homemaking in our day and age is a sacrifice. Isn't it worth it to see our loved ones happier because we have moved in these circles, developed these techniques, attended these courses, gave of our time, talents, substance, opportunity, sweat, devotion, the tears of our heritage, that they might have a better life, a wider vision, a truer moment, a happy feeling, a well nourished body

housing a sound brain that thinks in terms of the good,
the beautiful, the true, in an atmosphere truly New
Mexican, a great heritage the likes of which America will
never see again? Carry on, homemakers, carry on![103]

Cabeza de Baca recognized the ideological potential of advocating pride
in heritage through the language of domesticity long before these words
appeared in print. Though such emphasis on feminine "sacrifice" restricted her ability to advocate social change, this "homemaking" ideal did
permit her a pedestal from which to speak, even when her topic changed
from affirming home extension work to affirming cultural identity.

In the "Noche Buena" piece, the first writing Cabeza de Baca did in
this vein, she cultivated cultural pride through the language of food. She
wrote a story about a Hispano woman going about her cooking for
Christmas festivities, describing her preparation of *molletes* (sweet
rolls), *bizcochitos* (sugar cookies), *empanaditas* (meat turnovers), and
pozole (lime hominy stew) with the help of her husband and her "Indian
comadre" Juanita.[104] Initially, she had written in Spanish for an audience that she believed benefited from information about home management. Then she wrote down recipes for an English-speaking audience
eager to take up New Mexican cooking. Now she attempted to share the
cultural context behind those recipes and to show their emergence from
homes steeped in tradition. In this respect, her efforts resembled Austin's
quests to preserve traditional Hispanic and American Indian cultures.
But because she wrote from an empathetic intermediary position, rather
than as an outsider looking in, Cabeza de Baca's work ultimately
showed a more complex understanding of how traditional cultures
change over time, contrary to romantic expectations of timelessness.

Initially, however, her literary writing in English drew directly from
the romantic impulse that had driven previous attempts to portray the
Hispanic village experience in New Mexico. *The Good Life*, first published by Santa Fe's San Vincente Foundation in 1949, combined a series
of narratives about the fictional Turrieta family and their village life with

Fig. 18:
Fabiola Cabeza de
Baca at Work in a
Kitchen in Later
Years. Courtesy of
the Museum of New
Mexico, Neg. No.
148467.

a short cookbook for the recipes mentioned throughout the narrative. The
piece Cabeza de Baca had previously published on "Noche Buena" reap-
pears in a revised and expanded form in *The Good Life*, as a chapter titled
"Christmas Festivities." Through both its title and its content, *The Good
Life* implies that the life at the Turrieta home, driven by nature and

tradition, holds a quality superior to that of the overmodernized city residence. Indeed, Cabeza de Baca later wrote (in an unpublished short manuscript about the book) that she intended to describe the culture from a nostalgic perspective; she was well aware that she longed for a life that might not exist much longer. "It was a challenge to work with these rural families and I wanted to share my discovery of the good life with my city friends by writing about the beautiful rural Hispanic heritage," she wrote. "It was nostalgia for the customs, traditions, and folkways which were rapidly passing. They had to be retrieved, so I wrote a book."[105]

This statement shows her belief that the glorification of this life in print could affirm Mexican-American identity even as it also appealed to outsiders' romanticism. Emphasizing domestic issues, rather than political ones, allowed her to advocate the cultural pride that LULAC strived for without seeming to pose a political threat, either to Anglos or to Hispanic male leadership. Writing about these traditions also allowed her to elevate the Hispano village lifestyle above mainstream American society, a significant discrepancy with LULAC's "All-American" goals. Through the language of homemaking, Cabeza de Baca had found her niche.

There is no autobiographical "Home Extension agent" character in *The Good Life*, though there is a character who represents a foil to someone with such a title. The same "Indian *comadre*" who appeared in "Noche Buena" plays a prominent role in *The Good Life*. "Seña Martina" is a curandera who shares herbal remedies and sage wisdom with Doña Paula Turrieta, a character of greater wealth and social position. In a passage that also appears, perhaps with deliberate irony, in the *New Mexico Extension News* version of the story, the narrator portrays the "herb woman" as someone who would disregard the advice any home economist would have to offer. She resists writing down the recipes for her herbal remedies for Doña Paula, and she mixes dough for molletes without concern for scientific precision. "Seña Martina," the narrator comments, "had not patience with those who used measuring cups and spoons, worrying for fear they would put in an ounce too much of this or that. Her hands were so used to the amounts that without thinking she broke four eggs, beat them thoroughly, and added two handfuls of sugar and a good pinch of anise seed."[106]

Doña Paula appreciates Señá Martina's traditional ways even as she herself adopts modern cooking methods and technologies (such as a set of dentures fitted by a dentist in Santa Fe). The narrative emphasizes that Señá Martina's way of life is passing through Doña Paula's observations about her friend's old-fashioned style and also by Señá Martina's death later in the book. Doña Paula holds a wake for her friend, "who had been closer to her than even her own mother," remembering to follow her wishes for an "Indian burial." Señá Martina did not want a coffin, she had explained, because "once we are dead nothing matters anymore. The coffin rots and we return to the earth as was intended."[107] Soon after this passage, the narrative portion of *The Good Life* gives way to recipes and a glossary of Spanish terms, instructions for those who, unlike Señá Martina, need help achieving a "good life."

In the 1950s, Cabeza de Baca's work in home economics grew international in scope, while her writing continued to focus on intensely local settings and history. Through a United Nations effort to train Central and South American students to work with Indian communities in their home countries, she went to Pátzcuaro, Mexico, to start a home economics program in 1951. Students who enrolled in this United Nations Educational, Scientific, and Cultural Organization (UNESCO) program went with Cabeza de Baca to Tarascan village training centers to observe the skills she had gained working in Pueblo and Hispano villages.[108] After six months of teaching, she returned to the NMAES. Since 1947, her position had expanded from Santa Fe and Rio Arriba counties and was now titled "Agent at Large" for seven counties in northern New Mexico. In addition to this work, she spent the mid-1950s actively involved with the New Mexico Folklore Society and was elected president of this organization in 1955.[109] She also earned accolades in home economics: in 1957, she received two of the highest awards in her field, the National Home Demonstration Agents Association Distinguished Award for Meritorious Service and the Distinguished Service Award for Authorship from the United States Department of Agriculture. Thus, her work as a home economist and folklorist continued to earn her the leadership roles and recognition that LULAC had stopped short of granting her.

These awards for her home extension work particularly recognized the publication of her most famous work of writing, *We Fed Them Cactus*. This work of history and autobiography, published by University of New Mexico Press in 1954, dealt not with her extension work in northern New Mexico but with the Hispano communities on the western edge of the Llano Estacado, the Las Vegas area where she had grown up. Just as she was reaching the highest point of her career as a home economist, her writing expressed an interest in exploring the history of Hispanic New Mexico as untouched by the rhetoric of progress that fueled her career. Cabeza de Baca retired from the Agricultural Extension Service in 1959. Aside from time spent at New Mexico State in Las Cruces in 1961, training Peace Corps Volunteers bound for Guatemala, she began to devote herself more entirely to the writing of history.

We Fed Them Cactus represented her first and best-known foray into this field. She published the book under her maiden name even though she still went by Gilbert socially and professionally, thus stressing the roots of the Cabeza de Baca family, as well as a distance from her former husband. The book, divided into five sections, blends the genres of folklore, history, and memoir: Cabeza de Baca hardly tells her life story, but she does recall stories she heard on her father's ranch and offers glimpses of how she heard the stories to begin with. She opens with a brief physical description of the Llano, then moves into the stories that "El Cuate," a hand on her father's ranch, told on rainy nights, stories of rodeos, fiestas, buffalo hunts, and Indian trade in the old days. The third section turns to her family's history more explicitly, and the "Spanish customs" she learned about even as they faded away. A fourth section, "Bad Men and Bold," chronicles the history of banditry in the area. A final section describes the ranch during the arrival of Anglo homesteaders, Cabeza de Baca's first year of teaching, and the droughts that finally drove her father away.

Like *The Good Life*, *We Fed Them Cactus* is a nostalgic tribute to a fading way of life. "This is the story of the struggle of New

Mexican Hispanos for existence on the Llano, the Staked Plains," the preface begins. The book goes on to mourn the decline of a culture even as it praises the persistence of its descendants. "Through four generations, our family has made a living from this land—from cattle and sheep, and lately by selling curios, soda pop, gasoline and food to tourists traveling over U.S. Highway 66."[110] *We Fed Them Cactus* is a record of extensive cultural change, but Cabeza de Baca replaced praise for the "progress" she espoused in her career as a home demonstration agent with mourning for loss.

In an unpublished manuscript, Cabeza de Baca made clear that her goal in writing *We Fed Them Cactus* was to share a previously unwritten history of the culture and environment of the Hispanic settlements in the Llano Estacado region, one that drew authority from her life story and her distinct access to this community. As one literary scholar has written, Cabeza de Baca used her ancestral ties to the land to create a "collective cultural autobiography."[111] Armed with a scrapbook her brother Luis had kept of the tales of "El Cuate" as well as with information she acquired through weekend interviews with "old timers," she and her brother undertook the ambitious research project resulting in the book. (For this reason, she dedicated the book to Luis, himself a rancher on the Llano.) She emphasized her desire to write "history" by explaining that she pursued as many interviews as she could: "A writer while interviewing informants should be able to separate fiction from truth."[112] But in order to do so, she blended others' stories and her own in a way that contradicted most readers' expectations of how history should be written. She did not, in other words, produce a seamless narrative characterized by an anonymous, objective narrative voice.

The blending of genres and the difficulty presented by retelling a story of such extensive loss combined to earn *We Fed Them Cactus* mixed reviews. Cabeza de Baca's mission of telling the truth about the past was somewhat undermined by initial responses from critics, such as one published in the *Albuquerque Journal* that focused on how the author's name "rings of color and romance and legendary history in

New Mexico." Perhaps these "romantic" associations account for the anonymous reviewer's subtle critique of the way the book's preface "perhaps tells in somewhat bitter words" the story of economic decline that followed the days of "legendary history."[113] Another reviewer, however, claimed that Cabeza de Baca's book had "no rancor or animosity against the Anglos who came in and dispossessed her people of a great deal of their land": this review praised Cabeza de Baca's implied "favor of the American way... against the Spanish way" as well as her demonstration of how, "to the New Mexican, 1846 is the same as 1776 to the New England boy or girl."[114] It seems likely that reviewers' difficulty in identifying the text's viewpoint on Anglo conquest stemmed from the contradiction between romantic views of the Hispanic past and Hispanics' declining status. To some, especially those who were unaware of the devious processes by which land was taken away from Hispanics, it must have seemed impossible for a book to be both "romantic" and "bitter," and thus they categorized it as one or the other.

Cabeza de Baca's involvement in this history and its contradictions further threw off readers, as revealed in a review by T. M. Pearce, a scholar of New Mexican literature. He confined the book's significance to being a "personalized" account that "has the unique distinction of being a Spanish American history of the *Llano*." This review mentioned Cabeza de Baca's ancestry but not her career as a public servant.[115] Since she omitted this experience from her work, the lack of attention is not surprising, but reviewers' continual emphasis on her ancestry and her "authentic" experience shows what made the book most significant to the mainstream press.[116] By 1980, a reviewer of a reprint of *We Fed Them Cactus* seemed less impressed with these qualifications, focusing instead on what he saw as the book's lack of resolution. "The book contains little history and no fully developed stories," wrote critic John Rothfork of what he called the book's "generalizations," acknowledging only that "those looking for a light and easy-to-read introduction to the Llano of nearly a hundred years ago will enjoy the work."[117] The tone of the book, at once intensely personal, arguably vague, and seemingly "authentic," seemed to confuse readers who expected either an "objective" history or a personal account of rico ancestry, not something somewhere in between.

More recent work by Chicano literary critics has offered valuable ways to interpret *We Fed Them Cactus*'s defiance of genre and confusions of tone, but even these interpretations vary widely. Raymond Paredes labels all early Mexican American literature in English that emerged in New Mexico as a "profoundly disturbing" body of work that romanticizes the "Spanish" rico heritage at the expense of indigenous and mestizo ones. This generation, suggests Paredes, fell victim to a "hacienda syndrome" they internalized in the wake of U.S. conquest.[118] A feminist critic of Chicana literature, Tey Diana Rebolledo, has characterized Paredes's general approach as "exceedingly harsh." Given what all Hispanic authors, especially women, were up against, explains Rebolledo, "It is a wonder that they wrote at all." Additionally, Rebolledo locates in *We Fed Them Cactus* and other works, including Jaramillo's writing, a "culture of resistance" as well as one of romanticized accommodation.[119] *We Fed Them Cactus* acknowledges the difficult legacy of race and racism in New Mexico, for example, when Cabeza de Baca describes how her father became outraged at a homesteader who told him he had "mistaken" him for a "white man."[120] Rebolledo also cites overall patterns of resistance, such as referring to ancestors and Hispanic place-names, relating (and perhaps glorifying) stories of social banditry, alluding to an idyllic past, overriding established genres, emphasizing a feminine voice, and indirectly criticizing Anglo culture.[121] Genaro Padilla, who considers *We Fed Them Cactus* alongside Jaramillo's *Romance of a Little Village Girl* and other Mexican American autobiographies, acknowledges the power of the book to resist romanticized conquest even as it produces a "diffident, abruptly self-censoring, sentimental narrative."[122]

Approaches that measure Cabeza de Baca's writing only by the degree of its "resistance" to past conquests, however, are troubling, because they tend to ignore or discredit the forward-looking nature of her life. Other critics' interpretations point out that she wrote not to dwell in the past, but to move forward from it. As Merrihelen Ponce hypothesizes, Cabeza de Baca "wrote *We Fed Them Cactus* to document and affirm the New Mexican Hispano experience at a time when Euroamerican writers were defining who Hispanics were."[123] In her analysis of the book's "communal voice," Becky Jo Gesteland McShane argues that its idealized portrayal of the past likely stemmed from Cabeza de Baca's desire to correct negative stereotypes among Anglo readers and to foster a usable past that would unite Hispanic readers.[124]

Ultimately, *We Fed Them Cactus* both embraces "traditionalist" views of Hispanic culture and contradicts them through subtle resistance. Cabeza de Baca wanted to show that Hispanics took pride in their past but were not stuck in it, nor were they cultural isolationists. Through her career, her work with LULAC and other organizations, and in the modern home she made in Santa Fe, she embraced the pluralist world she lived in even as she mourned the world she saw being lost. In fact, *We Fed Them Cactus* shows the appeal that a pluralistic environment held for her; it describes her happiness in living among people of different ethnic backgrounds in Las Vegas as a child and her pleasant memories of evenings and recipes shared with the same Anglo homesteaders whom her father detested. An entire chapter fondly relates the story of her ambitious struggles as a one-room schoolhouse teacher for "Spanish," mestizo, and Anglo children.

Cabeza de Baca never expected that her grandparents' and parents' way of life would be her way of life. She felt angry about what had happened to Hispanics in New Mexico, and *We Fed Them Cactus* serves as a lyrical tribute to what had been lost as well as to what should not be forgotten. But it is also a book written in a different era than the one it describes and according to a different set of values. When she writes of the women of her grandmother's generation, she writes of the kind of woman that she steadfastly refused to be. "It was a difficult life for a woman," she explains of the nineteenth-century ranches on the *Llano*, "but she had made her choice when in the marriage ceremony she had promised to obey and follow her husband." She retracts this emphasis on "choice," however, when she follows that statement with a further explanation: "It may not have been her choice, since parents may have decided for her. It was the Spanish custom to make matches for the children. Whether through choice or tradition, the women had to be a hardy lot in order to survive . . . "[125] As with other customs, she admires the women of her family's history even as her own life represents a clear departure from their model of femininity.

We Fed Them Cactus negotiates the difficult territory of cultural loss through efforts to distinguish between enforced and chosen measures of cultural change; Cabeza de Baca had spent years learning to make such distinctions through her work in home economics and with LULAC. Clearly, the loss of land to Anglo homesteaders falls into the "enforced" category. *We Fed Them Cactus* holds up General Kearny's words during the U.S. occupation of Santa Fe in 1846—"We come as friends, to better your condition . . . "—as an unfulfilled promise.[126] Cabeza de Baca states that Kearny broke his pledge to protect "New Mexicans and their property" and to respect "the Spanish and Mexican land grants." Somewhat too diplomatically, she places some blame on a New Mexican Hispanic population "unaccustomed to technicalities" and dismisses the land grant issue as "a subject too vast to discuss in this history."[127] But she also undoubtedly wanted her readers to be aware of what happened to her family and others.

Still, the book's closing statement—that "each generation must profit by the trials and errors of those before them; otherwise everything would perish"—indicates that she felt herself to be a part of a Hispanic generation that looked forward as much as it looked back. Her insistence on doing both simultaneously may be what distanced her from the "All American"–progress rhetoric of LULAC. Furthermore, she showed particular interest in moving forward from the restrictive "choices" offered to women in the past. She came to treasure the cooking and curandera traditions lovingly passed down by her grandmothers as well as by the women she worked with through the NMAES. But she also distanced herself from LULAC's traditional views of gender. Being a woman made Cabeza de Baca's understanding of the losses and gains offered by cultural change particularly complex.

The divide between the twentieth-century pluralist and Progressive values that she thrived within and the Hispanic colonial heritage that

Anglo conquest had rendered into an increasingly powerless and roman-ticized commodity presented her with a sharp, double-edged contradic-tion. Not all members of her family, she knew, had benefited from an education and a career like hers. Some, she reminded readers of *We Fed Them Cactus*, had been reduced from large-scale ranchers to people who ran gas stations that catered to tourists. Anglo visitors, she knew, flocked to "Old Santa Fe" hoping to see quaint Indians and Spaniards. They wanted to tour the Palace of the Governors but were not willing to acknowledge that the people who served them at restaurants and "curio" shops, or that cleaned up after them at hotels, could be mestizo descendants of the very same "governors" or more recent immigrants who shared the original nuevomexicanos' heritage. New Mexico tourism (and the Anglo intellectual and artistic climate that helped give rise to it) sought an experience of "enchantment" that denied the reali-ties of both past and present. Cabeza de Baca's double-edged present, contradictory as it was, attempted to avoid that pitfall. Still, her strug-gle with genre in *We Fed Them Cactus* indicates how difficult it was for her to articulate her complex position toward cultural change.

"An Information Bureau for Free"

The work she did after *We Fed Them Cactus* continued this complicated devotion to remembering the past. Not long before her retirement from the Extension Service, she began to write a column about local history for *The Santa Fe Scene*, a weekly publication about local personalities and happenings. From 1958 through the early 1960s, she chronicled customs, events, and people of the past for readers, sometimes relying exclusively on written sources but often drawing from personal experience. In a 1958 column about the history of the Santa Fe Fiesta, for example, she recalled the first one she experienced, when she moved to Santa Fe to begin NMAES work in 1929. "It was the people's fiesta and really Spanish," she remembered, disregarding the fact that the Fiesta actually had been revived in the twentieth century by Anglos, "but one did not need to be Spanish to enjoy it and everybody joined in the gaiety." In the same column, she praised Mary Austin's efforts in organizing 1920s and 30s exhibits of Spanish colonial arts for Fiesta alongside the merienda and other preservation efforts of La Sociedad Folklórica.[128]

Through columns such as this, the *Santa Fe Scene* allowed Cabeza de Baca to express her involvement and interest in historic preservation, even as she commented on the processes of change. Such changes ranged from the "quaint," such as her history of train travel in the state, to the overtly political.[129] In a 1960 column titled "Nineteenth Century in Santa Fe," for example, she criticized the recent decision by *El Palacio*, the magazine of the Museum of New Mexico, to reprint a document titled "Tales of Santa Fe, 1839." In this piece, an all-too-familiar one to historians of the U.S. West, a journalist named Matthew C. Field chronicled "exotic" customs of the Spanish that he recorded during a visit to pre–U.S.-conquest New Mexico. Cabeza de Baca pointed out clear errors in Field's interpretations of Spanish culture and his inappropriate use of Spanish terms—errors that *El Palacio* did not make any effort to correct.[130] What irritated her most were Field's observations about Spanish "señoritas": their looks, their supposed smoking and "fandango" habits, and, by implication, their loose morals. She contrasted such generalizations with what she knew of her own grandmother's appearance and strict codes of behavior.

While her insistence on her grandmother's "perfect blonde" hair seems strangely defensive and racialist, other parts of the column suggest her motive was to imply that history is always more complex, and historical actors less stereotypical, than one suspects. She began her response to the Field piece by calling attention to the class of people that Spanish colonists in New Mexico called "*gente de razón*," literally people of reason, but more generally the educated, rich, and "European" classes of Spanish Mexicans. She suggested that Field might not have met such New Mexicans during his visit. Somewhat surprisingly, she followed her definition of "gente de razón" by asserting her own dislike for the term. "In Spain," she explained, "as in other European countries, there was a definite distinction of social classes, of which I do not approve and the appellation *gente de razon* is to me the height of arrogance." This column reflects her continuing wrestling with cultural change, perhaps expressed nowhere with more conflict than in her closing statement: "Many changes have occurred in Santa Fe since 1839 [the year of Field's visit], but the Spanish culture still remains as a salient factor of a once colorful era. In 350 years, it has withstood foreign influences and gradually is amalgamating into the American way of life."[131] Thus, even Cabeza de Baca's job of writing remembrances of local history for the pages of *The Santa Fe Scene* showed division between feelings of grief and appreciation for that distance.

This contradictory attitude toward "progress" also applied to the way the popular press and academics approached Cabeza de Baca and her work. New Mexico's split approach to praising traditionalism in cultural policy and boosting "progress" in social policy had encouraged her to develop her complicated public persona along both of these lines. Her attempt to do so ensured that she would be heard, but it also limited the content of her message. Uncertain of how to consider this woman and her complex identity, commentators instead placed her squarely, and nonthreateningly, within the two contradictory roles she had casted herself: that of the old-fashioned Hispanic doña and the progress-minded home economist, both roles played by a fastidious woman rather than one who asserted the need for any threatening forms of social change.

These portrayals help to explain why the more radical reforms that Cabeza de Baca pursued through LULAC never became an effective part of her persona. A 1968 *Santa Fe New Mexican* feature about her life and work that dubbed her "a patrona of the old pattern" also characterized her as a "perfectionist" guardian of the customs and artifacts of the past. The interviewer praised the adobe house in Santa Fe that Cabeza de Baca had remodeled and decorated with local artifacts as an expression of "an appreciation and love of the finest in the folk culture of New Mexico" and characterized her as a "vast storehouse of knowledge about our Hispanic Southwest."[132] Two oral historians, Paula Thaidigsman and Ruleen Lazell, who were interested in her work in rural New Mexico and her other accomplishments, came to speak to her during the 1970s and 80s. During interviews they recorded on tape, they alternately asked her to talk about her experiences in Progressive extension work and to share knowledge of the "old ways." To one of these women, Cabeza de Baca remarked, "I think that I am an information bureau...for free. I have more people coming to me...whether it's history, whether it's folklore, whether it's foods, or...you name it.... So those are the things that have kept me from really finishing my writing."[133] Clearly, she enjoyed speaking with others, but this comment indicates her desire to create more written contributions to history.

She never did publish all the writing that she wanted to. Some of the other writers in this study, especially Kay Bennett and Pablita Velarde, did not write their life stories in full, partially because there did not seem to be a reading audience for the nontraditional stories they would have had to disclose to do so. Cabeza de Baca conforms to this trend to a degree. Inspired by the vogue for tradition initiated by Austin and Luhan, Cabeza de Baca's work in *The Good Life* and *We Fed Them Cactus* documents tradition at the expense of the nontraditional paths of her life story. On the other hand, while there remained some aspects of her life that she never shared with audiences, such as her difficult marriage to Gilbert, she did attempt to write an account of her change-oriented work as an extension agent. She discussed plans for the manuscript with interviewer Thaidigsman in 1975, and a handwritten manuscript with sections titled "Introduction," "The Homes," "The People and the Community," and "The Work" now lies in storage at the Center for Southwest Research at the University of New Mexico in Albuquerque.

Though she referred to the manuscript as *A New Mexican Hacienda* when she spoke with Thaidigsman, it pays less attention to chronicling hacienda life than it does to showing the changes experienced by the Hispanic New Mexican population over the course of the twentieth century. The onset of World War II and the atomic age, she explained to Thaidigsman, resulted in what she saw as a major transition in job opportunities and increased economic power for northern New Mexicans. She planned a book that would document this important change as well as the traditions that had come before it.[134] Unfortunately, the manuscript remained unfinished. She cited continuing speaking obligations as one cause for her failure to complete it; eventually, her declining health was also a factor. In 1984, she moved to a nursing home in Albuquerque because of her increasing problems with dementia. She died in 1991, at the age of ninety-seven.

Had she been able to finish the book, it might have been difficult for her to publish, for what she intended was not homage to tradition or progress but instead history written with a decided ethnic perspective. In this respect, she planned to go beyond the preceding generation's emphasis on "recovery" and turn instead to questions of civic equality. Citing prejudices and lack of research by many of the nineteenth- and early twentieth century Anglo writers who had attempted to produce the English language histories of New Mexico, she asserted that she and others could do better.[135] "Until writers with Indian or Hispanic backgrounds contribute towards a history of their peoples," she explained, "there will not be a true impartial picture of their cultures, traditions, religion, and folkways."[136] The bulk of this short manuscript remains sketchy, but this point is very clear.

She intended to speak for a people and a past that had not received enough attention before, and she knew that her ethnic background played an integral role in giving her the perspective required to do so. But she also knew her experience in crossing social and cultural divides enabled her to broaden that perspective and to place it in context. Despite her continuing interest in her family's "Spanish" rico past, she once wrote of the people she worked with in extension, many of them mestizo or Pueblo, that "after 35 years I am one of them and closer to them than to my own family."[137] Ultimately, Cabeza de Baca may have done less to preserve the home life that NMAES policymakers feared losing than to create a new, more complex sense of home, one that offered women new ways to guard tradition.

🔲

CHAPTER 4
Leaving Home
Kay Bennett and the Limits of Tradition

Like Hispanics, American Indians faced significant obstacles in their efforts to maintain and prosper in their New Mexican homes in the early twentieth century. But to a higher degree than Hispanics, American Indians found vocal and powerful advocates for reform among Anglo immigrants to the state. Mary Austin, Mabel Dodge Luhan, and other Anglo cultural activists of the early twentieth century pushed for federal American Indian policies to sponsor the revival of cultural traditions, believing this was the most viable remedy for the crises they perceived for American Indians. By making crafts and ceremonies sustainable forms of economic sustenance, these activists hoped, American Indians could continue being American Indians in the "modern" world. Because they wanted to teach a non-American Indian public how to appreciate (and thus commercially support) such traditions, these activists launched a vogue for traditional Indian art and pressed for greater interest in and respect for customs like ceremonial dances.[1]

But American Indians' ability to benefit from these policies depended on their willingness to conform to a static view of their cultures and an impractical view of their needs. For even though Anglo activists' strategies for Indian policy reform attempted to employ the ideal of cultural relativism, they ultimately sustained the romantic expectations of the "noble savage" that had characterized previous approaches to "saving" Indian culture. While scholars have been eager to document both the achievements and limitations of such activism, they have stopped short of showing how it played out in the lives of individual American Indians. Their own perceptions of home were suddenly complicated by the gap between the rhetorical advantages to be had by fulfilling these romantic ideals and the economic advantages offered by less traditional approaches to saving their homes.

American Indian women who came of age in this era sustained a particularly complex web of expectations for their lives in New Mexico. As the lives of Kay Bennett and Pablita Velarde reveal, they underwent upheavals wrought by federal educational policy, economic depression, and world war mobilization. They hardly led "traditional" lives, and yet the continually growing tourist economy of New Mexico and its increased codification of cultural relativism created new expectations of traditionalism for them. These women were caught between tribal models of femininity and the "modern" models they learned at school, the low-paying craft practices that well-meaning Anglos encouraged them to pursue and their need to support themselves, and their desires to live both within and beyond the sphere of tribal influence. Like Hispanic women during the same period, they found that life required modern and multicultural skills even as their ability to present themselves powerfully as public figures depended on their success in appearing "traditional."

In the case of Bennett (1920?–1997), a Navajo, these conflicting demands led to a painful case of homesickness—and a powerful illustration of the need for New Mexicans, non-Navajo and Navajo alike, to reform their ideas of home and womanhood.[2] Bennett's cultural activism took many shapes. She sought to call attention to Navajo culture both as an insider and as someone who spent much of her life away from the place she called home. Though born, raised, and educated on the reservation, Bennett left as a teenager for work in Los Angeles. Eventually, as an adult, she made her way back to New Mexico, settling in Gallup, just outside the formal borders of the Navajo Nation. During these years, she entered the public eye by competing in Indian beauty pageants. She met her third husband, Russ Bennett, in Gallup, but left soon afterward when he worked abroad as a civil engineer. They returned to Gallup for Russ's retirement in the early 1960s, and she reinitiated her public career, this time through work as a Navajo doll maker, a singer, and a writer. She used these activities to undertake the difficult job of serving as a "spokeswoman" for Navajo culture, work that often earned her praise from non-Indian audiences even as it ultimately distanced her from other Navajos.

While much of her work invoked Navajo tradition, her most famous act was to be one that many considered nontraditional. On June 10, 1986, as a front-page story in the *Navajo Times* reported, Bennett entered the political race for the office of the Navajo tribal chairman as the first-ever woman candidate.[3] Her campaign, and the controversy that ensued, riveted momentary attention on the issues of tradition, femininity, and Indian activism with which she wrestled for her entire career. She received few votes that year, and few when she ran again in 1990, but she ensured her place in Navajo history books—and her role in our story of New Mexican women's efforts to control the terms by which their homes would be imagined.

Unfortunately, Bennett's place in this story has been more difficult to trace than those of the others, due to a lack of archival material and her own reluctance to share some of her more difficult struggles. Because she passed away in 1997, before I initiated research about her, I was not able to ask her directly about her life. I interviewed several of her friends and relatives but they almost all told me that while they knew Bennett for a long time, they did not know much about her private life. The public records of her life—newspaper articles, books, a few letters—have survived, but beyond speculation and inferences drawn from more general sources, much about her will remain unwritten.[4] Scholars have mentioned her work in annotated bibliographies of American Indian literature and consulted it when compiling information on American Indian boarding schools, but no one has attempted a comprehensive study of her life and work, despite her distinguished career.[5]

This is disheartening, especially since her work implicitly argued that Navajos, New Mexicans, and Americans at large needed to come to a better understanding of Navajo women's status. When she published her autobiography, *Kaibah: Recollection of a Navajo Girlhood*, in 1964, she introduced it as a "true story" of her life, and posited that "the history of her people would not be complete if it did not record the everyday life of a family as it was lived" between 1928 and 1935.[6] This book did, in fact, prove to be a pioneering effort in writing Navajo women's history. Moreover, considering the stories it tells in conjunction with previously untold stories about Bennett's life forms an argument against other historians' views of how Navajo homes changed in the twentieth century. While some have seen the years in which she lived as key ones in the development of strong Navajo nationalism, Bennett's life story shows that women experienced this period of cultural change differently, and less positively, than men. Her work reveals that she tried to develop new cultural forms to help resolve these inequities. She wanted to find a way to connect the past to the present so that the Navajo community could be a better place for women who, like herself, blended traditional Navajo values regarding women's status with skills and experiences drawn from non-Navajo sources.

While her use of modern methods, such as a political campaign, to advocate traditionalism makes her story similar to those of Jaramillo and Cabeza de Baca, the particular conflicts Bennett faced as an American Indian woman make her story distinct, and in some ways, more sad. Austin and Luhan's romantic rhetoric of traditionalism, and the Anglo cultural values that fueled it, offered Bennett an Anglo audience for her work, and a way to succeed economically despite the changes in Navajo life wrought by modernization. But, like other Navajo women of her era, Bennett actually achieved less stature and self-sufficiency than her grandmothers had, because of

Fig. 19: Kay Bennett at a Book Signing for *Kaibah*, c. 1964. Courtesy of a
Private Collection.

policies created by Anglo progressives. Furthermore, despite her demonstration of the fact that adaptability could be a Navajo woman's greatest asset, Bennett found her innovative approach to tradition led others to question whether her methods made her an inauthentic representative of her people.

A Navajo Girlhood

During her youth, Bennett led what she later considered to be a very traditional Navajo life, mostly removed from non-Navajo influences. Based on what her mother reported during a census, Bennett, then named Kaibah Chischillie, was born during or soon after 1920, near the Sheepsprings trading post.[7] She would learn as a child that her family's home in the high country of western New Mexico and eastern Arizona should not be taken for granted, for only sixty-some years before her birth Navajos had endured an enforced expulsion from the region in an event known as the "Long Walk." It began in 1864, when after a devastating period of wars, raids, starvation, and hiding, the U.S. Army forcibly relocated close to nine thousand Navajos to Fort Sumner, in the Bosque Redondo region of the Pecos River Valley of eastern New Mexico.[8] While those who directed this aggression believed it could result in the beneficial founding of a Navajo farming community, the resulting settlement bore more resemblance to a concentration camp. Terrible army management, a series of crop failures, poor water, epidemics, and Comanche raids led policymakers to reconsider the Navajo "settlement" at Fort Sumner. In the summer of 1868, treaty negotiations resulted in the return of some lands to the Navajo people.

In the years to come, Bennett learned about this displacement through the story of the family of one of her ancestors, her great-grandfather Gray Hat. She came to tell this story as it had been told to her, emphasizing the themes of exile and loss that echoed in her own life. In fall 1868, Gray Hat's family joined others on the long return journey from Fort Sumner. They resettled near the Chuska Mountains, where Bennett later grew up.[9] By the time she was born, her family had become prosperous, but she heard often of her grandparents' struggle to build new homes and herds.

Another family story Kay learned as a child was the dramatic tale of Shebah, one of Gray Hat's daughters. Shebah returned to her family in their new home in 1870, after spending many years away as a captive. Navajos and Hispanics had raided one another for slaves up until the U.S. Army attempted to stop to this practice through the atrocities of the Long Walk. Raiders had taken Shebah in 1847, when she was twelve years old and alone watching the family's sheep. They sold her to a rancher not far from the city of Chihuahua in northern Mexico. She became a weaver, one of many servants in the large household. In about 1858, she gave birth to a son of the rancher. Upon the rancher's death in 1870, when Shebah was thirty-five years old, she decided to return to Navajo country, and she and her son undertook the long northern journey on horseback. The trip took a tragic turn: when they stopped at a trading post not far from her father's home, the trader raped Shebah while her frightened young son hid outside. She shot the trader in self-defense, burned the building with his body in it, gathered her provisions and her son, and rode the last part of her long journey to a home she could recollect only vaguely. She made her son promise not to tell what had happened, but she feared the news of the burnt trading post would cause the family she had just rejoined to be persecuted. Not long after her homecoming, she went to the hills, where she had hid a gun she had taken from the trading post, and killed herself rather than bring shame upon her family.

Shebah was Bennett's grandmother. Shebah's son, born as Fernando, called Keedah by his mother, and then called "Chischillie" because of the curly hair he had inherited from his Mexican father, was Bennett's father. Bennett told Shebah's story, as I have repeated it above, in her second book, *A Navajo Saga*, published in 1969 and cowritten by her husband, Russ.[10] Shebah's story clearly resonated with Bennett

◪ CHAPTER FOUR ◪

because she experienced so many of its themes in her own life: a woman, born to Navajos, finds herself away from that culture. She returns home but finds herself changed by what she has seen in the non-Navajo world. Nevertheless, she wants to embrace her Navajo identity, despite increasingly feeling like an outsider. Like Shebah, Bennett had to make difficult choices about how best to "be Navajo" when her experiences seemed to separate her from that cultural identity. Unlike Shebah, Bennett lived to tell her own story, though she remained selective about which aspects of her life she shared, and which she confined, like Shebah's story, to secrecy.

Bennett would come to tell the story of her childhood openly because, for the most part, she lived comfortably. Her father had built a three-room stone house (as Bennett proudly put it later, "the only house in the area with fireplace and hearth," in not just one, but in all three rooms) for his two wives and twelve children.[11] When Bennett was three years old, her father died after a fall from a horse. As dictated by tradition, the family destroyed his stone hogan after his death because he had passed away inside it. Bennett's mother, who had two young children, including Kaibah, still living at home, as well as a few grandchildren entrusted to her care, moved to a new wood hogan.

Bennett described this girlhood home in detail in *Kaibah*. Her mother built it on a hill overlooking New Mexico State Highway 666, which extends north from Gallup toward Colorado. To the east of this road, the land stretches out as a flat plain; to the west rise the Chuska Mountains, where Bennett's family and their herds spent summers. When non-Navajos stopped along this road near her home, Bennett had some of her first contact with outsiders. As a young girl, she sold one of her own lambs to an Anglo family, refugees from the Dust Bowl making their way west, so they could eat while they camped nearby for the night.

Bennett's youthful experiences with outsiders, however, were not always positive. When she was eight years old, the local school superintendent visited her mother's home and directed her to send Kaibah to the boarding school at Toadlena, a nearby trading post. Bennett's mother had taught her children to hide until she called them if they saw a car coming directly toward the hogan, but the young girl had been too frightened to run. When the superintendent gave her an apple, she threw it at his forehead, and when he tried to grab her hand, she bit him. Bennett later wrote that her mother, embarrassed by Kaibah's behavior and fearful of the school, asked the interpreter to tell the superintendent to come back in a few days. At that time, she arranged to send her fourteen-year-old son, Keedah, in her daughter's place, convincing school officials that her daughter needed more time before she was ready to leave home.

Keedah's departure meant that Mother Chischillie would be losing not only her son but also an invaluable source of household labor. Recognizing this, he asked her if she intended to move in with one of her older children while he was gone. As Bennett recalled, Mother Chischillie responded "calmly": "No, my son, I shall stay here in my own hogan. I am the head of our family, and I must maintain a separate house where my people may feel free to come to me for advice.... I believe there should only be one woman in a hogan, and even though my daughter-in-laws [*sic*] ask me to stay in their homes, I would not be free if I lived with them."[12] Strong ties of support between female kin continue to be an important part of Navajo culture, and while Bennett's mother clearly respected those ties she also wanted to be on her own. As a crucial step in maintaining her home and independent status, Mother Chischillie needed to teach her daughter Kaibah how to help with work such as the care of the sheep. These were common steps in the life of a Navajo girl of that era, but in Bennett's case the need to undertake them was all the more pressing because her mother depended on her assistance.

Bennett's childhood memories centered on the labor she did at home; she was taught to see this labor as a typical and integral part of asserting and maintaining a woman's power within Navajo society. Anthropologist Dorothea C. Leighton, who spent time observing Navajo families in 1940, later wrote of the experience that though Navajo women seemed to be more "conservative" than Navajo men in terms of interactions with the outside world, they maintained power equal to that of their husbands, argued for their own opinions, and earned the respect of men as well as women. Their isolation, relative to Navajo men, may have made them more wary of outsiders, Leighton commented, "but it also necessitated the development of independence and self-reliance."[13] From a Navajo perspective, this was not so much a "development" as the way that it had always been: while Navajo men may have occupied leadership positions in clan politics, Navajo women have, in the words of Navajo historian Ruth Roessel, "formed the heart and foundation" of Navajo culture, and "always have been the basis of and the most important teachers in Navajo society."[14] This is undoubtedly true for many reasons, but it is especially important to note that Navajo women have typically owned the sheep herds that have been the source of Navajo livelihood. As late as 1974, anthropologist Louise Lamphere wrote: "Navajo women have a great deal of control over their lives. They do not need to wrest power from others who hold positions of authority or attempt to influence decisions that are not theirs to make."[15] But perhaps their status was less secure than Lamphere posited, or more altered by the influence of Anglo culture. Bennett's experiences in later life would challenge the messages she learned about women's power in her early years.

As a young girl, however, Bennett learned that being a Navajo woman meant being a powerful person with many important responsibilities. For several years after her brother's departure for school, she stayed at home, learning from her mother. Her memoir covers these years in detail, characterizing this time as a fruitful period of experience with herding, weaving, cooking, farming, and ceremonials. When she was old enough, and time permitted, her mother told her stories about her family's history, as well as the old Navajo stories, such as that of Changing Woman. But when her brother and cousins returned from school in the summers, she could not help but feel curious about what they did at school and jealous of their knowledge of a different language. After her brother finished school, he proposed that she start attending and her mother agreed; schooling could not be put off forever. On a fall morning in 1933, when Bennett was around twelve years old, she rode several miles on horseback with her mother to Toadlena, where in 1913 the federal government had built a boarding school for the purpose of educating Navajo children.

When Bennett saw the school for the first time, she confronted the largest building she had ever seen.[16] Toadlena School sat against the backdrop of the eastern slope of the Chuska Mountains, a collection of three-story stone dormitories and a white frame schoolhouse set among peach and apple orchards. Despite the beautiful surroundings, Bennett felt homesick and scared upon her arrival, and threatened by the changes she faced. As historian Michael C. Coleman has written, when American Indian children arrived at school during this period, "the assault on traditional culture began symbolically, with the transformation of the outer child, and proceeded with a regimen and curriculum which would also, the teachers hoped, change the student mentally and spiritually."[17] Usually, when officials brought schoolchildren to Toadlena School, they cut their hair. Because Bennett's mother brought her to the school voluntarily, officials waived the requirement. Bennett also found herself excused from the requirement of taking an "American" name: the girls' superintendent could not settle on a name she liked and instead decided that "Kaibah" was acceptable. Bennett later wrote that "Kaibah was a little disappointed. She had hoped to be given an English name like the other children."[18] Perhaps her use of the name "Kay" in later years reflected her understanding, even as a young child, of the important roles names played in perceptions of a Navajo person's willingness to adapt to "modern" life.

Bennett was not, however, left out of other boarding school procedures. The girls' dormitory attendant, a Navajo woman, led her to the showers. Accustomed to only partial undressing exclusively in the privacy of her hogan, Bennett found this embarrassment difficult to endure. After her shower, the attendant gave her new, non-Navajo school clothes, lighter and stiffer than her usual garments, and braided her hair, a custom not practiced by Navajos. With her appearance revised according to these unfamiliar standards, Bennett began school.

Pablita Velarde, whose life story I will turn to in the next chapter, also completed her education at an Indian boarding school during the Depression. While Velarde found that her teachers emphasized crafts as a means of economic survival, Bennett already knew how to weave when she got to school, and her family was prospering from farming. From her later recollection, it seems her primary motivation in going to school was to learn English, so she could communicate with the traders and government officials involved in the weaving and wool trades.[19] Bennett's experiences thus seem consistent with the expectations of many Navajos for schooling at the time. According to historians Garrick and Roberta Glenn Bailey, Navajo reservation boarding schools, where children remained geographically close to home, were full by the early 1920s. This "may have resulted from a growing conviction on the part of many Navajos that education in general, and English language skills in particular, would give their children an economic advantage."[20] Bennett and her mother dreaded the period of separation that school required, but Bennett went because she believed it could be beneficial in the long run.

But she did not get to fulfill her goals for her time at Toadlena School. Not long after she began, drought, economic depression, and the federal government's campaign to reduce Navajo livestock herds foiled her early attempts at an education. Though her memoir later referred to this chain of events as the "White Man's Depression," she and other Navajos did not escape its disastrous consequences. The tragedy of the years that followed seemed to be a somewhat sudden blow, but it actually drew its force from long-building conflicts within and between both Navajo and U.S. government leadership.

The White Man's Depression

The crisis of Navajo culture that began in the 1930s emerged from the fact that the federal government granted the Navajo Nation powers of self-government while simultaneously robbing it of an economic structure previously instrumental in preserving Navajo cultural identity.[21] From the New Deal government's perspective, these stock reduction measures were necessary evils, required for long-term sustenance of Navajo culture within an increasingly industrialized nation and consistent with reduction efforts attempted throughout the United States. From the Navajo perspective, these measures were confusing, unfair, and destructive. In Bennett's case, the policies of this era led to her increasing desire to be able to support herself independently, despite the fact that this distanced her from Navajo communal traditions.

The first major hint of the troubles faced by Navajos at this time took the shape of a government report of a range survey of the reservation conducted by Indian Service forester William H. Zeh. Written in 1930, the report detailed the deteriorating condition of the Navajo ranges, emphasizing problems with sufficient water, overgrazing, erosion, and poor livestock quality. Zeh concluded that the government needed to introduce stock management techniques to the Navajo people so they could continue to produce food to eat and livestock (and wool) to sell.[22] While he recommended what later seemed to be very moderate strategies for reduction, such as the education of farmers and the reduction of goats only, environmental and political developments soon pushed policymakers to recommend more drastic measures.

Environmentally, the condition of the Navajo ranges declined rapidly during the years following Zeh's 1930 report. The extremely harsh winter of 1931–32 killed thousands of sheep during a time when the Depression had already driven wool prices down; not even the skins of the dead sheep could be salvaged profitably. That winter, Bennett remembered, students at Toadlena School saw aircraft passing over to deliver food and supplies to Navajos living in the mountains.[23] To make matters worse, a drought followed the harsh winter. When Bennett rode home from school at the beginning of the summer of 1933, she could not help but notice, with eyes trained by her years as the primary caretaker of her family's sheep, that "the grass was already brown and much sparser than usual." She wondered if there would be enough for the sheep to eat that winter.[24]

❧ CHAPTER FOUR ❧

The political developments of the early 1930s initially seemed more promising for Navajos. The new commissioner of Indian affairs, John Collier, expressed optimism about bringing the New Deal to Navajo country. He believed reform policies could reinvigorate Navajo traditionalism. As historian Donald Parman has written, the Navajo reservation's established system of local alliances and government and its large population dedicated to "traditional" life led Collier to see it as an ideal place for reform programs. He wanted to expand Indian-held land, initiate Indian self-rule, and institute localized, nonassimilative education.[25] But Collier's determination to preserve "traditional" Navajo life also led him to support large-scale stock reductions. He believed the Navajo people would only survive the Depression and the drought if they complied with strict reduction measures, both to preserve their land and to improve the quality of their livestock. In his efforts to convince Navajos to follow this policy and soften its blows, he promised that the federal government would, in return for compliance, use its power to expand the Navajo land base.

At Collier's suggestion, the Navajo Tribal Council approved a set of regulations in 1933 governing "voluntary" reduction. These regulations asked Navajos to sell a certain percentage of their sheep to the government. The government purchased the sheep using Federal Emergency Relief Association funds, then resold them if possible or destroyed them if necessary. By 1934, however, it became clear that most Navajos would not willingly part with their sheep in this manner, especially at the low offered prices. The centrality of sheep to Navajo culture, especially to women who owned most of the herds, accounts for this reluctance. As Bennett had learned growing up, Navajo people had to work very hard after the Long Walk to rebuild their herds; cutting them down at the bidding of the federal government threatened a loss of power as well as property.

Collier encouraged the tribal council to impose reduction quotas. Such quotas, however, proved difficult to enforce unilaterally. No clear policy guided reductions, and no easy method existed for disposal of reduced stock in an already depressed market. Often, government

Fig. 20: Navajo Women Dipping Sheep at Ganado Trading Post, 1940. Photograph by Sallie Wagner. Courtesy of the Museum of New Mexico, Neg. No. 5424.

officials pressured Navajo families to sell their sheep and goats when they brought them to trading posts for mandatory "dipping." When sheep could not be sold to off-reservation buyers, officials slaughtered them on site, sometimes butchering them, sometimes shooting them en masse. Sheep killed in large groups were either left to rot or burned. Such reductions affected stockholders unevenly, devastating small herds, many of which were owned by women running family herds, while large herds, often held by men running more commercial enter- prises, remained viable. Thus, the reductions not only affected livestock holdings, but also, as historian Peter Iverson has argued, inflicted "social and cultural havoc" upon Navajo households.[26]

To federal employees inspired by the New Deal's spirit of reform, reduction measures, enforced correctly, seemed to have the potential to be, as Iverson has explained, "a symbolic victory needed to impress the fruits of soil conservation upon the entire country."[27] To a Navajo populace that, in general, did not sympathize with the "scientific" principles at work behind these measures, livestock reduction was, as Ruth Roessel has succinctly put it, both a "disgrace" and a "tragedy." In addition to depleting families of their herds and thus their wealth, reduction seemed to make environmental circumstances worse rather than better because it violently disrupted the natural order.[28]

To Bennett's family, encouraged by their recent prosperity and certain that the bad weather would pass, reduction struck a particularly tragic blow, one pushing Bennett to develop the cautious approach to blending tradition and change that she displayed in later years. She wrote in her memoir that her mother blamed the environmental and reduction problems on some Navajo leaders' desire to live like "white men." She accused these leaders of accepting personal benefits of power while allowing Washington to overstep its authority when it came to the general Navajo populace. But Mother Chischillie also knew little could be done to stop the chain of events unleashed by the powerful federal government. The Navajo people were immobilized, just as they had been during the Long Walk days her parents had suffered through. As Bennett reported, her mother angrily compared their position to that of "a mouse caught by a cat.... Washington put us in a cage and then let us out, but he only lets us run a little way before he pounces on us again."[29]

If this "cat" had a face, it was that of John Collier. His attempts to cast reduction to Navajos in a positive light had failed and so had his efforts to fulfill his promise of trading reduction efforts for an expansion in the Navajo land base. Due to pressures from ranching, mining, and farming interests, substantial gains in landholdings never made it through the U.S. Congress.[30] In 1934, the Navajo people, clearly displeased with what Collier had offered them so far, rejected the provisions of the Wheeler-Howard Act, the "Indian Reorganization Act" designed by Collier and championed as the key to positive reform by his administration. Ostensibly designed as a program for granting

American Indian self-government, Navajos tended to view it as a referendum on reduction measures, especially when Navajos who opposed Collier encouraged others to see it that way.

Unfortunately, the results of the referendum did not halt reduction. By 1937, in fact, officials considered more drastic measures in an effort to make the program more successful, because, despite reductions, Navajo sheep herds had still increased since 1933.[31] Collier's administration decided by 1935 that "voluntary" efforts would not achieve the goal of a 56 percent reduction in the remaining stock. Instead, the commissioner began to enforce reduction through land management units and a permit system, all in place by 1937.[32] By that time, however, Bennett had already left the reservation.

Rise of the Navajo Nation, Fall of the Navajo Woman

Bennett left her home in 1935, at around age fourteen, at the height of stock reductions. In *Kaibah*, she recalled how a friendly missionary couple staying near her family offered to take her back to Los Angeles with them. She would be able to attend school, they promised, and she could live with them in exchange for cleaning their house. Bennett's mother let her make the final decision, and Bennett's memoir neither explained exactly why her mother, so recently reluctant to let her daughter go to school, let her leave at this time, nor revealed exactly why Bennett, so recently devoted to her family's prosperity and her education at the Toadlena School, decided to go so far away. Other parts of *Kaibah* imply that these sudden shifts in attitude resulted from the drought and the sheep reduction. These events changed the way Navajos like Bennett and her family thought about future prospects on the reservation—what had once seemed a promising place for a young Navajo woman had become a place she might be better off leaving. *Kaibah* ends in 1935, when Bennett left home, as if what followed was so different that it could not be part of the same book and so traumatically controversial that she could not bring herself to write about it.

In any account of Navajo history, the livestock reduction era must appear as a tragedy. Regardless of good intentions held by Collier and Navajos who acted as agents of stock reduction measures, the inconsistency, inefficiency, and waste produced by these policies devastated something more important, even, than the Navajo herds: Navajo confidence in a way of life and in the potential to work with "Uncle Sam" to achieve it. Even recently, as an article published in both the *Arizona Republic* and the *Gallup Independent* pointed out, elderly Navajos have refused to participate in census efforts because they remember what such counts led to during the reduction era.[33] "No program before or since," writes Ruth Roessel, "has had such a continuing and devastating impact upon the Navajos as did stock reduction. Regardless of the need for the action, fundamental human rights were violated in the rush to reduce the livestock. The Navajos have not forgotten the experience!"[34] For Bennett, these years imposed a sharp break between her youthful expectations for a "traditional" life and her adult experiences with traumatic forms of change, beginning with her departure for California.

From some perspectives, the tragic stock reduction era can also look like a crucible for positive change. Historian Peter Iverson characterizes these years as a critical period of development for the idea of a "Navajo Nation" with a truly independent and powerful tribal government. Although the centralized tribal council created in 1923 assumed a form more consistent with the American system than with the headman system of the Navajo past, it offered a viable alternative to the paternalistic approach of the Fort Sumner era. Rather than boycotting the new government because it was "nontraditional," Iverson writes, most Navajos "turned to it as a way of maintaining a separate, integral Navajo way of life."[35] This centralization provided a way of uniting Navajos against a common enemy, the invasive stock reduction measures. Further strengthened by the revisions in Indian policy initiated by Collier's administration, this sense of unity and a strong, self-governing council carried Navajos into the 1940s, 1950s, and 1960s—an era in which, Iverson writes, the "tribe" became a "nation."[36] Self-government provided a centralized means of taking advantage of wartime employment opportunities and postwar oil and mineral strikes. According to this interpretation of Navajo history, the support that the enforced changes of the livestock reduction era generated for self-government became a key element in developing both Navajo nationalism and an economic base to sustain it.

Looking at these developments in detail, however, reveals that not all of them may be best characterized as "progressive." Bennett's story poses questions about the particular changes in women's lives wrought by the reduction years and the resulting economic and governmental trends: why did a girl who had planned to take over her family's sheep herds decide to take a job as maid instead? What happened to the opportunities of Navajo women as a result of the livestock reduction years? How did the reductions affect the power traditionally held by women, as the primary owners of sheep herds?

Though Bennett's work in later years would often cast the changes invoked by these questions as ones involving the loss of "tradition," they actually imply a more complex process of cultural change. The world of Bennett's youth may have seemed ageless to Kaibah in 1930, but it actually emerged from changes in Navajo women's roles and customs in the previous sixty years, since the return from Bosque Redondo. The full skirts and fitted blouses that Bennett wore as a child, for example, borrowed ideas about women's fashion not only from the Spanish and Mexican settlers of the region but from the American women who accompanied their husbands when they served as officers at Fort Sumner in the 1860s.[37] It did not take many generations for this costume to become "the way" that Navajo women dressed. In this manner, Navajos practiced "cultural borrowing" similar to both the processes that Elsie Clews Parsons had identified in Pueblo culture and the adaptive processes that Hispanic culture in New Mexico had undergone.

As with these other forms, Navajo women's practice of cultural borrowing actually served as a means of maintaining and asserting ethnic identity. While Navajo women borrowed the shape of American women's dresses, they recreated these patterns with different fabrics. They made their blouses from velveteen, not cotton. Around their shoulders, Navajo women of the early twentieth century wore blankets, as they had in the "old days." But the blankets they most often chose to wear were Pendleton blankets, made in Oregon, rather than those they themselves had crafted.[38] These choices reflected Navajo women's ability, in the early twentieth century, to maintain Navajo roles even as they used non-Navajo products and styles to do so.

The changes in Navajo life wrought by stock reduction, however, made it quite difficult for women, regardless of how open they were to cultural influences, to maintain the roles and stature they had previously held. Collier intended his measures to reduce Navajo dependence on livestock, thus fundamentally altering the economic underpinnings of Navajo life—and the herd-owning roles that had brought Navajo women's power to an all-time high in the years of prosperity following the Bosque Redondo removal. These alterations, combined with the economic changes going on outside the reservation, proved to be hard on Navajo women.

Community studies focusing on women's status reveal that their options outside of a sheep-based economy initially proved to be limited. In 1957, anthropologist Laila Shukry Hamamsy established that the livestock reduction era was especially devastating to Navajo women in the reservation border community of Fruitlands. From observation and interviews, Hamamsy concluded that new landownership laws, decreases in livestock holding, and increased industrialization had diminished the average Navajo woman's "economic position, the significance of her function within the family, and her sense of security and bargaining position in family interaction." Increasingly, women had to depend upon "the industry and good-will of the wage earners—the men"—for survival in the changing Navajo economy.[39] When government jobs began to replace livestock raising, wage-earning jobs became available for men more frequently and at higher wages than for women.[40] Similarly, Christine Conte's more recent study of Navajo women in Flagstaff concluded that "the transformation of a woman's economic power base from a women-centered kin network to one in which nonkin, and predominantly non-Navajo, religious institutions play a major role makes Navajo women more emotionally and economically dependent upon men."[41]

Bennett's moves off and on the reservation in the 1930s and 1940s reflect such vulnerability. Exactly how her time at the missionary couple's home in Los Angeles ended remains unclear, but she returned to New Mexico in the late 1930s. When she was around sixteen, she married Ned Kelleywood, who was Navajo. In 1938, while her husband was working as a property clerk for the Indian Service, she worked as a ward attendant at the hospital in Fort Defiance. But by 1942 she and her husband went back to California. During that year she began work as a file clerk at Douglas Aircraft in Long Beach, where she was employed for over three years.[42] When the war ended, she headed back to New Mexico. From her later recollection, despite the work she found at Douglas, her experiences in Los Angeles were difficult, made all the more so by the birth of her two daughters, Alyce and Rosalie. "We never had enough to eat and our clothes became so worn I was ashamed to be seen outside our room," she later told an interviewer. "Finally I took our two little girls back to Navajo country."[43] Bennett also later implied to her stepson that her first marriage was difficult and perhaps abusive.[44]

My research on Bennett's life has revealed little about her first marriage or time in Los Angeles, but other sources make it possible to speculate on her life there. Clearly, any woman who was young, poor, and the mother of two small children in 1940s Los Angeles faced a difficult situation. Studies of Navajo women living in urban environments may illuminate the stresses that particularly affected a woman in Bennett's position. In an article published in 1976, Ann Metcalf shared the results of her interviews with Navajo women who had attended reservation boarding schools during their youth but moved to San Francisco as adults. She found that women who had spent a great deal of time away from home expressed a lower level of self-confidence, as well as a greater level of ambivalence about both their Navajo heritage and the certainty of their future positions.[45] A study published by Joyce Griffin in 1982, focusing on Navajo women living in the city of Flagstaff, Arizona, set out to discover what made their lives most difficult. The major source of tension for these mostly educated, mostly working women, Griffin found, was "engendered by fear of not living up to expectations, whether those expectations were their own or those of others."[46] While these studies apply to later years and different places than Bennett's experiences in Los Angeles, they certainly correspond to her experiences. Bennett had grown up seeing herself as the potential successor to her mother's wealth and power and found herself, instead, ashamed to leave her room in Los Angeles.

In search of something better, she returned home to New Mexico with her daughters and without her husband. Her first marriage was over. She may have entrusted her daughters to a relative or to a boarding school, because she began working soon afterward at boarding-school jobs that would have required her to do so. According to a job application on which she later indicated her employment history, she spent the 1946–47 academic year working as a dormitory attendant at Toadlena Boarding School. Then she moved to Phoenix in 1947 and started working as a teacher and interpreter at the Phoenix Indian School.[47]

She took this job at a moment of very significant transitions in Navajo education. When John Collier began his tenure as Indian commissioner, Navajo schools became one of his primary targets for carrying out educational reforms for all Indian schools.[48] Specifically, Collier aspired to end off-reservation and boarding education for the Navajos and oversee the implementation of a full-scale day school program. The 1868 treaty between the U.S. government and the Navajos had promised a schoolhouse for every thirty Navajo children between six and sixteen. While budget constraints, distance, and population density made this goal unattainable, Collier hoped at least to begin work on ending Navajo education away from home by initiating a major effort to construct locally controlled day schools. During the 1930s, New Deal funds resulted in the building of nearly fifty day schools.[49] But during World War II, financial support disappeared, and more than half of the day schools had closed by 1945.[50] Members of a Navajo delegation who went to Washington, D.C., in 1946 to testify before Congress on American Indian issues emphasized that the Navajos faced an educational crisis. Fueled by their wartime experiences in the non-Navajo world, these Navajos argued that the time had long since passed for the government to fulfill its promise of educating Navajo children. In fact, because of population growth and school closures, more Navajo children were out of school in 1946 than in the late 1920s.[51]

In response to these conditions, government officials created a program called the Special Navajo Education Program, which began in 1946, took root at the Phoenix Indian School by 1947, and eventually became a curriculum at ten Bureau of Indian Affairs off-reservation boarding schools.[52] In contrast to Bennett's initial educational goals of pursuing English mastery for trade, and to Collier's philosophy of using schools to advocate cultural preservation, the Special Navajo Education Program marked a return to the style of nineteenth-century policies, with what Peter Iverson has described as an "unapologetic emphasis on vocational training and assimilation."[53] Veterans returning from the war and workers struggling to survive in urban environments sensed that Navajos needed basic skills in order to prosper; the Navajo delegation that advocated this program was composed entirely of men who emphasized goals for education consistent with their own experiences in seeking wage work. The Special Navajo Education Program provided poorly educated students between twelve and eighteen years old with a five-year program in basic skills (including English and math) and vocational training. At the end of that period, the program assisted these students in finding jobs, mostly off-reservation.

Bennett, who worked in the program at the Phoenix Indian School until 1952, when she was in her early thirties, taught language skills, but she seems to have secured much more than a steady job. She later wrote that she acquired her own education, "for the most part," during her time in Phoenix.[54] She also began performing publicly as a singer, sharing Navajo songs with audiences throughout the West. In 1951, she sang at the Inter-Tribal Indian Ceremonial in Gallup, an event organized by town boosters in 1922 for the purpose of generating tourism and educating tourists about Indian art and culture.[55] Bennett claimed to be the first Navajo woman to perform for such audiences. She later recalled that she had done so daringly, by wearing a skirt some considered "too loud," altering traditional songs to fit her voice, and writing completely new songs.[56] Her approach must not have been altogether displeasing: she was crowned "Queen" of the Flagstaff's "Southwest All-Indian Powwow" in 1953.[57] Inspired by this success, she competed in the 1954 "Miss Indian of America" Beauty Contest in Sheridan, Wyoming.[58]

These awards reveal how time at the Phoenix Indian School led Bennett to consider how she could blend the traditions and stories of her upbringing with her desire to make a better living in the outside world. Bennett realized that events like these provided a forum in which she could take initial steps toward presenting herself as an individual who could promote traditional culture, albeit in nontraditional ways.[59] She also likely realized that while the Special Navajo Education Program could prepare Navajos for wage work in a nonreservation economy, women like herself would be confined to lower-paying jobs. Perhaps she believed performance would offer her a way to overcome the limitations to her earning power posed by her sex; in fact, a performing career could turn femininity into an asset.

Local press coverage received by Bennett in the 1950s supports this conclusion, as these reports of her accomplishments tended to focus on her looks and her affability. "She has broken with the past in many respects," one article about her performance in the 1953 Inter-Tribal Ceremonial acknowledged, "but she still clings to the traditional mode of dress.... Noted for both her beauty and her clear soprano voice, [she] chooses the bright velvet squaw blouse and full ankle-length skirt as most becoming. And like her ancestors, she tops off the costume with silver and turquoise jewelry."[60] In 1954, a Gallup-area newspaper reported that Bennett had appeared on the television show "Queen for a Day" and inspired more fan mail than the show had received for any prior guest. Apparently Bennett impressed viewers when she spoke up from the audience to request a stove for her "grandmother" who had been cooking all her life over an open fire. The show's sponsors gave Bennett the "stove, a set of Club aluminum cooking ware and an electric perculator [*sic*] for her grandmother."[61] Bennett's decision, in this moment of attention, to refer to her mother as her grandmother—and not to refer to her own daughters at all—reveals her desire to fashion her image as a "young" woman.

Bennett also recognized the important role traditionalism played in ensuring her success as a public figure. Perhaps the show's sponsors granted her request so enthusiastically because it seemed to recognize the benefits of technological progress even as it called attention to the supposedly simple life practiced by Indians and romanticized by so many other Americans. The equipment Bennett requested would not change the role played by her "grandmother"—she would still be doing the cooking, after all. Bennett had begun to see the multiple ways in which "tradition" could be a powerful tool for a woman seeking economic advancement.

Other publicity she received from the mainstream press reinforced her choice of an accommodating image. The *McKinley County Warrior*, for example, could not praise Bennett's accomplishments without implicitly criticizing other Indians:

> Kay is not always the Navajo entertainer. She is a modern
> girl, well dressed and cultured with a vivid, charming per-
> sonality. She has faced and overcome many difficulties all
> intelligent, ambitious Indians face when they leave the
> vastness of the reservation to make a place for themselves
> in the world.[62]

Such publicity emphasized Bennett's supposed embodiment of "Indian" femininity and of the qualities of a "good Indian" making her way in the "white man's world."

Still, Bennett was only able to achieve limited success as a performer, and she apparently began to consider other means of advancement. She resigned her position at the Phoenix Indian School in 1952, telling her employer that the Gallup Women's Club had offered her a scholarship. Unfortunately, her plans for further education did not come to fruition. Later employment applications indicate that she married her second husband, a man with the last name Price, at this time (this marriage ended in a few years), and moved to California, but did not go to school.[63] By this point, her daughters were definitely no longer in her care. According to later job applications, Bennett worked at several clerical and factory jobs in southern California during the early 1950s, the era in which she began her career as a performer, and then returned to Gallup to work at a pharmacy by 1956. She lived alone in a small apartment above the store. Despite her efforts to avoid this kind of work, she ultimately found, like other Navajo women, that she had to rely on low-wage labor to ensure her economic survival.

But this job proved to be temporary. In later years, Kay told friends the story of how she escaped it. The owner of the drugstore convinced Russ Bennett, an engineer working in Gallup temporarily, that he should ask Kay, whom he had admired while shopping at the store, to accompany him on a date.[64] Kay and Russ Bennett married in April 1956, and her life again changed dramatically.

An Expert on Navajo Life

Russ Bennett, an Anglo, had grown up in Missouri, but his work in the construction industry took him around the country and eventually, with Kay, around the world. Between 1958 and 1960, Kay and Russ lived together in Afghanistan while he worked there. These years remained memorable to Bennett for a number of reasons. She told interviewer Lela Waltrip that during her time there she became the "adopted daughter of a Moslem [sic] Afghan chief."[65] She also learned more about women's culture and a traditional Afghan art form. "The woman of the village agreed to exchange their knowledge of doll-making for Kay's old treadle sewing machine," Bennett later wrote, describing herself in a brochure publicizing her work. "Kay agreed to the exchange, and a new Indian art form was born."[66]

Bennett's choice of the term "new Indian art form" indicates a trend characterizing much of her work in the coming years: she began, at this time, to independently use new forms to express traditional values or themes. From the time she returned to Gallup, after Russ's retirement in 1960, when she herself was around forty years old, Bennett took on a series of innovative projects. In addition to making "Navajo dolls" and designing clothing inspired by Navajo styles, she wrote and illustrated three books featuring Navajo themes and recorded four albums featuring Navajo songs.[67] Of course, these projects ranged in the extent of their departures from "traditionalism": while the records only used a nontraditional medium to record an old form, the books recorded Navajo stories in the English language.[68] But the relative "traditionalism" of Bennett's work seems less relevant than the fact that the "borrowing" she did was in an effort to preserve and to bolster her identity as a Navajo artist.

Russ Bennett apparently encouraged his wife to begin this work. His son Andy, who was grown and living in California by the time his father remarried, feels Russ helped Kay to cultivate the confidence she needed to expand her place in the public eye. Andy met Kay soon after the marriage began and stayed in touch with her until her death, several years after his father's. He recalls that Russ "prodded her to get into doing more art work and more singing." Russ also convinced her to write down the stories she had lived through and heard about during her childhood. While only her second book, *A Navajo Saga*, credited Russ as an author, Andy describes their work on both of the books Kay published as collaborative: Kay told Russ the stories, he helped her to write them down, and she illustrated them.[69] With her financial status now more secure, and the means to write and publish available to her,

Fig. 21: Kay and Russ Bennett, c. 1969. Courtesy of a Private Collection.

she could now begin thinking about the youth that her pursuit of stability and education had separated her from. The prefaces of her books state her belief that publication in English of the stories of her childhood had become crucial to their survival. With Russ's support, she could take on the ambitious task of reclaiming her Navajo identity and sharing its roots with others.

These books, in fact, brought the stories and their writer regional and some national attention. By 1969, both *Kaibah* and *A Navajo Saga* had been published by prominent regional presses of the era, Westernlore Press of Los Angeles and the Naylor Company of San Antonio (which also published Cleofas Jaramillo's *Romance of a Little Village Girl*). That year, an announcement of Kay and Russ Bennett's appearance at a book-signing in Scottsdale, Arizona, described Kay as having "a nation-wide reputation for her contributions to varied expressions of Navajo culture" and added that she had "appeared in educational films and participated in television and radio programs."[70] This announcement may have overstated the extent of her fame, but it does show how she had become someone to whom non-Navajo audiences turned as an expert on Navajo culture.

Bennett's ultimate personal success seems to represent a contradiction of the analyses of researchers who concluded that Navajo women suffered more than Navajo men from the changes wrought by livestock reduction. In fact, at least one researcher has argued that Navajo women, as a general rule, rose in status during the 1950s and 1960s, the same era in which Bennett was beginning to succeed economically. Mary Shepardson has posited that by the late 1950s Navajo women had used educational opportunities and wage work to regain the high status they had held in the years before stock reduction.[71] In this respect, it could be argued that the overarching theme of Navajo women's history parallels that of the Navajos in general: while the reduction period disrupted preexisting patterns of economy and social structure, it ultimately resulted in a more cohesive Navajo Nation and a cemented position of high status for Navajo women. These innovative women, according to Shepardson, applied traditional components of Navajo society (including a matrilineal social structure, a strong work ethic, a pragmatic worldview, and women's ultimate responsibility for raising children) to a contemporary wage-based economy, and emerged in a position of strength.[72]

And yet Shepardson also pointed out that Navajo women did "lag behind" in the realms of politics and public decision making.[73] While Annie Wauneka, the daughter of one of the first tribal chairmen and herself an advocate of public health, won a seat on the Navajo Tribal Council in 1951, she was, for many years, the only woman who held such a position. These trends attest to the double-edged nature of Navajo women's "progress" since the stock-reduction years. Women like Bennett adjusted to the new economic patterns of the post-livestock-based, postwar economy. They worked hard to "borrow" features of non-Navajo culture, such as higher education and wage labor, that enhanced Navajo women's status in the later twentieth century. But these interactions also exposed them to a set of standards for women that offset such progress. Like Anglo and Hispanic women, Navajo women found themselves shut out of channels of public power.

In particular, though Navajos had valued women's localized political contributions in the years before the stock reduction, the institution of the tribal council not only diminished the value of women's voices but also discouraged women from participating in the new forum. As a newly national institution that privileged this level of representation over local politics, it cut off the traditional channels of women's public voices and authority. In fact, when Navajo leaders and federal officials first established the tribal council in 1923, women were not allowed to vote.[74] Though women received the franchise soon after, in 1928, a precedent had been set: the tribal council, based on non-Navajo ideas of public representation at a federal level, followed its U.S. model by establishing elective politics as the provenance of men. (This happened in a region where American Indians did not unequivocally have the right to vote in state and federal elections until 1948—apparently one form of discrimination did not immediately inspire some leaders to see another.[75])

The gender standards of the non-Navajo world tended to limit the ways in which Navajo women could achieve status in the later twentieth century. Shepardson writes that "federal authority did not support the high position of Navajo women." The Bureau of Indian

Affairs ignored matriarchal family structure when listing men only as "heads of households" and did not adequately acknowledge women's roles in owning sheep. Jobs offered to men in compensation for stock reduction were more available and more highly paid than those for women.[76] "Modernization" of economic and political roles reduced Navajo women's ability to control their lives and their homes. Thus, even as Bennett's marriage and cultural work allowed her to create a powerful niche for herself, she also found that her voice lacked impact in Navajo Nation affairs.

The personal history of Annie Wauneka shows how one woman was able to negotiate this trend successfully. As a winner of the Presidential Medal of Freedom for her work in public health, Wauneka lives on in U.S. public memory not only as the most famous Navajo woman, but also as one of the most well known of all Navajos. When she passed away in 1997, the *Navajo Times* memorialized her as the "matriarch of the Navajo Nation."[77] Born in 1910, Wauneka lived through the same extensive changes as Bennett. Though her father, Chee Dodge, was a wealthy man who became chairman of the Navajo Tribal Council in 1946, Wauneka spent her early childhood watching sheep like other Navajo children. She went to boarding schools as an older child but returned to the reservation to marry when she was eighteen. After she won a seat on the tribal council in 1951, she began extensive work for the council's Health Committee, attempting to eradicate tuberculosis on the reservation through education as well as cooperation between traditional healers and the Indian Health Service. She involved organizations like the Girl Scouts in her efforts to pursue reforms in housing, sanitation, vaccination, and education.[78]

The significance of her achievements is unquestionable. But one wonders if a Navajo woman whose time in the public eye included work less consistent with traditional Anglo gender roles would have received as much notice from the public. As a public health worker and a politician whose efforts most impacted the immediately local level of home and family, Wauneka was able to perform a role consistent with both Navajo ideas of matriarchal authority and Anglo ideas of women's roles as caregivers. Thus, she united the "traditional" world with "modern" women's roles in the public sphere.

Bennett did not bridge Navajo and Anglo worlds quite as smoothly. Her books, for example, provide a rich account of "traditional" Navajo life but do not move forward in time to cover the post-stock-reduction years—the time in which Wauneka thrived. As far as I have been able to determine, Bennett never wrote nor spoke extensively about her life after she left Navajo country and tried to make her way in the non-Navajo world. Perhaps her final marriage to a non-Navajo, the end of her first and second marriages, and her difficult relationships with her daughters, whom she gave up as young girls, made returning to this portion of her life more difficult. While Navajo society has traditionally included both divorce and the raising of children by nonparents and, more recently, the education of children away from home, Bennett's separation from her children seems to have been unusually bitter, as evidenced by her strained relationship with her daughters in later years. Bennett's cross-cultural life, in which she likely found herself being measured against both Navajo and non-Navajo standards of motherhood, could only have made parenting more difficult.

Still, others persisted in ascribing "traditional" roles to her, and Bennett found such attention to be ultimately beneficial, despite its degree of artificiality. In a situation that one of Bennett's friends in Gallup described as "ironic," Bennett received the "Mother of the Year" award for New Mexico in 1968, though her daughters, grown by then, had not lived with her for a good portion of their young lives. The state governor, David Cargo, and "Mrs. Horace Biggs," the state president of the New Mexico American Mothers Selection Committee, presented her with the award, and she accordingly attended the "Wonderful World of Mothers" contest finals in New York. New Mexico newspapers heralded her appointment as a "first" for American Indians.[79] The *Gallup Independent* noted the event with a front-page headline reading "Gallup Navajo Plans Blessing." Apparently, she planned to use "corn pollen, an eagle feather, a ceremonial basket, and a drum" for a ceremony during the

Fig. 22: Kay Bennett in Traditional Dress, c. 1960s. Courtesy of a Private Collection.

contest. The article's tone, in describing her comments about the blessing, portrayed her intentions as maternal and gracious: "'And if that doesn't straighten out the country—nothing will,' she said with a smile."[80]

Bennett's choice of performance activity, as well as the newspaper's delight in portraying it, helps to explain why she was chosen as a contestant, despite her difficult history as a mother. The "Selection Committee" may have conflated her public work as an author and cultural interpreter with her private role as a mother, or they may have been moved by her "exotic" status to consider the category of motherhood in liberal terms. Given the context of the civil rights movement, they may have been eager to choose an American Indian woman who met the qualifications for the award. According to her stepson, Bennett remembered the attention she received for the award (including a ride on a float in the Rose Tournament Parade) quite proudly.[81] She apparently felt determined to see herself as a good mother, despite the fact that economic circumstances forced her to entrust her children to others' care.

But it is nevertheless troubling to think that this award may have been one of the limited ways in which she could receive broad notice for her non-mothering-related work. The dilemma posed by this award and her reception of it points to the overall dilemma raised by her life. Like other Navajo women, Bennett was caught between her adherence to the Navajo standards for womanhood she learned as a girl and the economic and social circumstances that either made it very difficult for her to adhere to them or devalued her efforts to do so.

"My People as They Truly Are"

Bennett's 1964 memoir, *Kaibah: Recollection of a Navajo Girlhood*, makes it possible to see how a woman in this difficult position chose to express the origins and development of her identity. While it describes only the period between 1928 and 1935, and thus stops short of providing reflection on her adult life, her choices regarding what to record and what to omit become instructive. Moreover, her other writings, published and unpublished, shed light on how she thought about her memoir's purpose and effectiveness in later years.

Despite the title of the memoir, Bennett wrote her book not so much as a "recollection" but as a series of vignettes in which the narrator describes young Kaibah's life in the third-person form. Perhaps it felt safer or easier to write about herself as another person, or perhaps she thought her memoir would have better publishing success as a book written for children. Every now and then, her adult voice permeates the narrative, as when she completes the first chapter by attempting to dispel any notions on the part of the reader that Indian life was inferior to that practiced by non-Indian cultures. "Life on the Navajo reservation did not provide all the luxuries of the city," she acknowledged, "but the people were happy. They lived an uncomplicated existence, free from the worries which beset most people who live and work in urban communities."[82]

Bennett's nostalgic comments here set the tone for the rest of *Kaibah*. Her book attempted neither to compare her life away from the reservation with the early years, nor to show what happened in the post-stock-reduction years, when the "worries" of industrialized America began to make their way to Navajo country, and when she made her way to a worrisome non-Navajo urban world. Rather, in *Kaibah*, Bennett chronicled what she saw as a happy and fulfilling childhood and tried to offer readers, especially non-Navajos, one clear perspective on life in a Navajo community. While her decision to write this book and its overall format reflects her positive experiences, as an adult, with the strategic use of Anglo culture, *Kaibah* is, at heart, a tribute to what she perceived as the unadulterated Navajo culture of her youth as well as a recollection of the outside forces that devastated it.

One critic has remarked that the book offers only a "somewhat romanticized" portrayal of Navajo country, faulting the author for producing an unbalanced book that does not include her negative experiences both at home and after she left the reservation.[83] While the narrative does not dwell on Kaibah's negative experiences, Bennett did certainly include some, such as the family separation required by boarding school. When Kaibah and her siblings leave for school in 1934, her mother watches with "tears rolling down her cheeks."[84]

Bennett also dealt with painful contrasts between "modern" medicine practiced by Anglos and Navajo healing practices. Eleven-year-old Kaibah watches her half-sister Tesbah suffer from complications during childbirth. Kaibah and her mother take Tesbah to the hospital in Shiprock, but it is too late to save her, and the doctor scolds the women for waiting too long. One of Tesbah's infant twins also dies, and the family gives the other child away to an Anglo couple to raise, fearing she will bring bad luck. Kaibah herself must have surgery performed on one of her eyes (for trachoma) soon after arriving at Toadlena School, though the narrator mentions this event only briefly.

In the last third of Bennett's memoir, sad events receive more than a passing mention. The Depression, the drought, the enforced stock reduction, and Kaibah's mother's despair at not being able to provide for her family shadow this portion of the book and its culmination in Kaibah's departure. Thus, the book's nostalgia for the days of Bennett's "simple" youth is accompanied by an emphasis on how Navajo life had changed since then, both for better and for worse.

Bennett's desire to make her readers aware of the intricacies of cultural change is also reflected in the narrative's powerful use of both obvious and subtle humor. Kaibah's launching of the apple at the school superintendent stands out as a funny moment, as does her experience with religion at the boarding school. When the narrator describes the daily routine of children at Toadlena School, she includes offhandedly that "on Sundays they marched to the church to hear the preacher tell them that they would all go to hell and be burned up if they were bad." A confused Kaibah can only respond by asking another student, "Who are God and Jesus? And why are they going to burn us all up?" Though Kaibah's friend's explanation does not convince her that the "white man's gods" are better than the Navajo ones, Kaibah decides to hold on to her church newspapers just in case, because the preacher has warned the students that they will burn in hell if they throw them away.

But the preacher does not get the last word. Though he also tells the students they will go to hell if they attend any summer Squaw Dances (festive events that accompany healing ceremonies and at which partners traditionally give each other gifts of money in exchange for a dance), Kaibah goes to one anyway, after coming to the conclusion that "God was far away, and no one would tell Him what they were doing in the mountains." The preacher visits her mother's hogan later that summer in an attempt to "save" Navajos, and Mother Chischillie turns to her daughter and says, "Go get my corn pollen. We must say a prayer for that poor man, as his mind is confused by the evil spirits." Her mother's corn pollen prayer convinces Kaibah that it will be safe to burn her church papers, after all.[85]

Moments like these lead non-Navajo readers to look at life from the Navajo point of view. When Kaibah practices her English before returning to school after the summer, her mother complains about the mumbling, remarking that "whenever I hear people speaking English I wonder how anyone can understand what they say. All the words sound alike."[86] Bennett's goal in writing *Kaibah*, it seems, was to use the English language and the form of a children's didactic novel to make the Navajo way of life more than a jumble of customs in a foreign language for the non-Navajo reader. Moreover, by describing her mother's own antipathy to English and the "white man's ways," Bennett showed that Navajos, too, had difficulty understanding outsiders' ideas and customs.

In *Kaibah*, Bennett achieved an honest retelling of her childhood, one that continues to resonate with individual readers today. The memoir does not romanticize the processes of cultural interaction and conquest; rather, Bennett described these processes in personal terms, as those removed from the public centers of political power experienced them. For example, *Kaibah* includes an incident in which Anglo teachers punished Navajo girls who ran away from school by shaving their heads, adding that the girls' parents removed them from school soon after. "To have one's hair cut short was a drastic break in Navajo tradition," Bennett explained, "but to have it all cut off was a great disgrace" and unacceptable as a punishment to Navajo parents.[87] Towards the end of the memoir, Bennett wrote of how a white man came to the trading post to explain that the Navajos gathered there "must vote so John Collier would know if they agreed to reduce their herds." She movingly described how "the men and women talked, but still did not understand," voted anyway, and "quietly left for their homes."[88]

Kaibah does not ever discuss the results of this election (the Navajos' 1934 rejection of the Wheeler-Howard Act); it is enough, the book implies, just to know that it happened and that many of the participants did not understand its implications. A young girl like Kaibah, who was actually away at school during the election, would not remember the exact result, but she would remember how the election took place shortly after the drought began and shortly before the reduction of the herds. The Navajo experience, as revealed through Bennett's narrative, cannot be reduced to a series of elections; it must be understood in terms of everyday experience, and in this case through the eyes of a young girl and her mother who do not want to see their sheep go. The book carries out what it promises in its preface: the "completion" of Bennett's people's history through the recording of everyday experience.[89] While her memoir does not make an explicit case that Navajo women's status suffered as a direct result of the stock reductions, the stories it tells imply that these policies' consequences carried further than previous accounts had indicated.

Bennett's post-1965 writings supplement *Kaibah*'s implications but also show that her ideas about how best to advocate her messages about culture, change, and traditionalism shifted over time. Her pageant competitions and "nostalgic" tributes to Navajo tradition gradually gave way to more direct critiques of others' approaches to Indian life, be it through policy making or history writing. She also began to more directly challenge views, including those of other Navajos, about what constituted Navajo identity.

⚜ Leaving Home ⚜

This shift is reflected in a piece she wrote in 1969, when John Milton, editor of the *South Dakota Review*, asked contemporary American Indian writers and artists to contribute to an upcoming issue of the journal. Rather than sending a creative piece, Bennett, now entering her fifties, wrote Milton a letter, which he published in the collection. Bennett's letter states that she had published her books and recorded songs in an effort "to preserve a part of our history and culture and to encourage others to do likewise." *Kaibah*, Bennett wrote, "is the story of my life as a girl on the reservation. In it I present my people as they truly are, intelligent, sympathetic and a great deal more humanitarian than the people of other races with which they have come into contact."[90] Bennett's claim in this letter that the story of her girlhood has significance for her "people" shows her desire to use her writing to reconnect herself to a culture from which she had felt apart.

Her effort to reclaim Navajo history continued in her next book, *A Navajo Saga*, published in 1969 and coauthored with her husband. Describing this work in her letter to Milton, Bennett wrote that the book surveyed Navajo history from 1846 to 1870. By publishing the story in a new way, from the perspective of Navajo people, Kay and Russ hoped to make a much-needed contribution to the history of the region. In *A Navajo Saga*, they recorded how Kay's grandmother, Shebah, and father, Chischillie, returned to Navajo country just after the Long Walk. The book alternates between the story of Shebah's captivity in Mexico, the experiences of Gray Hat (Shebah's father) and his family during the Long Walk era, and the overarching context of negotiations between the U.S. government, Hispanic settlers, and Navajos. While Russ Bennett seems to have significantly helped his wife with the writing of *Kaibah*, his name is actually listed as a coauthor for *A Navajo Saga*. He likely researched and wrote the chapters dealing with the military campaigns and negotiations, while Bennett's family stories supplied the material for the rest of the book.

Through its blending of the "personal" and the "political," the book as a whole is illustrative of Bennett's changing views of the relationship between Navajos and the larger U.S. culture. The book's main content, however, concerns events that took place about a hundred years before Kay and Russ wrote the book, as if Kay felt reaching back further into history deepened her connection to her people. Still, the book's preface does also explicitly reveal how Bennett's sense of identity was changing in her present day. The true story of her family and Navajos in general, the preface argues, challenges the U.S. government's ideas about how Indians and other minorities should be treated. The stories of the raiding and of the Navajos' adoption of Hispanic slaves, and in Bennett's case, the story of her father's Hispanic ancestry, show, in the Bennetts' words, that "there are few pure-blooded Indians or Spanish people in the Southwest, just as there are few pure-blooded people in any country in the world." Moreover, the Bennetts implied that the United States had established a false and unfair dichotomy between "Indians" and mestizos: "There is little difference between the people with Indian blood who are wards and those who are non-wards of the United States," they wrote, "except that the former are told they are not capable of self-government, and the latter share in governing the states in which they live."[91]

By 1969, Bennett wanted her identity as a Navajo to be understood as a matter of culture, of religion, and of history, not of blood. Five years earlier, the publisher of *Kaibah*, Westernlore Press, included the book as a volume in its "Great West and Indian Series" and publicized it as the work of "a full-blooded Navajo."[92] But Bennett's second book both contradicted this statement and labeled such an idea of heritage as a fallacy. *A Navajo Saga* emphasized a Navajo perspective based on spirituality: in the preface, the Bennetts argued that "an understanding of the Navajo people comes through an understanding of the religion by which they live."[93] The book illustrated this point through characters who hold on to their religious views despite significant obstacles. As opposed to a Christian religion based on written legends, this spirituality is passed down by word of mouth, and, by implication, it can be flexible enough to respond to crises, such as captivity and the Long Walk, as they emerge. The family depicted in the book is Navajo not because of static values and a "pure" family tree but because their spirituality enables them to endure such crises together.

Bennett came to feel this Navajo spirituality and the flexible identity it created was at risk, endangered by economic and social policies at work on the reservation since the stock reduction. In her letter to Milton, she described her treatment of Navajo religion in *A Navajo Saga* as a last-ditch effort to chronicle a dying tradition. "Our religion sustained the race through thousands of years of wandering, hardships and wars," she began. "We survived attack by nature, and many other tribes and races, and remained strong and independent." But then, Bennett argued, the final stage of conquest kicked in. "It is only in the past few years when the ultimate weapon, welfare, has been used against us that some of my people have been defeated."[94]

Bennett ended her letter there, leaving her argument about welfare unexplained, but burning with emotion. As someone who had escaped poverty initially through wage work, but eventually through marriage, Bennett watched the Navajo "battle" with welfare from a removed, but conflicted, vantage point. Her criticism of the government implies that, like her mother, she believed Navajos were caught in a "cat and mouse" game, but her choice of rhetoric also implies criticism of those who accepted assistance rather than adapting as much as she had. Instead of making her an impartial observer, Bennett's experiences likely led her to feel defensive about her privilege and removed from her Navajo relatives and upbringing.

This sense of removal emerges in an interview she granted to a writer from the Women's Section of the *Scottsdale Daily Progress* soon after the 1964 publication of *Kaibah*. The article, titled "Navajo Writes About Navajos," begins auspiciously: "Mrs. Russell C. Bennett is a full-blooded Navajo and the first member of her colorful Northeastern Arizona tribe ever to have written a book." Here, Bennett emerges as a Navajo renegade of sorts—as much through her own statements as in the way the article's author frames her. "I may drive a Cadillac and wear contemporary clothes instead of traditional velvet tunics and gathered skirts when I return to my old mother's hogan at

Sheepsprings, N.M.," the writer quoted Bennett, "but that does not make her words of wisdom nor the practices of the medicine men any less valid for me. What is invalid is living in a mud hut and tending sheep. That is not my way of life and I cannot accept it." Bennett's rejection of her mother's "traditional" life makes her story similar to those of Austin, Luhan, Jaramillo, and Cabeza de Baca, who all strayed from their mothers' paths even as they became advocates for tradition.

Reading the article today, one is struck by Bennett's apparent bitterness toward her difficult youth, but perhaps what is even more striking is the article's deliberate smoothing over of the difficulties she invokes. The review's author acknowledges that the memoir tells stories of the harsh years of stock reduction; it also describes the book as a "no-sweat little volume, written with the charm and warmth of most reminiscent stories of past days." It praises the book as being the first one "written by someone who actually lived in a hogan"; it also expands on her qualifications by noting how "Mrs. Bennett lives in an apartment in Gallup with her non-Indian engineer husband. With him, she has traveled the major capitols [*sic*] of the world and now can look at her tribe with an objective perspective few others can boast."[95] An *Albuquerque Tribune* review of *Kaibah* written in a similar vein does not mention Bennett's husband but does promise readers that "Mrs. Bennett" has "no axe to grind in her book." According to this impressed reviewer, the memoir "expresses sympathetic understanding of all points of view" even as it shows that Bennett "comprehends" the issues it presents "as only the Navajo people can."[96]

Such shallow media portrayals enhanced Bennett's ability to present herself as someone with the ability to juggle the "new" and the "old" gracefully, despite this image's contradiction of her actual experiences. She often employed this graceful image herself, especially in the kinds of activism she took on in the 1970s and 1980s. Despite the strident politics she had begun to articulate in her writing, much of her work took more accommodating forms. She continued to craft and sell Navajo dolls and clothing. She did extensive volunteer work, serving on the board of directors of the Gallup Inter-Tribal Ceremonial from

1974 to 1982, and on the McKinley County Hospital Advisory Board from 1976 to 1978. In the late 1970s, she also supervised student teachers on the Navajo reservation.[97] Her commitment to public involvement continued into her seventies. As late as 1997, the year of her death, she opened a small museum in Gallup where her dolls were featured, wearing Navajo costumes from different eras.[98] During these later years, she also independently republished her previous books and wrote, illustrated, and self-published a book of children's stories called *Kesh the Navajo Indian Cat*. Through these activities, she fulfilled both Anglo and Indian models of conventional female community involvement and appropriate leadership roles.

Frustration

Bennett's efforts at community work were not, however, limited to non-confrontational approaches. The last years of her life reflected her increasing determination to enter into politics—and her continual disappointment with election results. Her attempts to use elections to build bridges between her tribal community and the Anglo community, thus cementing the kinds of intermediary roles she had played throughout her life, ended in her acute awareness of the gap between her enthusiasm for activism and Navajos' general willingness, at that time, to allow women to officially serve as elected leaders.

Bennett first ran for office in 1968, when she competed, as a Republican candidate, for the office of county assessor in McKinley County. During the campaigning season, she met with Governor David Cargo during his stop in Gallup—the same governor who oversaw her nomination as New Mexico's "Mother of the Year" earlier that year. In a campaign statement, she spoke about how she wanted to devote more county money to schools and more attention to the "worsening in the relations between the Tribal Governments and the local communities." She also explained that she was "seeking a county office ... because I believe all Indian people should take a greater interest in State, County and City affairs."[99] She received 3,443 votes—many more than she would receive as a tribal candidate—but lost by a little under 1,500 votes to the Democrat candidate.[100]

Bennett's work with Governor Cargo, also a Republican, earned her a more direct opportunity to serve as an intermediary for contemporary Navajos. In 1969, he appointed her to serve on the New Mexico Human Rights Commission (NMHRC). She became one of the inaugural members of the commission, which the New Mexico Human Rights Act established in 1969 as a replacement for an earlier civil rights effort, the Fair Employment Practice Commission (FEPC). The new commission had an ambitious task: by law, it was "empowered to investigate complaints of discrimination in employment, public accommodations, and the acquisition of housing and real estate in New Mexico."[101] Bennett wrote an article for the *Gallup Independent* explaining the commission's goals as well as the constraints of its budget, which meant that she and her four cocommissioners were not paid for their work.[102] After news of the commission reached New Mexicans, letters began to pour into the offices of its executive director, Byron Stewart. These letters give vivid firsthand accounts of lost jobs and personal harassment resulting from racism. The commissioners met to discuss how the cases should be handled, and Bennett brought a good deal of initial enthusiasm. In a June 1969 letter to Stewart, she wrote she had been upset to find that the minutes from a meeting of the NMHRC's earlier incarnation, the FEPC, revealed "no mention of anything being accomplished." She thanked Stewart for his devotion and wrote that she "sincerely hope[d] our record will be better."[103]

But the commission faced opposition from local industry within its first year of existence because of its focus on employment concerns. Such sentiments made this work difficult and controversial, and Bennett apparently lost heart.[104] In a letter written to Stewart only a month after she had expressed optimism, she revealed her doubt that some of the measures that Stewart had proposed for the NMHRC would be effective for the Navajo community. Stewart had apparently suggested that the NMHRC open a booth at the upcoming Gallup Inter-Tribal Ceremonial, an event with which Bennett had become extensively involved. Bennett dismissed this suggestion, telling Stewart that "all booths are held for exhibitors of arts and crafts." Navajos and other American Indians came to the event, she wrote, to enjoy themselves, not to "listen to how they might change their status in the white man's society." Moreover, she argued that "few Indians" would even be likely to complain of discrimination for, in her estimation, they tended by necessity to be more self-reliant economically than other American people.[105]

Bennett felt the commission would have limited relevance in the eyes of most Navajos. If the commission wanted to educate Navajos about its work nevertheless, she suggested, it should do so at local chapter house meetings. But Bennett warned it would be an uphill battle. "The people who attend these meetings," she explained, "give a great deal of thought to the future but tend to oppose any change." In an indirect reference to the stock reduction years, she wrote that "they associate change with increases in costs of food, clothing and pickups without a corresponding change in the price they receive for their wool and their sheep." She did think, however, that Navajo concerns for "the future welfare of their children" made them interested in hearing about ways that the NMHRC could help students, especially those hoping for work after graduation. "It is very discouraging for her mother when her well-educated child returns home to loaf simply because he does not know how to go about getting a job or is not offered a job," Bennett explained, hinting that perhaps it was also discouraging for a Navajo mother to feel unable to help her child with that process herself. She also attempted to explain her sense of the root of the problem to Stewart: "I blame the white society because I do not believe it is making an effort to absorb the educated Indians," she wrote. "There is too much propaganda being spread about Indians being drunkards or irresponsible."[106]

Bennett, who had just written two books in an effort to create reverse propaganda, seems unusually defeatist in this statement, as if she were questioning the capacity of the NMHRC to initiate change. She stayed with the NMHRC until her term expired in 1973, but the fact that she missed two of the three meetings leading up to the end of her term indicate that she could not fully commit herself to the work. Her remarks to Stewart suggest that she had come to feel the NMHRC model drew too much from white institutions to be effective for Navajos.

Such awareness must have been painful to come by for a woman who had devoted much of her life to using European cultural forms, such as the memoir, to advocate cultural strength and preservation. While her books had attracted initial notice and praise from the Anglo mainstream press, they did not take long to go out of print. And those who did see her work as worthwhile may not have seen it as a political contribution or a form of activism.

The American Indian activists who *were* receiving attention, beginning in the late 1960s, were younger, frequently male activists who advocated "Red Power" in more aggressive ways than the development of "new Indian art forms" and the publication of books. In 1974, when Bennett served as exhibits' chair of the Inter-Tribal Ceremonial, she directly confronted this brand of activism when she spoke out against the boycott of that year's Ceremonial called for by six groups, including the American Indian Movement and Indians Against Exploitation. In a newspaper interview, she countered that protestors were underestimating the economic benefits that arts and crafts sold at the fair brought to American Indians, expressed her determination to continue with the event and her career, and articulated her willingness to differ with these younger activists' vision of cultural isolation. "It has taken me years to get where I am," she told the reporter covering the story. "I don't like to be blocked. Not all of us will have jobs on reservations in the future."[107]

A month later, Bennett's comments on the controversy conveyed less anger and more sadness. She told the *Gallup Independent* that she felt contemporary ceremonials lacked the "happiness" they had once held, and that she feared for the Gallup event's future if "the community, the Indians, the tribal leaders" didn't get behind it. While the purpose of the Ceremonial had once been, in Bennett's experience, for people of different tribes to meet each other, she now also saw it, as the reporter paraphrased, "as an excellent way for Indians and Anglos to learn about each other."[108] Her willingness to speak of this as an ideal relationship, despite her disillusioning experiences with the NMHRC, cast her as a political conservative, while her desire to gain a leadership role that permitted her to act on this ideal would ultimately conflict with perceptions about the proper public role of women.

In 1986, she set herself on a course that contradicted such perceptions by declaring herself a candidate for the office of Navajo Tribal Chairman. Perhaps the death of her husband less than a month before the filing deadline led her to decide such an effort might be a good way to distract herself from grief. One friend of Bennett's, Gallup publisher Martin Link, told me Bennett ran for office not to win but to "shake them up," referring, it seems, to both the existing male-dominated government and the Navajo voters who had elected it.[109] Coverage of her campaign in the *Navajo Times* did, in fact, portray it as a novelty, taking care to emphasize that despite Bennett's relative fame, she had no experience as an elected official. Her platform, the article continued, stressed "the lack of progress by Navajo women."[110]

But the newspaper's representation of her platform cast it in a different light than she herself did. She actually argued that Navajo government leadership did not reflect the true progress of Navajo women; Navajo women weren't the problem, Navajo government was. "We have too many women whose talents and intelligence are being wasted," she wrote in her *Position on Issues Affecting Women*. "It's a sad fact, however, that we have been governed by men too long."[111]

Her assertions were unfortunately validated by the extreme reluctance with which the existing Navajo administration greeted her campaign. Soon after she registered as a candidate, the election commission told her that she did not qualify because she had not established continuous permanent residency on the reservation four years prior to her filing date.[112] While the election board eventually waived this requirement, it then disqualified Bennett because she had never served as an elected official or as a tribal employee. Apparently her work in education had been at the service of the state, even though it exclusively dealt with Navajo students. Bennett challenged this ruling and its definition of work quite directly, stating at a press conference that the songs and stories she had written were very much at the service of the Navajo Nation. She had performed at official tribal functions, and written books used by Navajo schools, thus leaving a legacy of Navajo stories and songs.[113] "Every [Navajo] beauty queen," she deftly argued, "is singing my songs at fairs."[114]

Moreover, as she asserted, she also had the best interests of the Navajo people in mind and, she believed, the skills to help them achieve their goals. "I am a businesswoman," she told reporters, "and I know quite a bit about how to make money." Such knowledge and skills, she told those who listened, made her "want to work for the Navajo people, especially for the women. Also, for Navajos who live off-reservation. They shouldn't just be pushed aside."[115] Bennett campaigned because she wanted to call attention to Navajos like her, whom the forces of economic pressure and cultural change had pushed away geographically and psychologically. It is telling that the election board ruled her out because she did not fulfill its requirements for a Navajo resident or worker, and that in her press conference she told reporters, defensively, that she "[felt] like a Navajo," despite what the election board said.[116] What was at issue, it seems, were the borders of Navajo identity, and whether Bennett had crossed them. Eventually, the election board reinstated her candidacy, and she competed, with poor results, in the primary. She received only 103 votes.[117]

In 1990, Bennett, now entering her seventies, tried again. She felt this bid might call more attention to the need for political reform, a need that she and others perceived after a series of controversies involving Navajo leadership in the four years following the previous election. These complicated events resulted in the removal of Chairman Peter McDonald (who had won the 1986 race) from office, his trial and conviction on charges of bribery, and his removal from the 1990 ballot.[118]

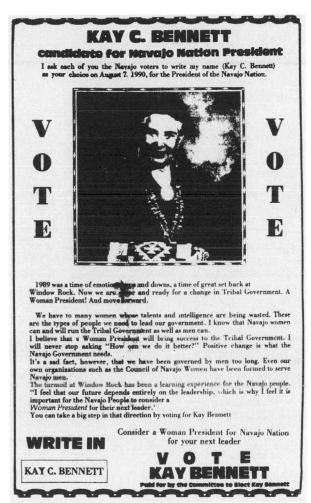

Fig. 23:
Kay Bennett
Campaign
Advertisement, *The
Navajo Times*, 2
Aug. 1990.

Promising that the turmoil in the Navajo government could be turned
into a learning experience, Bennett challenged voters during her candidacy announcement to consider change by electing "a woman president
for their next leader."[119] Once again, however, Bennett's quest for votes
endured heavy scrutiny, and she was removed from candidacy because

she did not have "experience" as a previously elected official or employee of the Navajo Nation. The Navajo Supreme Court reinstated her candidacy the day before the election but did not order her name back on the ballot; she won only 195 votes in that bid for the Navajo Nation's highest office.[120]

In an interview after the election, Bennett candidly described her experiences with the Election Board. "I have never in my life been treated with such hostility," she claimed, "as when I began to contest the decision of the board to disqualify me." But instead of rejecting Navajo politics, she spoke of holding them to a higher standard, as revealed through this conflicted statement of loyalty to a place that remained ambivalent about accepting her: "I cannot accept such treatment here at home."[121] In the world of Navajo politics, Bennett found, "authenticity" took on a whole new meaning. "True" candidates needed to travel in the established channels of power, power rooted in Anglo ideas at least as much as Navajo ones. On a more positive note, those channels were beginning to appear less "male" than they had in the past: in the 1990 election, Bennett was actually joined by two other women candidates.[122]

Not all Navajos saw this as a positive development. According to a letter to the *Navajo Times*, Bennett's candidacy unleashed the "old tiresome question" of whether Navajo women should be leaders. The writer, a woman, argued against those who had apparently voiced their opposition to Bennett: "A Navajo woman is the best kind of leader because she has experienced the pain of childbirth and life. She is the daily arbitrator in her family's life and constantly makes sacrifices so her family members can have better or more. Thus she is in a better position to be logical, firm, consistent, and yet temper her decisions with gentleness and love."[123] In her analysis of why some people have disagreed with this opinion, historically as well as in contemporary Navajo society, historian Ruth Roessel has written that both men and women have resisted women as "number-one" leaders of the tribal council because they feel it violates the "teaching and traditions of Navajo culture." What Roessel astutely points out, however, is that

☙ *Leaving Home* ☙

Navajo women traditionally participated in leadership and decision making, as they do still today on the local level. Writing in 1981, Roessel identified "growing jealousy" on the part of Navajo men "as women begin to reassert this position of leadership that traditionally was accorded to them."[124] In other words, while some Navajos have seen Navajo women's moves toward political leadership in the 1980s as too radical, others have seen them as a return to tradition.

Despite her low vote counts, Bennett succeeded in bringing more attention to her perception of a discrepancy between Navajo women's traditional skills and their status in contemporary public life. Her 1986 platform put it bluntly: "Most Navajo women are very conservative; in fact, I am very conservative myself. Maybe this is one of the reasons why Navajo women have always been underappreciated."[125] The time had come, Bennett argued, for Navajo women to stop letting adherence to "tradition" mean blindness to the inequities that had developed between Navajo men and women since the stock reduction era. She implied that Navajo women were more conservative and traditional than Navajo men, and that Anglo ideas about a woman's place had misled Navajo men into thinking women did not belong in the Navajo Nation government. The two contrasting narratives of post-stock-reduction history that Bennett first articulated in *Kaibah*—the rise of the Navajo Nation and the declining status of Navajo women—could be reconciled successfully, Bennett felt, if Navajo women participated in the formal channels of the Navajo Nation.

Bennett's campaigns for office thus asked Navajo voters to consider attempting the difficult feat of combining tradition and innovation. She wanted the Navajo Nation to turn, as a whole, to the tradition of women's leadership, and at the same time to develop new channels for putting this leadership into action. Such maneuvering would have been akin to her own work at using nontraditional means, such as beauty contests, books, and dolls, of asserting Navajo cultural identity.

Her election bids did not win many votes. But she likely expected such results, as they were consistent with the mixed public reception that her work had continually created. When she died of cancer in 1997, as she was nearing her eighties, local papers noted her accomplishments as a singer, writer, entrepreneur, and the first woman to run for the Navajo Nation's highest office. But, by contrast, when Annie Wauneka's obituaries had appeared, only a week before, local citizens remembered Wauneka as a "visionary," a woman of significance to Navajos and Americans alike. Both women had visions, both accomplished much, but one clearly seemed more important to the people that knew of them. Wauneka's leadership, a role inherited from her father, and played in accordance with Anglo ideas of women's public roles, smoothed over the rough edges of cultural change and conflict. Bennett's vision of innovative traditionalism—whether it came through her dolls, records, books, or campaigns—not only exposed cultural fissures, but also asked people to try, as she had, to leap back and forth over them. This vision may have ultimately demanded too much extra juggling of tradition and change from a Navajo society that had been heavily engaged in such juggling for many years.

Where others assumed Navajo culture was "authentic" because it was separate from modern Anglo life, Bennett argued that experiences with Anglo culture actually strengthened her Navajo identity. Contrary to the view that Navajo women were most traditional when they were most accommodating, she used her controversial runs for political office as calls for traditionalism, apparently recognizing that these efforts more closely resembled the roles played by Navajo women in her grandmothers' generation than her competitions in beauty pageants had. Bennett's campaigns reflected her willingness, at the end of her life, to call direct attention to the shortcomings of assumptions that had come to permeate New Mexicans' lives during her lifetime; specifically, the notion that cultural integrity (at least for Hispanics and American Indians) depended on cultural isolation and preservation and on women's willingness to remain confined to static, and increasingly powerless, roles as "homekeepers."

Both Jaramillo and Cabeza de Baca were willing to display perfect loyalty to these ideas, despite their actual conflicts with them, because doing so permitted greater recognition for Hispanic culture.

Bennett, however, wearied of such accommodations. Perhaps living in a slightly later era granted her a vantage point from which she could see not only the decline in status that had happened between her grandmothers' generation and her own but also the limitations of cultural policies that prided themselves on strict preservation. She grew tired of the discrepancy between the ideal home such reasoning promised and the actual flexibility she had needed to exercise to preserve herself and her Navajo identity. Her willingness to speak of this homesickness, to even draw attention to it through the controversial medium of a political campaign, cost her popularity, especially among Navajos, but it also ensured her relevance to those seeking a better home for New Mexicans today.

CHAPTER 5
"No Woman Ever Built a House"
Pablita Velarde and the Unraveling of Traditional Womanhood

On the painted wall of a building in Albuquerque, a woman dances. All around her, people from Santa Clara perform the Buffalo and Deer Dance. She is taking part in the ceremony, but she is the only woman doing so. The movements engross the other dancers; they are caught up in the importance of maintaining rhythm and tradition. The woman keeps up with their steps, her eyes watching the dancer in front of her. A proud smile is beginning to form on her lips, as if she is about to turn to her audience, to see them watching her dance so boldly among the men. The whole scene is a mural, commissioned in 1976 for one of the walls surrounding the courtyard of the Indian Pueblo Cultural Center. And the woman who dances so boldly is the woman who painted it, Pablita Velarde.

This boldness makes Velarde, born in 1918 and still living today, a kindred spirit to the other women considered in this book, all of whom broke new ground in their efforts to make their audiences

Fig. 24: *Buffalo and Deer Dance,* Mural by Pablita Velarde, 1975. Courtesy of the Indian Pueblo Cultural Center. Copyright Pablita Velarde.

consider cultural traditions in a new way. But their boldness had distinct limitations; they had to consider how ideas about women's roles affected their ability to interact with audiences whose attitudes they were trying to change. They often relied on and sometimes took pride in conventional femininity. Luhan presented herself as a "muse" for, rather than a leader of, cultural causes, while Austin happily noted the "ladyhood" status she had found in Santa Fe. Similarly, the women of color who followed Luhan and Austin into cultural preservation work found that adhering to tradition in their public images made it more likely that they would be heard. Jaramillo emphasized her reluctance to enter into the public sphere as anything but a last resort. While Cabeza de Baca privately backed away from LULAC after the organization confined her to an "auxiliary" role, she publicly embraced the domestic mission of home economics. Bennett assured the public that she was a "conservative" Navajo woman even as her actions called her performance of this role into question. For all of these women, "tradition" became an effective way to publicly emphasize a desire for a more ideal New Mexican home even as private life required both traditional and nontraditional strategies of homemaking.

When Velarde began her career as a professional painter, in the 1940s, she also found adherence to conservative ideas about tradition to be an important aspect of her public image. She adopted a "traditionalist" painting style, using illustrative methods to depict daily and ceremonial life at Santa Clara Pueblo, her ancestral home. While she has continued to use this style throughout her career, the world to which she has presented her work has undergone rapid and substantial change; New Mexico has become a thoroughly "modern" place. As a result, the perceived value of Velarde's work has escalated. Encouraged by both the Indian arts revival of the mid-twentieth century as well as the late twentieth-century push for multicultural social values, audiences have come to see Velarde's style as work that sustains New Mexico's distinctive multicultural heritage. The New Mexico image encourages, even thrives upon, the work of "traditionalists" like her, who seem to keep American Indian culture alive. Every August, crowds of artists and audiences alike congregate in Santa Fe for "Indian Market," and Velarde's work has been among the most prominent featured at the event. Her work, once of interest only to collectors and museums that valued its documentary approach, has gradually become mainstream multicultural art.

Modernization has also brought the second-wave feminist movement of the 1960s and 1970s to New Mexico, and this trend has also defined Velarde's reputation. Earlier treatments of her work hinted that her status as a female Pueblo painter was unusual; her work now appeals to contemporary audiences precisely because her individualistic pursuit of a career breaks with both Pueblo and Anglo traditions of femininity. Somehow, Velarde has managed to be both "traditional" and "modern" in the eyes of her audience; perhaps that accounts for the sly smile in the mural.

Velarde's adoption of modern methods does not make her different from the other women of color in this study, but her success in publicly embracing a modern image does stand out. When Bennett, for example, drew attention to her nontraditional approach to contemporary issues by entering politics, her action did not immediately affect her appeal to white audiences and only distanced her from other Navajos. Sadly, Velarde also experienced such isolation in her private life. But as a public figure, she continued her career to the historical point at which discarding some aspects of traditionalism became a viable, if not necessary, means of self-presentation. Her story shows the continuing usefulness that adopting a traditionalist persona has had for women of color pursuing public careers; it also shows a gradual unraveling of this strategy's effectiveness.

Velarde has been the subject of countless magazine and newspaper articles, mostly in New Mexican periodicals, several video documentaries, and two short books.[1] She has also given numerous interviews, with both journalists and oral historians. These extensive sources show increasing reluctance on the part of both Velarde and the media to present her as a "traditional" Santa Clara woman. Instead, later sources focus on her independence and "spunk."

Interestingly, Velarde has developed this unconventional image despite her continuing use of a traditionalist painting style. Even the one book she has written maintains such a focus on tradition. *Old Father Story Teller* is a collection of stories she remembered from growing up at Santa Clara, first published in 1960, and reprinted without any textual alterations in 1989, despite the interim changes in her life and career.[2] The lives and writings of all the women in this study invite questions about why they wrote what they wrote: Velarde's career choices, in particular, prompt inquiry into why a woman whose life and cultural climate changed so dramatically, and whose audience began to appreciate her nontraditional approach to womanhood, nevertheless stuck to very traditional forms of art and writing. One possible explanation rests in comparing Velarde's career to that of her daughter, the painter Helen Hardin, who spoke often of her desire to eschew the label of Indian artist but nevertheless made her ethnicity a key feature of her work. "Indianness" lives on in New Mexico as a powerful component of its rhetoric of seamless multiculturalism. Thus, it serves as a powerful springboard for creating—and selling— art, even though Indian artists' relationships to tradition are often more complicated than they appear in such work.

Velarde's life story demonstrates such complexity, but her paintings maintain a strict focus on conventional ideas of heritage. When I met her, an animated woman in her eighties, she told me that she sees her writing and painting as part of a larger effort to tell stories, thus leaving something behind for people to remember her and where she came from. Sitting on her couch below *Old Father Story Teller*, the painting that led her to write down stories she had heard as a young girl, Velarde offered commentary that fulfilled her renegade image, but she also explained the writing and painting methods that make her a preservationist.[3] In fact, since I set out to research her story before those of the other women in this book, her graceful embodiment of this supposed contradiction between tradition and modernity led me to see how much it had also affected the lives of the other women, who were not able to express it as openly as Velarde.

In particular, the story of her life directly contradicts the philosophy of Indian cultural traditions articulated by Austin and Luhan: that American Indians must either maintain traditions absolutely or lose them absolutely. While Velarde benefited from an education at a federally run boarding school that valued Indian traditionalism, she also drew personal strength from her experiences in the non-Pueblo world. In fact, she needed non-Pueblo skills to pursue the "traditional" craft of Pueblo painting that she learned at school, because pursuing painting as a career ultimately set her at odds with Pueblo gender roles. The paintings she produced (and continues to produce), the book she wrote, and the awards she has won all attest to her success in her chosen profession. They also reveal that she did not merely waffle between Santa

Clara and the "modern world" during her quest to become who she is today. Rather, her life offers an individual testament to the conclusions that Elsie Clews Parsons drew regarding Pueblo culture in general: Velarde has set her own life course, supplementing her cultural roots with "borrowed" traditions as needed.

Like the other women in this study, the story of what she chose to write about her life and of changes in how she and others publicly discussed her life choices reveals that her homesickness included not only a longing for improved cultural relations but also a nagging discomfort with existing ideas about traditional womanhood. Unlike the others, Velarde found an audience for expressing such criticism. Thus, the story of her homesickness serves as the closing of one chapter in the story of how New Mexican women experienced multiculturalism and the opening of another.

Beyond Biculturalism

Like Kay Bennett, Velarde was born into an insular Indian community that remained distinct from Hispanic and Anglo New Mexican communities both by choice and by official designation. Santa Clara Pueblo, where Velarde was born in 1918, was only about twenty-five miles north of Santa Fe and quite near the town of Española. Yet Velarde, the child of two people who had lived in New Mexico all their lives, Herman and Marianita Velarde, was not born an American citizen: American Indians did not hold citizenship rights. The U.S. government granted citizenship to Indian veterans who had been honorably discharged after World War I in 1919, but it was not until 1924 that the government granted this title to all American Indians. Furthermore, in New Mexico, the right of American Indians to vote was not clearly established until 1948, when a court case settled the matter once and for all.[4]

Four days after Velarde's birth, according to Santa Clara customs, her grandmother, Qualapita Velarde, named her Tse Tsan, or Golden Dawn. For the first five years of her life, Pueblo customs secured Velarde's identity: she did not, until that time, leave the immediate vicinity of Santa Clara. But in 1924 (the same year she and other American Indians became citizens), her father, a farmer, decided to send his daughters to school in Santa Fe. Their mother had died, after suffering from tuberculosis, and he felt unable to raise them on his own. Because he himself had received some education outside the Pueblo that proved to be useful in his work, he believed his daughters would also benefit from more contact with the world outside Santa Clara.

In a sense, when she went off to St. Catherine's, a Catholic school for Indians in Santa Fe, in 1924, Tse Tsan became Pablita— the name given to her during the Catholic baptism she had been given as a baby—for the first time. This was her first full entry into a world where her "Indian" identity made her "different." At St. Catherine's, in Velarde's words, she experienced "fear for the first time," no doubt in part because she could not speak English and the nuns would not allow her to speak Tewa.[5] This deep sense of homesickness was compounded by the fact that she "was always hungry." "I prayed in Tewa...because God did not care what language I spoke," Velarde has recalled, though the nuns soon taught her to pray in English. (Velarde asserts that she still prays "every day in both languages."[6]) Despite the presence of her sisters and her increasing affection for the nuns, Velarde did run away from St. Catherine's once, when she was eight years old. While the friend she ran away with was allowed to stay home, Velarde's father was "furious," telling her that she had a responsibility "to study hard and learn." Velarde never ran away again.[7]

Most biographical accounts of her life describe it from this point forward as divided. During the winters, she was in school in Santa Fe, speaking in English as children in Indian school were ordered to do (except for certain hushed conversations in Tewa with her sisters and other Pueblo students who spoke this language). She learned academic skills such as reading and math and took the classes in sewing and cooking that were intended to help her and other young American Indian women grow up to be better housewives. During the summers, on the other hand, she went back to her father's home, helping him on his farm in the mountains, watching her female relatives make pottery, and participating in ceremonials. This divided youth, chroniclers of Velarde's life thus far have implied, laid the groundwork for later conflicts in her life between the "white man's" world and the world of the Pueblo. But it also supposedly gave her a special calling: she painted in order to share the Pueblo world with the Anglo one.

This interpretation tends to overemphasize supposed divisions in Velarde's life at the expense of understanding what it was that held it together. True, she was forced to learn at a young age that there were "white ways" she had to follow while at school and "Pueblo ways" to remember when at home. But she also discovered at a young age that she was fully capable of doing both and that both made her who she was in the first place. Her father, who insisted that his daughters attend school, was also "proud of his girls at the dances" that took place during Santa Clara ceremonials.[8] Rather than being a "woman in the margins," Velarde learned to be a woman who *crossed* margins. She is hardly alone among American Indians in U.S. history in her ability to do this. For Velarde and others, becoming U.S. citizens in 1924 was long-overdue recognition of their ability to participate simultaneously in more than one culture.

As in Bennett's case, Velarde's family's decision to send her away to school reflected their belief that biculturalism was a necessary and valuable skill for American Indians in the twentieth century. This philosophy has often come under fire, not only from Indians who faulted these schools for removing children from their homes and failing to grant them a sense of pride in their origins, but from Anglos who saw this education as a drastic blow to Indian traditions. While accurate, these attitudes also lead to the false impression that "true" Indian culture is either lost or hopelessly doomed. In the late 1960s,

"No Woman Ever Built a House"

Dakota activist Vine Deloria, who led the National Congress of American Indians from 1964 to 1967, emerged as a vehement spokesperson on this issue. In his self-described "Indian Manifesto" of 1969, *Custer Died for Your Sins*, Deloria critiqued Anglo attitudes and policies toward Native Americans, targeting, among other people, anthropologists who indirectly perpetuated the belief that schools had "ruined" Indian cultures. Deloria characterized the content of fieldwork among Native American tribes as a continuous replay of the same message. "Indians are a folk people, whites are an urban people, and never the twain shall meet. Derived from this basic premise," he continued, "have been such sterling insights as Indians are between two cultures, Indians are bicultural, Indians have lost their identity, and Indians are warriors." The results of this message, Deloria astutely observed, could be perceived as nothing but "excuses for Indian failures."[9]

In fact, a series of reforms in U.S. Indian policy that took place during Velarde's school years made it possible for her to develop a professional image that evades simple notions of biculturalism and its supposed disastrous consequences. After graduating from St. Catherine's Catholic School in 1929, upon finishing sixth grade, she went on to the Santa Fe Indian School, an institution run by the Bureau of Indian Affairs. Her education there was to be directly shaped by attempts to reconsider the purpose and strategies of Indian education. In 1926, urged on by radical Indian reformers like John Collier, the secretary of the interior, Hubert Work, asked the Institute for Government Research to perform an intense investigation of the Bureau of Indian Affairs. This request resulted in the publication of an eight-hundred-plus-page report, *The Problem of Indian Administration*, in 1928. This document, referred to as the Meriam Report because the project's director was Lewis Meriam, recommended a number of changes in Indian policy, including the suggestion that schools should not require complete assimilation. "The most fundamental need in Indian education is a change in point of view," stated the Meriam Report's opening sentence in its chapter on education.

"The Indian educational enterprise," the report argued, needed an approach that was "less concerned with a conventional school system and more with the understanding of human beings."[10] In addition to practical suggestions such as higher training and salary standards for teachers and the abandonment of boarding-school environments for young children, the report also made some observations regarding specialized curricula. "The possibilities of Indian arts," it posited, "would make a book in themselves."[11]

The report is particularly optimistic about the opportunities craft education might make available to young women like Velarde. More than training them to be housewives, the report suggested, schools should be teaching women about "the development of skill in the spending of money, and of the practice and understanding of the principles of thrift."[12] On the basis of the assumption that Indian cultures and Indian women in particular "show a great fondness and aptitude for handicrafts," the report posited that Indian schools should also teach women how to earn money, by making and marketing traditional crafts.[13] Moreover, idealistic reformers viewed such paternalistic efforts as a "wholesome thing in inter-racial relations": "It is good for both Indians and whites," the reasoning went, "to realize that Indians have a distinctive contribution to make to the world."[14]

In the late 1920s and early 1930s, some simultaneous trends made implementing such reforms in federally run Indian schools like the one Velarde attended a distinct possibility. First, activists like Austin and Luhan had undertaken a public relations campaign to convince Americans that possibilities for national resurgence lay untapped in the depths of native arts and cultures. Such awareness culminated in the groundbreaking Exhibition of Indian Tribal Arts at the Grand Central Galleries in New York in 1931. Dorothy Dunn, an Indian art researcher and promoter who was to play a crucial role in Velarde's career, described this exhibition as the first full national recognition of the Indian "as a full-statured artist."[15] Painter John Sloan presided over the exhibition, and notables such as Eleanor Roosevelt lent it further aesthetic respectability.[16] While anthropologist

Molly Mullin has written that this exposition "celebrated a rather narrowly defined version of cultural pluralism, particularly as expressed through commodities validated as art," its popularity reflected an undeniable opportunity for the school programs in which emerging artists like Velarde got their start.[17]

Along with this slow change in aesthetic values, the development of a new political climate allowed reforms in Indian policy and education to take place. Not long after Eleanor Roosevelt took part in the Exhibition of Indian Tribal Arts, her husband took the controversial step of appointing reform-minded John Collier as commissioner of Indian affairs. In 1933, prompted by the economic devastation of the Depression, Collier began to expand Roosevelt's "New Deal" to American Indians. While Bennett's story reflects the negative reaction that Collier's policies ultimately prompted among Navajos, they found wide acceptance among the Pueblo tribes, perhaps in part because of their closer affiliation with Anglo reformers through connections like those made by Luhan and Austin.[18]

Central to Collier's policies were the sort of ideas articulated in the Meriam Report: that cultural preservation was worthwhile and that schoolchildren like Velarde, as well as adults, should be encouraged in their efforts to be "traditional." But the legacy of previous approaches to Indian policy seriously hampered such efforts, because they meant that Collier could not simply start from scratch. Before his tenure, an emphasis on removal and extinction clearly dominated the government's approach toward working with American Indians, despite notable cries to the contrary not only by American Indians but also by Anglo activists, such as the anti-Bursum Bill efforts Austin and Luhan orchestrated in the early 1920s. Even after Collier's time as commissioner, as illustrated by the sharp shifts in educational strategies Bennett experienced, twentieth-century U.S. Indian policy has continued to waver between the two false poles that Deloria articulated in his attack on anthropological theories: it has either attempted to "assimilate" American Indians so they fit the mold of Anglo culture, or encouraged American Indians to preserve traditional ways, lest they die out and America lose all vestiges of the "noble savages" that once populated the country.[19]

While the theory of preservation of "pure" American Indian cultures advocated by Collier is very appealing from a multicultural perspective, policy makers and American Indians like Velarde were to learn that preservation of tradition could not take place in a vacuum. American Indian boarding schools could teach students how to produce traditional crafts. But in order to allow such crafts to survive, schools also had to teach students how to market them to an outside population—not just through business practices, but through fulfilling what the Anglo market expected "Indian crafts" to look like. Ultimately preservation of tribal cultures meant adaptation to the larger Anglo culture that surrounded them.

Just as assimilationists failed when they expected that forcing Indian children to speak English at federally sponsored boarding schools would lead them to stop speaking their native language when they went home, preservationists like Collier failed when they assumed arts alone would allow Indian culture to sustain itself. Business skills, the very tools of accommodation that Herman Velarde sent his daughters to school to receive, would also be necessary. In New Mexico, where an interest in native crafts exploded simultaneously with an increase in the Anglo population, the need for such skills became especially pressing. At the same time, New Mexican activists like Austin and Luhan discouraged nontraditionalist curricula because they believed tribes in the area were modernizing too quickly and that all tradition would be lost.

"Native Art as Art"

Velarde's time at the Santa Fe Indian School (1929–1936) demonstrated both the strengths and limitations of the preservationists' ideals. The institution became a key site of implementation for

Collier's education reforms, and Velarde arrived at the time of their initiation. Extensive reforms altered the campus during Velarde's time as a student. Administrators abolished the English-only policy of the school, commissioned Indian murals for school walls, offered lessons on tribal traditions, and hired more American Indian staff. Perhaps most notably, they also encouraged students to strengthen their ties to their tribal culture by performing dances for one another at school.[20] Clearly, this approach differed from the warnings against dances and urgings of Christianity experienced by Bennett, who ended her boarding-school education in 1935. The proximity of the artist colonies at Santa Fe and Taos undoubtedly influenced the quicker implementation of reforms at Velarde's school.

The most important reform to affect Velarde's education was certainly the opening of Dorothy Dunn's painting studio at the Santa Fe Indian School in 1932, not long after Velarde started attending. Dunn, who had spent time as a teacher at both Santo Domingo Pueblo and a Navajo boarding school in Shiprock, had just finished an art education degree at the Art Institute of Chicago. When she heard the Santa Fe Indian School planned to implement an arts and crafts curriculum, she jumped at the chance to get involved. She asked the superintendent of the school, Chester Faris, to allow her to begin a painting class in which she would emphasize traditional Indian subject matter and style, as well as the use of traditional pigments. Faris allowed the idealistic Dunn to undertake the project.[21]

While Velarde has only spoken positively of her time as Dunn's student, others have debated the authenticity of Dunn's attempt to lead American Indian children in traditional painting. Dunn maintained her goal was not so much to teach but "to create a guidance technique which would provide motivation, clarification, and development for each individual student's painting processes."[22] As art historian Bruce Bernstein has described, Dunn saw her role as "reveal[ing] to her students their own intrinsic knowledge and understanding of this indigenous art form."[23] Despite this generally essentialist approach, Dunn also wanted to allow for variation among her students' work because of tribal affiliations and individual interests. She believed she could establish continuity between the students' styles and motifs traditionally used to decorate Indian artifacts, which she had researched extensively in Chicago and Santa Fe museum collections.[24] She also found that art audiences in New Mexico were newly interested in such motifs, due to the recent discovery of the prehistoric Kuaua Murals (at the Coronado State Monument) and the revival of such symbolism among self-taught painters like Tonita Peña of San Ildefonso Pueblo.

Convincing students like Velarde to use such painting techniques and motifs took determination. Because, as Dunn put it, "it had not occurred to most students to think of their native art as *art*," she saw overcoming this reluctance as the most challenging aspect of her work. By her account, her students wanted to draw images they had seen in magazines, along the lines of what she referred to as "'Indian Heads' and 'noble Redman' scenes," not depictions of what they had seen at home.[25] An American Indian aesthetic tradition "was a concept which would have to be acquired gradually—absorbed in the course of fully appreciating, first of all, Indian art itself as art, and then as an art that extends beyond the bounds of Indian culture into the whole culture, which belongs to everyone for the knowing."[26] Dunn saw her mission as helping American Indians to recapture an aesthetic tradition that could ultimately benefit all Americans.

Some later critics found Dunn's motivations to be problematic, even patronizing. They questioned the sort of easel painting encouraged by Dunn, and taken up by Velarde, as a "traditional" native art form and charged that Dunn and other advocates of the "native" style encouraged a visual tradition that was based mostly on Anglo ideas of what "Indian" art should look like. In his study of the genre, *Indian Painters and White Patrons*, J. J. Brody argued that "representational painting for decorative, historical, or expressive purposes was rarely if ever a goal of any Southwestern painter" before contact with European civilizations.[27] Dunn stated that one of her objectives was to help her students "maintain individual and tribal distinction" in their paintings; Brody countered that this is an impossible venture, for to be individual is not to be tribal.[28] Moreover, even those who have praised Dunn's work, such as Bruce Bernstein, have noted that, despite Dunn's boosting of free expression, she "dictated the style her students were to use," thus stifling creativity. "She was teaching them, even if indirectly," writes art historian W. Jackson Rushing, "to meet certain expectations she held about Native painting."[29] Brody argues that it was only in the 1960s that Indian painters moved beyond "meek acceptance" of the Anglo medium of easel painting and produced an art that was truly the work of "Indian painters."[30]

Perhaps it is best to resolve the differing interpretations of the work undertaken by Dunn's studio at the Santa Fe Indian School by considering it as a forum of negotiation. Dunn offered students like Velarde a space in which they could use an Anglo cultural form, easel painting, to express an Indian sensibility. Dunn taught techniques at the studio, such as the use of abstraction and earth pigment paints, that established further connections between Indian life and modern painting. In fact, young people flocked to her studio, and Dunn's popularity proved to make her job more difficult. She resigned from Santa Fe Indian School in 1937 because a resentful administration opposed her efforts to place art at the center of her students' education and refused to give her the financial support she needed to continue her work.[31]

Velarde, who describes Dunn as a wonderful mentor and friend, thrived in the studio, despite obstacles she faced as a young woman in this environment.[32] While some older female students were required to occasionally participate in the class as part of a teacher-training program, Pablita and her sister Rosita were the only girls among the forty young students who signed up for the new painting studio. Rosita eventually quit the class, leaving her sister alone. By Velarde's account, "Miss Dunn had to keep me beside her desk for protection. The boys were always teasing me and sometimes they were mean. They didn't want me in the class anyway because they didn't believe women should be artists."[33]

Velarde's mere presence as a female student in the studio challenges Dunn's assessment of the form as purely tribal. As Brody's research suggests, the painting that had been done by Pueblo peoples prior to European contact took place for either decorative or ritual purposes. While Pueblo women traditionally took charge of the production and decoration of pottery, Pueblo men were responsible for sacred paintings in the kiva. Velarde's own aunts were potters. But she actively pursued painting as a young woman, despite being teased by the boys in her class. She was not the first Pueblo woman to take up easel painting. Tonita Peña, a woman originally from San Ildefonso who later lived at Cochiti, pursued painting professionally in the 1920s, even as she raised her children. In fact, Velarde met Peña while she did some work on murals at the Santa Fe Indian School and evidently drew inspiration from watching Peña paint. "She gave me kind of an inner strength, you might call it," Velarde told me, "to do what she's doing, because she wants to do it, not because somebody is telling her to do it." Velarde came to call Peña "aunt" in Tewa, while Peña called the young woman "daughter that I have chosen."[34]

Fueled by Peña's example and by Dunn's encouragement, and, most of all, by her own desire, Velarde kept pursuing painting. As a very young child, she had endured an eye infection for nearly two years, a condition that temporarily robbed her of her sight. Velarde has attributed her delight in remembering and recording visual details to this experience. Even as a very young painter, she earned accolades for her work. New Mexican mural painter Olive Rush praised Velarde's early work in an exhibition review and asked her to contribute a painting to an exhibit that Rush was preparing for the 1933 Chicago "Century of Progress" World's Fair. Velarde undoubtedly enjoyed the work and the critical praise she received for it.

Still, her enjoyment of painting and her goals for future success in it were ultimately at odds with the mission established by the Meriam Report for the education of Indian girls. It had recommended that crafts be taught to Indian girls as a means of preserving culture and allowing women to supplement household income even as they kept up with their other duties as housewives. A report commissioned specifically on "the Indian girl" by the commissioner of Indian affairs office in 1932 elaborated further on such ideals. It proposed that Indian education could help girls to "capitalize and develop those outstanding racial traits which are [their] heritage" (it cited traits such as "loyalty," "love of children," "hospitality," and a "fine appreciation of beauty") in order to prepare them for the "demands of modern living—vocationally, spiritually, and socially."[35] Collier began to act on such ideals, which he viewed as a positive departure from previous models of education, when he took office. Clearly, his administration subscribed to the same "traditionalist" view of Indian women's responsibility for preserving heritage as Austin and Luhan. As historian Margaret Jacobs has written, "new feminist preservationists believed that promoting art production among Indian women would strengthen their roles in the home."[36]

Velarde's experiences proved otherwise, perhaps because the work she did in Dunn's studio, Dunn's assertions regarding the traditional nature of painting to the contrary, was not a traditional Indian craft. And as Velarde contemplated a career in painting, she did not plan to do as Tonita Peña had done and combine this professional career with the traditional tasks of a wife and mother. In a 1979 interview, Velarde stated that she had wanted something quite different. "Painting was not considered woman's work in my time. A woman was supposed to be just a woman, like a housewife and a mother and chief cook. Those were things I wasn't interested in."[37] Velarde's sister Rosita, who had entered Dunn's painting studio with Velarde, left the Santa Fe Indian School to get married and gave up painting, according to Velarde, when her husband insisted on it. "Her husband was superstitious and made her quit," Velarde explained in an interview. "He believed that if his wife painted during pregnancy and made a mistake, left a finger off a hand or misshaped a person, the baby would be born with these deformities."[38] His views, though extreme, did not differ altogether from those of Anglo reformers who believed Indian women should bear the burden of preserving Indian culture. While Dunn and others were eager to help Velarde pursue painting, no one had quite yet considered how she might balance the life she planned for herself with both Anglo and Pueblo expectations of traditionalism.

One Woman's Work

Accounts of Velarde's life and work often characterize her as a woman who didn't play by the rules. But which rules didn't she play by? When she referred to the "woman's work" that she "wasn't interested in," was she referring specifically to the woman's work of a traditional Pueblo woman or of the "American" Indian woman that the Santa Fe Indian School was attempting to prepare her to be?

American Indian scholars such as Paula Gunn Allen, Gretchen M. Bataille, and Kathleen Mullen Sands have cautioned women's historians against confusing the particulars of American Indian gender roles with those of European Americans. Bataille and Sands argue that "Indian women repeatedly deny their interest in, or need for, 'liberation,' saying they cannot afford the luxury of feminist goals because they must devote their energies to keeping families intact, getting jobs, and fighting the political battles of their people."[39] Allen explains the historical sources of this resistance to "liberation" by arguing that traditional American Indian cultures, though diverse, held in common a high respect for women and their work, unlike European patriarchal culture—recall that Bennett, even while taking the unprecedented step of running for elected office, could rightfully claim to be adhering to traditional ideas about Navajo women's leadership. Discriminatory conditions for American Indian women in tribal environments today, Allen argues, may be a result of harsh conflict with European-American culture: "Evidently, while Americans and people all over the globe have been led into a deep and unquestioned belief that American Indians are cruel savages, a number of American Indian men have been equally deluded into internalizing that image and acting on it."[40] Thus, this reasoning goes, what Velarde was reacting against by rejecting "woman's work" was not so much traditional American Indian roles but a European American perversion of them.

Velarde, however, felt constrained by both traditions. When she decided that she did not want to do what was "woman's work," she referred simultaneously to the standards of the Bureau of Indian Affairs for the proper education of Indian girls and to Santa Clara's ideas about ideal lives for women. Regardless of the fact that "woman's work" was taught and valued both in Velarde's Santa Clara home and at the Santa Fe Indian School, Velarde knew that what she planned was something different; she wanted to be a painter. Furthermore, she could find precedents and support for her chosen career within two cultural traditions: in the forms of both Anglo and American Indian woman artists and writers who preceded her, in feminist rhetoric circulating within Anglo culture, and through traditional esteem for women within Pueblo culture.

One fascinating aspect of her work as a painter is that it appears to negotiate between feminism and traditionalism so smoothly. For even as the act of painting allowed Velarde to break free from "woman's work," the subjects of her work often revolved around the ideas about "tradition" and "womanhood" that she had to fight against to paint in the first place. Nearly all of her paintings feature some aspect of "tradition" at the Pueblo, be it through depicting everyday events, ceremonials, or tribal stories and symbols. Velarde's earliest exhibited paintings feature women doing "woman's work"; Olive Rush praised this aspect of her style in reviews of Santa Fe Indian School art exhibitions printed in the *Santa Fe New Mexican*. "The only girl who is a full-time painting student in the school," wrote Rush, "is Pablita Velarde of Santa Clara who gives us work of great delicacy and charm—water colors, and a pleasant and rhythmic design of corn grinding."[41] In fact, the painting Rush invited Velarde to send to the Century of Progress exhibition depicted a Santa Clara girl.

Dunn probably encouraged Velarde to paint works of this sort because Velarde was familiar with feminine aspects of Pueblo life neglected by Dunn's male students. Dunn might have also suspected that as a woman painter, Velarde might have more luck in selling her work if she produced "women's" paintings.

Despite these good intentions, Velarde had a hard time establishing herself professionally during the early years of her career. While she has modestly attributed this to her "amateurish" style at the time, she has also cited two other factors.[42] First, while the general audience for Indian painting was growing all the time, it was still relatively small (and she did not want, as she later put it, to "paint an apple on a plate" rather than Pueblo-style paintings).[43] Second, she had difficulty navigating the business aspects of the art world, and, perhaps more significantly, finding other work that would sustain her until she could live by painting.

This trouble began as soon as she graduated from the Santa Fe Indian School in 1936, testifying to what Velarde has identified as a limitation of her Indian–New-Deal-inspired education. During a project to record the school's history, Velarde told an interviewer that she did not believe the school had adequately stressed how hard it would be to find work upon graduation.[44] In fact, she had actually supplemented her art education at the Santa Fe Indian School with an eighteen-month period of "business" study at Española High School, close to home. She did so at the request of her father, who did not believe she would be able to make a living as an artist—apparently, the Indian school's vehement turn away from assimilation-oriented education did not win his support. Velarde left Santa Fe and lived at Santa Clara from the fall of 1934 until the spring of 1936. While there, she took all the business classes that Española High School offered, such as typing, shorthand, and bookkeeping.[45] Then she returned to Santa Fe to complete her diploma there.[46]

Unfortunately, her father's suspicions about an artistic career initially proved to be true. Upon graduating she had trouble finding employment, or at least lucrative work that put her diploma to good use. In an interview, she listed the kinds of odd jobs that she worked during her first ten years out of school:

> I sold a few paintings, but not enough to be self-support-
> ing. I had to take other jobs. I worked as a maid for a
> lady in Pecos. She had little cabins for fishermen and I
> was to clean those. They smelled! Then I worked as a
> nursemaid. I worked in two hospitals as an attendant,
> emptying bedpans and scrubbing floors. Then I worked
> at the Santa Clara school as a part-time teacher.[47]

After two years of teaching art to small children, Velarde decided to try nursing again, but soon realized that she didn't really like the work—as she put it, "any clean-up jobs...with blood just made me sick to my stomach."[48]

Such rough work may be a crucial part of the early stages of any artist's career. But in the context of the Meriam Report's suggested strategies for the education of Indian women, and Collier's desire to allow Indians to return to the "traditional" life, Velarde's struggle takes on a special significance. Because her education in "traditional" painting did, in fact, lead her away from a "traditional life," her story illustrates the fundamental weakness of Indian–New Deal-era educational reforms. Collier, Dunn, and other reformers neglected to fully consider what the implications of this "traditional" education were for young men and women who truly lived in a changing world—and who may have wanted, like Velarde, to find work, off the reservations, that was nontribal in nature.

Since Bennett, whose education was less influenced by the Indian New Deal than Velarde's, also faced such difficulties, it's worth noting that these policymakers erred not by suggesting that Indian education embrace Indian values, but by failing to prepare Indian students for economic success in the non-Indian world in which they would often need, if not want, to make their way. Historian Brian Dippie has described such shortsightedness as the "assimilationist's error in reverse": the assumption by Collier and others that "inside every Indian, no matter how assimilated, there lurked a Pueblo waiting to be freed, a communal being eager to shuck off the trappings of individualistic, materialistic white civilization in order to recapture a long-lost communal past."[49] While Velarde clearly wanted to paint the Pueblo "communal past" and prevent it from being "long-lost," she also wanted to do so in a way that was decidedly nontraditional, especially for a woman.

This contradiction made it difficult for her to establish herself as a painter, but it ultimately became the key ingredient for her professional success. Velarde did ultimately, though sporadically, find employment that enabled her to paint for a living. People who felt strongly about the "traditional" content of her paintings sponsored her in her nontraditional endeavor. Ernest Thompson Seton, a naturalist, writer and artist who helped found the Boy Scouts of America, invited Velarde to accompany his family on a lecture tour of the eastern United States about a year and a half after she graduated from high school, in the late 1930s. She worked as the Setons' nanny, but in retrospect, she considered the work a great trade: it was her first trip outside New Mexico. As Velarde shared with one interviewer, the journey exposed her to discrimination as well as to broader horizons: "The waiter in a hotel in Ohio thought I was black and refused to feed me. Mr. Thompson [Seton] raised plenty of ruckus with the hotel manager."[50]

Mentorship also made it possible for her to overcome barriers in the art world. Soon after she returned to New Mexico, Olive Rush invited her to participate in a Federal Arts Project commission to create murals for Maisel's Indian Trading Post, a building on Highway 66 in downtown Albuquerque. Not long after that, in 1939, Bandelier National Monument supervisor Dale Stuart King asked Velarde to paint a series of mural-style paintings that depicted traditional Pueblo life in the park's museum.[51]

fig. 15: Pablita Velarde, *Life Inside a Pueblo Home*, 1939–40. Courtesy of Pablita Velarde and Bandelier National Monument, National Park Service, Catalog No. 14020.

King wanted the Bandelier paintings to show monument visitors the cultural activities of the descendants of the "Cliff Dwellers," the ancient people who once lived in homes whose ruins later served as the centerpiece of the park. For this project, Velarde explicitly took on the role of cultural researcher and interpreter, a task she had performed in her earlier paintings but not as extensively. The murals she began at Bandelier opened her eyes to the possibilities of an artistic career shaped not just by aesthetic goals but by the purpose of educating non-Pueblo audiences about this culture. With the onset of World War II, however, the government cut the funding for the project, and Velarde found herself looking for work once again.

She moved back to Santa Clara, which was not necessarily a comfortable place for her to be. By this time, her father had remarried, and his new wife and his daughters from his previous marriage did not get along well. Her sisters had all married, and Velarde, now in her early twenties, found herself shuffled from relative to relative. With the money she had earned at Bandelier, she began to build a house of her own on a piece of land her father had given her. "I wanted my own peaceful home where I could create a studio," she has said, but her desire to have such a home was unusual; by her account, she was "the first woman to build and own her own home" at Santa Clara.[52] When I asked her about the building, she told me about hiring "people to make . . . adobe bricks, to cut . . . vigas, and to build up walls." Being able to do so, she explained bluntly, made her stand out: "Women didn't have money. Women didn't have jobs. All they had were a bunch of kids, one after another."[53] To another interviewer, Velarde revealed that this activity made her Santa Clara neighbors think of her as a "nut": "I built my own house when I was a very single girl in the pueblo," she explained. "No woman ever built a house. That was man's work."[54] She told me the only usual way a woman could have a house on her own in Santa Clara was if her husband left her for another woman.[55]

While other Pueblos have different customs of home ownership, and women take part in adobe maintenance in many New Mexican communities, the findings of W. W. Hill, an ethnographer who worked in Santa Clara Pueblo during the 1940s, support Velarde's observations. In Santa Clara, "houses were predominantly owned by males," he wrote. "A father usually built a house for his son at the time of the son's marriage, or he established the son in a unit of his own home."[56] Velarde disregarded this custom, worked on building her house, and continued trying to paint. Unfortunately, the best paying job she could find during this time (1941) was painting decorations on drums in a trader's shop in Española.

Marriage and Homemaking

When it was offered to her later that year, Velarde took a job as a telephone operator at the Bureau of Indian Affairs office in Albuquerque. During this stint as an "office girl," she met Herbert

Hardin, a young Anglo man working as a security guard in the building. According to Jay Scott, a biographer of Velarde's daughter Helen, Hardin was attracted to Velarde because of her easy-going personality, compatible to his own.[57] Whether he initially wanted to support her artistic career is unclear—Velarde told me in retrospect that he had little interest in her world of painting, just as she had little interest in his later work as a policeman.[58] But when they first met, Velarde apparently appreciated both Hardin's personality and his desire to go to college and become a lawyer.

Before the couple's wedding (a Catholic ceremony in Santa Fe, in February 1942), Velarde told her family she was getting married, but that they didn't need to come. Hardin took a less cautious approach—after the wedding he drove Velarde to his parents' house in Albuquerque and introduced her as his wife. Though they later came to support Velarde, they were initially surprised to have a daughter-in-law at all, much less an Indian daughter-in-law; Velarde clearly views this introduction to Hardin's parents as a painful memory.[59] Additionally, she has commented that her own family was "unhappy that I had married a non-Indian."[60] It is not surprising that Velarde and Hardin faced familial resistance: while New Mexicans of this era supported cultural coexistence to a certain point, marriage disrupted carefully drawn boundaries between ethnic groups.

Their marriage was ultimately tested less by ethnic difference, however, than by differing views of family responsibilities. In the early years of their marriage, they moved several times to accommodate Hardin and this, as well as the arrival of children, proved to be stressful for Velarde, who wanted to continue her painting career. These moves began just a few months after their marriage, when Hardin was drafted. The family traveled to Texas, Pennsylvania, and California (with several stays back in New Mexico in between) in order to accommodate his military obligations and then his G.I. Bill–sponsored education. Amidst these transitions, Velarde gave birth to a daughter (Helen, born in 1943) and a son (Herbert, Jr., born in 1944).

⚑ CHAPTER FIVE ⚑

Velarde did not stop painting, and she did not give up her ties to Santa Clara. Like Bennett, she found that her travels did not change her sense of home. When she began to suffer from asthma in California, she brought her children back to Santa Clara for a period. At this time, with the war over and more funding available, she was able to complete her commission at Bandelier National Monument. Her husband returned to Albuquerque in 1947, and, having switched his career goals from law to police work, he took a job with the police department there. They bought the house in Albuquerque where Velarde still lives today.

She later credited the resumption of the Park Service commission with giving her "the nerve" to keep painting.[61] In 1948, when she was thirty years old, she won her first important prize, one given at the annual Indian art show at the Philbrook Art Center in Tulsa, Oklahoma. In 1954, the French government awarded Dunn, Velarde, and other graduates of the Santa Fe Indian School Studio with the Palmes d'Académiques award, given in honor of artistic excellence. Velarde continued through this decade to win prizes at regional shows and museums.

The same woman who had, against the community's better judgment, built a home for herself at Santa Clara Pueblo, now painted in the kitchen of her Albuquerque home, amidst housekeeping responsibilities: she had no studio, no "room of her own." Despite these surroundings, she hardly became the kind of self-effacing housewife that Betty Friedan sought to awaken with the publication of *The Feminine Mystique* in 1963. She confessed in a later interview that while she enjoyed spending time with her grandchildren, she had not altogether enjoyed being a mother: "It's a lot of hard work," she explained, "and it takes too much time." What made the work more difficult was that she found that if she didn't paint, she got "bored." Her days became efforts to get back into her studio: "I would get up in the morning and as soon as I fed the kids and took them to school, I'd get in here [the studio] and I'd work. Then, at 3:00, I'd go pick them up and get them home, and come back in and work again."[62]

In a feature published during the early 1960s, her teenaged son
Herbert, Jr., testified to his mother's unconventionality. When the
interviewers arrived on a Saturday to speak with Velarde, Herbert told
them that his mother was at the laundromat on the corner. "I had better go sit with the laundry and let her come talk with you," he reportedly offered. "She should be almost finished now, but she might go
someplace else before coming home. Mother is unpredictable."[63]
Velarde found her children and husband alike annoyed when paintings
she was working on took over their home and driveway, but she kept
right on painting nevertheless. In a more recent interview, she joked
that "my children, in self defense, learned how to cook so they didn't
have to wait for Mama to stop painting."[64]

In the 1950s, it took a husband of unusual flexibility to support his
wife's clear preference for painting over childcare, her success at
prizewinning rather than at housework. Hardin and Velarde's marriage
did not make it through this decade. While the exact cause of their
breakup is unclear, it is certain that he resented her work and decided to
leave.[65] By 1958, when she was forty, they had separated, and in 1959
their divorce became final. The end of her marriage to Hardin prompted Velarde to pursue two goals: to secure consistent support for her
paintings and to attempt to return to her roots at Santa Clara Pueblo.

Returning Home

Velarde accomplished success in her professional career with the help
of Margarete and Fred Chase from the Enchanted Mesa Gallery in
Albuquerque. In 1956, Enchanted Mesa had begun to exhibit all of
Velarde's work, and the sales of her paintings eventually increased.
Meanwhile, her project of getting back in touch with Santa Clara
had begun auspiciously a few years before, when she started visiting
the Pueblo to listen to her father retell the stories she had heard from
him as a young girl. She has explained her motives for recording

these stories as an evolving awareness of the need for someone to get them down on paper. Initially, she just wanted to preserve the stories for her children, who had had a hard time learning them outside the context of the Pueblo. "My kids used to laugh at me when I was trying to tell them the story," Velarde explained in an interview. "They couldn't picture it in their heads...so I painted the picture first and then I read them the story the way I had written it by that time—and then they understood...before they saw the picture, they didn't even know what you were talking about."[66]

One of the pictures Velarde initially painted for her children, *Old Father Story Teller*, won immediate critical recognition, including the grand prize at the 1955 Inter-Tribal Ceremonial in Gallup, the same event in which Kay Bennett actively participated. This painting's success led her to consider publishing her stories, complete with illustrations, for a larger audience. "I decided to write all those old stories into a book," she has said, "so that every Indian child and children of every race could forever have these Indian stories."[67]

Renewed contact with a former supporter further encouraged her in this project. During a 1956 Christmas vacation with her children, Velarde got a flat tire in Globe, Arizona, and called the only person she knew in town: Dale Stuart King, the man who had commissioned her for the murals at Bandelier. Retired from the Park Service, King was now interested in publishing books and had started a small regional press. When he heard about Velarde's manuscript idea, he offered to publish it. Velarde completed *Old Father Story Teller*, which consisted of six stories accompanied by painted illustrations, and it was published in 1960. According to historian Sally Hyer, Velarde thus became the first Pueblo woman to publish a book.[68] A regional audience eager for American Indian art and stories received the book warmly, and one association of printers and booksellers, the Rounce and Coffin Club of Los Angeles, selected the book for its annual Western Books exhibit.

But some residents of the Pueblo did not approve of Velarde's publication of the stories and traditions of Santa Clara. Even her

Fig. 26: Pablita Velarde with Her Father, Herman Velarde, April 1958.
Photograph by Emmett P. Haddon. Courtesy of the Museum of New Mexico,
Neg. No. 151997.

father, whose stories formed the heart of the book, had initially expressed reservations about the project. "My father helped me reluctantly because he believed that telling a story was better than writing it," Velarde has explained.[69] In addition to his caution about disclosing sacred stories, he feared writing them would diminish their power to live on—after all, they had lasted for generations through oral storytelling alone. Eventually, in her words, she "convinced him that this was the only way to preserve our culture. After that he became interested and often sent for me to come back to Santa Clara to hear more stories." Even then, Velarde described, he might ask her to wait with him in silence before he spoke:

> sometimes we would sit there for hours, perhaps all day, not saying anything, for that was the way the Indians were. It was a way of being respectful to the Ancient Ones, to the past and to the gods. Time meant nothing. When I would get impatient for him to talk, he would say: "You talk too much. The fruit tree has too much fruit. The tree limbs break and fall to the ground. Be still and listen to what is inside you." Other times he would be moved to talk. The fruit tree would be bowed down with fruit, and I would take home many of Old Father's stories.[70]

Velarde eventually decided to leave out some of what she and her father discussed, because of his wishes and out of respect for the Santa Clara community.

Her father was, in the end, pleased with the project. Velarde described his reaction to seeing the published book as a happy moment for both him and her: "I could tell by his expression that he was connecting the story with the pictures...I knew he was getting kind of a thrill out of knowing that he had something to do with a book. And when he finished, he said, 'Isn't it nice that we did it?' He put 'we' in there!"[71] Through the creation of the book, Velarde was able both to renew her relationship with her father and to provide what she saw as a service to Santa Clara, preservation of its old stories.

The book features six such stories, all told to a group of children by a character named Old Father. On special occasions, such as the Buffalo and Deer Dance, or on long winter nights, Old Father shares his stories with these listeners. "The Stars," "Sad Eyes," and "First Twins" explain fundamental beliefs of Santa Clara culture: they tell, respectively, how the people arrived in Santa Clara, how the deer dance ceremonial started, and how the first Koshares (Pueblo intermediaries between everyday life and supernatural life) came to be. The other three stories, "Enchanted Hunter," "Turkey Girl," and "Butterfly Boy," teach lessons through recounting individual events.

Velarde's children and grandchildren formed the original intended audience for the stories, but publication meant that other children, and adults, read them as well. At moments in the text, this intended larger audience clearly seems to be a non-Indian one. When the narrator lists the constellations by their Tewa names but with European names following in parentheses, or when she steps back from Old Father's story to explain basic elements of Santa Clara ceremonials such as the Koshares, she addresses readers who may have never been to Santa Clara or any of the Pueblos. Unlike an anthropologist who might use the stories to explain aspects of Santa Clara culture, or a historian who might analyze how they depict the events involved, the storyteller of this book leaves the stories as stories. Like Jaramillo, Cabeza de Baca, and Bennett, Velarde invites readers to immerse themselves in her culture.

Unlike books by the other authors, however, *Old Father Story Teller* does not represent an effort in intentional autobiography. Rather, Velarde seeks only cultural preservation. Still, the publisher capitalized on the opportunity to highlight the book's "authenticity" by emphasizing the author's distinct identity. The book includes an introduction, "About Pablita and Her Legends," as well as a foreword written by Velarde. The introduction quotes Velarde as commenting that she "thought it would be a good thing if an Indian wrote an Indian book" and praises her success in being "self-reliant in the complex task of bridging two cultures."[72] In the foreword, Velarde introduced herself as both witness and interpreter:

> Indian legends are not always easy to understand, for small details are very likely to carry much meaning. For the non-Indian reader, I have tried to simplify and explain things more than *Old Father* did for his listeners.
>
> I was one of the fortunate children of my generation who were probably the last to hear stories from Great-grandfather or Grandfather. I treasure that memory, and I have tried to preserve it in this book so that my children as well as other people may have a glimpse of what used to be.[73]

Velarde's emerging fame as a painter guaranteed people would be interested in this book not just because of the stories and the illustrations but also because of her particular identity. Thus, the book became autobiographical in a personal as well as a communal sense, because its bicultural format mirrored Velarde's life and because it was consistently promoted and received as "an Indian book" written by a particularly famous Indian, based on her true-life experiences.

Old Father thus precariously balances a content based on Santa Clara folklore with a book format (and an audience) from beyond Santa Clara. Like the author's personal negotiation of the contexts of Pueblo childhood, "American Indian" schooling, and an American wifehood, motherhood, and painting career, the book pulls from more than one tradition in its efforts to carry its stories. *Old Father* does not tell readers everything they may want to know about Velarde's life, but by drawing the content and the narrative of those stories from more than one cultural tradition, it shows them how Velarde's life works.

One of the most striking stories in the collection, "Turkey Girl," serves as a metaphorical reflection of Velarde's difficult experiences in leaving the Pueblo and writing the book. She opens the story, which is placed midway through the collection, with a young girl making a story request that the independently minded Velarde might have made as a child: "Old Father, are there any little girls in the mountains?"[74] Old Father responds with the story of Turkey Girl. She is a Cinderella-type figure, abused by her stepmother and unable to attend a ceremonial because she has nothing to wear. The flock of turkeys she cares for takes pity on her and magically prepares her for the celebration. The story that follows is a familiar one:

> When she got to Puye the ceremonial dancing had begun,
> and after watching for a while she realized that everyone
> was staring in her direction. She did not understand that
> it was her beauty they were admiring. Even her foster
> mother was gaping, without recognizing her.
>   Soon all the young men and even some of the older
> ones were asking her name and where she was from.[75]

When her jealous stepmother accuses her of being a witch, a fight erupts, and Turkey Girl flees into the mountains. She escapes, but is forever exiled from her people.

Velarde's resemblance to Turkey Girl only increased with time. She had encountered resistance at Santa Clara when she set out to publish *Old Father*; sadly, when she attempted to collect and publish more stories, she experienced even greater frustration. In the 1960s, she moved back to Santa Clara for a time in order to pursue a more extensive ethnographic project. In an interview conducted before this move, Velarde, now in her forties, revealed that she had optimistically settled on this return as a means of fulfillment. "When my children are through school and settled in their own homes, I am going back to Santa Clara to live. There I will have much time to paint and to write for and about my people.... There is a great satisfaction in all of this, now that I know what I want to do with my life."[76]

But Velarde found that it was quite difficult to go home again. "I thought that home was still home," she told me, "and so I went out there, I bought a house, and I lived there two years, but in those two years I felt like an outsider." She began her work, only to experience what she later described as an antipathy not only to her project, but also to her identity. When I asked if she tried to ask the council for permission to pursue the work, her answer revealed that, in her mind, the opposition to her project revolved around her sex:

> No, I just did it, without asking. That was my problem,
> I guess. I didn't ask the council.... And I keep telling the
> women up there, you have power here, you have
> strength to demand, but you don't do it. You just sit
> back and let the men walk all over you. I guess they
> think I'm a man hater, and maybe I am, because I don't
> agree with every man that talks to me, I always find
> something to say no to.

And when I asked her if anyone had supported the idea of her project, she again blamed the opposition on sexism: "Well, if it's a man doing it [ethnographic work], it's all right, but if it's a woman doing it, then it's not all right. Especially a woman like me who lives away from the pueblo, and who writes books, and who paints pictures, and who's talking."[77]

One historian, Sally Hyer, attributes the resistance that Velarde faced upon her 1960s return to Santa Clara to her break with certain community values. Velarde had chosen as her life's work the task of painting for secular purposes, which was not only at odds with the preconquest Pueblo views on what painting was for, but also at odds with expectations for women at Santa Clara. Furthermore, despite her hope to use her work for broader cultural purposes, Velarde's career goals and lifestyle were individualistic in comparison to the more community-oriented Pueblo. By living alone, she lived differently from most other people at Santa Clara. By painting, she increased the gap between herself and her ancestral community. And finally, trying to initiate an ethnographic project "brought accusations that she was exploiting the culture for her own benefit," rather than allowing it to "remain dynamic and alive" through oral tradition alone.[78] In the eyes of some, the project just went too far.

If she had been a man, Velarde contends, they might have let her do it. But even then, she might have faced resistance. The recording of ethnographic information promised the benefit of preservation, but it risked the betrayal of sacred cultural knowledge to people who might not treat it with the respect it deserved. It also risked reducing Pueblo culture to a static set of traits listed on paper, rather than the dynamic set of relationships, constantly evolving and strengthening, described by Elsie Clews Parsons in her theory of cultural borrowing. As Hyer astutely concludes, "both [Velarde's] education and her marriage had removed her from Pueblo life while giving her the opportunity—and financial necessity—to develop as an artist."[79] Now, granted the additional opportunity of returning to the Pueblo, she found that some of the gaps between her and Pueblo life were too wide to cross easily.

Faced with such pressures, she abandoned her plans for the ethnographic project. She was frustrated and saddened by what had happened, recalling recently that her resulting fear of "retribution" made this one of the "worst times in [her] entire life."[80] She kept her home at Santa Clara so she could stay there when she went back for ceremonials but moved back to Albuquerque to live most of the time. For a brief period, she experimented with other painting styles. Perhaps the best example of this work is *Communicating with the Full Moon*, a 1962 self-portrait in which Velarde, dressed in traditional clothing, looks directly at the moon, as if in pursuit of both forgiveness and guidance. Set against an abstract and angular background, the painting resonates with intensity; the woman looks both mournful and hopeful. Hyer describes it as a "powerful expression of her struggle to balance a traditional Pueblo upbringing with an untraditional career and personal life."[81] Velarde describes it as a painting that emerged from a "distorted mood" and acknowledges that this painting was one good thing that came out of her rough attempt to return to Santa Clara.[82]

Indian Painters

While *Communicating with the Full Moon* represents experimentation with style, Velarde's paintings also undertook some experimentation with content—with mixed results. In 1960, she was commissioned by *New Mexico Magazine* to create three Indian-style Christmas paintings for the December issue. At first, Velarde says, she "couldn't think of anything Indian that was Christmas. Because we didn't have Christmas. And I thought, the only Christmas I know was what I learned at St. Catherine's, was Christ being born and how his life went from there on." She decided to paint these stories with Indian figures and settings.

Velarde remembers being criticized for one of the paintings, which retold the story of young Jesus in the temple from an Indian perspective. The painting features a young Indian boy standing in a kiva, surrounded by a circle of old men smoking corn-husk cigarettes. According to Velarde, people asked her "if it was supposed to be a church, why were they smoking in there? And I said, 'well, that's the way the Indians do...it's a sacred place, but not in the sense of Heaven so pure from any other disturbance.' And I said, 'smoking is part of their religion, and it's not disrespectful for the old men to sit there and blow smoke.'"[83]

Though *New Mexico Magazine* had featured the controversial

painting, it also attempted to intercept any criticism of Velarde's motives. In an anonymously authored feature that accompanied the images, Velarde was presented as a nonthreatening traditionalist:

> Pablita feels a strong sense of dedication toward the tra-
> ditions of her ancestors, who are the descendants of the
> prehistoric Basket Makers and Cliff Dwellers of the
> southwest. Pablita states that many of the old customs
> are being forgotten. She says that this could be due to the
> fact that the pressure of the white man's civilization is so
> overwhelming but possibly due to the fact that the Indian
> feels he must adjust to a 'protective coloration' in the
> accelerated pace of today's living. She is in no way a cru-
> sader, but she does feel an urgency in recording as much
> as possible of the ancient ways of her people before their
> true meaning is changed or lost forever.[84]

Velarde stuck by her interpretation of the temple scene, but chose not to repeat this painting when she later redid the others. Today, Velarde told me, these Christian paintings "don't mean as much" to her.[85] The layers of negotiation, influence, and expectation that came together to produce them may have ultimately felt more emotionally taxing than the publicity was worth.

By the late 1960s, Velarde had returned to painting in the "tradi-tional" (in Dunn's sense of the word) style of Pueblo painting by which she had made her name as an artist. Because this style adhered to mainstream ideas of Indian art, it would save her from having to prove, at least artistically, that she was "in no way a crusader." Given her experiences in attempting to live and work at Santa Clara, her choice of style is somewhat contradictory, but given the kinds of encouragement for "traditionalism" she received in publications like *New Mexico Magazine*, her choice is not surprising.

◼ CHAPTER FIVE ◼

This dynamic of contradictory expectations also helps to explain why Velarde ultimately shied away from writing a more autobiographical book. When she returned to the Pueblo in the 1960s, she felt like Turkey Girl—misunderstood and unappreciated. Turkey Girl could escape forever into the mountains; Velarde could only go back to Albuquerque. Storybooks provide happy endings, or at least resolved ones, while real life rarely does. Perhaps the traditional stories Velarde wants to tell seem more suitable for images than for words because images provide a chance to freeze a moment in time, uncomplicated by change. Velarde's life story, made complex by her experiences in more than one cultural context, and by tensions between communalism and individualism, might require a different sort of style, one more like the cubist layers and shards of *Communicating with the Full Moon* than the idealized timelessness of *Old Father*.

But it is the Pueblo's story, and not her own, that she has chosen to paint. While many of her paintings are based on abstract motifs rather than legends or daily activities, Velarde told me that at some point in her career she decided each of her paintings would carry a discernible message: "This is the way I think when I paint: it's not just painting a picture, just to be selling a picture because it's a pretty looking picture, but it's a picture that's going to tell somebody something someday."[86] Clearly, Velarde has painted what she has wanted to, but her desires have also been affected by her awareness of what people want to see.[87]

Articles and documentaries that have featured her work since the 1960s have nearly all emphasized the "traditionalism" of her style, especially of her "earth paintings." While this publicity has implied that this technique establishes a direct connection between her and her ancestors, she first learned this technique not at Santa Clara, but in Dunn's studio.[88] Velarde has acknowledged this openly, but she still uses words that evoke "ancient" tradition, as in statements included in a recent book featuring her work: "Miss Dunn taught me to grind rocks and raw clay to make beautiful earth colors for my paintings. I ground the different earth colors with the *mano* [stone

262

grinding tool] and *metate* [stone grinding surface] like the ancient Indians had once ground corn for tortillas." Velarde later refined the technique through independent experimentation and pursuit of materials: "I dig the dirt in secret places," she has said.[89] She grinds earth pigments she finds using the one-hundred-pound metate and ten-pound mano she salvaged from a Pueblo home in the early 1960s.[90] Still, the grinding itself takes place in Albuquerque, not Santa Clara. Velarde settled on a middle ground in establishing her career: she would use "traditional" painting techniques and "traditional" subject matter, but also present herself as a "modern" woman artist attempting to educate a "modern" audience.[91]

The painting style adopted by Velarde's daughter, Helen Hardin, picks up at the level of complexity where *Communicating with the Full Moon* left off. Whereas Velarde made a name for herself by being "traditional," her daughter's fame arose from her individualized and innovative use of native motifs, used abstractly rather than for narrative purposes: one writer has termed her work "a fusion of ancient and ultra-modern" themes and techniques.[92] Hardin began painting as a young girl in the 1950s, moving into Indian art as a teenager because, as she put it in a 1972 interview, "people were interested in buying paintings done by little Indian children."[93] She had her first show, at Coronado State Monument, in 1962, when she was nineteen years old. At this time, she had already attended a summer institute for young American Indian artists at the University of Arizona, sponsored by the Rockefeller Foundation. She later sensed, however, that the most important turning point in her early painting career was a show she had in Bogotá, Colombia, in 1968. Fleeing an abusive ex-boyfriend and a sense of aimlessness in New Mexico, Hardin had gone to stay there with her father, who was training police officers as part of his job with the United States Agency for International Development (USAID). After seeing her paintings, the U.S. cultural attaché arranged for her to give a show. "The paintings sold," Hardin explained later, "and the reason why the show gave me confidence was because, I would say, ninety-nine percent of the people there had

Fig. 27:
Helen Hardin
on the Cover of
*New Mexico
Magazine*,
March/April
1970.
Photograph by
Michael
Mouchette.

not heard of Pablita Velarde....I was Helen Hardin, an Indian artist and I was selling those paintings on my own."[94]

Hardin's pursuit of painting represented a departure from her mother both stylistically and emotionally. Just as Velarde's own father had tried to steer her away from a career as an artist, Velarde tried to discourage her daughter from painting, perhaps because she knew the difficulties of a painting career all too well. But Hardin pressed on, and interviews or articles featuring her work usually included her assertion that she was creating art that differed greatly from her mother's work. In 1972, she explained the stylistic difference as the result of experience. "I am actually alive and I am not painting things that I experienced as a child," Hardin emphasized. "I never experienced these things because I grew up in the city."[95] She described her work as a combination of research on Indian motifs, color theory, and personal inspiration. The "personal" element was central to her sense of identity: "I want to break into the art world as a whole," she explained. "I don't want to go down in an Indian history art [*sic*] book as a good Indian painter...I want to go down in an art history book as a good artist of my time."[96]

Like her mother before her, Hardin found her niche. A 1970 cover story in *New Mexico Magazine*, "Helen Hardin: Tsa-sah-wee-ch Does Her Thing," featured her against a dramatic mesa landscape, referring to her by her Pueblo name, which translates as Little Standing Spruce.[97] In 1976, a public-television documentary portrayed Hardin as an independent artist, determinedly contemporary, and wary of activist labels. "I'm not the American housewife," Hardin asserted, "but on the other hand, I'm not the woman's libber either. I can't get into movements, whether they're women's movements or Indian movements. I'm just not programmed for that. I'm very independent."[98] The documentary also included a segment where Hardin elaborated on how important it was to her to be a good mother to her daughter. Margarete was born in 1964 and named after Margarete Chase, the gallery owner who helped both Hardin and Velarde establish themselves.[99] Based on statements Hardin made to her biographer, it seems such remarks may have implied criticism of her mother's pursuit of a painting career—in Hardin's apparent opinion, a consuming interest that took place at the expense of her family.[100]

Amid such implications, it is worth noting that the two women's careers developed in dramatically differing contexts. Velarde spent her early years in a small village and at a boarding school for Indian children; Hardin did spend time at Santa Clara as a small child, but mostly grew up in an urban environment where she only knew a few other American Indian children. Velarde became a professional woman painter against the codes of her culture and without the support of her husband; Hardin was the daughter of a woman who painted and who valued women's painting. Velarde began to make a living painting "traditionally" at the same time that artists, art dealers, and patrons were discovering that tradition; Hardin "did her own thing" during the 1960s, when Anglos turned to "Indian" traditions less for cultural knowledge than a means to their own individualized "countercultural" ends.

As these contrasts reveal, the material life conditions of American Indians had changed. Moreover, American women's efforts to combine careers with childrearing had gained recognition. Still, comparing Velarde and Hardin shows little change in the status of American Indian artists in the American imagination. Despite Hardin's desire to step outside the categorization of American Indian artist, this was most often the context in which her work was featured, and, willingly or not, she relied upon this label for exposure. The public-television documentary that featured her work was one of a series on American Indian artists, and most exhibitions and articles featuring her work presented her in this context.

Sadly, whether or not Hardin eventually would have more clearly fulfilled her goal of transcending the categorization of her work as "Indian" remains uncertain, because she died, after battling with breast cancer, in 1984. In a 1981 piece on American Indian women artists in *Southwest Art*, Hardin (interestingly, given the focus of the article) asserted that "each of us is an individual, and to put neat and tidy labels on any one of us is doing a disservice to mankind."[101] But when she signed her paintings with her Tewa name, regardless of her own ideals or intentions about identity, she put a label on herself for those who choose to see her, first and foremost, as an Indian artist. Judging by her style, it was a label that, at some level, she was willing to embrace.

Looking at the careers of Velarde and Hardin next to one another helps explain why Velarde wrote the kind of book she did when she did—and perhaps why she did not write another like it. Preceded by several decades in which Indian art and folklore had exploded in popularity, not just in the Southwest but throughout America, Velarde sensed there was yet another angle from which to tell an Indian story in print: through the voice of an Indian. She presented her work as the preservation of traditions, as the recording of stories that might be forever lost if no one (at least no one who understood them as she and her father did) took the care to write them down. And yet the very act of doing so went against Pueblo ideas regarding the sacredness of such traditions. When she attempted to undertake a similar project later, she felt shut out, not just because of her project, but because of her sex. The Indian artist who had made a name for herself by painting tradition in one context felt like a renegade in another. At the same time that she was abandoning her plans for an ethnographic project, her daughter was earning fame as the Indian painter who broke new ground by trying to turn away from tradition.

These two women's stories show how an Indian woman artist in the later twentieth century, no matter how complicated her experience with or attitude toward tradition may be, will find that her art will be measured against the yardstick of tradition. She will be considered, first and foremost, an Indian. Clearly, Velarde embraces this identity less ambivalently than her multiethnic daughter did. She wrote *Old Father* because she was proud of where she came from and because she wanted others to know more about what it was like. She believed in the project enough to ask for help, as illustrated by her answer to her father's initial question about how she planned to get it published, a story she told me when I met her.

> I said, "I don't know!" I said, "Maybe if you said some Indian prayers for me well, I might get lucky," and he looked me and said, "I thought you didn't believe in that stuff," and I said, "Well, I do believe some of it," I said, "but not all of it." He said, "Why?" I said, "Well,

it's your fault!" I said, "You sent me to a Catholic school and they taught me something else." And I said, "When I come home, you say this, and you say that, and I can't put the two together." And so, he kind of understood that, or at least accepted it, I don't know which. But, anyway, I asked him to say Indian prayers for me, and I said, "I'll pray the way the sisters taught me how to pray," and I said, "maybe somehow this will come out."[102]

The book did come out. But in Velarde's life, as in the life of many twentieth-century American Indians, it has indeed been hard, as she put it, to "put the two together."

Her Own Place

Velarde's increasing identification with feminist values intensified her sense of distance from Santa Clara Pueblo. Despite the traditional esteem for women held by Pueblo culture, Velarde's individualism set her apart from her home. She considers this a problem with Pueblo culture, as indicated when she told me about her unfruitful efforts to convince the women at Santa Clara Pueblo to cast off what she called the role of "slave in the house": "I kept telling those women up there, 'You don't have any rights in those pueblos. Sure, you make pottery and make money now,' I said, 'but you still don't have many rights.'"[103] Velarde's greatest sense of injustice at Santa Clara was the fact that her children, born from her marriage to an Anglo, could not inherit her land at the Pueblo. In fact, another Santa Clara woman challenged (unsuccessfully) this Santa Clara rule all the way to the U.S. Supreme Court in 1978.[104] The very same factors that made Velarde attractive to the Anglo mainstream press as a "bridge between the Indian and

Fig. 28: Pablita Velarde at Work on a Painting, 1960. Courtesy of the Museum of New Mexico, Neg. No. 174208.

non-Indian worlds," as one article put it, made her identity difficult to sustain within the Santa Clara community.[105]

On the other hand, her individualistic character changed, and perhaps increased, her appeal to Anglo audiences. The same newspapers that had emphasized her "femininity" and "traditionalism" in 1930s and 1940s coverage of her painting career also increasingly emphasized the ways in which her individualist approach to her career set her apart from her Pueblo roots. Even in the 1950s, features on her work often focused on her marriage to a non-Indian, which made her "untraditional." A 1952 article Dunn wrote about her former student for the Museum of New Mexico's *El Palacio* magazine concluded with a description of the Hardins' "pleasant new home on the heights approaching the Sandía Mountains in Albuquerque, where both Pablita and the children paint."[106] The author of an article published in the *Albuquerque Journal* two years later waited only until the fourth paragraph to describe the Hardins' marriage, their home, and Herbert's career as a police officer.[107] (One article from the same era, which appeared in *Desert* magazine, did note that Velarde always signed her paintings with her given name and that the artist was "only rarely called 'Mrs. Hardin.'"[108]) After 1959, when the Hardins' marriage ended, features on Velarde's work emphasized that she lived in Albuquerque, where she was raising her children, and not in Santa Clara.

Her deviance from Pueblo tradition, combined with her divorce from Hardin, lent itself to the creation of a new Anglo media image for Velarde. Despite her "traditional" painting style, she became known as a feminist pioneer for the American Indian art world. When author Mary Carroll Nelson published a slim biography of Velarde in 1971, for example, she clearly aimed the book at a young audience, but at least one publication saw it as a "feminist" work. *New Mexico Magazine* reviewed it as a model for "feminine" writing: "In this well-illustrated modest biography of one of New Mexico's outstanding ladies...a lady writer chitchats in a style which should enthrall other ladies all over the country, whether they are interested in Indian art or not. It's women's lib as it should be—with feminine grace."[109] A 1979 article for *El Palacio* on "Pioneering Women of New Mexico" opened with Velarde's life story and concluded by affirming that Velarde and other women like her could offer "today's 'liberated' women" an example.[110] In a 1985 feature in the *Albuquerque Journal*, Velarde, described by the journalist as a "traditional" artist, confided, "Painting took me out of a shell... I've become—well,... sort of brazen."[111]

By the 1990s, references to her breaks with tradition became even more emphatic. The catalog for a 1993 retrospective exhibit of her work, titled "Woman's Work," at the Wheelwright Museum of the American Indian in Santa Fe, began with Velarde's assertive statement about her lack of interest in conventional feminine responsibilities.[112] A 1995 profile in the *Albuquerque Journal* featured this provocative subtitle: "Half a Century Ago, a Santa Clara Artist Defied Tradition to Paint, and She Hasn't Stopped Since."[113] Features in *New Mexico Magazine*, the *Santa Fe Reporter*, and *Pasatiempo*, the Sunday magazine of the *Santa Fe New Mexican*, all told Velarde's story as one of determination and liberation, or as *Pasatiempo* called it, "spunk and sparkle."[114] After being criticized by Pueblo men for choosing her career as a painter, this story went, Pablita had responded by becoming a "sharp-tongued," "rebellious," and "irrepressible" woman who "knocked down [walls] of tradition."[115] And in a recent book about Velarde's life, art historian Joyce Szabo writes that "Velarde holds a singular position in the history of Native American painting, especially because of her early, pivotal role as a woman artist in a field dominated by men."[116]

Despite this radical image, Velarde's continual focus on Santa Clara themes in her work—and the reissuing of *Old Father Story Teller* by a Santa Fe press in 1989—continued to grant her status as a spokeswoman for "authenticity." Margaret Jacobs describes this contradictory trend when she writes that, despite the intentions of Anglos to nurture Indian culture through patronizing women artists, "the arts and crafts movement actually served to blunt differences between Indian and white women." This is not a process of assimilation, however, as much as it is a "commercialization of Pueblo culture [that] fostered new cultural forms and a set of fresh strategies for both maintaining ethnic identity and integrating into the American economy."[117]

While economically empowering, these contradictions did take a toll on Velarde in her personal life. Velarde maintained an Indian ethnic identity—but her life story suggests she did this more in the eyes of the Anglo community than in those of Santa Clara. Part of the process of developing her feminist image was an increased distancing from her Pueblo heritage. Still, as late as 1976, when she painted the Buffalo and Deer Dance mural at the Indian Pueblo Cultural Center, she testified to her desire to preserve traditional Santa Clara culture. And when she painted herself, bold and smiling, into the mural, she testified to her success in not only doing just that, but also remaining true to herself. The remedy for Velarde's homesickness proved to be her determination to build her own home, bolstered by the cultural traits she had inherited and "borrowed" as she saw fit.

The shift in coverage of Velarde's career helps to explain why her story serves as a "coda" to the others in this book. The choices she made in presenting herself echo the choices made by Jaramillo, Cabeza de Baca, and Bennett, but they also further illuminate a current of change running through the earlier stories. These women learned how to manipulate the image of traditional, multicultural womanhood for Hispanics and American Indians set into motion by Austin and Luhan, but they also increasingly found that "traditional" roles held limited power for women. As mainstream culture gradually accepted the tenets of second-wave feminism, women of all ethnic groups demanded greater autonomy.

Today, New Mexico is a place where the rhetoric of tradition continues to grant women of color a greater voice than they might otherwise have, but the stories of Jaramillo, Cabeza de Baca, Bennett, and Velarde, read in progression, do show their increasing success at speaking as individualists as well as "traditionalists." Jaramillo maintained an allegiance to traditional womanhood, but Cabeza de Baca seemed less interested in following this role in her private life than in using it to her advantage in her public life: recall that she published cookbooks but did not like to cook. Bennett sensed this sea change when she described herself as a traditional and conservative Navajo woman even as she took the unprecedented step of running a woman's campaign for the highest Navajo office. And Velarde, who first experienced a feminist consciousness when she undertook a painting career that contradicted Santa Clara values, further developed it through her difficult marriage, her anger at Santa Clara land rules, and her positive "feminist" image in the Anglo press. As Velarde's experiences illustrate, the multicultural ideals that had confined Hispanic and American Indian women to "traditional" roles when they wanted to speak out publicly about culture became less confining in the late twentieth century. Feminism, an explicit argument for cultural change regarding women's autonomy, ultimately implied the fallacy and undesirability of promoting culture as unchanged.

AFTERWORD

*O*n June 1967, Reies Lopez Tijerina led an armed raid on the courthouse at Tierra Amarilla, a small northern New Mexican village in the heart of the land that had once belonged to Cleofas Jaramillo's great grandfather. Tijerina, a Texan, acted as the leader of *Alianza Federal de Mercedes* (the Federal Alliance of Land Grants), a group he had started in New Mexico after learning of the history of Hispanic dispossession in the state. The dramatic events unleashed by the Alianza symbolized powerful changes in New Mexican cultural relations. Tijerina acted with what he saw as necessary and justified force, backed by his interpretation of existing laws regarding landownership and transfer, the provisions of the 1848 Treaty of Guadalupe Hidalgo, and the petition signatures of thousands of Hispanic New Mexicans. He aimed to reclaim the home many felt they had lost unfairly, thus transforming the costs of conquest into an empowering statement of cultural identity. Fortunately, no one was killed as a result of his passion for justice.[1]

While the violence at Tierra Amarilla discredited Tijerina in the eyes of some and lionized him in the eyes of others, no one could deny the power of the raid as a symbolic gesture. It signified the transformation of long-building sentiments about injustice among New

☙ AFTERWORD ❧

Mexican Hispanics into a Chicano movement in the state, and it coincided with a push for self-determination among American Indians, as exemplified by the American Indian Movement (AIM). Founded in Minneapolis-Saint Paul, Minnesota, in 1968, the AIM demonstrated its perspective on New Mexican cultural affairs in 1974 when it called for a boycott of the Inter-Tribal Ceremonial in Gallup. It is worth remembering that Kay Bennett took AIM's charge of exploitation seriously enough to dispute it publicly.

Since the Chicano movement called for recognition of the mestizo identity long denied by idealized sketches of New Mexico's tri-cultural (Spanish, American Indian, and Anglo) heritage, Chicanos and American Indians found a new, albeit tenuous, allegiance in their resistance to Anglo domination of economic and cultural affairs. Further inspired by Civil Rights Movement protests undertaken by African Americans in other parts of the United States, New Mexican Hispanic and American Indian activists sought to redraw the map of cultural relations in New Mexico. The radical actions of these activists challenged the romantic nostalgia of Anglo views of Hispanic and American Indian cultures by calling attention to all that stood in the way of civic equality in the state. They questioned the myth of "cultural coexistence," advocating instead radical acts of cultural nationalism.

These activists' calls for self-determination did not result in the full equality they pushed for, as attested to by the scenes invoked in this book's introduction, or by a brief glimpse at contemporary poverty rates in New Mexico. But the pressure they exerted did ultimately, if ironically, attain recognition for multiculturalism as the only appropriate way to govern the state's cultural affairs. Any remaining resistance to the ideals of cultural relativism among Anglo conservatives seems to have given way to a general recognition that multiculturalism at least offers a benign alternative to the actual eradication of racial inequality and acts as a safety valve against the supposed extremes called for by activists of the 1960s and 1970s. The semblance of peaceful multiculturalism also offers economic opportunities. As earlier generations of New Mexicans recognized, the tourism industry that drives New Mexico's economy depends on the perception that "true" separate cultures continue to thrive in New Mexico. For all New Mexicans, there can be profit in the appearance of perfect "multiculturalism."

Among the more adamant calls for social justice and cultural reform that emerged in the 1960s, the apparent efforts of an earlier generation of women to preserve tradition may seem old-fashioned. Their actions, which emphasized keeping the peace, relied on accommodation rather than confrontation and demands for equality. Memoirs, cookbooks, and children's books hardly strike most audiences as radical tools of change.

But it is possible to see Luhan, Austin, Jaramillo, Cabeza de Baca, Bennett, and Velarde as more than gentle foremothers for the more confrontational activists that followed them. They were, in fact, pathbreakers whose innovative approaches to maintaining cultural tradition contributed to "Chicanismo" and "Red Pride." Luhan and Austin boldly advocated cultural relativism, Jaramillo and Cabeza de Baca bravely voiced a nascent Chicana identity, and Bennett and Velarde determinedly challenged ideas about "lost" Indian cultures. In these narratives of progress, these women defy their era as heroines of multiculturalism; they become women pioneers whose stories embody cultural ideals held by New Mexicans today much more than the statue of the sunbonneted Anglo mother proposed for Santa Fe by the DAR in 1927.

Still, viewing these women as "pathbreakers" stops short of recognizing the full lesson they have to teach. In fact, studying their efforts leads one to see a more complex, and more troubling, portrait of the multicultural ideal that New Mexico, as well as the United States in general, lives by today. They may be heroines of multiculturalism, but they also illustrate this ideal's continuing central limitation: its lack of acknowledgement of cultural change and interaction. Their untold

❧ AFTERWORD ❧

stories, the ones they left out of their autobiographies and other efforts of self-presentation, show how they went to considerable lengths to emphasize absolute traditionalism, even when this emphasis denied the realities of life in New Mexico, especially for women of color.

Unfortunately, such relentless emphasis on pure traditionalism continues to drive public discussion of culture in New Mexico. With the notable exception of wider recognition for mestizo identity, the "separate" cultural identities expressed by these women have mostly remained separate in the New Mexican cultural imagination. The Anglo, Hispanic and American Indian heritages of New Mexico do deserve separate appreciation—they are sources of identity and pride, and of the very real traditions embraced by these women. But these heritages also deserve to be considered as entities that change with time and through interaction with one another, as producers not of absolute and therefore authentic cores of tradition, but instead of living and sometimes contentious relationships between people. In this respect, the full stories of Austin, Luhan, Jaramillo, Cabeza de Baca, Bennett, and Velarde caution us about the limitations multiculturalism places on our understanding of cultural identity. So long as we continue to consider it as a relationship between separate cultures rather than an overarching environment of borrowing, change, interaction, and inequality, we are failing to tell the full story.

Furthermore, these women show us how women have played and can continue to play a fundamental role in a multicultural society's attempt to negotiate tradition and change. By invoking "traditional" sources of women's power even as they actively pursued authority in the public sphere, these six women offered a model for cultural change for later generations. For the Hispanic and American Indian women, this method often required publicly implying that this was all done in the name of "tradition," thus masking their innovative and individualistic achievements. From the full story of their efforts, men and women of today might see ways to effectively and openly balance traditional and new ways of empowering themselves through cultural identity. Velarde's gradual ability to stand *both* for American Indian tradition and feminist ideals testifies to the capacity for such dual paths.

While her story may indicate that Americans have a greater capacity for acknowledging the place of change in a multicultural society than they did in the era of Austin and Luhan, the fact remains that Americans still call upon "tradition" when they want to find a way to adjust to radical change. One such recent change in American home life has prompted such a response. Census data has revealed that, for the first time, more than half of families with married parents and children have two parents working outside the home.[2] At the same time, cultural commentators draw attention to a supposed recent rise in American women's expressed wish to stay home with their children.[3] Perhaps coming to terms with why American women express the desire to "stay home"—even when economic circumstances increasingly dictate that they cannot afford to—requires that we see what this "tradition" appears to offer women that life in the postindustrial workplace does not. And perhaps trying to understand what this emphasis on tradition may obscure, as the lives of the women in this study hint it might, will allow us to be more honest about what the ideals of home and work actually offer individuals.

New Mexican adherence to tradition takes comfort in an idealized past while actually grappling with a troubling present; American devotion to "traditional" homemaking today expresses anxiety about actual changes in gender roles at home and in the workplace. Our homes can remain traditional, this reasoning suggests, even when such traditions seem to be threatened by forces of rapid change, such as Americans' increased entry into dehumanizing jobs in service and high-tech industries. Women, as mothers, supposedly serve as primary guardians for cultural traditions. But women's ability to carry culture clearly also depends on the performance of traditional gender roles by *both* men and women: assuming women will "stay home" presupposes that men will not. As in the case of New Mexico, this story of women and tradition serves as a cover story for larger cultural issues.

Thus, these women's biographies allude to two myths of contemporary American culture: the idea of multiculturalism as a loose

Fig. 29: *Señora with Chiles*. Photograph by Jack Parsons. Courtesy of the Santa Fe Convention and Visitors Bureau.

collection of separate traditions, and the idea of homes as havens for such traditions—with women keeping close watch over them. More honesty about both our interconnected cultural roots and what our conceptions of home demand of men and women would allow us to develop more realistic visions of American homes than those available to Luhan, Austin, Jaramillo, Cabeza de Baca, Bennett, and Velarde. The records they left behind, especially their autobiographical writings, grant us an opportunity to compare them across ethnic divides, showing us a shared impulse to teach Americans about advantages offered by cultural awareness and interaction. And in the stories they did not tell, they encourage us to acknowledge the full complexity of women's contributions to American homemaking, both in the domestic and social sphere. We need to stop telling stories about women and people of color that fail to recognize their ability to strengthen cultural identity even when they do not act traditionally; we need to recognize that the authenticity of traditions rests less in their purity than in their adaptability and their relevance to everyday life.

New Mexico, certainly, will continue to thrive on the story of tradition and the story of women's roles in maintaining it. The state's tourism industry will continue to use photos like *Señora with Chiles* to popularize the image of the state as a perfect multicultural home, complete with traditional homemakers. The Señora's eyes are closed in the photo, as if she is trying to shut out the gaze of those who seek to make her something she is not—a hollow image of traditional womanhood, rooted in days gone by.

Another photo used to entice tourists to New Mexico, *Traditional Dress Girl*, shows a more youthful image of femininity, a child from San Juan Pueblo dressed for feast-day festivities. Visitors may see the girl in this photo and expect she will lead a life steeped in tradition—she will grow up to be like the "Señora with Chiles," responsible for carrying the weight of her culture on her back.

Fig. 30: *Traditional Dress Girl* (San Juan Pueblo's Feast Day). Photograph by Mark Nohl. Courtesy of the New Mexico Department of Tourism.

◼ AFTERWORD ◼

But the girl from San Juan Pueblo will likely share something else with the Señora—an acute sense of distance from the perfectly traditional homes and cultural harmony promised by glossy New Mexican travel brochures. She, too, may end up homesick. Or, perhaps she'll learn to ignore the gaze of tourists and the fallacy of their ideals. Perhaps she'll simply make her own home, blending tradition and change, as generations of New Mexican women have done before her.

ABBREVIATIONS USED IN ARCHIVAL REFERENCES

ACHC: Alice Corbin Henderson Collection, Harry Ransom Humanities Research Center, University of Texas at Austin

ACHL: Angélico Chávez History Library, Palace of the Governors, Santa Fe, New Mexico

CSWR: Center for Southwest Research, General Library, University of New Mexico

FCBP: Fabiola Cabeza de Baca [Gilbert] Papers (at CSWR)

GASP: Governor Arthur Seligman Papers (at NMSRCA)

MDLC: Mabel Dodge Luhan Collection, Yale Collection of American Literature, Beinecke Rare Book and Manuscript Library, Yale University

MHACB: Mary Hunter Austin Collection, Bancroft Library, University of California, Berkeley

MHACH: Mary Hunter Austin Collection, Huntington Library, San Marino, California

NMHRC: New Mexico Human Rights Commission Records (at NMSRCA)

NMSRCA: New Mexico State Records Center and Archives, Santa Fe, New Mexico

NOTES

INTRODUCTION

1. The U.S. Census Bureau recently ranked New Mexico as the poorest state in the country, citing a 17.9 % poverty rate for 2002, as compared to a 12.1% 2002 average for the country as a whole. (Bernadette D. Proctor and Joseph Dalaker, *Poverty in the United States: 2002*, U.S. Census Bureau, September 2003.) Additionally, a 2003 report noted that New Mexico, Louisiana, and Mississippi tied for last place among U.S. states in the percentage of children living in poverty (26%). Nationally, 17% of children live in poverty. (Annie E. Casey Foundation, *Kids Count Data Book*, 2003, p. 137.)

2. For an analysis of how "cultural relativism" became "multiculturalism" and of the continuing limitations of this ideological framework for American culture, see David Hollinger, *Postethnic America: Beyond Multiculturalism* (New York: Basic Books, 1995). The *Oxford English Dictionary* defines "multicultural" as "of or relating to a society consisting of varied cultural groups, in which the distinctive cultural identity of each group is maintained." The first appearance of the word in English is attributed to the *American Journal of Sociology* in 1937; an antinationalist writer in the *New York Herald Tribune* used the word in 1941. Other credited early uses include newspapers throughout Canada and other parts of the former British Empire. "Multicultural" in *Oxford English Dictionary*, 2d ed., accessed online 24 March 2004.

3. Whenever possible, I will refer to indigenous people or groups by specific cultural affiliation, such as Navajo, or Santa Clara Pueblo. When more general terminology is warranted, I will use American Indian, or Indian, as it is a term used by both Bennett and Velarde and commonly used by indigenous people in the United States today.

4. Jack E. Holmes, *Politics in New Mexico* (Albuquerque: University of New Mexico Press, 1967), 10.

5. The 2000 census measured Hispanic origin separately from race. This may partially explain why 17 percent of New Mexicans chose "some other race" as their one racial category, as people of *mestizo* ancestry may have been uncomfortable choosing "white," or "American Indian," or even both, as new census procedures allowed them to do—less than 4 percent of New Mexicans chose to identify as being more than one race. The statistic for American Indian population I have given is based on those who chose it as their only racial category. Also according to this data, just under 2 percent of New Mexicans who chose only one race classified themselves as "Black or African American," while people of Asian descent constituted just over 1 percent of the state's population. Of the 42.1 percent of New Mexicans who identified themselves as Hispanic (again, in a question separate from the one about race), only 18.1 percent claimed Mexican ethnicity and less than 1 percent choose "Puerto Rican" or "Cuban." But a striking 23.5 percent chose "Other Hispanic or Latino." This indicates the continuing force of the "Hispano" or Spanish American identity in New Mexico, an identity which the census did not offer as an option. U.S. Census Bureau, *Profiles of General Demographic Characteristics, 2000 Census of Population and Housing: New Mexico*, May 2001.

6. Three other writers attracted my interest during research. Alice Corbin Henderson, an editor, poet, and cultural activist whose move to Santa Fe from Chicago preceded Luhan's and Austin's, created a compelling body of poetry, correspondence, and preservation work. But the fact that she neither wrote nor published a major autobiographical text led me to exclude her from this study. Nina Otero-Warren, a state politician and educator who campaigned for woman's suffrage, published *Old Spain in Our Southwest* (under the name Nina Otero) during this period (New York: Harcourt, Brace, and Co., 1936). While this book and her political work make her a fascinating figure, I found that her writing and other public statements did not include enough autobiographical reflection to allow her to fit with the themes of this particular study. A recent biography covers her life in detail. See Charlotte Whaley, *Nina Otero-Warren of Santa Fe* (Albuquerque: University of New Mexico Press, 1994). Helen Sekaquaptewa, a Hopi woman, published *Me and Mine* in 1969. Her roots in Arizona, rather than New Mexico, as well as the fact that her book was recorded and edited by an ethnographer, led me to exclude her from this study in literary self-representation in New Mexico. See Helen Sekaquaptewa, *Me and Mine: The Life Story of Helen Sekaquaptewa*, ed. Louise Udall (Tucson: University of Arizona Press, 1969).

7. "Secretary Anderson Pays Tribute to Women in Home Demonstration Work," *New Mexico Extension News* 27.3–4 (March-April 1947): 1.

8. The closest exception to this is Vera Norwood and Janice Monk, eds., *The Desert Is No Lady: Southwestern Landscapes in Women's Writing and Art* (Tucson: University of Arizona Press, 1987). Austin's career is

studied in an essay on Anglo writers (Lois Rudnick, "Re-Naming the Land: Anglo Expatriate Women in the Southwest," 10–26) while an essay on Chicana literature analyzes Jaramillo's work (Tey Diana Rebolledo, "Tradition and Mythology: Signatures of Landscape in Chicana Literature," 96–124).

9. Mary Austin, "In Papagueria," *The Nation*, 18 July 1928, 65. She titled the poem "Homesickness" in an earlier manuscript. See Mary Austin, "Homesickness," undated manuscript, AU 223, MHACH. Given the final title of her poem, Mary Austin probably refers specifically here to the Tohono O'odham (formerly Papago) people of southern Arizona, though her deliberately dreamlike imagery makes this poem more revealing of a general sentiment toward American Indian cultures of the Southwest.

10. Cleofas Jaramillo, "The New Home, Abode of Happy Years," inscribed on back of photo of El Rito country home of Cleofas and Venceslao Jaramillo, Photo No. 9934, Photo Archives, Palace of the Governors, Santa Fe, NM.

CHAPTER ONE

1. J. D. De Huff, "Chamber of Commerce Gives Version of Statue Episode," *Santa Fe New Mexican*, 12 Oct. 1927, 5.

2. Austin, "Mary Austin Asked for Her Opinion on Statue and Gave It; Mrs. Moss Discourteous," *Santa Fe New Mexican*, 18 Oct. 1927, 3.

3. The organization requires that members "prove lineal, blood line descent from an ancestor who aided in achieving American independence," thus effectively shutting out all Hispanic and American Indian women in New Mexico, many of whom have ancestors whose presence in what is now the United States long predated 1776. Eligibility Requirements, National Society of the Daughters of the American Revolution Official Web Site; available from www.dar.org; accessed 1 April 2004.

4. For a journalist's less passionate coverage of the statue controversy, see "Artists Object, Statue is Forfeited; Mrs. Austin, Applegate Protest," *Santa Fe New Mexican*, 12 Oct. 1927, 5.

5. Austin quite literally embraced this image when she described the Southwest as a country of "lost borders." She began to see it this way long before she came to New Mexico, during her time as a young woman in California. Based on her experiences with American Indians, Hispanics, and Anglo migrants to the Owens Valley, she published a collection of stories titled *Lost Borders* (New York and London: Harper and Brothers, 1909).

6. For a study of cultural relativism that emphasizes its particular appeal to modernist women, see Desley Deacon, *Elsie Clews Parsons: Inventing Modern Life* (Chicago: University of Chicago Press, 1997). For an analysis of how this theory helped create art and tourism markets of particular appeal to women, see Molly Mullin, *Culture in the Marketplace: Gender, Art, and Value in the American Southwest* (Durham: Duke University Press, 2001).

7. For Austin, see Augusta Fink, *I-Mary: A Biography of Mary Austin* (Tucson: University of Arizona Press, 1983); and Esther F. Lanigan [originally published under "Esther Lanigan Stineman"], *Mary Austin: Song of a Maverick* (New Haven: Yale University Press, 1989). Fink's work tells Austin's basic life story, while Lanigan's extensively analyzes her in the context of literary and historical themes. For Luhan, see Emily Hahn, *Mabel: A Biography of Mabel Dodge Luhan* (Boston: Houghton Mifflin, 1977); and Lois Palken Rudnick, *Mabel Dodge Luhan: New Woman, New Worlds* (Albuquerque: University of New Mexico Press, 1984). Hahn's book sensationalizes Luhan's life, while Rudnick's is an academic biography that traces her relationship with other well-known literary and historical figures. Rudnick's efforts to place Luhan at the center of the cultural movements of the twentieth century continued with her publication of another book: *Utopian Vistas: The Mabel Dodge Luhan House and the American Counterculture* (Albuquerque: University of New Mexico Press, 1996). For work that considers both women simultaneously, see Rudnick, "Re-Naming the Land: Anglo Expatriate Women in the Southwest," in *The Desert Is No Lady: Southwestern Landscapes in Women's Writing and Art*, ed. Vera Norwood and Janice Monk (Tucson: University of Arizona Press, 1987), 10–26; and Margaret Jacobs, "Antimodern Feminists and the Emergence of Cultural Relativism," in *Engendered Encounters: Feminism and Pueblo Cultures, 1879–1934* (Lincoln: University of Nebraska Press, 1999), 56–81.

8. Elizabeth Ammons, *Conflicting Stories: American Women Writers at the Turn into the Twentieth Century* (New York: Oxford University Press, 1991), 10.

9. Quoted in Luhan, *Movers and Shakers*, Vol. 3 of *Intimate Memories* (New York: Harcourt, Brace and Co., 1936), 534.

10. Luhan, *Edge of Taos Desert: An Escape to Reality*, Vol. 4 of *Intimate Memories* (New York: Harcourt, Brace and Co., 1937), 6.

11. Some critics, however, attacked what they saw as the books' narcissism and name-dropping, attacking what Luhan intended to be a self-conscious and very honest portrait of the "disease" that plagued her before her arrival in Taos. Frank Waters, a friend of Luhan's, reacted to these claims when he attempted to sum up the significance of her work according to her Proustian model and her desire to show what she saw as the "decadent" end of Western civilization. "She had resolved, as she told me," Waters recalled, "to record its false values and superficial attitudes, its materialistic greed and corruption, as Proust had recorded his time and world . . . without sparing her own faults and foibles. This illuminating statement of purpose reveals her *Intimate Memories* to be more than the writings of an egotistical exhibitionist, as they have often been regarded." Waters, *Of Time and Change: A Memoir* (Denver: MacMurray and Beck, 1998), 80–81. For the story of Luhan's memoirs and their negative critical reception, see Rudnick, *Mabel Dodge Luhan*, 251–61.

12. Rudnick, *Mabel Dodge Luhan*, 256.

13. Mary Rowlandson, *The Sovereignty & Goodness of God* (1682; Boston: Bedford Books, 1997).

14. Luhan, *Background*, Vol. 1 of *Intimate Memories* (New York: Harcourt, Brace and Co., 1933), 287–90.
15. Luhan, *European Experiences*, Vol. 2 of *Intimate Memories* (New York: Harcourt, Brace and Co., 1936), 184.
16. Ibid., 159.
17. Ibid., 83.
18. Ibid., 452–53.
19. Luhan's later recollections show a complex self-awareness of the currents of their relationship, as evoked when she describes a time that John Reed fell ill. "Women of the type I was at that time like to have men sick in bed. Then a truce is declared. An illusion of complete possession takes the place of the feeling of strain that one has all the time that one is trying to hold the whole attention of a man." Luhan, *Movers and Shakers*, 228.
20. Ibid., 375. In a 1932 review Luhan wrote for the *New Republic*, she described such goals as a long-established pattern in gender relations. In the past, she wrote, "women stood behind men, pouring their vitality and their encouragement into them, glad to contribute to achievement." Luhan, "Decline of the Male," Letter to the editor in response to Neith Boyce's 9 March 1932 review of Robert Herrick's *The End of Desire*, *New Republic*, 20 April 1932, 275–76.
21. In this role, she became what Rudnick terms "one of Freud's earliest popularizers." In one column, she advised "women who seek masters" that according to Freud's theories, "there is no master" for a "mature woman": "There is only herself, free and alone, in the brotherhood of man, bearing her own security within her own soul." Mabel Dodge, "Mabel Dodge Talks of Women Who Seek Masters: An Atavistic Infantile Idea Like Being Afraid of the Dark, Maturity Needs No Protection But Cave Man Impression Lingers," *Washington Times*, 18 Aug. 1917, 14. As Rudnick points out, Luhan published this piece only one week after her marriage to Sterne. Rudnick, *Mabel Dodge Luhan*, 139–41.
22. Her most famous performance in this role took place after her marriage to Antonio Luhan, when she invited English writer D. H. Lawrence to stay with her in Taos. His 1922–1925 tenure in New Mexico established an exploitative tangle of affections among Luhan, Lawrence, his wife Frieda, and his friend Dorothy Brett (an English painter who took up residence in Taos). Thus, Luhan's efforts to insert herself into the lives of others, particularly creative men, took place even after her supposed "change" in Taos. She did not fail to disclose the extent of this problem in her memoirs—but did apparently exaggerate the ability of her home in Taos to "cure" her of it.
23. Luhan, *Edge of Taos Desert*, 19. Parrish was one of the most prominent American commercial artists of the early twentieth century.
24. Ibid., 41.
25. Ibid., 94.
26. Ibid., 272.
27. Ibid., 298.

28. Letter from unknown editor at Houghton Mifflin to Austin, 1 Feb. 1929, AU 2992, MHACH.

29. "She has joined up the pioneer life of action and the reflective mode of the artist," wrote one reviewer. "No American can read this book without gaining from it a sense of direction." (Isabel Patterson, "Mary Austin's Story, the Story of America: Review of *Earth Horizon*," *New York Herald Tribune*, 6 Nov. 1932, 2.) Another praised the "design" of the book ("as satisfactory as an Indian rug") and cited its ideas as offering a "possible synthesis for a native American culture." (R. L. Duffus, "Mary Austin, Who Found God Under a Walnut Tree: *Earth Horizon* is the Autobiography of a Unique and Commanding American Personality," *New York Times Book Review*, 13 Nov. 1932, 13–14.)

30. Austin, *Earth Horizon: Autobiography* (1932; Albuquerque: University of New Mexico Press, 1991), 33.

31. An undercurrent running through reviews is that Austin's claim to fame lay in being famous, rather than through a wide familiarity with her books and ideas. Austin's editor reminded her that she needed to write an autobiography that would live up to her reputation, not as a writer, but as "the most intelligent woman in America." Letter from Ferris Greenslet at Houghton Mifflin to Austin, 24 Feb. 1933, AU 3073, MHACH. The letter reminded Austin: "You will remember that Isabel Patterson said in print a while ago: 'Mary Austin ought to be able to write the best autobiography since Benjamin Franklin.' Suppose you keep that before your eye as a slogan...." Publicity materials for *Earth Horizon* also contained Patterson's remark.

32. Houghton Mifflin promised potential readers that they would find within *Earth Horizon's* pages the "living figures" of Theodore Roosevelt, William James, John Muir, Emma Goldman, and Jane Addams. It further lured readers with positive comments about Austin and her books by Carl Van Doren, Joseph Conrad, Henry Nash Smith, William Allen White, and H. G. Wells. Houghton Mifflin Company, Publicity Materials for *Earth Horizon*, in "Misc. from the Ina S. Cassidy purchase" folder, MHACB.

33. Austin to Daniel T. MacDougal, 9 Jan. 1922, AU 1145, MHACH. As if playing up her "exotic" image, Austin attended the dinner dressed in Spanish costume and accompanied by a young Chickasaw man in full ceremonial dress.

34. Austin, *Earth Horizon*, 152.

35. Ibid., 147. For an account of Willard's life and her reliance on the rhetoric of domesticity for power, see Ruth Bordin, *Women and Temperance: The Quest for Power and Liberty, 1873–1900* (Philadelphia: Temple University Press, 1981).

36. Austin, *Earth Horizon*, 144–46.

37. Susanna Savilla Graham Hunter to "kind friends," 23 Sept. 1888, AU 3199, MHACH.

38. Austin, *Earth Horizon*, 194.

39. The Owens River offered irrigation strategies to farmers of the region in the late nineteenth century. But by the early twentieth century the city of

Los Angeles had targeted the area for an ambitious aqueduct project, and succeeded through a variety of schemes to seize control of the area's water. This "water crisis" caused Austin to develop a distaste for California development strategies, which she would later cite as a factor in her decision to settle in New Mexico. See Marc Reisner, *Cadillac Desert: The American West and Its Disappearing Water* (New York: Viking, 1986), esp. 81–82; see also Austin, *Earth Horizon*, 308, 336.

40. When Mary Austin contacted Wallace Austin, at that point her ex-husband, to ask him about events she wanted to include in *Earth Horizon*, his reply illustrated his continuing lack of understanding for her efforts as a writer. He sent her dates and names, but also wrote, "Why not leave it to the real biographers who will write you up anyhow after you are dead? Can you get a publisher to produce such a book?" Stafford Wallace Austin to Mary Austin, 2 July 1929, AU 1299, MHACH.

41. Austin, *Earth Horizon*, 257, 294.

42. Ibid., 286–87.

43. Ibid., 289.

44. Ammons, *Conflicting Stories*, 102.

45. Austin, *Earth Horizon*, 246.

46. Ibid., 267.

47. Austin, *The Land of Little Rain* (Boston: Houghton Mifflin, 1903), 168–9.

48. Ruth Austin died of pneumonia (likely brought on by influenza) at the institution in 1918. Austin wrote of the commitment and Ruth's death in *Earth Horizon*, confiding, "It is a relief to speak of it now, of the cruelty, the weight, the oppression of its reality, the loss of tenderness, of consideration, the needless blight and pain" (295). The publisher fulfilled Austin's prophecy that commentators would criticize her for this decision by issuing materials that attempted to hide her decision to pursue writing rather than care for her daughter. Houghton Mifflin sent such materials to Henry Nash Smith (he was preparing a 1931 article on Austin for the *Southwest Review*) that misrepresented Austin's choices, apparently hoping to safeguard her from criticism. "She was married in 1891 to S. W. Austin and had one child," stated a "Who is Mary Austin?" fact sheet. "It was not until after the loss of this child that her literary career was begun." These materials also failed to mention her divorce. "Book News: Who is Mary Austin?" in "Materials Sent to H. N. Smith" Folder, MHACB.

49. Austin's archival collection includes a copy of Wallace Austin's suit for divorce, filed in October 1907. It charges that Mary Austin "willfully and without cause...deserted and abandoned" her husband. See Box 122, Folder 8, MHACH.

50. For an analysis of Austin's indeterminate relationship with Lincoln Steffens (one that he characterized as platonic and she perceived as devastating), see Karen S. Langlois, "Mary Austin and Lincoln Steffens," *Huntington Library Quarterly* 49 (Autumn 1986): 357–82.

51. Austin, *Earth Horizon*, 280.

52. Austin, with Anne Martin, *Suffrage and Government: The Modern*

Idea of Government by Consent and Woman's Place in it, with special reference to Nevada and other Western States (Reno: Nevada Equal Franchise Society, 1914), 15.

53. For analysis of this literature, see Lanigan, *Mary Austin*; and Leah Dilworth, *Imagining Indians in the Southwest: Persistent Visions of a Primitive Past* (Washington: Smithsonian Institution Press, 1996).

54. What she learned through her inquiries into Indian culture encouraged her to critique established ideas about gender. Austin published a series of articles on "Making the Most of Your Genius" in *The Bookman* (republished as a book in 1923) in which she argued, against existing logic on the subject, that genius was not strictly an inherited "gift." Instead, she saw it as a skill at using the "immediate self," the sum of an individual's experience, to make use of the "deep-self," the sum of inheritance, defined as "racial" or cultural experience. This definition implicitly explained the high incidence of "geniuses" among men relative to women by introducing the elements of access to experience and challenged Anglo readers to also consider that different cultures produced different sorts of geniuses. Austin, "Making the Most of Your Genius I: What is Genius?," *The Bookman*, November 1923, 246–47.

55. Austin, *Earth Horizon*, 339–40.

56. Ibid., 354.

57. Austin, "Why I Live in Santa Fe," *The Golden Book*, October 1932, 306–7.

58. "Writer Speaks Before Sessions of N.M.E.A.," *Santa Fe New Mexican*, 6 Nov. 1931, 8.

59. Austin, *Earth Horizon*, 368.

60. Tey Diana Rebolledo, introduction to Cleofas Jaramillo, *Romance of a Little Village Girl* (1955; Albuquerque: University of New Mexico Press, 2000), xxv.

61. See Jacobs, *Engendered Encounters*, 18; and Brian Dippie, *The Vanishing American: White Attitudes and U.S. Indian Policy* (Middletown, CT: Wesleyan University Press, 1982), 274–79.

62. Luhan to Austin, 1 Feb. 1922?, AU 3573, MHACH.

63. Luhan to Austin, ? Dec. 1922?, AU 3584, MHACH; reprinted in T. M. Pearce, *Literary America, 1903–1934: The Letters of Mary Austin* (Westport, CT: Greenwood Press, 1979), 172–73.

64. Austin to Luhan, 5 Dec. 1922, MDLC.

65. Austin, "Speech of Mary Austin Before the National Popular Government League on the Burson [*sic*] Bill, Washington, D.C., Jan. 17, 1923," AU 51, MHACH.

66. Austin to Luhan, 4 April 1923, MDLC.

67. For details on the Arizona case, see Peggy Pascoe, "Miscegenation Law, Court Cases, and Ideologies of 'Race' in Twentieth-Century America," in *Sex, Love, Race: Crossing Boundaries in North American History*, ed. Martha Hodes (New York: New York University Press, 1999), 464–90.

68. While Jacobs argues that "it was more their adultery and cohabitation without marriage than the interracial quality of their liaison that

caused many white Americans to view Mabel and Tony's relationship as scandalous," such statements more accurately describe the feelings of moderates like Austin than Americans at large; Luhan's fear about losing her inheritance, a fear she apparently did not experience with her other marriages, testifies to her sense that Tony's race played a significant part in creating scandal. See Jacobs, "The Eastmans and the Luhans: Interracial Marriage between White Women and Native American Men, 1875–1935," *Frontiers* 23.3 (2002), 43.

69. Tony Lujan's relationship with Mabel apparently cost him access to Taos Pueblo ceremonials for a time, but he was welcomed back into the kiva in 1936, according to a letter Mabel Luhan sent John Collier about the event. Luhan to Collier, 3 Feb. 1936, John Collier Papers, Manuscripts and Archives, Yale University Library, New Haven, CT. Microfilm Edition (Sanford, NC: Microfilming Corporation of America, 1980), Reel 15.

70. Luhan to Henderson, "Journal Intime," 15 April 1923, ACHC.

71. The one-thousand dollar allowance reported by Luhan was the amount she feared giving up if her mother disowned her; she still would have earned three hundred dollars a month from her father's estate. Luhan to Henderson, "Journal Intime," 15 April 1923, ACHC. Rudnick reports the thirty-five-dollar monthly payment to Candelaria Lujan in her biography of Mabel Dodge Luhan and also indicates that Luhan apparently did not realize when she wrote to Henderson that she had an annual income of about fourteen thousand dollars a year that her mother would not have been able to control. But apparently Luhan had come to depend on her mother for large cash gifts in addition to her other income. Rudnick, *Mabel Dodge Luhan*, 155, 182.

72. Luhan to Henderson, 17 April 1923, 18 April 1923, ACHC.

73. Luhan to Austin, 21 April 1923, AU 3588, MHACH.

74. Austin to Luhan, 29 April 1923, MDLC.

75. Austin to Luhan, undated letter (likely sometime in 1925), MDLC.

76. Luhan, "Mary Austin: A Woman," in *Mary Austin: A Memorial*, ed. Willard Houghland (Santa Fe: Laboratory of Anthropology, 1944), 20.

77. Austin to Luhan, undated letter, MDLC.

78. Austin wrote an opinion piece about this controversy, for a national intellectual audience, in which she proudly stated the fact that two civic organizations for Spanish-Americans in Santa Fe had issued opinions against the Chautauqua. See Austin, "The Town That Doesn't Want a Chautauqua," *The New Republic*, 7 July 1926; repr. in *Beyond Borders: The Selected Essays of Mary Austin*, ed. Reuben Ellis (Carbondale, IL: Southern Illinois University Press, 1996), 102–10.

79. For an account of this campaign, see Mullin, *Culture in the Marketplace*, 98–104.

80. For one portrait of Campa and his work, see Mario T. García, *Mexican Americans: Leadership, Ideology, and Identity, 1930–1960* (New Haven: Yale University Press, 1989), 273–90.

81. A University of New Mexico English professor had recommended Campa to Austin, pointing out that he had grown up in Mexico, and

was a fine scholar as well as a fluent speaker of Spanish, French, and three Indian dialects. When Austin hesitated, the professor chided her for her suggestion: "It would hardly suit Mr. Campa to act in the capacity of translator for your work." C. V. Wicker to Austin, 12 July 1929, AU 4989, and 9 Aug. 1929, AU 4990, MHACH.

82. Southwestern writer and popularizer Charles Lummis once criticized Austin for unabashedly pleading ignorance about some Spanish phrases she requested from him. In a letter, Lummis reminded Austin that "when you use Spanish names, it is your business as a decent woman, and as a writer, to have them right." Charles Lummis to Austin, 24 Nov. 1904, AU 3617, MHACH; reprinted in T. M. Pearce, *Literary America*, 19–21.

83. Austin, *Earth Horizon*, 358–59.

84. Ibid., 359.

85. Rosa Montoya, interview by author, Santa Fe, NM, 25 Mar. 1999.

86. Austin to J. F. Zimmerman, 25 Nov. 1930, AU 1270, MHACH. Austin also expressed reservations about proposed changes in the curriculum of the Spanish American Normal School at El Rito in letters to the governor of New Mexico. See Austin to Governor Arthur Seligman, 6 Feb. 1931 and 1 Oct. 1931, GASP, NMSRCA.

87. Austin, "Mexicans and New Mexico," *The Survey*, 1 May 1931, 141–44, 187–90. This special issue on Mexicans in the United States included photographs by Ansel Adams, as well as artwork by Georgia O'Keeffe and Diego Rivera, and articles by Frank Applegate, J. Frank Dobie, D. H. Lawrence, Adelina (Nina) Otero, and Paul S. Taylor. Thus, *The Survey*'s editors considered Austin's viewpoints on Mexican immigrants worthy of placement among the foremost "experts" of her day.

88. Rudnick, *Mabel Dodge Luhan*, 155.

89. Luhan, *Lorenzo in Taos* (New York: Knopf, 1932), 235.

90. Rudnick, *Utopian Vistas*, 54, 57.

91. Luhan, *Winter in Taos* (New York: Harcourt, Brace and Co., 1935), 48.

92. Luhan, *Winter in Taos*, 46.

93. Ellen Kay Trimberger, "The New Woman and the New Sexuality: Conflict and Contradiction in the Writings and Lives of Mabel Dodge and Neith Boyce," in *1915, The Cultural Moment: The New Politics, the New Woman, the New Psychology, the New Art, and the New Theatre in America*, ed. Adele Heller and Lois Rudnick (New Brunswick, NJ: Rutgers University Press, 1991), 112.

94. Jacobs, "Eastmans and the Luhans," 44.

95. Luhan to John Collier, 30 Nov. 1933, John Collier Papers, Microfilm Edition, Reel 15.

96. "An Amazing Marriage: New York Society Woman Happy with Indian Husband at Taos," *Denver Post*, 7 Aug. 1932, 15. Several articles ran on the marriage on 1932: why then is unclear, though perhaps they drew from each other as sources. Luhan clipped this particular article and others out of newspapers and put them in her scrapbook. See also "Indian Marriage Pleases Writer," *Pittsburgh Post-Gazette*, 28 May

1932, 26; and "Society Woman Glad That She Married Indian," *Buffalo Times*, 1 Sept. 1932, 17.

97. "Taos County District Court, Civil: State of New Mexico on the Relation of Mabel Dodge Luhan vs. The Village of Taos," 1935, Manuel Sanchez Papers, NMSRCA.

98. John Bodine, "A Tri-Ethnic Trap: The Spanish-Americans in Taos," in *Spanish-Speaking Peoples in the United States: Proceedings of the 1968 Annual Spring Meeting of the American Ethnological Society*, ed. June Helm (Seattle: University of Washington Press, 1968), 150.

99. H. A. Kiker to James L. Goree, 13 Feb. 1935, Manuel Sanchez Papers, NMSRCA.

100. Sylvia Rodríguez, "Land, Water, and Ethnic Identity in Taos," In *Land, Water, and Culture: New Perspectives on Hispanic Land Grants*, ed. Charles L. Briggs and John R. Van Ness (Albuquerque: University of New Mexico Press, 1987), 313.

101. Luhan, *Edge of Taos Desert*, 80–81.

102. Rodríguez, "Land, Water, and Ethnic Identity in Taos," 345.

103. Roxanne Dunbar Ortíz, *Roots of Resistance: Land Tenure in New Mexico, 1680–1980* (Los Angeles: Chicano Studies Research Center and American Indian Studies Center, University of California, 1980), 93.

104. Jacobs, *Engendered Encounters*, 113, 148.

105. See William Chafe, *The Paradox of Change: American Women in the Twentieth Century* (New York: Oxford University Press, 1991); and Nancy F. Cott, *The Grounding of Modern Feminism* (New Haven: Yale University Press, 1987).

106. Elsie Clews Parsons, "The Pueblo Indian Clan in Folk-Lore," *Journal of American Folklore* 34 (April-June 1921): 209.

107. Parsons acknowledges that it is "very baffling" to try to figure out why some traits are borrowed but not others. Her general theory regarding such borrowing is "that resistance to taking over an alien trait or indifference to it is greatest when there is nothing resembling it in the culture of the potential borrower or when the new trait clashes with an existing trait or is incompatible with the spirit of the culture." Elsie Clews Parsons, *Pueblo Indian Religion* (Chicago: University of Chicago Press, 1939), 1085.

CHAPTER TWO

1. For an excellent study of how the complex processes of resistance and acculturation worked in such marriages, see Deena J. Gonzales, *Refusing the Favor: The Spanish-Mexican Women of Santa Fe, 1820–1880* (New York: Oxford University Press, 1999).

2. Cleofas Jaramillo, *Romance of a Little Village Girl* (San Antonio: Naylor, 1955), vii.

3. This phrase is used as part of the title of Genaro M. Padilla's chapter on Jaramillo, "Lies, Secrets, and Silence: Cultural Autobiography as Resistance in Cleofas Jaramillo's *Romance of a Little Village Girl*," in *My History, Not Yours: The Formation of Mexican American*

Autobiography (Madison: University of Wisconsin Press, 1993); as well as the title of an earlier article by Padilla, "Imprisoned Narrative? Or Lies, Secrets and Silence in New Mexico Women's Autobiography," in *Criticism in the Borderlands: Studies in Chicano Literature, Culture, and Ideology,* ed. Hector Calderón and José David Saldívar (Durham: Duke University Press, 1991), 43–60.

4. Jaramillo, *Shadows of the Past/Sombras del Pasado* (1941; Santa Fe: Ancient City Press, 1972), 34. Jaramillo also included this detail in her later book, *Romance of a Little Village Girl,* although she omitted the Spanish in the later version, perhaps in deference to her publisher's wishes. Jaramillo, *Romance,* 46.

5. "Usually migrating in family units, the pioneers were predominantly *mestizos,* a mixture of Indian and Spanish. There were also many mulattos and a few Europeans—some born in Spain, others in Mexico—as well as Hispanicized Indians from the interior of Mexico, and later, Indians from the north, who themselves were pioneers. The culture, with variant regional adaptations, corresponded to that of central Mexico." Juan Gómez-Quiñones, *Roots of Chicano Politics, 1600–1940* (Albuquerque: University of New Mexico Press, 1994), 15.

6. Matt S. Meier and Feliciano Ribera, *The Chicanos: A History of Mexican Americans* (New York: Hill and Wang, 1972), 21.

7. Jaramillo, *Shadows,* 13; see also Jaramillo, *Romance,* 4. The later book also implies that some of Don Manuel's ancestors had participated in the 1598 Oñate expedition, and that authorities granted the Tierra Amarilla land in recognition of such efforts. Tierra Amarilla later gained a significant place in the history of the Chicano Movement: in 1967, the *Alianza Federal de Pueblos Libres,* led by Reies Lopez Tijerina, staged a well-publicized raid on the Tierra Amarilla Court House, in the name of unjust violation of land grant ownership and the terms of the 1848 Treaty of Guadalupe Hidalgo. See Juan Gómez-Quiñones, *Chicano Politics: Reality and Promise, 1940–1990* (Albuquerque: University of New Mexico Press, 1990), 115–18. I also briefly describe the significance of this event in the Afterword.

8. Jaramillo, *Shadows,* 13.

9. Ibid., 14. Jaramillo does not specify which tribes raided the village. Most likely such raiders would have been Navajos, Apaches, or Utes. For more explication of the relationship between Navajos and Hispanics in New Mexico, and an account of how both groups depended on raiding for economic purposes, see Chapter 4.

10. Jaramillo, *Shadows,* 15.

11. Ibid., 17.

12. Gómez-Quiñones, *Roots of Chicano Politics,* 194–95.

13. A Spaniard was *español* if male, and *española* if female; a Pueblo Indian was an *indio;* a *genízaro* was a detribalized Indian; and a person of general mixed race was a *color quebrado.* More specifically, a child of a Spaniard and an Indian was a *mestizo* or a *mulato,* a child born to a mestizo and a Spanish woman was a *castizo,* while a child born in captivity to an Indian slave mother and a Spanish father was a *coyote*

or a *lobo*. See Ramón Gutiérrez, *When Jesus Came, the Corn Mothers Went Away: Marriage, Sexuality, and Power in New Mexico, 1500–1846* (Stanford, CA: Stanford University Press, 1991), 197–98.

14. Gutiérrez, *When Jesus Came*, 196.

15. In the late eighteenth century, for example, a mulato named Don Antonio Gil y Barbo became the lieutenant governor of colonial Tejas as well as the leader of the resettlement of the presidio at Nacogdoches, even though the position officially needed to be filled by an español. His status among his local supporters made it possible to waive this requirement: personal correspondence referred to him as mulato, while official documents listed him as español. Gómez-Quiñones, *Roots of Chicano Politics*, 45.

16. Quoted in Ralph Emerson Twitchell, *The History of the Military Occupation of the Territory of New Mexico From 1846 to 1851, By the Government of the United States* (Denver: Smith-Brooks, 1909), 74.

17. David C. Gutiérrez, *Walls and Mirrors: Mexican Americans, Mexican Immigrants, and the Politics of Ethnicity* (Berkeley: University of California Press, 1995), 32.

18. Historian Charles Montgomery, for example, explains the early-twentieth-century revival of "Spanish" identity as a collaborative effort by Anglos and Hispanos to assert a common racial identity despite the "problem" of the "dark-complexioned Mexican." Montgomery, "The Trap of Race and Memory: The Language of Spanish Civility on the Upper Rio Grande," *American Quarterly* 52.3 (September 2000), 495.

19. Arthur L. Campa, *Hispanic Culture in the Southwest* (Norman: University of Oklahoma Press, 1979), 5. For an intense and evocative debate involving the history and significance of what Spanish-speaking New Mexicans call themselves, see Richard L. Nostrand, "The Hispano Homeland in 1900," *Annals of the Association of American Geographers* 70.3 (September 1980): 382–96; followed by Niles Hansen and Richard L. Nostrand, "Commentary: The Hispano Homeland in 1900; Comment in Reply," *Annals of the Association of American Geographers* 71.2 (June 1981): 280–83; followed by J. M. Blaut and Antonio Rios-Bustamante, "Commentary on Nostrand's 'Hispanos' and their 'Homeland,'" Richard L. Nostrand, "Hispano Cultural Distinctiveness: A Reply," and Marc Simmons, Fray Angélico Chávez, D. W. Meinig, and Thomas D. Hall, "Rejoinders"—all in *Annals of the Association of American Geographers* 74.1 (March 1984): 157–72.

20. Jaramillo, *Romance*, 10–11.

21. Jaramillo, *Shadows*, 40.

22. Jaramillo, *Romance*, 12.

23. Ibid., 8.

24. For a nuanced explanation of the historical roots of such stereotypes, see David J. Weber, "'Scarce More Than Apes': Historical Roots of Anglo American Stereotypes of Mexicans in the Border Region," *New Spain's Far Northern Frontier*, ed. David J. Weber (Albuquerque: University of New Mexico Press, 1979), 293–307.

25. Jaramillo, *Romance*, 54.

26. Roxanne Dunbar Ortíz, *Roots of Resistance, Land Tenure in New Mexico, 1680–1980* (Los Angeles: Chicano Studies Research Center and American Indian Studies Center, University of California, Los Angeles, 1980), 99.

27. For an account of Catron and the emergence of "Santa Fe Ring," see Howard Roberts Lamar, *The Far Southwest, 1846–1912: A Territorial History* (1966; New York: Norton, 1970), 136–70.

28. The Loretto nuns came from Kansas City to New Mexico at the request of the first non-Spanish and non-Mexican archbishop of the state, Rev. Jean Baptiste Lamy, in the years following his 1851 arrival in Santa Fe. Willa Cather tells a sympathetic version of the story of his impact on New Mexico in *Death Comes for the Archbishop* (New York: Knopf, 1927).

29. Jaramillo, *Romance*, 30.

30. Ibid., 52.

31. Ibid., 71.

32. Ibid.

33. The church wedding record of Cleofas Martínez and Venceslao Jaramillo shows that they received a church dispensation for their marriage because of this relationship; such dispensations were common for marriages between members of New Mexico's Hispanic elite. Copy of wedding record, 27 July 1898, Cleofas Jaramillo biography file, Southwest Room, New Mexico State Library, Santa Fe, NM. For an extensive analysis of New Mexico church policy on these matters during this period, and its effect on the Martínez-Jaramillo wedding, see Carol Jensen, "Cleofas Jaramillo's View of Marriage: An Example of the Interplay of Folk Religion and Institutional Religion in Territorial Northern New Mexico" (Master's thesis, Indiana University, 1981); and/or Carol Jensen, "Cleofas M. Jaramillo on Marriage in Territorial Northern New Mexico," *New Mexico Historical Review* 58.2 (April 1983): 153–71.

34. Jaramillo's niece, Rosa Martínez Montoya, indicated that Venceslao had attended Regis, as had many of the young men in the Martínez family. Rosa Montoya, interview by author, Santa Fe, NM, 25 March 1999.

35. Letters from Venceslao Jaramillo to Cleofas Martínez (Jaramillo), 16 July 1896, 28 Aug. 1896, 3 Jan. 1898, Venceslao Jaramillo Papers, AC 115-P, ACHL. These letters are written in English.

36. Jaramillo, *Romance*, 67.

37. Ibid., 71–72.

38. Carol Jensen's study of Jaramillo's wedding and changes in religious customs points out that the proximity of Jaramillo's wedding date, July 27, to the feast day of Saint Anne, *Dia de Santa Ána*, July 26, may indicate that she wanted to maintain a core of tradition in choosing the day for her wedding. (Jensen, "Cleofas M. Jaramillo on Marriage in Territorial Northern New Mexico," 165.) Though Jaramillo's later writings do not mention such a choice specifically, they do mention this day as one of particular interest for women, who traditionally gathered together to go riding on this day. Additionally, Jaramillo later chose Santa Ana as the patron saint of the folklore society she formed. (Jaramillo, *Shadows*, 87; Jaramillo, *Romance,* 44, 183.) As a young woman planning her wedding,

Jaramillo may have wished to establish a link between her modern wedding and her traditional faith, especially since she had approached the marriage with trepidation. Perhaps she neglected to mention choosing a patron saint for her wedding day because the events of that day made it seem like no saint could be watching over her and Venceslao.

39. Jaramillo, *Romance*, 76.
40. In *Shadows*, Jaramillo notes that traditional *nuevomexicano* wedding invitations were "printed in the name of both parents and distributed by messengers." She followed American custom even though Venceslao Jaramillo, and not her father, paid for the wedding. Jaramillo, *Shadows*, 32; Invitation to the Wedding of Cleofas Martínez and Venceslao Jaramillo, AC 115-P, Venceslao Jaramillo Papers, ACHL.
41. Jensen, "Cleofas Jaramillo's View of Marriage," 43.
42. Jaramillo, *Romance*, 81.
43. Ibid., 96.
44. Jaramillo, *Shadows*, 96.
45. Ortíz, *Roots of Resistance*, 91-108.
46. Lamar, *Far Southwest*, 138.
47. Jaramillo, *Romance*, 184.
48. Lamar, *Far Southwest*, 198.
49. Lynn I. Perrigo, *Hispanos: Historic Leaders in New Mexico* (Santa Fe: Sunstone, 1985), 67.
50. Jaramillo, *Romance*, 96, 64.
51. Gómez-Quiñones, *Roots of Chicano Politics*, 259.
52. A senior archivist for the state of New Mexico confirmed these dates (which are not included in Jaramillo's writings) for me by consulting the Legislative Manuals (Blue Books) for the state of New Mexico. Daphne S. O. Arnaiz-DeLeon, NMSRCA, letter to the author, 10 May 1999.
53. Venceslao Jaramillo served as one of thirty-two Hispanic delegates, all of them Republican. There were one hundred delegates total; recall that approximately 60 percent of the state's residents at this time were Hispanos. For details about the convention, see Lamar, *Far Southwest*, 499-504, and Gómez-Quiñones, *Roots of Chicano Politics*, 326-28.
54. Jaramillo, *Romance*, 112. The school later became a campus of Northern New Mexico Community College.
55. Mary Austin, letter to Governor Arthur Seligman, 6 February 1931, GASP, NMSRCA.
56. Guillermo Lux, *Politics and Education in Hispanic New Mexico: From the Spanish American Normal School to the Northern New Mexico Community College* (El Rito, NM: Northern New Mexico Community College, 1984), 2-4. For an earlier study of the school, one focusing on an important moment of transition, see John H. Burman and David E. Williams, *An Economic, Social, and Educational Survey of Rio Arriba and Taos Counties*, 2d ed. (El Rito: Northern New Mexico Community College, 1961).
57. According to two architectural historians, the home, finished around 1900, cost ten thousand dollars to build. While residents of El Rito pointed out a ruined home covered by trees to me (from where I stood, behind a locked gate) as the Jaramillo home, these historians stated that

the house had been torn down by 1980. See Edward Fitzgerald and John
Bucholz, "The Jaramillo House," *New Mexico Architecture* 22.4 (July-
August 1980): 9–15. See also Agnesa Lufkin, "Cleofas Jaramillo and Her
Queen Anne House," *Denver Post*, 8 June 1980, 19, 21–24, 26.

58. Jaramillo, *Romance*, 96.
59. Ibid., 107–8.
60. For Rebolledo's analysis of this and other moments in *Romance* that
reveal a "disjuncture between cultures," see Tey Diana Rebolledo,
"Narrative Strategies of Resistance in Hispana Writing," *Journal of
Narrative Technique* 20.2 (Spring 1990): 134–46; as well as her introduction to a recent edition of Jaramillo, *Romance of a Little Village
Girl* (1955; Albuquerque: University of New Mexico Press, 2000), xxiii.
61. Jaramillo, *Romance*, 110–11.
62. Ibid., 114–15.
63. Ralph Melnick, *Justice Betrayed: A Double Killing in Old Santa Fe*
(Albuquerque: University of New Mexico Press, 2002), 23.
64. Jaramillo, *Romance*, 125.
65. Ruth Laughlin Barker, *Caballeros* (New York: D. Appleton and
Co., 1931).
66. Jaramillo, *Romance*, 119.
67. Montgomery, "Trap of Race and Memory," 480–81.
68. Jaramillo, *Romance*, 125.
69. Ibid., 128.
70. She took a business course as a senior in high school, but did so, she
remembered, "not dreaming that I would ever make use of it." Ibid., 70.
71. Ibid., 135. Jaramillo refers several times in her autobiography to her
very small stature, and people who knew her often refer to it in their
recollections. "She was small-boned," recalled her niece, "smaller than
I." (Rosa Montoya, interview by author.) Jaramillo seems to have disliked being perceived as "too small": she writes of her annoyance at
her wedding as being referred to as "exquisite," wondering, "Would
people ever let me forget my diminutive size?" (Jaramillo, *Romance*,
78). Perhaps she resented the implication of unimportance.
72. Copy of Decision on Case no. 2624, District Court of Rio Arriba
County, 28 September 1927, Renehan-Gilbert Papers, NMSRCA.
73. Jaramillo, *Romance*, 137.
74. Ibid., 146.
75. Rosa Montoya, interview by author.
76. Jaramillo, *Romance*, 141.
77. Ibid., 145.
78. Ibid., 157.
79. Until recent years, however, such doubts were not discussed openly or
by scholars, despite clear evidence of racial bias. Perhaps the story did
not receive attention outside Santa Fe because outsiders still tend to
view New Mexican cultural history as strictly a matter of Hispanic,
Indian, and Anglo heritages. In 1995, the O. J. Simpson murder trial
led to the publication of a local article regarding the crime and the bias-
es it unleashed. See Steve Terrell, "A Tale of Murder, Race, Media, and

Justice: How Much Has Changed in Fifty Years?" *Santa Fe New Mexican*, 29 Oct. 1995, A1, A6. Melnick published his book about the case in 2002. He argues convincingly that Johnson was not the murderer, although his conclusions do not appear to be based on new evidence.

80. "Negro Is Brought to Prison, Denies Attacking Young Girl," *Santa Fe New Mexican*, 16 Nov. 1931, 1–2.

81. "A Lesson," editorial, *Santa Fe New Mexican*, 16 Nov. 1931, 4.

82. "Santa Fe for Law and Order," *Albuquerque Journal*, 18 Nov. 1931, 4.

83. "An Old Subscriber," "Citizen Criticises Paper For Attitude in Negro Case; Crime Personal, Not Racial," letter, *Santa Fe New Mexican*, 17 Nov. 1931, 4.

84. Melnick, *Justice Betrayed*, 55.

85. "Slain Girl Student at Loretto Member of Old Spanish Family," *Santa Fe New Mexican*, 16 Nov. 1931, 1, 6.

86. Jaramillo, *Shadows*, 96.

87. Jaramillo, *Romance*, 161.

88. "Crist Charges Court Erred in Trial of Johnson," *Santa Fe New Mexican*, 20 June 1932, 1.

89. Jaramillo, *Romance*, 161.

90. Consider that, during the 1920s, an estimated 200,000 Klansmen lived in Texas, and in 1924 Coloradans elected a "Klan" candidate for governor. James E. Wright and Sarah A. Rosenberg, *The Great Plains Experience: Readings in the History of a Region* (Lincoln, NE: University of Mid-America Press, 1978), 357.

91. "No Decision on Johnson," *Santa Fe New Mexican*, 18 July 1933, 1.

92. T. W. Hanna, letter to Governor Arthur Seligman, 4 April 1933, GASP, NMSRCA.

93. Lujan, telegram to Governor Arthur Seligman, 15 July 1933, and Walter White, Governor Arthur Seligman, 14 July 1933, GASP, NMSRCA.

94. Rosa Montoya, interview by author. See also Melnick, *Justice Betrayed*, 178.

95. Maria Puente, "Execution New Mexico Style: The Rope, the Chair, and Gas All Claimed Victims and Aroused Passions," *Santa Fe New Mexican*, 4 March 1979, B3.

96. Rita Younis, "Who Killed Angelina?," *La Herencia del Norte*, Spring 1998, 38–39.

97. Dan Burrows, "The Clue of the Lipstick: An Enigma of New Mexico," *Master Detective* (March 1935), 42–49, 83.

98. Jaramillo, *Romance*, 155.

99. "Crowd Gathers at Pen for Execution: Johnson, Garduno First In State Sent to Chair," *Santa Fe New Mexican*, 21 July 1933, A1.

100. Montgomery calls this phenomenon the "trap of Spanish heritage": it elevated Spanish identity by confining the power of those who claimed it to the past. Montgomery, "Trap of Race and Memory," 480–81.

101. Rosa Montoya, interview by author.

102. Ibid.

103. Jaramillo, *Romance*, 167. Rosa Montoya emphasized that her aunt had a favorable opinion of Mary Austin's work. Rosa Montoya, interview

by author. The "cinco pintores" were a group of five Anglo painters (Freemont Ellis, Willard Nash, Jozef Bakos, Will Shuster and Walter Mruk) who began exhibiting together in Santa Fe in 1921. See Marta Weigle and Kyle Fiore, *Santa Fe and Taos: The Writer's Era, 1916–1941* (Santa Fe: Ancient City Press, 1984), 22, 116.

104. "An Open Letter to *Holland's* Friends," *Holland's*, January 1935, 2.

105. Elizabeth Willis DeHuff, "Intriguing Mexican Dishes," *Holland's*, March 1935, 47.

106. Ibid., 34. All spellings and the parenthetical explanation belong to the original author.

107. Jaramillo, *Romance*, 173.

108. Edith Wyatt Moore, "The Natchez Pilgrimage," *Holland's*, March 1935, 18.

109. Jaramillo, *Romance*, 174.

110. Chris Wilson, *The Myth of Santa Fe: Creating a Modern Regional Tradition* (Albuquerque: University of New Mexico Press, 1997), 195.

111. Moore, "Natchez Pilgrimage," 21.

112. Renato Rosaldo's term *imperialist nostalgia*, which applies to the conqueror's longing for that which he or she has already conquered, comes to mind here. Rosaldo, "Imperialist Nostalgia," *Representations* 26 (Spring 1989): 107–22.

113. Wilson, *Myth of Santa Fe*, 201, 205.

114. Will Shuster, "Zozobra Belongs to All the People," *The Santa Fe Scene*, 30 August 1958, 4.

115. Jaramillo, *Romance*, 174.

116. Ibid., 174–76.

117. Montgomery, "Trap of Race and Memory," 502.

118. Jaramillo explained the origins of her ideas, including a reference to Dobie's work, in *Romance*, 176. Despite a search of the J. Frank Dobie papers at the Harry Ransom Humanities Research Center at the University of Texas at Austin, I have not uncovered any other evidence of a correspondence between Jaramillo and Dobie, other than the fact that Dobie owned a copy of Jaramillo's first book, *Cuentos del Hogar (Spanish Fairy Stories)* (El Campo, TX: The Citizen Press, 1939).

119. Francis A. Abernethy, "Texas Folklore Society," *The Handbook of Texas Online* (The Texas State Historical Association, 1999); available http://www.tsha.utexas.edu; Internet; accessed 7 April 2004.

120. Jaramillo, *Romance*, 176.

121. Ibid., 177.

122. Reynalda Ortíz y Pino de Dinkel and Dora Gonzales de Martínez, *Una colleccion de adivinanzas y diseños de colcha/A Collection of Riddles and Colcha Designs* (Santa Fe: Sunstone Press, 1988), 9.

123. Jaramillo, *The Genuine New Mexico Tasty Recipes* (1942; Santa Fe: Ancient City Press, 1981), 1.

124. Padilla, *My History, Not Yours*, 224.

125. Anne Goldman, "'I Yam What I Yam': Cooking, Culture, and Colonialism," in *De/Colonizing the Subject: The Politics of Gender in Women's Autobiography*, ed. Sidonie Smith and Julia Watson

(Minneapolis: University of Minnesota Press, 1992), 179. See also Anne
Goldman, *Take My Word: Autobiographical Innovations of Ethnic
American Working Women* (Berkeley: University of California Press,
1996), 3–31. Rebolledo, Introduction to Jaramillo, *Romance*, xix.

126. Rosa Montoya, interview by author.

127. Jaramillo, "Author's Foreword," *Cuentos del Hogar*.

128. Jaramillo, *Romance*, 168.

129. Reyes N. Martínez produced at least two narratives for the folklore
project: "The Martínez Family of Arroyo Hondo," which describes his
family's history, including his sister's wedding; and "Rural Weddings,"
which describes some of the same customs that Jaramillo wrote about
in her books. Reyes Martínez, "The Martínez Family of Arroyo
Hondo," WPA 5–5–47 no. 22, AC 228, ACHL; Reyes N. Martínez,
"Rural Weddings," 13 May 1936, no. 457, Unpublished WPA Records,
NMSRCA. For an account of this folklore project and the context of
the Works Progress Administration, see Lorin Brown, *Hispano Folklife
of New Mexico: The Lorin W. Brown Federal Writers' Project
Manuscripts* (Albuquerque: University of New Mexico Press, 1978).

130. Rosa Montoya, interview by author.

131. Jaramillo, Letter to Mary Austin, 21 April 1934, AU 3259, MHACH.

132. Cary Abbott (Editor's Department, Alfred A. Knopf, Inc.), Letter to
Mary Austin, 18 June 1934, AU 3419, MHACH.

133. Jaramillo, *Romance*, 168.

134. Jaramillo, *Shadows*, 12.

135. Ibid., 97.

136. Jaramillo, *Romance*, vii.

137. Ibid., 14.

138. Ibid., 194.

139. Rosa Montoya, interview by author. Rosa herself was not able to attend
many meetings for this reason; she worked in stores and as a milliner.

140. For an analysis of how women's groups in the U.S. employed "domestic feminism" during the era in which Jaramillo came of age, see Karen
Blair, *The Clubwoman as Feminist: True Womanhood Redefined,
1868–1914* (New York: Homes and Meier, 1980).

CHAPTER THREE

1. Fabiola Cabeza de Baca's married name was Gilbert; she published writings for the *LULAC News* under the name of "Mrs. Carlos Gilbert" and
usually went by the name of Gilbert in social situations. Since she published her autobiography under the name Fabiola Cabeza de Baca, however, and since her marriage ended in divorce after ten years, I have
chosen to refer to her by her given last name, Cabeza de Baca. This
choice is consistent with other recent sources. For example, in the second
(2000) edition of *American Women Writers*, a reference work, Cabeza
de Baca is listed under "Cabeza de Baca," even though the first (1980)
edition listed her under "Gilbert." See Helen Bannan, "Fabiola Cabeza
de Baca," in *American Women Writers: A Critical Reference Guide from*

Colonial Times to the Present, 2d. ed., vol. 1, ed. Lina Mainiero (Detroit: St. James Press, 2000), 159; and Bannan, "Fabiola Cabeza de Baca Gilbert," *American Women Writers: A Critical Reference Guide from Colonial Times to the Present*, 1st ed., vol. 2, ed. Lina Mainiero (New York: Frederick Ungar Publishing Co., 1980), 113. Biographer Merrihelen Ponce, who has written the only book-length study of Cabeza de Baca's life, states that "research indicates [that] Fabiola reverted back to her maiden name sometime in the late 1950s" (174). Merrihelen Ponce, "The Life and Works of Fabiola Cabeza de Baca, New Mexican Hispanic Women Writer: A Contextual Biography" (Ph.D. diss., University of New Mexico, 1995). When citing published sources, I add [Gilbert] to Fabiola Cabeza to Baca if the source was published under her married name. If her name was listed using a different variation, such as "Fabiola de Baca Gilbert," or "Mrs. Carlos Gilbert," then I put this version of her name in quotations.

2. Cabeza de Baca [Gilbert], *The Good Life: New Mexico Traditions and Food* (1949; Santa Fe: Museum of New Mexico Press, 1982); Cabeza de Baca, *We Fed Them Cactus*, 2d. ed. (1954; Albuquerque: University of New Mexico Press, 1994).

3. Cabeza de Baca [Gilbert], *Boletin de Conservar*, Circular No. 133 (State College, NM: New Mexico Agricultural Extension Service, 1935); and *Los Alimentos y su Preparacion*, Circular No. 129 (State College, NM: New Mexico Agricultural Extension Service, 1934). Both were reprinted in subsequent editions.

4. Though Cabeza de Baca's cousin, Paul Taylor, reports that she often fixed him elaborate breakfasts during his visits to Santa Fe, her niece, Esther Branch Sánchez, told me that Cabeza de Baca did not enjoy cooking. J. Paul Taylor, phone interview by author, 23 Mar. 2003. (Taylor, a retired teacher, stayed with his cousin while conducting business as the president of the New Mexico Education Association; today he serves in the New Mexico state legislature, representing his home district of Mesilla.) Esther Branch Sánchez, interview by author, Santa Fe, NM, 6 June 2000.

5. This anecdote is mentioned in a review of *We Fed Them Cactus*. See "'*We Fed Them Cactus*,' Worthy Addition to Western Americana," *Las Cruces* (N.M.) *Sun-News*, 13 Dec. 1954, 2.

6. Ponce, in "Life and Works," reports this relationship between Jaramillo and Cabeza de Baca without documenting the exact connection (32). There is no record of correspondence between the women, which is not surprising given that only a small fraction of either women's papers remain, and that both of them lived in Santa Fe from the late 1920s until Jaramillo's death; they likely saw each other often in person. It also seems likely that Cabeza de Baca was one of the women whom Jaramillo invited over when she had her initial idea for La Sociedad Folklórica; though Cabeza de Baca's busy career must have made it difficult for her to attend its weekday meetings, she certainly served as one of the group's most notable members. Both clearly shared a sense of heritage and a sense of purpose: the fact that Jaramillo came from the generation prior to Cabeza de Baca's (she was seventeen years older

than her cousin) helps to explain why many of her life choices and her view of traditionalism proved to be more conservative. I interviewed both Jaramillo's niece (Rosa Montoya) and Cabeza de Baca's niece (Esther Branch Sánchez) for this project. The women live within half a mile of each other in Santa Fe, but they did not know one another.

7. Angélico Chávez's *Origins of New Mexico Families*, the standard genealogical reference for Hispanos, states that members of Fabiola's family were not descended from the explorer, though some previous sources suggested this. Apparently one "Baca" changed his name to "Cabeza de Baca" in 1803, perhaps because the name suggested a higher social prominence, and his descendents followed suit. "Baca" and "Cabeza de Baca" are common last names in New Mexico today. See Angélico Chávez, *Origins of New Mexico Families: A Genealogy of the Spanish Colonial Period*, rev. ed. (1954; Santa Fe: Museum of New Mexico Press, 1992), 152.

8. Cabeza de Baca, *We Fed Them Cactus*, 80.

9. In a 1975 interview, Cabeza de Baca explained, as Jaramillo did in her writings, that in "colonial days, when the Spanish...came to New Mexico, they married their cousins...because they did not want to mix their blood with others. And that's the way my family was." Cabeza de Baca [Gilbert], interview by Paula Thaidigsman, 29 August 1975, cassette tape, Women in New Mexico Collection, CSWR.

10. As explained by Tey Diana Rebolledo, 16 May 1894 is the most likely date for Cabeza de Baca's birth, though in some sources, including one interview she gave, the year of her birth is stated as 1898. See Tey Diana Rebolledo, Introduction to Fabiola Cabeza de Baca, *We Fed Them Cactus* (1954; Albuquerque: University of New Mexico Press, 1994), xxx, n.1.

11. Cabeza de Baca, interview by Thaidigsman.

12. Cabeza de Baca, not surprisingly, never mentioned such an incident or expulsion herself, but her niece claimed this to be true. Esther Branch Sánchez, interview by Merrihelen Ponce, 22 Mar. 1991, cited in Ponce, "Life and Works," 32.

13. Cabeza de Baca's memoir remained vague on the exact chronology of her graduation date and early teaching experiences, but Ponce's research establishes these dates using available records and interviews. For a review of Cabeza de Baca's educational and early teaching experiences in the context of her family history and trends in nuevomexicano society, see Ponce, "Life and Works," 82–89. Ponce indicates that Cabeza de Baca was offered the job in about 1915, but in *We Fed Them Cactus*, Cabeza de Baca associates the memories of her first year teaching with her memories of her uncle's campaign for the New Mexico governorship in 1916. Cabeza de Baca, *We Fed Them Cactus*, 165.

14. Cabeza de Baca, *We Fed Them Cactus*, 84.

15. Cabeza de Baca, interview by Thaidigsman.

16. Cabeza de Baca, *We Fed Them Cactus*, 132.

17. Ibid., 151.

18. Ibid., 129.

19. Ibid., 134.

20.   Cabeza de Baca, "The People and the Community," undated portion of
        unpublished book manuscript, Folder 11, FCBP, CSWR, 1.
21.   "The Las Vegas Community Land Grant: Its Decline and Fall,"
        Unattributed, undated manuscript from Land Grant Vertical File, Las
        Vegas Public Library, Las Vegas, NM. This struggle for control of the
        land became a major cause of the "White Caps" or "Las Gorras Blancas"
        rebellion of the 1890s. For a brief summary of this violence, see Richard
        White, "*It's Your Misfortune and None of My Own": A History of the
        American West* (Norman: University of Oklahoma Press, 1991), 343.
22.   Cabeza de Baca, *We Fed Them Cactus,* 73.
23.   The history of voting rights in New Mexico shows how women's issues
        were inextricably connected with civil rights issues during the era of
        Cabeza de Baca's youth. Women received the right to vote in school elec-
        tions with the New Mexico state constitution drafted in 1910, but by
        1914 it was one of the only states in the West without women's suffrage
        in state elections. Full suffrage for women did not reach New Mexico
        until it reached all the states, through the Nineteenth Amendment to the
        U.S. Constitution in 1920. Historian Joan Jensen explains that previous
        historical work has attributed this relative rate of delay to a
        Hispanic/Anglo divide over the issue. She asserts instead that New
        Mexico's lack of full women's suffrage emerged as a result of the absence
        of long-established suffrage organizations, the difficulty of attaining state
        amendments through the provisions of the 1910 constitution, and the
        sense among both Anglo and Hispanic voters that women's suffrage could
        disrupt the political compromises that currently existed between these
        two ethnic groups. Thus, Cabeza de Baca likely believed that ethnic ten-
        sions needed resolution if sexual inequality in the civic realm was to be
        further addressed. See Joan M. Jensen, "'Disenfranchisement is a
        Disgrace': Women and Politics in New Mexico, 1900–1940," *New
        Mexico Historical Review* 56.1 (January 1981): 5–36; repr. in *New
        Mexico Women: Intercultural Perspectives,* ed. Joan M. Jensen and Darlis
        A. Miller (Albuquerque: University of New Mexico Press, 1984), 310–31.
        See also Necah Stewart Furman, "Women's Campaign for Equality: A
        National and State Perspective," *New Mexico Historical Review* 53.4
        (October 1978): 365–74.
24.   Cabeza de Baca [Gilbert], "Pioneering in Home Economics," unpub-
        lished manuscript, likely a speech or lecture for home economics stu-
        dents, Folder 15, FCBP, CSWR, 1.
25.   A strong body of literature documents Progressive women's roots and
        influences, though scholars of U.S. history have devoted less attention
        to how Progressivism influenced New Mexican women. For the gener-
        al context of the movement and women's roles within it, see Karen
        Blair, *The Clubwoman as Feminist: True Womanhood Redefined,
        1868–1914* (New York: Homes and Meier, 1980); Dolores Hayden,
        *The Grand Domestic Revolution: A History of Feminist Designs for
        American Homes, Neighborhoods, and Cities* (Cambridge, MA: MIT
        Press, 1981); Ellen Condliffe Lagemann, *A Generation of Women:
        Education in the Lives of Progressive Reformers* (Cambridge, MA:

Harvard University Press, 1979); Kathryn Kish Sklar, "Hull House in the 1890s: A Community of Women Reformers," *Signs: Journal of Women in Culture and Society* 10.4 (Summer 1985): 658–77.

26. Ponce, "Life and Works," 81, 113 n. 34.
27. Cabeza de Baca, *We Fed Them Cactus*, 154–55.
28. Ibid., 161.
29. Ibid., 167.
30. Ibid., 156–59.
31. Ezequiel Cabeza de Baca, Fabiola's father's brother, ran as the Democrat candidate for New Mexico governor in 1916, after becoming the first lieutenant governor of the new state of New Mexico. During his term in that office, he was active in attempts to secure bilingual lessons and teachers in all New Mexico public schools; prior to being a politician, he ran a Spanish-language newspaper and press. He won the election against Republican Holm Olaf Bursum in 1916 but died before he was able to take office in 1917. See Lynn I. Perrigo, "Ezekiel Cabeza de Baca: First But Frustrated," in *Hispanos: Historic Leaders in New Mexico* (Santa Fe: Sunstone Press, 1985), 72–74. Republican officials tried to change the polling place near Fabiola Cabeza de Baca's school the night before the 1916 gubernatorial election, but she, her father, and others were able to notify voters in time. See Cabeza de Baca, *We Fed Them Cactus*, 163–65. Despite conflicts with some printed sources, I have spelled Ezequiel Cabeza de Baca's name as Cabeza de Baca did in *We Fed Them Cactus* (96).
32. Various secondary sources state Cabeza de Baca's college dates, but perhaps the best source of information about her years spent studying and teaching is an unpublished manuscript titled "The Work," undated portion of unpublished book manuscript titled *A New Mexican Hacienda*, Folder 11, FCBP, CSWR.
33. Ponce, "Life and Works," 88.
34. Cabeza de Baca, *We Fed Them Cactus*, 165. Cabeza de Baca does mention, perhaps significantly, that the young man did not vote for her uncle in the gubernatorial election of 1916.
35. While Cabeza de Baca never directly explained her reasons for working at El Rito, her family's history in politics does make her resemble other Progressive women of her era. Kathryn Kish Sklar has pointed out that the three major reformers at Chicago's Hull House in the 1890s, Jane Addams, Julia Lathrop, and Florence Kelley, all had politically active fathers. Sklar, "Hull House in the 1890s," 662. Cabeza de Baca's cousin, J. Paul Taylor, now serves in the New Mexico State House of Representatives, another testament to her family's prioritization of community leadership. Taylor, interview by author.
36. Cabeza de Baca, *We Fed Them Cactus*, 172–73.
37. Ibid., 178.
38. Cabeza de Baca, "Pioneering in Home Economics," 2.
39. Cabeza de Baca related this story of the beginning of her extension career in an unpublished and undated manuscript. See Cabeza de Baca, "The Work," 1. The story is also documented in Susan Pieper,

"Fabiola's Good Life," *New Mexico Resources* (Magazine of the College of Agriculture and Home Economics, New Mexico State University) 8 (Spring 1995): 7.

40. Hayden, *Grand Domestic Revolution*, 151.

41. William L. Bowers, *The Country Life Movement in America, 1900–1920* (Port Washington, NY: Kennikat Press, 1974).

42. Sandra Schackel, *Social Housekeepers: Women Shaping Public Policy in New Mexico, 1920–1940* (Albuquerque: University of New Mexico Press, 1992), 121, 171.

43. Jensen, "Canning Comes to New Mexico: Women and the Agricultural Extension Service, 1914–1919," *New Mexico Historical Review* 57 (October 1982): 351–86; repr. in Jensen and Miller, eds., *New Mexico Women: Intercultural Perspectives*, 201–26. See pp. 209–10 for a discussion of the various barriers that prevented employment of Spanish-speaking agricultural and home extension agents. Interestingly, the state hired several Spanish-speaking men as agricultural agents before it employed any Spanish-speaking women as home demonstration agents. Jensen has also written about the history of the relationship between New Mexican women and the Agricultural Extension Service in two other helpful articles: "Crossing Ethnic Barriers in the Southwest: Women's Agricultural Extension Education, 1914–1940," *Agricultural History* 60 (Spring 1986): 169–81; and "'I've Worked, I'm Not Afraid of Work': Farm Women in New Mexico, 1920–1940," in Jensen and Miller, eds., *New Mexico Women: Intercultural Perspectives*, 227–55.

44. Schackel, *Social Housekeepers*, 121.

45. Jensen, "Canning Comes to New Mexico," 209. By the 1950s and 1960s, however, the NMAES had not only created, but also prided itself on, a better effort to serve non-Anglo populations, as seen in the way the agency described its work in the *New Mexico Extension News*. In this later era, the NMAES still did little in this forum to recognize the need of Spanish-speaking clients, other than listing its few Spanish bulletins alongside the ones in English, but it did increasingly congratulate itself on its efforts with Native American populations. See "Indian Boys and Girls Are Outstanding 4-H Club Members," *New Mexico Extension News* 34.11 (November 1954): 5; "An Improved Way of Life Through Home Demonstration Work," *New Mexico Extension News* 36.4 (April 1956): 4–5; "Indian Women Like Homemakers College," *New Mexico Extension News* 39.9 (September 1959): 3, 5. Efforts to recognize Hispanic culture took place in the tributes to the success of Cabeza de Baca's *Historic Cookery* bulletin as well as in pieces about culinary and other cultural traditions. See "Try These Easy Ways to Peel Chile," *New Mexico Extension News* 38.8 (August 1958): 4–5; and "Twinkling Luminarias Brighten Holidays in New Mexico," *New Mexico Extension News* 42.6 (Fall 1962): 3, 5.

46. Jensen, "I've Worked, I'm Not Afraid of Work," 242.

47. In a 1975 interview, Cabeza de Baca was surprised when the interviewer asked her whether she had hired housekeepers. "Yes, I've always had help at home. I didn't do housework!" she exclaimed. Cabeza de

Baca, interview by Thaidigsman. When I spoke with Cabeza de Baca's niece, she told me that Cabeza de Baca hired a woman to help her around the house, partially because of the loss of her leg and partially because she didn't like to cook. "She had someone that took care of her at home.... And she taught them how to cook the way she liked. And that was really something... because she could always tell you how to do it but she never liked to cook. She always had someone to do her cooking." Sánchez, interview by author.

48. Virginia Scharff, "'So Many Miles to a Person': Fabiola Cabeza de Baca Makes New Mexico," in *Twenty Thousand Roads: Women, Movement, and the West* (Berkeley: University of California Press, 2003), 128.

49. Cabeza de Baca, "Pioneering in Home Economics," 4.

50. Cabeza de Baca [Gilbert], "New Mexican Diets," *Journal of Home Economics* 34 (November 1942), 668.

51. Ibid., 668.

52. Scharff, "'So Many Miles to a Person,'" in *Twenty Thousand Roads*, 130.

53. Cabeza de Baca, interview by Thaidigsman.

54. Cabeza de Baca [Gilbert], interview by Ruleen Lazell, Albuquerque, NM, 9 Feb. 1983, cassette tape, RG-T153, Rio Grande Historical Collections, New Mexico State University Library, Las Cruces, NM.

55. Suzanne Forrest, *The Preservation of the Village: New Mexico's Hispanics and the New Deal* (Albuquerque: University of New Mexico Press, 1989), 177.

56. Sarah Deutsch, *No Separate Refuge: Culture, Class, and Gender on an Anglo-Hispanic Frontier in the American Southwest, 1880–1940* (New York: Oxford University Press, 1987), 185, 209.

57. Ibid., 192.

58. Anne Goldman, "'I Yam What I Yam': Cooking, Culture, and Colonialism," in *De/Colonizing the Subject: The Politics of Gender in Women's Autobiography*, ed. Sidonie Smith and Julia Watson (Minneapolis: University of Minnesota Press, 1992), 175. See also Anne Goldman, *Take My Word: Autobiographical Innovations of Ethnic American Working Women* (Berkeley: University of California Press, 1996), 3–31. Goldman cites the bulletins on "proper" and "modern" nutrition as additional evidence of Cabeza de Baca's endorsement of Anglo standards, but Cabeza de Baca's continual remarks on the nutritional value of traditional food (like beans and chile) makes it likely that she wanted her nutrition lessons to affirm traditional habits rather than challenge them.

59. Cabeza de Baca [Gilbert], *Los Alimentos y su Preparacion*, 3.

60. Jensen, "Crossing Ethnic Barriers in the Southwest," 180.

61. Deutsch, *No Separate Refuge*, 191.

62. Cabeza de Baca [Gilbert], "New Mexican Diets," 669.

63. Mary Austin, "Mexicans and New Mexico," *The Survey*, 1 May 1931, 190.

64. While I have seen Cabeza de Baca's ability to speak Pueblo languages cited in a few secondary sources (including Pieper, "Fabiola's Good

Life," 10), Merrihelen Ponce, the author of the most extensive work on Cabeza de Baca, claims that there is no written evidence of this and that relatives disagreed on whether Cabeza de Baca spoke Tewa or not. Ponce, "Life and Works," 236–37. Esther Branch Sánchez believes that her aunt did speak Tewa. Sánchez, interview by author.

65. The letter lists other women under their husband's names, such as "Mrs. John Underwood," which may obscure their Hispanic identities. Mary Austin, letter to the editor, *Santa Fe New Mexican*, dated only 1932. Found in clippings file, Box 127, MHACH.

66. "DeBaca-Gilbert," *New Mexico Extension News* 9 (October 1929): 4.

67. The Mary Austin letter cited above, for example, was written in 1932 and refers to Cabeza de Baca as Miss Cabeza de Baca, even though she had apparently married at that point. One source indicates that Carlos Gilbert had been Cabeza de Baca's "longtime beau," but no direct records of their courtship, marriage, or divorce seem to exist. Pieper, "Fabiola's Good Life," 7.

68. Esther Branch Sánchez, interview by Ponce, cited in Ponce, "Life and Works," 101, 116.

69. Apparently the church exclusion affected Cabeza de Baca deeply; Sánchez told me that she only knew that her aunt's marriage had ended for sure when Cabeza de Baca asked her to take her to church for confession. Sánchez, interview by author.

70. The school is located near downtown Santa Fe. See Michelle Melendez, "History Lesson: Elementary Students Celebrate School's Past," *Albuquerque Journal*, 4 Dec. 1992, 1, 4. For coverage of Carlos Gilbert's election to the school board, see "School Board Ticket Filed," *Santa Fe New Mexican*, 30 July 1939, 1; "Citizens Will Ballot Tuesday," *Santa Fe New Mexican*, 11 Feb. 1939, 1; and "Democrats Take All Three Places on City School Board," *Santa Fe New Mexican*, 15 Feb. 1939, 1.

71. According to Sánchez, Gilbert had one son and one daughter, but Cabeza de Baca never discussed them openly with her family. Sánchez, interview by author.

72. Carlos Gilbert may have been driving the car when this happened, as Sánchez told Merrihelen Ponce. She also indicated that Cabeza de Baca may have sued the Atchison, Topeka, and the Santa Fe Railroad for negligence. Sánchez, interview by Ponce, cited in Ponce, "Life and Works," 101, 116. On the other hand, when I interviewed Sánchez, she recalled that Cabeza de Baca was driving the car when the train hit it. Sánchez, interview by author.

73. Cabeza de Baca, interview by Thaidigsman.

74. Cabeza de Baca's work in Spanish-language newspapers and radio is only sparsely documented. For one reference, see Harold J. Alford, "Fabiola Cabeza de Baca Gilbert: Home Economist," in *The Proud Peoples: The Heritage and Culture of Spanish-Speaking Peoples in the United States* (New York: New American Library, 1972), 223–24.

75. Esther Branch Sánchez has asserted that Cabeza de Baca borrowed many of the recipes she published from her sister, Virginia Cabeza de Baca Branch. Sánchez, interview by Ponce, cited in Ponce, "Life and

Works," 66. Sánchez also indicated to me that Branch (Sánchez's mother) had taught Cabeza de Baca how to cook and that Cabeza de Baca did not enjoy cooking. Sánchez, interview by author.

76. An article about *Historic Cookery* published in the *New Mexico Extension News* explained that the book was distributed, by request, through county extension offices throughout the state, and that the second printing of the book added illustrations to the cover page and throughout the book. See Edith Mae Woodard, "Want to Learn to Cook Spanish Food? Popular Circular Gives the Know-How," *New Mexico Extension News* 27.1–2(January–February 1947): 3. A 1957 piece in the same publication noted that "since 1939, 80,000 copies have been mailed out in answer to requests from almost every state in the Union." See "'Historic Cookery' is a Storehouse of Good Eating," *New Mexico Extension News* 37.4 (April 1957): 3. Reference sources indicate that later publications of the book resulted in total production of over 100,000 copies; see, for example, Stephanie Poythress, "Fabiola Cabeza de Baca Gilbert," in *Notable Hispanic American Women*, eds. Diane Telgen and Jim Kamp (Detroit: Gale Research, 1993), 178–79. Newspaper articles written about Cabeza de Baca in the 1950s also cite this figure. Her later books did not sell nearly as many copies.

77. Cabeza de Baca, *Historic Cookery* (NMAES Circular No. 161, 1939; repr., Santa Fe: Ancient City Press, 1970), 1.

78. Cabeza de Baca, interview by Thaidigsman; Cabeza de Baca, interview by Lazell.

79. I have not found *any* references by Cabeza de Baca to her involvement in the organization, not even in her unpublished writings.

80. Antioneta Delgado de Martínez was at least a distant relative of Cabeza de Baca's given her maiden name and the fact that a feature noting her death in the May 1939 *LULAC News* mentions that she was from Las Vegas. Like Cabeza de Baca, she earned a teaching degree at New Mexico Normal before teaching in rural New Mexico schools for ten years. Her husband, Filemón T. Martínez, had also been a teacher and also had a degree from New Mexico Normal; later he pursued a career in the insurance business, like Carlos Gilbert. These ties between the two couples probably factored in the appeal of active LULAC involvement for Cabeza de Baca. See "Antioneta Delgado de Martínez," *LULAC News* 6.5 (May 1939): 14; and "Parade of Past Presidents General: Filemón T. Martínez," *LULAC News* 13.12 (June 1947): 23, 25. I consulted all issues of *LULAC News* cited here through the League of United Latin American Citizens Archives, Nettie Lee Benson Latin American Collection, the University of Texas at Austin.

81. See David Montejano, *Anglos and Mexicans and the Making of Texas* (Austin: University of Texas Press, 1987).

82. For one example, see "Aims and Purposes of the League of United Latin American Citizens," *LULAC News* 7 (April 1940): 16.

83. For one example of the often-reprinted code, see "LULAC Code," *LULAC News* 6.5 (May 1939): 6. The required display of loyalty included speaking the English language. Item Four of the "Aims and Purposes"

cited above states that English was the official language of LULAC, "being necessary for the enjoyment of our rights and privileges." "Aims and Purposes," 16.

84. Mario T. García, *Mexican Americans: Leadership, Ideology, and Identity, 1930–1960* (New Haven: Yale University Press, 1989), 15.

85. Benjamin Márquez, a political scientist who has analyzed the history of the organization, emphasizes that LULAC's members "belonged to a racial and cultural minority group whose aims were to declare its loyalty to the United States, adopt American culture, and renounce any political loyalty to Mexico and its institutions." Márquez, *LULAC: The Evolution of a Mexican American Political Organization* (Austin: University of Texas Press, 1993), 9. In his study of the relationships between Mexican Americans and Mexican immigrants, historian David Gutiérrez points out that many working-class Mexican Americans and Mexican immigrants likely felt differently. "Indeed," Gutiérrez writes, "many ethnic Mexicans could see very little reason why they couldn't continue living culturally as Mexicans, even while living within the political boundaries of the United States." David G. Gutiérrez, *Walls and Mirrors: Mexican Americans, Mexican Immigrants, and the Politics of Ethnicity* (Berkeley: University of California Press, 1995), 92.

86. League of United Latin American Citizens, "About LULAC: History of LULAC, LULAC's Milestones," LULAC Official Web Site; available from www.lulac.org; accessed 17 April 2004.

87. García, *Mexican Americans*, 25.

88. This is the last mention I have found of Cabeza de Baca in the *LULAC News*. "Activities of Santa Fe Ladies Council No. 18," *LULAC News* 13.4 (October 1946): 11.

89. Service Certificate for "Mrs. Carlos Gilbert" from the American National Red Cross, 1 Nov. 1946, Folder 24, FCBP, CSWR.

90. A 1948 description of activities of the Santa Fe Ladies' LULAC group includes a car raffle to raise money for the national convention, a competition for high school Spanish students, donations to various charities, and sponsorship of a "princess" and a "Pet Parade" float for the annual Fiesta. Clearly, such activities were beneficial but secondary to the political and civic goals that initiated LULAC. "Activities of the Santa Fe Ladies LULAC Council No. 18," *LULAC News* 14.7 (January 1948): 13.

91. "Son Muy Hombres," editorial, *LULAC News* 5 (March 1938): 11–13. For an analysis of how gender affected the groups that formed LULAC, see Cynthia E. Orozco, "The Origins of the League of United Latin American Citizens (LULAC) and the Mexican American Civil Rights Movement in Texas with an Analysis of Women's Political Participation in a Gendered Context, 1910–1929" (Ph.D. diss., University of California at Los Angeles, 1992), 325–26. For women's roles in LULAC as they emerged from these origins, see García, *Mexican Americans*, 38–40. This passage mentions several women, including New Mexican women, who were active in LULAC, but it does not mention Cabeza de Baca.

92. Cynthia E. Orozco, "Regionalism, Politics, and Gender in Southwest

History: The League of United Latin American Citizens' Expansion into New Mexico from Texas, 1929–1945," *Western Historical Quarterly* 29.4 (Winter 1998): 459–83.

93. See Márquez, *LULAC*.
94. See Cabeza de Baca, interview by Thaidigsman; Cabeza de Baca, interview by Lazell.
95. Based on correspondence with Cynthia Orozco, Virginia Scharff also cited this "respectability" issue as a possible explanation for Cabeza de Baca's family's rejection of her marriage to Carlos Gilbert, an active LULAC member. If so, they also rejected Cabeza de Baca's eventual interest in the organization. Scharff, "'So Many Miles to a Person,'" in *Twenty Thousand Roads*, 126.
96. Tomas Jaehn, "Concha Ortíz y Pino: Making History in Politics," *Women's Times* (Ketchum, ID), October/November 1994, 6. Found in vertical file for Concha Ortíz y Pino de Kleven, CSWR.
97. George I. Sánchez, *Forgotten People: A Study of New Mexicans* (1940; Albuquerque: Calvin Horn, Publisher, 1967), vii
98. García, *Mexican Americans*, 231–32.
99. "Mrs. Carlos Gilbert" [Fabiola Cabeza de Baca], "New Mexicans in Texas," *LULAC News* 6.5 (May 1939): 18–19.
100. Cabeza de Baca, "New Mexican Diets," 668–69.
101. "Fabiola deBaca Gilbert" [Fabiola Cabeza de Baca], "Noche Buena for Doña Antonia: She Met Christmas with Arms Open," *New Mexico Extension News* 25.12 (December 1945): 2, 4.
102. "Extension Leaders Look Ahead," *New Mexico Extension News* 25.12 (December 1945): 6.
103. "Father Francis Stanley Crocchiola," Address to New Mexico State University's Homemakers College, *New Mexico Extension News* 44.3 (Summer 1964): 4.
104. The translations I have used here are Cabeza de Baca's own, based on the revised version of this story that she published four years later in *The Good Life*.
105. Cabeza de Baca, "Notes on *The Good Life*," unpublished manuscript, Folder 18, FCBP, CSWR.
106. Cabeza de Baca [Gilbert], *Good Life*, 26.
107. Ibid., 43.
108. Cabeza de Baca wrote of this project in a piece for the *New Mexico Extension News*, reflecting quite positively on the program, the students, and Mexican cultural politics. "The Mexican revolution was a movement [that] not only destroyed, but also built up the country," she wrote, praising the elimination of class difference in opportunities for education, and describing the village life in detail. In this piece she also laid forth her philosophy of extension work, which she described as helping people to "develop the best elements in their own culture" as well as to "achieve the social and economic progress [that] will enable them to take their place in the modern world and to live together in peace." Cabeza de Baca [Gilbert], "UNESCO's Pilot Project," *New Mexico Extension News* 32.7 (July 1952): 4–5.

109. See "Minutes of Ninth Annual Meeting," *New Mexico Folklore Record* 9 (1954–55): 29. According to earlier issues of this publication, Cabeza de Baca served as second vice-president in 1952–53, and first vice-president for the 1953–54 term.

110. Cabeza de Baca, "Preface," *We Fed Them Cactus*.

111. Becky Jo Gesteland McShane, "In Pursuit of Regional and Cultural Identity: The Autobiographies of Agnes Morley Cleaveland and Fabiola Cabeza de Baca," in *Breaking Boundaries: New Perspectives on Women's Regional Writing*, ed. Sherrie A. Inness and Diana Royer (Iowa City: University of Iowa Press, 1997), 183.

112. Cabeza de Baca, "Notes on *We Fed Them Cactus*," unpublished manuscript, Folder 18, FCBP, CSWR.

113. Associated Press, "Book Tells of Pioneering on Storied Llano Estacado," Review of *We Fed Them Cactus*, by Fabiola Cabeza de Baca, *Albuquerque Journal*, 17 Feb. 1955, 29.

114. James W. Arrott, Review of *We Fed Them Cactus*, by Fabiola [Cabeza] de Baca, *Western Folklore* 14.4 (1955): 297–99.

115. T. M. Pearce, Review of *We Fed Them Cactus*, by Fabiola Cabeza de Baca, *New Mexico Historical Review* 31.1 (January 1956): 78–79.

116. A review in the *Las Cruces Sun-News* mentions Cabeza de Baca's extension career and the awards she had received because of it, but also states that the book draws "most of all upon her own rich memories as the daughter of one of New Mexico's oldest Spanish families." "'We Fed Them Cactus' Worthy Addition To Western Americana," 2.

117. John Rothfork, Review of *We Fed Them Cactus*, by Fabiola Cabeza de Baca, *New Mexico Historical Review* 55.2 (April 1980): 180–81.

118. Raymond A. Paredes, "The Evolution of Chicano Literature," in *Three American Literatures*, ed. Houston A. Baker, Jr. (New York: Modern Language Association, 1982), 52. Historian Suzanne Forrest describes the hacienda syndrome as a gradual process, initiated by Anglo writers in the West, by which "that which was considered 'good' [about Mexican culture] became Spanish or Spanish colonial." The corollary is as follows: "That which was considered 'bad' continued to be called, derogatorily, Mexican." See Forrest, *Preservation of the Village*, 48.

119. Tey Diana Rebolledo, "Las Escritoras: Romances and Realities," in *Pasó Por Aquí: Critical Essays on the New Mexican Literary Tradition, 1542–1988*, ed. Erlinda Gonzales-Berry (Albuquerque: University of New Mexico Press, 1989), 202.

120. Cabeza de Baca, *We Fed Them Cactus*, 148.

121. Rebolledo, "Narrative Strategies of Resistance in Hispana Writing," *Journal of Narrative Technique* 20.2 (Spring 1990): 134–46.

122. The book's emphasis on Hispanic genealogy and place, writes Padilla, provides evidence of "the force of identitarian will sustained by ethnic and cultural communities that paradoxically refuse to forget the past while tending toward the occlusion of the present." Genaro Padilla, *My History, Not Yours: The Formation of Mexican American Autobiography* (Madison: University of Wisconsin Press, 1993), 204, 230.

123. Ponce, "Life and Works," 8.

124. McShane, "In Pursuit of Regional and Cultural Identity," 190.
125. Cabeza de Baca, *We Fed Them Cactus*, 59.
126. Quoted in Ralph Emerson Twitchell, *The History of the Military Occupation of the Territory of New Mexico, From 1846 to 1851, By the Government of the United States* (Denver: Smith-Brooks, 1909), 73.
127. Cabeza de Baca, *We Fed Them Cactus*, 176.
128. Cabeza de Baca, "Las Fiestas," *Santa Fe Scene*, 9 Aug. 1958, 22.
129. The train travel article described her grandfather's involvement in granting the Atchison, Topeka, and Santa Fe Railroad a charter. Cabeza de Baca also told of her own use of the railroad in the 1910s, when she went from El Rito to Las Vegas by carriage and train. Cabeza de Baca, "Changing Modes of Travel," *Santa Fe Scene*, 6 Dec. 1958, 24–25.
130. See Matthew Field, "Tales of Santa Fe, 1839 (From the Files of the *New Orleans Daily Picayune*)," *El Palacio* 67.1 (February 1960): 1–15.
131. Cabeza de Baca, "Nineteenth Century in Santa Fe," *Santa Fe Scene*, 13 Feb. 1960, 20.
132. Alice Bullock, "A Patrona of the Old Pattern," *Santa Fe New Mexican*, 19 May 1968, D4.
133. Cabeza de Baca, interview by Thaidigsman.
134. Ibid.
135. Cabeza de Baca did, however, recognize the contributions that her predecessors had made and clearly valued many of them. In an article published in 1958, Cabeza de Baca paid tribute to the efforts of Mary Austin; see Cabeza de Baca, "Las Fiestas." In an unpublished manuscript, she mentioned that Paul Horgan and Cleve Hallenbeck had both published good books about New Mexican history, *Great River* and *Land of the Conquistadores* respectively; see "Introduction," undated and unpublished manuscript, Folder 11, FCBP, CSWR, 4. In 1958 and 1960 articles, she paid tribute to the pioneering work in Hispanic folklore undertaken by Jaramillo; see Cabeza de Baca, "La Merienda," *Santa Fe Scene*, 23 Aug. 1958, 10; and "Sociedad Folklórica Celebrates 25th Year," *Santa Fe Scene*, 19 Nov. 1960, 8.
136. Cabeza de Baca, "Introduction," undated and unpublished manuscript, Folder 11, FCB, CSWR.
137. Cabeza de Baca, "The People," undated and unpublished five-page manuscript among others of that title, Folder 11, FCB, CSWR, 1.

CHAPTER FOUR

1. For history and analysis of these efforts, see Margaret Jacobs, *Engendered Encounters: Feminism and Pueblo Cultures, 1879–1934* (Lincoln: University of Nebraska Press, 1999); Leah Dilworth, *Imagining Indians in the Southwest: Persistent Visions of a Primitive Past* (Washington: Smithsonian Institution Press, 1996); and W. Jackson Rushing, *Native American Art and the New York Avant Garde: A History of Cultural Primitivism* (Austin: University of Texas Press, 1995).
2. While the Navajo refer to themselves as Diné (the People), I use *Navajo*, the term Bennett used when describing her life and culture to

English-speaking audiences and a term commonly used today in both informal and official capacities. I refer to Kay Bennett as "Bennett" or "Kay Bennett" throughout this chapter, but her given Navajo name was Kaibah Chischillie. Though government-run schools assigned "English" names to many Navajo children, the Toadlena School that Bennett attended allowed her to go by Kaibah. She later chose to refer to herself primarily by a shorter, Anglicized version, "Kay." Though she later also listed "Curly," the Anglicized form of "Chischillie," as her given surname, she published works only under her last name from her third marriage, Bennett.

3. Bill Donovan, "Twelve Seeking Chairman's Job: The New, the Old, and the First Woman All File by Monday's Deadline," *Navajo Times Today*, 10 June 1986, 1. At that time, the chairman of the council was the highest political office in the Navajo Nation. In 1989, the Navajos restructured the nation's government to more decisively split powers between the executive and legislative branches, and the executive office became that of president, instead of chairman. For an analysis of this restructuring and the events that led to it, see Peter Iverson, *Diné: A History of the Navajos* (Albuquerque: University of New Mexico Press, 2002), 297.

4. Mabel Yazzie, Bennett's niece, helped me to confirm many of the details of her life history. Mabel Yazzie, interview by author, Window Rock, AZ, 23 Mar. 1998. I found the biographical information on Bennett's young life in her memoir. See Kay Bennett, *Kaibah: Recollection of a Navajo Girlhood* (Los Angeles: Westernlore, 1964). I have also located one unusually extensive biographical article on Bennett. See Lela Waltrip, "Kay Bennett: A Versatile Navajo Woman," *Southwest Heritage* 11.4 (Winter 1981–1982): 10–13, 28. Waltrip and her husband were New Mexican teachers who wrote often about local and state history. They also published a book about famous American Indian women, in which they included the life of Pablita Velarde (but not Bennett). See Lela Waltrip and Rufus Waltrip, *Indian Women: Thirteen Who Played a Part in the History of America from Earliest Days to Now* (New York: David McKay, 1964).

5. See Rayna Green, *American Indian Women: A Contextual Bibliography* (Bloomington: Indiana University Press, 1983) 26; Gretchen M. Bataille and Kathleen M. Sands, *American Indian Women: Telling Their Lives* (Lincoln: University of Nebraska Press, 1984), 157, 193; and Michael C. Coleman, *American Indian Children at School, 1850–1930* (Jackson: University Press of Mississippi, 1993).

6. Bennett, *Kaibah*, 9.

7. I have seen Bennett's birth date listed as 1920, 1922, and 1924. Bennett's memoir implies that she was born in 1920; this is the date I have chosen to use to calculate her age at other points in her life. She told her stepson, Andrew Bennett, that the year was based on her mother's census answer and that she made up a birth month and day for her driver's license. Andrew Bennett, interview by author, telephone, 7 Jan. 1999.

8. The largest number of Navajos ever recorded by the army at the Bosque Redondo was 8,354. See Lawrence Kelly, *Navajo Roundup: Selected*

Correspondence of Kit Carson's Expedition Against the Navajo,
1863–1865 (Boulder, CO: Pruett, 1970), 163. Ruth Roessel reminds her
readers that this figure does not include Navajos who never surrendered
to the army. It also does not account for those who died during the
journey or while at the Bosque Redondo Reservation. Ruth Roessel,
"Navajo History and Culture II (Growth of the Navajos to 1960)," in,
Navajo Studies at Navajo Community College, ed. Ruth Roessel (Many
Farms, AZ: Navajo Community College Press, 1971), 32.

9. Bennett's books called these mountains the Tunicha Mountains. I refer
to them as the Chuska Mountains because this refers to the larger
range of which the Tunicha Mountains are a part. T. M. Pearce, *New
Mexico Place Names: A Geographical Dictionary* (Albuquerque:
University of New Mexico Press, 1965), 34, 171.

10. Kay and Russ Bennett, *A Navajo Saga* (San Antonio: Naylor, 1969).

11. Bennett, *Kaibah*, 14, 36. When describing the house, Bennett also
explains that her mother had been Keedah Chischillie's first wife, and
that he "some years later, had [also] married her sister. As he could
afford two wives, the sisters thought this was an ideal situation, as they
could share the work of the family" (36). Chischillie's second wife died
before Bennett was born, while giving birth to her half-sister Tesbah. In
their mid-twentieth-century study of Navajo culture, Clyde Kluckhohn
and Dorothea Leighton acknowledged that they found it difficult to
estimate plural marriages among the Navajo. Navajos concealed such
marriages during this era because missionaries and the government had
disapproved of them. But in one area, they established that seven out
of one hundred men had more than one wife. They were also able to
conclude that "in general, plural marriages are associated with higher
economic status." Clyde Kluckhohn and Dorothea Leighton, *The
Navaho,* rev. ed. (1962; Cambridge, MA: Harvard University Press,
1974), 100–01. Bennett's remark thus establishes the high status of her
family in the community, at least before her father's death.

12. Bennett, *Kaibah*, 24.

13. Dorothea C. Leighton, "As I Knew Them: Navajo Women in 1940,"
American Indian Quarterly 6.1–6.2 (Spring/Summer 1982): 50.

14. Ruth Roessel, *Women in Navajo Society* (Rough Rock, AZ: Navajo
Resource Center, 1981), 132, 134.

15. Louise Lamphere, "Strategies, Cooperation, and Conflict Among
Women in Domestic Groups," *Women, Culture, and Society,* ed.
Michelle Zimbalist Rosaldo and Louise Lamphere (Stanford, CA:
Stanford University Press, 1974), 103.

16. Bennett, *Kaibah*, 210. The Toadlena School is still in service today;
I toured it with the school's librarian, Andrew Deschenie, in
November 1998.

17. Coleman, *American Indian Children at School,* 80.

18. Bennett, *Kaibah*, 213.

19. According to Bennett's memoir, she began school because her brother felt
that she should "learn to read and write," and her mother wanted her to
"learn the ways of the white man." Bennett was apparently curious about

what her brother, cousins, and nieces and nephews had been learning, but not anxious to leave her life at home behind altogether. She presented her arrival at school not so much as an entry to a different world as an initially uneasy expansion of the Navajo one that she had been living in until that time. She returned home in the summers (Bennett, *Kaibah*, 209).

20. Garrick Bailey and Roberta Glenn Bailey, *A History of the Navajos: The Reservation Years* (Santa Fe: School of American Research Press, 1986), 169.

21. For a collection of firsthand accounts by Navajos of these tumultuous years, see Ruth Roessel and Broderick H. Johnson, eds., *Navajo Livestock Reduction: A National Disgrace* (Chinle, AZ: Navajo Community College Press, 1976). For the perspective of an Anglo anthropologist who lived with Navajos during this time, see Gladys Reichard, *Spider Woman: A Story of Navajo Weavers and Chanters* (New York: Macmillan, 1934). For analytical accounts focusing on Navajo history, see David Aberle, *The Peyote Religion Among the Navajo* (Chicago: University of Chicago Press, 1982); Peter Iverson, *Diné*; Iverson, *The Navajo Nation* (Westport, CT: Greenwood, 1981); Donald L. Parman, *The Navajos and the New Deal* (New Haven: Yale University Press, 1976); and Robert W. Young, *A Political History of the Navajo Tribe* (Tsaile, AZ: Navajo Community College Press, 1978). For an analysis of the place of these events in the overall context of U.S. Indian policy, see Brian W. Dippie, *The Vanishing American: White Attitudes and U.S. Indian Policy* (Middletown, CT: Wesleyan University Press, 1982).

22. William H. Zeh, "General Report Concerning the Grazing Situation on the Navajo Indian Reservation," 23 Dec. 1930, MSS 289 BC, United States Soil Conservation Service Records, 1919–1953, CSWR.

23. Bennett, *Kaibah*, 220. Bennett wrote that army helicopters did this work, but helicopter technology was too experimental to perform such work at this date. She probably mixed up this winter with a later one during which she saw helicopters conducting relief efforts.

24. Bennett, *Kaibah*, 228.

25. Parman, *Navajos and the New Deal*, 31.

26. Iverson, *Diné*, 142.

27. Iverson, *Navajo Nation*, 27.

28. Roessel, "Foreword," in Roessel and Johnson, *Navajo Livestock Reduction*, x.

29. Bennett, *Kaibah*, 233, 237.

30. As Iverson writes, "Liberal reformer John Collier pursued the twin goals of Navajo livestock reduction and Navajo land expansion. He succeeded partially with both but fully in neither." This lack of success, and the fact that many Navajos, like Bennett's mother, increasingly associated the troubles with Collier's name, contributed to the Navajos' rejection of the Wheeler-Howard Act. Iverson, *The Navajo Nation*, 27.

31. Aberle, *Peyote Religion*, 60.

32. These measures included new rules for horse and cattle reduction as

well as a continuation of sheep and goat efforts. In the 1940s, as Iverson describes, Navajos engaged in violent reactions to these policies and their emerging consequences "on a number of occasions." Iverson, *Diné*, 164. By 1952, Aberle estimates, Navajos had 36 percent of their 1930 stock. Because of the growth in Navajo population during this time, Navajos lost 80 percent of their livestock holdings in per capita terms. Aberle, *Peyote Religion*, 72–73.

33. "Indians Helping with Census; Will Map the Way to Remote Houses," *Arizona Republic*, 9 Nov. 1998, B1; "Census Bureau Hires 300 Navajo: $9.50 an Hour Jobs To Guarantee Count," *Gallup Independent*, 11 Nov. 1998, 2.

34. Roessel, "Navajo History and Culture II," 37.

35. Iverson, *Navajo Nation*, 30.

36. Iverson, *Diné*, 181, 188.

37. Kluckhohn and Leighton, *Navaho*, 86–87; Ruth M. Underhill, *The Navajos* (Norman: University of Oklahoma Press, 1956), 193–94.

38. Kluckhohn and Leighton, *Navaho*, 67, 86–87.

39. Fruitlands is a northern New Mexico community near the non-Navajo town of Farmington. Laila Shukry Hamamsy, "The Role of Women in a Changing Navajo Society," *American Anthropologist* 59.1 (February 1957): 109.

40. One anthropologist has described this discrepancy as a general trend on the Navajo reservation during this period. Mary Shepardson, "The Gender Status of Navajo Women," in *Women and Power in Native North America*, ed. Laura F. Klein and Lillian A. Ackerman (Norman: University of Oklahoma Press, 1995), 174–75.

41. Christine Conte, "Changing Woman Meets Madonna: Navajo Women's Networks and Sex-Gender Values in Transition," in *Writing the Range: Race, Class, and Culture in the Women's West*, ed. Elizabeth Jameson and Susan Armitage (Norman: University of Oklahoma Press, 1997), 550.

42. These dates and the name and occupation of her husband were indicated on personal history forms and applications for employment filed with the federal government. Kay Kelleywood [Price] [Bennett] Personnel File, Civilian Personnel Records, National Personnel Records Center, National Archives and Records Administration, St. Louis, MO.

43. Waltrip, "Kay Bennett," 12.

44. Andrew Bennett, interview by author.

45. Ann Metcalf, "From Schoolgirl to Mother: The Effects of Education on Navajo Women," *Social Problems* 23.5 (June 1976): 542.

46. Joyce Griffin, "Life Is Harder Here: The Case of the Urban Navajo Woman," *American Indian Quarterly* 6.1, 6.2 (Spring/Summer 1982): 96.

47. Kay Kelleywood [Price] [Bennett] Personnel File.

48. Collier was responding to the 1928 Meriam Report, which I will discuss at length in Chapter 5. It called for across-the-board changes in the style and purpose of American Indian education. See Lewis Meriam et al., *The Problem of Indian Administration: Report of a Survey Made at the Request of Honorable Hubert Work, Secretary of*

the Interior, and Submitted to Him, February 21, 1928 (Baltimore: Johns Hopkins Press, 1928).

49. U.S. Dept. of the Interior, *The Navajo: A Long Range Program for Navajo Rehabilitation*, Report of J. A. Krug, Secretary of the Interior (Washington: GPO, 1948), 39.

50. Dorothy R. Parker, *Phoenix Indian School: The Second Half-Century* (Tucson: University of Arizona Press, 1996), 30.

51. Margaret Szasz, *Education and the American Indian: The Road to Self-Determination, 1928–1973* (Albuquerque: University of New Mexico Press), 115.

52. Parker, *Phoenix Indian School*, 31.

53. Iverson, *Diné*, 193.

54. "Kay C. Bennett," *Reference Encyclopedia of the American Indian*, 5th ed., ed. Barry T. Klein (West Nyack, NY: Todd Publications, 1990), 766.

55. "A History of Gallup's Inter-Tribal Indian Ceremonial" (Church Rock, NM: Inter-Tribal Indian Ceremonial Association, n.d.).

56. Quoted in "Kay Bennett Led Way for Women," *Gallup Independent*, 14 July 1979 (Special issue for the 1979 Inter-Tribal Ceremonial), 11.

57. Unattributed and undated newspaper clipping, "Gallup Navajo Beauty is Queen of Flagstaff's Indian Powwow," Kay Bennett Scrapbook, Private Collection.

58. Waltrip, "Kay Bennett," 12.

59. In more recent years, the Navajo Nation has adopted the form of a beauty contest and truly shaped it as its own, resulting in an interesting blend of tradition and borrowing in the gendered realm of beauty. Participants in the Miss Navajo Nation contest compete in events involving sheep butchering, fire building, fry bread making, and speaking in Navajo, in addition to the performing, public speaking, and gown-wearing competitions common in "Miss America" type pageants. The winning Miss Navajo Nation serves as a goodwill ambassador for the Navajo Nation for one year, maintaining an office in the building housing the Navajo Nation Library and Museum. See Leslie Linthicum, "More than Beauty: Miss Navajo Nation Has to Talk Tribal Politics, Build a Fire, and Butcher a Sheep," *Albuquerque Journal*, 6 September 1998, B1, B4.

60. Undated and unattributed article, Kay Bennett Scrapbook, Private Collection.

61. "No More Cooking on Open Reservation Fires," *McKinley County* (NM) *Warrior*, 15 Apr. 1954, 1, 4. In this article, Bennett is referred to as "Kay Price," the last name of her second husband. She is also referred to by a performance name she used at that time, "Princess White Feather."

62. Ibid., 4.

63. Kay Kelleywood [Price] [Bennett] Personnel File.

64. Bonnie Shirley, interview by author, Gallup, NM, 13 Nov. 1998; Andrew Bennett, interview by author. Andrew Bennett believed that his father had been working on the construction of Interstate 40, but one newspaper article reported that Russ had been working on the

construction of an oil refinery in Gallup. This helps to explain his later work in the Middle East. See "Gallup Woman is Mother of the Year," *Gallup Independent*, 20 Apr. 1968, 1, 6.

65. Waltrip, "Kay Bennett," 12.

66. Kay Bennett, "Kaibah's Beautiful Indian Doll Museum," brochure (Gallup: Martin Link, 1997).

67. For books, see *Kaibah* (1964), *A Navajo Saga* (1969), and *Kesh: The Navajo Indian Cat* (Gallup, NM: Kay Bennett, 1985). For records, see *Kaibah* (Gallup, NM: 1966), *Kaibah Sings Songs of the Diné/Navaho Songs* (c. 1965), *Songs from the Navajo Nation* (Phoenix, AZ: Canyon Records, 1978), and *Kaibah: Navajo Love Songs* (Phoenix: Canyon Records, 1992).

68. One of John Collier's pet projects for the Navajo New Deal was the establishment of a written form of the Navajo language. A BIA team of linguists developed a Navajo alphabet that appeared in bilingual readers for children by 1940. See Iverson, *Navajo Nation*, 40. Perhaps Bennett could have used this written form of the language to write her books, but seems to have wanted to reach a larger audience (among both Navajos and non-Navajos). Her books apparently have not been translated into Navajo.

69. Andrew Bennett, interview by author.

70. Notice, Alamogordo Public Library, *Otero County Star*, 6 Mar. 1969, n.p.

71. Mary Shepardson, "The Status of Navajo Women," *American Indian Quarterly* 6.1, 6.2 (Spring/Summer 1982): 149–69.

72. Ibid., 165–66.

73. Ibid., 166.

74. Shepardson, "Gender Status of Navajo Women," 175.

75. See Daniel McCool, "Indian Voting," in *American Indian Policy in the Twentieth Century*, ed. Vine Deloria, Jr. (Norman: University of Oklahoma Press, 1985), 111.

76. Shepardson, "Gender Status of Navajo Women," 174.

77. Deenise Becenti, "Navajos Will Miss 'Dr. Annie': Many Remember, 'She Was a Good Grandma," *Navajo Times*, 13 Nov. 1997, A1, A2.

78. For a recent account of Wauneka's life, see Carolyn Niethammer, *I'll Go and Do More: Annie Dodge Wauneka: Navajo Leader and Activist* (Lincoln: University of Nebraska Press, 2001).

79. "Navajo Is Chosen Mother of the Year," *Albuquerque Journal*, 21 Apr. 1968. A1, A16; "N.M. Mother of the Year Goes to New York," *Albuquerque Journal*, 5 May 1968, 1.

80. "Gallup Navajo Plans Blessing," *Gallup Independent*, 6 May 1968, 1.

81. Andrew Bennett, interview by author.

82. Bennett, *Kaibah*, 11.

83. Green, *American Indian Women*, 26.

84. Bennett, *Kaibah*, 239.

85. Ibid., 220–25.

86. Ibid., 225.

87. Ibid., 227.

88. Ibid., 242.

89. Ibid., 9.

90. Bennett, "Letter to the Editor," *South Dakota Review* 7.2 (summer 1969); repr. in John R. Milton, ed., *The American Indian Speaks* (Vermillion, SD: Dakota Press), 171–72.

91. Kay and Russ Bennett, "Preface," *Navajo Saga*, viii.

92. Ronald Dean Miller, *Paul Bailey and the Westernlore Press: The First Forty Years—With Annotated Bibliography* (Morongo Valley, CA: Sagebrush, 1984), 62.

93. Kay and Russ Bennett, "Preface," *Navajo Saga*, ix.

94. Bennett, "Letter to the Editor," 172.

95. Maggie Wilson, "Navajo Writes About Navajos," *Scottsdale Daily Progress*, 15 Feb. 1965, 6.

96. Howard Bryan, "Navajo Singer Shows Great Talent as a Writer in Book," *Albuquerque Tribune*, 16 Feb. 1965, A14.

97. According to Bennett's obituary, she served in this capacity from 1974 to 1982. Paul Logan, "Navajo Woman Made Run For Tribe President," *Albuquerque Journal*, 15 Nov. 1997.

98. "Navajo Doll Maker to Set Up Her Own Doll Museum in Gallup," *The Indian Trader*, Jan. 1997, 21–22.

99. Bennett, 1968 Campaign Statement, Kay Bennett Scrapbook, Private Collection.

100. Undated, unattributed newspaper clipping [clearly from 1968 election], Kay Bennett Scrapbook, Private Collection.

101. "History of the New Mexico Human Rights Commission," NMHRC, NMSRCA.

102. Bennett ["Mrs. Kay Bennett"], "Rights Commission Purpose Explained," *Gallup Independent*, 3 June 1969, 8.

103. Bennett, Letter to Byron Stewart, 17 June 1969, NMHRC, NMSRCA.

104. W. Wilson Cliff, "After Industry Collision: State Agency On Rights to Try Again," *Albuquerque Journal*, 29 Mar. 1970, A1, A6.

105. Bennett, Letter to Byron Stewart, 31 July 1969, NMHRC, NMSRCA.

106. Ibid.

107. Susan Landon, "Leaders Defend Concept of Indian Ceremonials," *Albuquerque Journal*, 15 May 1974, E1.

108. Susan Ressler, "Warmth of Earlier, Simpler Ceremonials Recalled," *Gallup Independent*, 12 June 1974, 3C.

109. Martin Link, interview by author, Gallup, NM, 12 Nov. 1998. Link, publisher of *Indian Trader*, a magazine about American Indian artifacts and history, also printed all of Bennett's campaign materials for her.

110. Donovan, "Twelve Seeking Chairman's Job," 1.

111. Bennett, *Position on Issues Affecting Women*, one-page pamphlet (Gallup, NM: Martin Link, 1986).

112. Bill Donovan, "Certification for Three Candidates May Be Held Up Over Residency," *Navajo Times*, 16 June 1986, 1. Living in Gallup, a nonreservation town, did not qualify her. She owned land on the reservation, but did not live there permanently.

113. Catherine Feher-Elston, "Bennett Shocked by Decision (to Throw Her Off Ballot)," *Gallup Independent*, 26 June 1986, 1, 2.

114. Bennett quoted in "MacDonald, Greyhat, Bennett To Appeal Candidacy to Navajo Voters—Bennett: A Tribal Worker for Life," *Navajo Times*, 26 June 1986, 1.
115. Feher-Elston, "Bennett Shocked by Decision," 1.
116. Ibid.
117. Bill Donovan, "Odds on the Race," *Navajo Times*, 2 Aug. 1990, A4. By contrast, the winner of the 1986 general election, Peter MacDonald, had over thirty-one thousand votes, while the second-place finisher, incumbent Peterson Zah, had over thirty thousand. "McDonald Wins: Chairman Margin is 778 Votes," *Gallup Independent*, 11 Nov. 1986, 1.
118. For an account of the scandal, see Iverson, *Diné*, 289–97.
119. "Bennett To Make Official Bid," *Navajo Times*, 26 Apr. 1990, 2.
120. "Official Results for Candidates Seeking Office of the Navajo Nation President," *Navajo Times*, 16 Aug. 1990, 6. That number represented 0.43 percent of the total cast votes.
121. "Bennett Not Quite Through Just Yet," *Navajo Times*, 9 Aug. 1990, 1–2.
122. Historian Peter Iverson sees the 1990s as a time of increasing political involvement by Navajo women: six served on the tribal council during this decade, and fourteen served as chapter presidents. See Iverson, *Diné*, 303–4.
123. Genevieve Jackson, letter to the editor, *Navajo Times*, 4 July 1990, A4.
124. Roessel, *Women in Navajo Society*, 133.
125. Bennett, *Position on Issues Affecting Women*.

CHAPTER FIVE

1. A recent book about Velarde stops short of being a full biography but it is a useful source for understanding her life and painting; it is based on interviews and written in Velarde's "voice," and the stories she tells are accompanied by selections from her artwork. While I have quoted from passages in this book under the assumption that they are true to things that Velarde told Ruch during the extensive interviewing they did to create the book, Ruch acknowledges that "the story that I have created is not verbatim." It is, however, "the story [Velarde] wants to tell" (7). See Marcella Ruch, *Pablita Velarde: Painting Her People* (Albuquerque: *New Mexico Magazine*, 2001). Another book about Velarde was published for young readers in 1971. See Mary Carroll Nelson, *Pablita Velarde: The Story of an American Indian* (Minneapolis: Dillon Press, 1971). The choice of her as a subject (for a children's series on American Indians) indicates the popular appeal of her life and work to Anglo audiences. Additionally, Sally Hyer, the author of articles and an exhibition catalog about Velarde, is at work on a full-length biography.
2. Velarde, *Old Father the Story Teller*, 1st ed. (Globe, AZ: Dale Stuart King, 1960); *Old Father Story Teller*, 2d ed. (Santa Fe: Clear Light Books, 1989). This work will refer to the book by the title of the second edition, which omits the word "the."
3. Velarde, interview by author, Albuquerque, NM, 7 Nov. 1998.

4. See Daniel McCool, "Indian Voting," *American Indian Policy in the Twentieth Century*, ed. Vine Deloria, Jr. (Norman: University of Oklahoma Press, 1985), 111.
5. Ruch, *Pablita Velarde*, 12.
6. Ibid., 14.
7. Ibid., 20, 22.
8. Ibid., 36.
9. Vine Deloria, Jr., *Custer Died For Your Sins: An Indian Manifesto* (New York: Macmillan, 1969), 87–88.
10. Lewis Meriam et al., *The Problem of Indian Administration: Report of a Survey Made at the Request of Honorable Hubert Work, Secretary of the Interior, and Submitted to Him, February 21, 1928* (Baltimore: Johns Hopkins Press, 1928), 346.
11. Ibid., 372.
12. Ibid., 615.
13. Ibid., 645.
14. Ibid., 651.
15. Dorothy Dunn, *American Indian Painting of the Southwest and Plains Areas* (Albuquerque: University of New Mexico Press, 1968), 234.
16. Art historian W. Jackson Rushing argues that this and other exhibitions reflect not merely a new appreciation of Indian art but a desire on the part of cultural modernists like Mabel Dodge Luhan and Mary Austin to access the "primitive." Though he devotes minimal attention to the motivations of specific American Indian artists, his work provides an important framework for understanding developments in American art as a whole. W. Jackson Rushing, *Native American Art and the New York Avant Garde: A History of Cultural Primitivism* (Austin: University of Texas Press, 1995).
17. Molly Mullin, *Culture in the Marketplace: Gender, Art, and Value in the American Southwest* (Durham, NC: Duke University Press, 2001), 91.
18. All but one (Jemez Pueblo) of the nineteen New Mexico Pueblo tribes voted "yes" during the 1934–35 Indian Reorganization Act/Wheeler-Howard Act elections; the Hopi (in Arizona) also voted "yes," while the Navajo voted "no." See Theodore H. Haas, *Ten Years of Tribal Government Under I.R.A.* (Chicago: United States Indian Service, 1947), 13–20.
19. For a history of the evolution of and tension between these two ideas, see Brian Dippie, *The Vanishing American: White Attitudes and U.S. Indian Policy* (Middletown, CT: Wesleyan UP, 1982), 299–300.
20. Sally Hyer, "'Our Way of Life Is Something We Are Proud Of' (1930–1945)," *One House, One Voice, One Heart: American Indian Education at the Santa Fe Indian School* (Santa Fe: Museum of New Mexico Press, 1990), 29–57.
21. Dunn later recorded her efforts to establish this painting studio in two different publications. See Dunn, "The Studio of Painting, Santa Fe Indian School," *El Palacio* 67.1 (February 1960): 16–27; and Dunn, *American Indian Painting*.
22. Dunn, *American Indian Painting*, 252.

23. Bruce Bernstein, "Art for the Sake of Life: Dorothy Dunn and a Story of American Indian Painting," In Bruce Bernstein and W. Jackson Rushing, *Modern by Tradition: American Indian Painting in the Studio Style* (Santa Fe: Museum of New Mexico Press, 1995), 10.

24. Ibid., 5.

25. Dunn, "Studio of Painting," 19.

26. Dunn, *American Indian Painting*, 254.

27. J. J. Brody, *Indian Painters and White Patrons* (Albuquerque: University of New Mexico Press, 1971), 44.

28. Dunn, *American Indian Painting*, 252; Brody, *Indian Painters and White Patrons*, 130–31.

29. W. Jackson Rushing, "Modern by Tradition: The 'Studio Style' of Native American Painting," In Bernstein and Rushing, *Modern by Tradition*, 32.

30. Brody, *Indian Painters and White Patrons*, 206.

31. Rushing, "Modern by Tradition," 41–45.

32. Velarde, interview by author.

33. Ruch, *Pablita Velarde*, 42.

34. Velarde, interview by author.

35. Josette Frank, *The Indian Girl: Her Social Heritage, Her Needs, and Her Opportunities* (Prepared by the Child Study Association of America at the request of the Commissioner of Indian Affairs, 1932), 16–17.

36. Margaret Jacobs, *Engendered Encounters Feminism and Pueblo Cultures, 1879–1934* (Lincoln: University of Nebraska Press, 1999), 179.

37. Velarde in Irene-Aimée Depke, prod. and dir., *The Enchanted Arts* (Las Cruces, NM: KRGW Public Television, 1979), videocassette, quoted in Sally Hyer, *"Woman's Work": The Art of Pablita Velarde*, Exhibition Catalog (Santa Fe: Wheelwright Museum of the American Indian, 1990), title page. Since this exhibit used the singular form of woman, I will do the same when referring to "woman's work."

38. Velarde, interview by Betty LaDuke, 11 May 1987, in *Women Artists: Multicultural Visions* (Trenton, NJ: Red Sea Press, 1992), 79.

39. Gretchen M. Bataille and Kathleen Mullen Sands, *American Indian Women: Telling Their Lives* (Lincoln: University of Nebraska Press, 1984), 129.

40. Paula Gunn Allen, *The Sacred Hoop: Recovering the Feminine in American Indian Traditions* (Boston: Beacon Press, 1986), 193.

41. Olive Rush, "Remarkable Paintings by Indians at Art Museum," *Santa Fe New Mexican*, 7 May 1934, 4. In a review published one year earlier, Rush wrote that "the Velarde sisters, Pablita and Po-ve [Rosita] of Santa Clara, find their best expression in picturing the people of their pueblo at their daily tasks, women making pottery, or husking corn, or winnowing wheat—all beautifully expressed." Rush, "Indian Students Show Work," *Santa Fe New Mexican*, 4 May 1933, 4.

42. Velarde, interview by Betty LaDuke, in Brian Varaday, dir., *Persistent Women Artists: Pablita Velarde, Lois Mallou Jones, Mine Okubo* (Ashland, OR: Southern Oregon State College Productions, 1996), videocassette.

43. Velarde, interview by Margaret Szasz, 9 Apr. 1972, transcribed tape recording, American Indian Oral History Transcripts, Reel 10, CSWR, 5.

44. Velarde, interview by Frank Tenorio and Gloria Keliia-Tom, tape recording, 2 Oct. 1986, Tape 22, Santa Fe Indian School First Hundred Years Project, Santa Fe Indian School Archives.

45. Velarde, interview by author.

46. In a 1972 interview, Velarde said that it was her idea to take business classes at Española, but when I asked her she said that it was her father's idea. Either way, she was happy to get back to Santa Fe Indian School when she did, because she could begin painting again, and because she no longer had to babysit the children of her father's wife. Velarde, interview by Margaret Szasz; Velarde, interview by author.

47. Velarde, "Pablita Velarde," interview by Sally Hyer, *Art Journal* 53.1 (spring 1994): 61–63.

48. Velarde, interview by Szasz, 10.

49. Dippie, *Vanishing American*, 312.

50. Ruch, *Pablita Velarde*, 50.

51. These "murals" are actually paintings on paper that King used to decorate the showcases holding artifacts.

52. Ruch, *Pablita Velarde*, 46.

53. Velarde, interview by author.

54. Velarde, interview by Hyer.

55. Velarde, interview by author.

56. W. W. Hill, *An Ethnography of Santa Clara Pueblo, New Mexico*, ed. Charles H. Lane (Albuquerque: University of New Mexico Press, 1982), 20.

57. Jay Scott, *Changing Woman: The Life and Art of Helen Hardin* (Flagstaff, AZ: Northland Publishing, 1989), 43.

58. Velarde, interview by author.

59. Ibid.

60. Ruch, *Pablita Velarde*, 52.

61. Velarde, interview by Szasz.

62. Velarde in Michael Kamins, prod., *Pablita Velarde: Golden Dawn*, COLORES! series (Albuquerque: KNME-TV, 1996), videocassette.

63. Lela Waltrip and Rufus Waltrip, *Indian Women: Thirteen Who Played a Part in the History of America from Earliest Days to Now* (New York: David McKay, 1964), 158.

64. Velarde, interview by LaDuke, *Women Artists*, 83.

65. Scott, *Changing Woman*, 61–62.

66. Velarde, interview by LaDuke, *Persistent Women Artists*.

67. Ruch, *Pablita Velarde*, 58.

68. Hyer, *"Woman's Work,"* 15. *Old Father Story Teller* became Velarde's only major published writing. She did consider publishing a second book, one based upon stories she learned from her grandmother. In contrast to her grandfather's legends, she called her grandmother's stories "how and why stories" because they explain natural facts like seasons. Brief versions of some of these stories were published in the 1961

Gallup Inter-Tribal Ceremonial magazine. A book version never came
about because Velarde ended up selling all the paintings that may have
worked as illustrations for the stories. See Velarde, "How and Why
Stories," *Indian Life: The Magazine of the Inter-Tribal Indian
Ceremonial*, August 1961, 23–26.

69. Ruch, *Pablita Velarde*, 58.
70. Waltrip and Waltrip, *Indian Women*, 158–59.
71. Velarde, interview by author.
72. D. Hancock, "About Pablita and Her Legends," Introduction to
Pablita Velarde, *Old Father Story Teller*, 13.
73. Velarde, Foreword to *Old Father Story Teller*, v.
74. Velarde, *Old Father Story Teller*, 31.
75. Ibid., 36.
76. Waltrip and Waltrip, *Indian Women*, 159.
77. Velarde, interview by author.
78. Sally Hyer, "Pablita Velarde: The Pueblo Artist as Cultural Broker,"
Between Indian and White Worlds: The Cultural Broker, ed. Margaret
Connell Szasz (Norman: University of Oklahoma Press, 1994), 289.
79. Ibid., 285.
80. Ruch, *Pablita Velarde*, 60.
81. Hyer, "Pablita Velarde," 291.
82. Velarde, interview by author.
83. Ibid.
84. "Pablita Velarde: Indian Artist of the Red Earth Country," *New Mexico
Magazine*, December 1960, 12. *New Mexico Magazine* is a state-sponsored publication aimed at a tourist audience, which partially explains its
emphasis on Velarde as "traditional." Though the article is not signed, it
uses almost the exact same phrasing in this paragraph as a newspaper
review of *Old Father Story Teller* that was also published that month,
Betty Armstrong, Review of *Old Father Story Teller*, by Pablita Velarde,
Las Cruces Citizen, 22 Dec. 1960, 3A. Armstrong may have written the
New Mexico Magazine article, but it is quite likely that she and another
author were working from a common press release about the book.
85. Velarde, interview by author.
86. Ibid.
87. As W. Jackson Rushing implies, Velarde's adherence to the traditionalist "Studio" style has likely led some critics to dismiss her work as
"handsome, if facile paintings that cater to the romantic fantasies of
White patrons." Rushing argues that this sort of condemnation
emerges from a false dichotomy perceived between the Studio Style and
the more individualistic style supported by the Institute of American
Indian Arts (IAIA), which resulted in the work of painters such as Fritz
Scholder, or even Helen Hardin. Rushing, "Modern by Tradition," 47.
In the eyes of some, Velarde's work is past its time, but its continued
inclusion in shows and media profiles attests to its continuing popularity with some audiences.
88. An archive of Dorothy Dunn's personal papers includes an "Earth
Colors" information sheet that offers guidance on sources of pigments,

extraction processes, preparation of paints and painting surfaces, and application of pigments. Dorothy Dunn, "Earth Colors," 93DDK.171, Dorothy Dunn Kramer Papers, Archives of the Laboratory of Anthropology/Museum of Indian Art and Culture, Santa Fe, NM.

89. The translations are mine. Ruch, *Pablita Velarde*, 44.

90. Kim Anderson, "Earth Yields Harvest of Colors, Textures, for Traditional Artist," *Albuquerque Journal*, 29 Sept. 1985, 1E.

91. Rushing points out that Velarde's "earth color" paintings and their interpretations of abstract Pueblo motifs "bypass the narrative genre of most Studio Style pictures" and were "much sought after" by collectors when she began producing them. Rushing, "Modern by Tradition," 69.

92. Rosemary Diaz, "Changing Woman: Three Generations of Tewa Women Painters," *Native Peoples*, November/December 2001, 73.

93. Helen Hardin, interview by Margaret Szasz, 11 Apr. 1972, transcribed tape recording, American Indian Oral History Transcripts, Reel 10, CSWR, 1.

94. Ibid., 20.

95. Ibid., 24.

96. Ibid., 31.

97. Walter Briggs, "Helen Hardin: Tsa-sah-wee-eh Does Her Thing," *New Mexico Magazine*, March/April 1970, cover story.

98. "American Indian Artists: Helen Hardin," dir. Tony Schmitz (Phoenix: KAET-8, Arizona State University, 1976), videocassette.

99. Helen's daughter, Margarete Bagshaw Tindel, is also a painter. In an article comparing her style to her mother's and grandmother's, a writer describes her paintings as "medium- to larger-sized canvases with colorful juxtapositions of abstract shapes and thoughtful placements of stylized Pueblo-eque designs and motifs." Diaz, "Changing Woman," 75–76.

100. Scott, *Changing Woman*, 5–6.

101. Tricia Hurst, "Crossing Bridges: Jaune Quick-to-See Smith, Helen Hardin, Jean Bales," *Southwest Art*, April 1981, 87.

102. Velarde, interview by author.

103. Ibid.

104. For accounts of *Martinez v. Santa Clara Pueblo*, a case initiated in 1972, see Karen Anderson, *Changing Woman: A History of Racial Ethnic Women in Modern America* (New York: Oxford University Press, 1996), 83–85; and Catherine A. MacKinnon, "Whose Culture? A Case Note on *Martinez v. Santa Clara Pueblo*," in *Feminism Unmodified: Discourses on Life and Law* (Cambridge: Harvard University Press, 1987), 63–69.

105. Thom Mahoney, "Pablita Velarde ... The 'Golden Dawn' of American Indian Art," undated article from unknown source, found in Pablita Velarde file of Dorothy Dunn Kramer papers, Archives of the Laboratory of Anthropology/Museum of Indian Art and Culture, Santa Fe, NM.

106. Dorothy Dunn, "Pablita Velarde: Painter of Pueblo Life," *El Palacio*

59.11 (November 1952): 340.

107. Flo Wilks, "Rain Gods Bless the Pueblo Soil in Painting by Pablita Velarde," *Albuquerque Journal*, 16 May 1954, 16.

108. W. Thetford LeViness, "Pablita of Santa Clara Pueblo," *Desert*, September 1956, 26.

109. Review of *Pablita Velarde: The Story of an American Indian*, by Mary Carroll Nelson, *New Mexico Magazine*, January/February 1972, 52.

110. Nancy C. Benson, "Pioneering Women of New Mexico," *El Palacio* 85 (Summer 1979): 8–13, 35–37.

111. Anderson, "Earth Yields Harvest of Colors, Textures, for Traditional Artist," 1E.

112. Velarde quoted in Hyer, "*Woman's Work*," 1.

113. David Steinberg, "A Well-Crafted Life," *Albuquerque Journal*, 16 June 1996, D1, D4.

114. Candelora Versace, "Pablita Velarde: Still Dreaming After All These Years," *New Mexico*, July 1995, 32, 34, 36; Sharon Niederman, "Pablita Velarde: The Nourishment of Rocks," *Santa Fe Reporter*, 20–26 January 1993, 23, 25; Gussie Fauntleroy, "Spunk and Sparkle," *Pasatiempo* [Sunday magazine of the *Santa Fe New Mexican*] (15–23 Jan. 1993), 24–26.

115. Versace, "Pablita Velarde," 32, 34.

116. Joyce M. Szabo, Introduction to Ruch, *Pablita Velarde*, 8.

117. Jacobs, *Engendered Encounters*, 179.

AFTERWORD

1. For details of this event, see Peter Nabokov, *Tijerina and the Courthouse Raid* (Albuquerque: University of New Mexico Press, 1969); Richard Gardner, *¡Grito!: Reies Tijerina and the New Mexico Land Grant War of 1967* (Indianapolis: Bobbs-Merrill, 1970); and Richard Griswold del Castillo, *The Treaty of Guadalupe Hidalgo: A Legacy of Conflict* (Norman: University of Oklahoma Press, 1990).

2. Tamar Lewin, "Now a Majority: Families with Two Parents Who Work," *New York Times*, 24 Oct. 2000, A20.

3. Sonya Chawla, "Newest Mothers Want Life at Home; Reject Old Ideal of 'Having it All,'" *Washington Times*, 18 Oct. 2000, A2. For a recent account of women who actually have the economic power to stay home, see Lisa Belkin, "The Opt-Out Revolution," *New York Times Sunday Magazine*, 26 Oct. 2003, 42.

BIBLIOGRAPHY

ARCHIVAL COLLECTIONS

Bancroft Library, University of California at Berkeley
    Mary Hunter Austin Collection (MHACB)
Beinecke Rare Book and Manuscript Library, Yale University, New Haven, CT
    Yale Collection of American Literature
    Mabel Dodge Luhan Collection (MDLC)
Center for Southwest Research, General Library, University of New Mexico,
    Albuquerque (CSWR)
    Fabiola Cabeza de Baca [Gilbert] Papers (FCBP)
    United States Soil Conservation Service Records, 1919–1953
    Women in New Mexico Collection
    American Indian Oral History Transcripts
Harry Ransom Humanities Research Center, University of Texas at Austin
    Alice Corbin Henderson Collection (ACHC)
    J. Frank Dobie Papers
Huntington Library, San Marino, CA
    Mary Hunter Austin Collection (MHACH)
Laboratory of Anthropology/Museum of Indian Art and Culture, Santa Fe, NM
    Dorothy Dunn Kramer Papers
Las Vegas Public Library, Las Vegas, NM
    Vertical Files on Local History
Manuscripts and Archives, Yale University Library, New Haven, CT
    John Collier Collection
National Personnel Records Center, National Archives and Records
    Administration, St. Louis, MO
    Civilian Personnel Records: Kay Kelleywood [Price] [Bennett] Personnel File

◩ BIBLIOGRAPHY ◩

Navajo Nation Museum, Window Rock, AZ
    Kay Bennett Exhibit
Nettie Lee Benson Latin American Collection, University of Texas at Austin
    League of United Latin American Citizens Archives
New Mexico State Library, Santa Fe, NM
    Southwest Room
New Mexico State Records Center and Archives, Santa Fe, NM (NMSRCA)
    Renehan Gilbert Papers
    Governor Arthur Seligman Papers (GASP)
    Manuel Sanchez Papers
    New Mexico Human Rights Commission Records (NMHRC)
    WPA Records
New Mexico State University Library, Las Cruces, New Mexico
    Rio Grande Historical Collections
Palace of the Governors, Museum of New Mexico, Santa Fe, NM
    Angélico Chávez History Library (ACHL)
    Venceslao Jaramillo Papers
    WPA Manuscripts
    Photo Archives
Private Collection
    Kay Bennett Scrapbook
Santa Fe Indian School, Santa Fe, NM
    School Archives, First Hundred Years Project
Santa Fe Public Library, Santa Fe, NM
    Vertical Files on Local History

SELECTED PUBLISHED WRITINGS BY FEATURED AUTHORS

Mary Austin

The Arrow-Maker: A Drama in Three Acts. Boston: Houghton Mifflin, 1915.
Earth Horizon: Autobiography. 1932; Albuquerque: University of New
    Mexico Press, 1991.
"In Papagueria." *The Nation,* 18 July 1928, 65.
The Land of Little Rain. Boston: Houghton Mifflin, 1903.
Lost Borders. New York and London: Harper and Brothers, 1909.
"Making the Most of Your Genius I: What is Genius?" *The Bookman,*
    November 1923, 246–51.
"Mary Austin Asked for Her Opinion on Statue and Gave It; Mrs. Moss
    Discourteous." *Santa Fe New Mexican,* 18 Oct. 1927, 3.
"Mexicans and New Mexico." *The Survey,* 1 May 1931, 141–44, 187–90.
[With Anne Martin.] *Suffrage and Government: The Modern Idea of
    Government by Consent and Woman's Place in it, with special reference
    to Nevada and other Western States.* Reno: Nevada Equal Franchise
    Society, 1914, 15.
"The Town That Doesn't Want a Chautauqua." *The New Republic,* 7 July
    1926. Repr. in *Beyond Borders: The Selected Essays of Mary Austin,* ed.

Reuben Ellis, 102–10. Carbondale, IL: Southern Illinois University Press, 1996.
"Why I Live in Santa Fe." *The Golden Book*, October 1932, 306–07.
A Woman of Genius. 1912; Old Westbury, NY: Feminist Press, 1985.

Mabel Dodge Luhan

Background. Vol. 1, *Intimate Memories.* New York: Harcourt, Brace, and Co., 1933.
"Decline of the Male." Letter to the editor in response to Neith Boyce's 9 March 1932 review of Robert Herrick's *The End of Desire. New Republic*, 20 Apr. 1932, 275–76.
Edge of Taos Desert: An Escape to Reality. Vol. 4, *Intimate Memories.* New York: Harcourt, Brace and Co., 1937.
European Experiences. Vol. 2 of *Intimate Memories.* New York: Harcourt, Brace and Co., 1936.
Lorenzo in Taos. New York: Knopf, 1932.
"Mabel Dodge Talks of Women Who Seek Masters: An Atavistic Infantile Idea Like Being Afraid of the Dark, Maturity Needs No Protection But Cave Man Impression Lingers." *Washington Times*, 28 Aug. 1917, 14.
"Mary Austin: A Woman." In *Mary Austin: A Memorial*, ed. Willard Houghland, 19–22. Santa Fe: Laboratory of Anthropology, 1944.
Movers and Shakers. Vol. 3, *Intimate Memories.* New York: Harcourt, Brace and Co., 1936.
Winter in Taos. New York: Harcourt, Brace and Co., 1935.

Cleofas Jaramillo

Cuentos del Hogar (Spanish Fairy Stories). El Campo, TX: The Citizen Press, 1939.
The Genuine New Mexico Tasty Recipes. 1942; Santa Fe: Ancient City Press, 1981.
Romance of a Little Village Girl. San Antonio: Naylor, 1955.
Shadows of the Past/Sombras del Pasado. 1941; Santa Fe: Ancient City Press, 1972.

Fabiola Cabeza de Baca [Gilbert]

Los Alimentos y su Preparacion. Circular No. 129. State College, NM: New Mexico Agricultural Extension Service, 1934.
Boletin de Conservar. Circular No. 133. State College, NM: New Mexico Agricultural Extension Service, 1935.
"Changing Modes of Travel." *Santa Fe Scene*, 6 Dec. 1958, 24–25.
"Las Fiestas." *Santa Fe Scene*, 9 Aug. 1958, 22.
The Good Life: New Mexico Traditions and Food. 1949; Santa Fe: Museum of New Mexico Press, 1982.
Historic Cookery. NMAES Circular No. 161, 1939. Santa Fe: Ancient City Press, 1970.
"La Merienda." *Santa Fe Scene*, 23 Aug. 1958, 10.
"New Mexican Diets." *Journal of Home Economics* 34 (November 1942): 668–69.

"New Mexicans in Texas." *LULAC News* 6.5 (May 1939): 18–19.

"Nineteenth Century in Santa Fe," *Santa Fe Scene*, 13 Feb. 1960, 20.

"Noche Buena for Doña Antonia: She Met Christmas with Arms Open." *New Mexico Extension News* 25.12 (December 1945): 2, 4.

"*Sociedad Folklórica* Celebrates 25th Year." *Santa Fe Scene*, 19 Nov. 1960, 8.

"UNESCO's Pilot Project." *New Mexico Extension News* 32.7 (July 1952): 4.

We Fed Them Cactus, 2nd. ed. 1954; Albuquerque: University of New Mexico Press, 1994.

Kay Bennett

Kaibah: Recollection of a Navajo Girlhood. Los Angeles: Westernlore, 1964.

"Kaibah's Beautiful Indian Doll Museum." Brochure. Gallup: Martin Link, 1997.

Kesh: The Navajo Indian Cat. Gallup, NM: Kay Bennett, 1985.

"Letter to the Editor." *South Dakota Review* 7.2 (Summer 1969). Repr. in John R. Milton, ed., *The American Indian Speaks.* Vermillion, SD: Dakota Press, 171–72.

[with Russ Bennett.] *A Navajo Saga.* San Antonio: Naylor, 1969.

Position on Issues Affecting Women. One-page pamphlet. Gallup, NM: Martin Link, 1986.

"Rights Commission Purpose Explained." *Gallup Independent*, 3 June 1969, 8.

Pablita Velarde

"How and Why Stories." *Indian Life: The Magazine of the Inter-Tribal Indian Ceremonial*, August 1961, 23–26.

Old Father Story Teller, 2d ed. Santa Fe: Clear Light Books, 1989.

Old Father the Story Teller, 1st ed. Globe, AZ: Dale Stuart King, 1960.

INTERVIEWS

Bennett, Andrew [Kay Bennett's stepson]. Interview by author, 7 Jan. 1999, telephone.

Cabeza de Baca [Gilbert], Fabiola. Interview by Paula Thaidigsman, 29 Aug. 1975. Cassette tape, Women in New Mexico Collection, CSWR.

———. Interview by Ruleen Lazell, 9 Feb. 1983, Albuquerque, NM. Cassette tape, RG-T153, Rio Grande Historical Collections, University Library, New Mexico State University Library, Las Cruces, NM.

Hardin, Helen [Pablita Velarde's daughter]. Interview by Margaret Szasz, 11 Apr. 1972. Transcribed tape recording, Reel 10. American Indian Oral History Transcripts, CSWR.

Link, Martin [Kay Bennett's friend]. Interview by author, 12 Nov. 1998, Gallup, NM.

Montoya, Rosa. Interview by author, 25 Mar. 1999, Santa Fe, NM.

Sánchez, Esther Branch [Fabiola Cabeza de Baca's niece]. Interview by Merrihelen Ponce, 22 Mar. 1991. In Ponce, "The Life and Works of Fabiola Cabeza de Baca, New Mexican Hispanic Women Writer: A Contextual Biography." Ph.D. diss., University of New Mexico, 1995.

———. Interview by author, 6 June 2000, Santa Fe, NM.

Shirley, Bonnie [Kay Bennett's friend]. Interview by author, 13 Nov. 1998, Gallup, NM.

Taylor, J. Paul [Fabiola Cabeza de Baca's cousin]. Phone interview by author, 23 Mar. 2003.

Velarde. Pablita. Interview by Margaret Szasz. 9 Apr. 1972. Transcribed tape recording, Reel 10. American Indian Oral History Transcripts, CSWR.

———. Interview by Frank Tenorio and Gloria Keliia-Toia, 2 Oct. 1986. Tape 22, tape recording. Santa Fe Indian School First Hundred Years Project, Santa Fe Indian School Archives.

———. Interview by Betty LaDuke, 11 May 1987. In LaDuke, Women Artists: Multicultural Visions. Trenton, NJ: Red Sea Press, 1992.

———. "Pablita Velarde." Interview by Sally Hyer. Art Journal 53.1 (Spring 1994): 61–63

———. Interview by Betty LaDuke. In Persistent Women Artists: Pablita Velarde, Lois Mallou Jones, Mine Okubo, dir. Brian Varaday. Ashland, OR: Southern Oregon State College Production, 1996. Videocassette.

———. Interview by author, 7 Nov. 1998, Albuquerque, NM.

Yazzie, Mabel [Kay Bennett's niece]. Interview by author, 23 Mar. 1998, Window Rock, AZ.

NEWSPAPERS CITED AND CONSULTED

Albuquerque Journal
Albuquerque Tribune
Arizona Republic
Buffalo Times
Denver Post
Gallup Independent
Las Cruces Citizen
Las Cruces (NM) *Sun-News*
McKinley County (NM) *Warrior*
Navajo Times, Navajo Times Today
New York Herald Tribune
New York Times, New York Times Book Review
Otero County (NM) *Star*
Pittsburgh Post-Gazette
Santa Fe New Mexican
Santa Fe Reporter
Scottsdale Daily Progress
Washington Times

✑ BIBLIOGRAPHY ✑

POPULAR MAGAZINES

The Bookman
Desert
The Golden Book
La Herencia del Norte
Holland's
The Indian Trader
Master Detective
The Nation
Native Peoples
New Mexico Magazine
New Republic
New York Times Sunday Magazine
Pasatiempo (Sunday magazine of the *Santa Fe New Mexican*)
The Santa Fe Scene
Southwest Art
The Survey

NEWSLETTERS

LULAC News
New Mexico Extension News
New Mexico Folklore Record

VIDEOCASSETTES

Depke, Irene-Aimée, prod. and dir. *The Enchanted Arts*. Las Cruces, NM: KRGW Public Television, 1979. Videocassette.
Kamins, Michael, prod. *Pablita Velarde: Golden Dawn. COLORES!* series. Albuquerque: KNME-TV, 1996. Videocassette.
Schmitz, Tony, dir. "American Indian Artists: Helen Hardin." Phoenix: KAET-8, Arizona State University, 1976. Videocassette.
Varaday, Brian, dir. *Persistent Women Artists: Pablita Velarde, Lois Mallou Jones, Mine Okubo*. Ashland, OR: Southern Oregon State College Productions, 1996. Videocassette.

BOOKS, JOURNAL ARTICLES, AND OTHER SOURCES

Aberle, David. *The Peyote Religion Among the Navajo*. Chicago: University of Chicago Press, 1982.
Alford, Harold J. "Fabiola Cabeza de Baca Gilbert: Home Economist." In *The Proud Peoples: The Heritage and Culture of Spanish-Speaking Peoples in the United States*, 223–24. New York: New American Library, 1972.
Allen, Paula Gunn. *The Sacred Hoop: Recovering the Feminine in American Indian Traditions*. Boston: Beacon Press, 1986.
Ammons, Elizabeth. *Conflicting Stories: American Women Writers at the Turn into the Twentieth Century*. New York: Oxford University Press, 1991.

338

✦ BIBLIOGRAPHY ✦

Anderson, Karen. *Changing Woman: A History of Racial Ethnic Women in Modern America*. New York: Oxford University Press, 1996.

Annie E. Casey Foundation. *Kids Count Data Book*, 2003.

Arrott, James W. Review of *We Fed Them Cactus*, by Fabiola [Cabeza] de Baca. *Western Folklore* 14.4 (1955): 297–99.

Bailey, Garrick, and Roberta Glenn Bailey. *A History of the Navajos: The Reservation Years*. Santa Fe: School of American Research Press, 1986.

Bannan, Helen M. "Fabiola Cabeza de Baca Gilbert." In *American Women Writers: A Critical Reference Guide from Colonial Times to the Present*, 1st ed., vol. 2, ed. Lina Mainiero, 123–25. New York: Frederick Ungar Publishing Co., 1980.

————. "Fabiola Cabeza de Baca." In *American Women Writers: A Critical Reference Guide from Colonial Times to the Present*, 2d. ed., vol. 1., ed. Lina Mainiero, 159–60. Detroit: St. James Press, 2000.

Barker, Ruth Laughlin. *Caballeros*. New York: D. Appleton and Co., 1931.

Bataille, Gretchen M., and Kathleen Mullen Sands. *American Indian Women: Telling Their Lives*. Lincoln: University of Nebraska Press, 1984.

Benson, Nancy C. "Pioneering Women of New Mexico." *El Palacio* 85 (Summer 1979): 8–13, 35–37.

Bernstein, Bruce. "Art for the Sake of Life: Dorothy Dunn and a Story of American Indian Painting." In Bruce Bernstein and W. Jackson Rushing, *Modern by Tradition: American Indian Painting in the Studio Style*, 3–25. Santa Fe: Museum of New Mexico Press, 1995.

Blair, Karen. *The Clubwoman as Feminist: True Womanhood Redefined, 1868–1914*. New York: Homes and Meier, 1980.

Blaut, J. M., and Antonio Rios-Bustamente. "Commentary on Nostrand's 'Hispanos' and their 'Homeland.'" *Annals of the Association of American Geographers* 74.1. (March 1984): 157–64.

Bodine, John. "A Tri-Ethnic Trap: The Spanish-Americans in Taos." In *Spanish-Speaking Peoples in the United States: Proceedings of the 1968 Annual Spring Meeting of the American Ethnological Society*, ed. June Helm, 145–53. Seattle: University of Washington Press, 1968.

Bordin, Ruth. *Women and Temperance: The Quest for Power and Liberty, 1873–1900*. Philadelphia: Temple University Press, 1981.

Bowers, William L. *The Country Life Movement in America, 1900–1920*. Port Washington, NY: Kennikat Press, 1974.

Brody, J. J. *Indian Painters and White Patrons*. Albuquerque: University of New Mexico Press, 1971.

Brown, Lorin. *Hispano Folklife of New Mexico: The Lorin W. Brown Federal Writers' Project Manuscripts*. Albuquerque: University of New Mexico Press, 1978.

Burman, John H., and David E. Williams. *An Economic, Social, and Educational Survey of Rio Arriba and Taos Counties*, 2d ed. El Rito: Northern New Mexico Community College, 1961.

Campa, Arthur L. *Hispanic Culture in the Southwest*. Norman: University of Oklahoma Press, 1979.

Cather, Willa. *Death Comes for the Archbishop*. New York: Knopf, 1927.

Chafe, William. *The Paradox of Change: American Women in the*

Twentieth Century. New York: Oxford University Press, 1991.

Chávez, Angélico. *Origins of New Mexico Families: A Genealogy of the Spanish Colonial Period.* 1954. Rev. ed., Santa Fe: Museum of New Mexico Press, 1992.

Coleman, Michael C. *American Indian Children at School, 1850–1930.* Jackson: University Press of Mississippi, 1993.

Conte, Christine. "Changing Woman Meets Madonna: Navajo Women's Networks and Sex-Gender Values in Transition." In *Writing the Range: Race, Class, and Culture in the Women's West,* ed. Elizabeth Jameson and Susan Armitage, 533–552. Norman: University of Oklahoma Press, 1997.

Cott, Nancy. *The Grounding of Modern Feminism.* New Haven: Yale University Press, 1987.

Deacon, Desley. *Elsie Clews Parsons: Inventing Modern Life.* Chicago: University of Chicago Press, 1997.

Deloria, Vine, Jr. *Custer Died For Your Sins: An Indian Manifesto.* New York: Macmillan, 1969.

Deutsch, Sarah. *No Separate Refuge: Culture, Class, and Gender on an Anglo-Hispanic Frontier in the American Southwest, 1880–1940.* New York: Oxford University Press, 1987.

Dilworth, Leah. *Imagining Indians in the Southwest: Persistent Visions of a Primitive Past.* Washington: Smithsonian Institution Press, 1996.

Dinkel, Reynalda Ortíz y Pino de, and Dora Gonzales de Martínez. *Una colleccion de adivinanzas y diseños de colcha/A Collection of Riddles and Colcha Designs.* Santa Fe: Sunstone Press, 1988.

Dippie, Brian. *The Vanishing American: White Attitudes and U.S. Indian Policy.* Middletown, CT: Wesleyan University Press, 1982.

Dunn, Dorothy. *American Indian Painting of the Southwest and Plains Areas.* Albuquerque: University of New Mexico Press, 1968.

————. "Pablita Velarde: Painter of Pueblo Life." *El Palacio* 59.11 (November 1952): 340.

————. "The Studio of Painting, Santa Fe Indian School." *El Palacio* 67.1 (Februrary 1960): 16–27.

Field, Matthew. "Tales of Santa Fe, 1839 (From the Files of the *New Orleans Daily Picayune*)." *El Palacio* 67.1 (February 1960): 1–15.

Fink, Augusta. *I-Mary: A Biography of Mary Austin.* Tucson: University of Arizona Press, 1983.

Fitzgerald, Edward, and John Bucholz. "The Jaramillo House." *New Mexico Architecture* 22.4 (July-August 1980): 9–15.

Forrest, Suzanne. *The Preservation of the Village: New Mexico's Hispanics and the New Deal.* Albuquerque: University of New Mexico Press, 1989.

Frank, Josette. *The Indian Girl: Her Social Heritage, Her Needs, and Her Opportunities.* Prepared by the Child Study Association of America at the request of the Commissioner of Indian Affairs, 1932.

Furman, Necah Stewart. "Women's Campaign for Equality: A National and State Perspective." *New Mexico Historical Review* 53.4 (October 1978): 365–74.

García, Mario T. *Mexican Americans: Leadership, Ideology, and Identity, 1930–1960.* New Haven: Yale University Press, 1989.

Gardner, Richard. *¡Grito!: Reies Tijerina and the New Mexico Land Grant*

War of 1967. Indianapolis: Bobbs-Merrill, 1970.

Goldman, Anne. "'I Yam What I Yam': Cooking, Culture, and Colonialism," in *De/Colonizing the Subject: The Politics of Gender in Women's Autobiography*, ed. Sidonie Smith and Julia Watson, 169–95. Minneapolis: University of Minnesota Press, 1992.

————. *Take My Word: Autobiographical Innovations of Ethnic American Working Women*. Berkeley: University of California Press, 1996.

Gómez-Quiñones, Juan. *Chicano Politics: Reality and Promise, 1940–1990*. Albuquerque: University of New Mexico Press, 1990.

————. *Roots of Chicano Politics, 1600–1940*. Albuquerque: University of New Mexico Press, 1994.

Gonzales, Deena J. *Refusing the Favor: The Spanish-Mexican Women of Santa Fe, 1820–1880*. New York: Oxford University Press, 1999.

Green, Rayna. *Native American Women: A Contextual Bibliography*. Bloomington: Indiana University Press, 1983.

Griffin, Joyce. "Life Is Harder Here: The Case of the Urban Navajo Woman." *American Indian Quarterly* 6.1, 6.2 (Spring/Summer 1982): 90–104.

Griswold del Castillo, Richard. *The Treaty of Guadalupe Hidalgo: A Legacy of Conflict*. Norman: University of Oklahoma Press, 1990.

Gutiérrez, David G. *Walls and Mirrors: Mexican Americans, Mexican Immigrants, and the Politics of Ethnicity*. Berkeley: University of California Press, 1995.

Gutiérrez, Ramón. *When Jesus Came, the Corn Mothers Went Away: Marriage, Sexuality, and Power in New Mexico, 1500–1846*. Stanford, CA: Stanford University Press, 1991.

Haas, Theodore H. *Ten Years of Tribal Government Under I.R.A.* Chicago: United States Indian Service, 1947.

Hahn, Emily. *Mabel: A Biography of Mabel Dodge Luhan*. Boston: Houghton Mifflin, 1977.

Hamamsy, Laila Shukry. "The Role of Women in a Changing Navajo Society." *American Anthropologist* 59.1 (February 1957): 101–11.

Hancock, D. "About Pablita and Her Legends." Preface to Pablita Velarde, *Old Father, the Story Teller*, 1st ed. Globe, AZ: Dale Stuart King, 1960.

Hansen, Niles, and Richard L. Nostrand. "Commentary: The Hispano Homeland in 1900; Comment in Reply." *Annals of the Association of American Geographers* 71.2 (June 1981): 280–83.

Hayden, Dolores. *The Grand Domestic Revolution: A History of Feminist Designs for American Homes, Neighborhoods, and Cities*. Cambridge, MA: MIT Press, 1981.

Heilbrun, Carolyn G. *Writing a Woman's Life*. New York: Ballantine Books, 1988.

Hill, W. W. *An Ethnography of Santa Clara Pueblo, New Mexico*. Edited and annotated by Charles H. Lane. Albuquerque: University of New Mexico Press, 1982.

"A History of Gallup's Inter-Tribal Indian Ceremonial." Church Rock, NM: Inter-Tribal Indian Ceremonial Association, n.d.

Hollinger, David. *Postethnic America: Beyond Multiculturalism*. New York: Basic Books, 1995.

Holmes, Jack E. *Politics in New Mexico.* Albuquerque: University of New Mexico Press, 1967.

Hyer, Sally. "'Our Way of Life Is Something We Are Proud Of' (1930–1945)." In *One House, One Voice, One Heart: Native American Education at the Santa Fe Indian School,* 29–57. Santa Fe: Museum of New Mexico Press, 1990.

————. "Pablita Velarde: The Pueblo Artist as Cultural Broker." *Between Indian and White Worlds: The Cultural Broker,* ed. Margaret Connell Szasz, 273–93. Norman: University of Oklahoma Press, 1994.

————. *"Woman's Work": The Art of Pablita Velarde.* Exhibition Catalog. Santa Fe: Wheelwright Museum of the American Indian, 1990.

Iverson, Peter. *Diné: A History of the Navajos.* Albuquerque: University of New Mexico Press, 2002.

————. *The Navajo Nation.* Westport, CT: Greenwood, 1981.

Jacobs, Margaret. "The Eastmans and the Luhans: Interracial Marriage between White Women and Native American Men, 1875–1935." *Frontiers* 23.3 (2002):29–54.

————. *Engendered Encounters: Feminism and Pueblo Cultures, 1879–1934.* Lincoln: University of Nebraska Press, 1999.

Jaehn, Tomas. "Concha Ortíz y Pino: Making History in Politics." *Women's Times* (Ketchum, ID), October/November 1994, 6.

Jensen, Carol. "Cleofas M. Jaramillo on Marriage in Territorial Northern New Mexico." *New Mexico Historical Review* 58.2. (April 1983): 153–71.

————. "Cleofas Jaramillo's View of Marriage: An Example of the Interplay of Folk Religion and Institutional Religion in Territorial Northern New Mexico." Master's thesis, Indiana University, 1981.

Jensen, Joan M. "Canning Comes to New Mexico: Women and the Agricultural Extension Service, 1914–1919." *New Mexico Historical Review* 57 (October 1982): 351–86. Repr. in *New Mexico Women: Intercultural Perspectives,* ed. Joan M. Jensen and Darlis A. Miller, 201–26. Albuquerque: University of New Mexico Press, 1984.

————. "Crossing Ethnic Barriers in the Southwest: Women's Agricultural Extension Education, 1914–1940." *Agricultural History* 60 (Spring 1986): 169–81.

————. "'Disenfranchisement is a Disgrace': Women and Politics in New Mexico, 1900–1940." *New Mexico Historical Review* 56.1 (January 1981): 5–36. Repr. in *New Mexico Women: Intercultural Perspectives,* ed. Joan M. Jensen and Darlis A. Miller, 310–31. Albuquerque: University of New Mexico Press, 1984.

————. "'I've Worked, I'm Not Afraid of Work': Farm Women in New Mexico, 1920–1940." In *New Mexico Women: Intercultural Perspectives,* ed. Joan M. Jensen and Darlis A. Miller, 227–55. Albuquerque: University of New Mexico Press, 1984.

Jensen, Joan M., and Darlis A. Miller, eds. *New Mexico Women: Intercultural Perspectives.* Albuquerque: University of New Mexico Press, 1984.

"Kay C. Bennett." In *Reference Encyclopedia of the American Indian,* 5th ed, ed. Barry T. Klein, 766. West Nyack, NY: Todd Publications, 1990.

Kelly, Lawrence. *Navajo Roundup: Selected Correspondence of Kit Carson's Expedition Against the Navajo, 1863–1865.* Boulder, CO: Pruett, 1970.

❧ BIBLIOGRAPHY ❧

Kluckhohn, Clyde, and Dorothea Leighton. *The Navaho.* 1962. Rev. ed,
 Cambridge, MA: Harvard University Press, 1974.
LaDuke, Betty. *Women Artists: Multicultural Visions.* Trenton, NJ: Red Sea
 Press, 1992.
Lagemann, Ellen Condliffe. *A Generation of Women: Education in the Lives of
 Progressive Reformers.* Cambridge, MA: Harvard University Press, 1979.
Lamar, Howard Roberts. *The Far Southwest, 1846–1912: A Territorial
 History.* 1966; New York: Norton, 1970.
Lamphere, Louise. "Strategies, Cooperation, and Conflict Among Women in
 Domestic Groups." In *Women, Culture, and Society,* ed. Michelle
 Zimbalist Rosaldo and Louise Lamphere, 97–112. Stanford, CA: Stanford
 University Press, 1974.
Langlois, Karen S. "Mary Austin and Lincoln Steffens." *Huntington Library
 Quarterly* 49 (Autumn 1986): 357–82.
Lanigan, Esther F [Esther Lanigan Stineman]. *Mary Austin: Song of a
 Maverick.* New Haven, CT: Yale University Press, 1989.
Leighton, Dorothea C. "As I Knew Them: Navajo Women in 1940."
 American Indian Quarterly 6.1–6.2 (Spring/Summer 1982): 34–51.
Lux, Guillermo. *Politics and Education in Hispanic New Mexico: From the
 Spanish American Normal School to the Northern New Mexico Community
 College.* El Rito, NM: Northern New Mexico Community College, 1984.
MacKinnon, Catherine A. "Whose Culture? A Case Note on *Martinez v. Santa
 Clara Pueblo.*" In *Feminism Unmodified: Discourses on Life and Law,*
 63–69. Cambridge, MA: Harvard University Press, 1987.
Márquez, Benjamin. *LULAC: The Evolution of a Mexican American Political
 Organization.* Austin: University of Texas Press, 1993.
McCool, Daniel. "Indian Voting." In *American Indian Policy in the Twentieth
 Century,* ed. Vine Deloria, Jr. Norman. University of Oklahoma Press, 1985.
McShane, Becky Jo Gesteland. "In Pursuit of Regional and Cultural Identity:
 The Autobiographies of Agnes Morley Cleaveland and Fabiola Cabeza de
 Baca." In *Breaking Boundaries: New Perspectives on Women's Regional
 Writing,* ed. Sherrie A. Inness and Diana Royer, 180–96. Iowa City:
 University of Iowa Press, 1997.
Meier, Matt S., and Feliciano Ribera. *The Chicanos: A History of Mexican
 Americans.* New York: Hill and Wang, 1972.
Melnick, Ralph. *Justice Betrayed: A Double Killing in Old Santa Fe.*
 Albuquerque: University of New Mexico Press, 2002.
Meriam, Lewis, et al. *The Problem of Indian Administration: Report of a
 Survey Made at the Request of Honorable Hubert Work, Secretary of the
 Interior, and Submitted to Him, February 21, 1928.* Baltimore: Johns
 Hopkins Press, 1928.
Metcalf, Ann. "From Schoolgirl to Mother: The Effects of Education on
 Navajo Women." *Social Problems* 23.5 (June 1976): 535–44.
Miller, Ronald Dean. *Paul Bailey and the Westernlore Press: The First Forty Years—
 With Annotated Bibliography.* Morongo Valley, CA: Sagebrush, 1984.
Montejano, David. *Anglos and Mexicans and the Making of Texas.* Austin:
 University of Texas Press, 1987.
Montgomery, Charles. "The Trap of Race and Memory: The Language of

⬙ BIBLIOGRAPHY ⬙

Spanish Civility on the Upper Rio Grande." *American Quarterly* 52.3 (September 2000): 478–513.

Mullin, Molly. *Culture in the Marketplace: Gender, Art, and Value in the American Southwest.* Durham, NC: Duke University Press, 2001.

Nabokov, Peter. *Tijerina and the Courthouse Raid.* Albuquerque: University of New Mexico Press, 1969.

Nelson, Mary Carroll. *Pablita Velarde: The Story of an American Indian.* Minneapolis: Dillon Press, 1971.

Niethammer, Carolyn. *I'll Go and Do More: Annie Dodge Wauneka: Navajo Leader and Activist.* Lincoln: University of Nebraska Press, 2001.

Norwood, Vera, and Janice Monk, eds. *The Desert Is No Lady: Southwestern Landscapes in Women's Writing and Art.* Tucson: University of Arizona Press, 1987.

Nostrand, Richard L. "Hispano Cultural Distinctiveness: A Reply." *Annals of the Association of American Geographers* 74.1. (March 1984): 164–69.

————. "The Hispano Homeland in 1900." *Annals of the Association of American Geographers* 70.3. (September 1980): 382–96

Orozco, Cynthia E. "The Origins of the League of United Latin American Citizens (LULAC) and the Mexican American Civil Rights Movement in Texas with an Analysis of Women's Political Participation in a Gendered Context, 1910–1929." Ph.D. diss., University of California at Los Angeles, 1992.

————. "Regionalism, Politics, and Gender in Southwest History: The League of United Latin American Citizens' Expansion into New Mexico from Texas, 1929–1945." *Western Historical Quarterly* 29.4 (Winter 1998): 459–83.

Ortíz, Roxanne Dunbar. *Roots of Resistance: Land Tenure in New Mexico, 1680–1980.* Los Angeles: Chicano Studies Research Center and American Indian Studies Center, University of California, 1980.

Otero, Nina. *Old Spain in Our Southwest.* New York: Harcourt, Brace, and Co., 1936.

Padilla, Genaro M. "Imprisoned Narrative? Or Lies, Secrets and Silence in New Mexico Women's Autobiography." In *Criticism in the Borderlands: Studies in Chicano Literature, Culture, and Ideology,* ed. Hector Calderón and José David Saldívar, 43–60. Durham, NC: Duke University Press, 1991.

————. *My History, Not Yours: The Formation of Mexican American Autobiography.* Madison: University of Wisconsin Press, 1993.

Paredes, Raymond A. "The Evolution of Chicano Literature." In *Three American Literatures,* ed. Houston A. Baker, Jr., 33–79. New York: Modern Language Association, 1982.

Parker, Dorothy R. *Phoenix Indian School: The Second Half-Century.* Tucson: University of Arizona Press, 1996.

Parman, Donald L. *The Navajos and the New Deal.* New Haven: Yale University Press, 1976.

Parsons, Elsie Clews. "The Pueblo Indian Clan in Folk-Lore." *Journal of American Folklore* 34 (April-June 1921): 209–16.

————. *Pueblo Indian Religion.* Chicago: University. of Chicago Press, 1939.

Pascoe, Peggy. "Miscegenation Law, Court Cases, and Ideologies of 'Race' in Twentieth-Century America." In *Sex, Love, Race: Crossing Boundaries in North American History,* ed. Martha Hodes, 464–90.

New York: New York University Press, 1999.

Pearce, T. M. *Literary America, 1903–1934: The Letters of Mary Austin.* Westport, CT: Greenwood Press, 1979.

————. *New Mexico Place Names: A Geographical Dictionary.* Albuquerque: University of New Mexico Press, 1965.

————. Review of *We Fed Them Cactus*, by Fabiola Cabeza de Baca. *New Mexico Historical Review* 31.1 (January 1956): 78–79.

Perrigo, Lynn I. *Hispanos: Historic Leaders in New Mexico.* Santa Fe: Sunstone, 1985.

Pieper, Susan. "Fabiola's Good Life." *New Mexico Resources* (Magazine of the College of Agriculture and Home Economics, New Mexico State University) 8 (Spring 1995): 3–11.

Ponce, Merrihelen. "The Life and Works of Fabiola Cabeza de Baca, New Mexican Hispanic Women Writer: A Contextual Biography." Ph.D. diss., University of New Mexico, 1995.

Poythress, Stephanie. "Fabiola Cabeza de Baca Gilbert." In *Notable Hispanic American Women*, ed. Diane Telgen and Jim Kamp. 178–79. Detroit: Gale Research, 1993.

Proctor, Bernadette D. and Joseph Dalaker. *Poverty in the United States: 2002.* U.S. Census Bureau, September 2003.

Rebolledo, Tey Diana. Introduction to Cleofas Jaramillo, *Romance of a Little Village Girl* (1955), xv–xxvii. Albuquerque: University of New Mexico Press, 2000.

————. Introduction to Fabiola Cabeza de Baca, *We Fed Them Cactus* (1954), xiii–xxxii. Albuquerque: University of New Mexico Press, 1994.

————. "Las Escritoras: Romances and Realities." In *Pasó Por Aquí: Critical Essays on the New Mexican Literary Tradition, 1542–1988*, ed. Erlinda Gonzales-Berry, 199–214. Albuquerque: University of New Mexico Press, 1989.

————. "Narrative Strategies of Resistance in Hispana Writing." *Journal of Narrative Technique* 20.2 (Spring 1990): 134–46.

————. "Tradition and Mythology: Signatures of Landscape in Chicana Literature." In *The Desert Is No Lady: Southwestern Landscapes in Women's Writing and Art*, ed. Vera Norwood and Janice Monk, 96–124. Tucson: University of Arizona Press, 1987.

Reichard, Gladys. *Spider Woman: A Story of Navajo Weavers and Chanters.* New York: Macmillan, 1934.

Reisner, Marc. *Cadillac Desert: The American West and Its Disappearing Water.* New York: Viking, 1986.

Rodríguez, Sylvia. "Land, Water, and Ethnic Identity in Taos," In *Land, Water, and Culture: New Perspectives on Hispanic Land Grants*, ed. Charles L. Briggs and John R. Van Ness, 313–403. Albuquerque: University of New Mexico Press, 1987.

Roessel, Ruth. "Navajo History and Culture II (Growth of the Navajos to 1960)." In *Navajo Studies at Navajo Community College*, ed. Ruth Roessel, 19–41. Many Farms, AZ: Navajo Community College Press, 1971.

————. *Women in Navajo Society* (Rough Rock, AZ: Navajo Resource Center, 1981.

Roessel, Ruth, and Broderick H. Johnson, eds. *Navajo Livestock Reduction: A National Disgrace*. Chinle, AZ: Navajo Community College Press, 1976.

Rosaldo, Renato. "Imperialist Nostalgia." *Representations* 26 (Spring 1989): 107–22.

Rothfork, John. Review of *We Fed Them Cactus*, by Fabiola Cabeza de Baca. *New Mexico Historical Review* 55.2 (April 1980): 180–81.

Rowlandson, Mary. *The Sovereignty & Goodness of God*. 1682; Boston: Bedford Books, 1997.

Ruch, Marcella. *Pablita Velarde: Painting Her People*. Albuquerque: *New Mexico Magazine*, 2001.

Rudnick, Lois Palken. *Mabel Dodge Luhan: New Woman, New Worlds*. Albuquerque: University of New Mexico Press, 1984.

————. "Re-Naming the Land: Anglo Expatriate Women in the Southwest." In *The Desert Is No Lady: Southwestern Landscapes in Women's Writing and Art*, ed. Vera Norwood and Janice Monk, 10–26. Tucson: University of Arizona Press, 1987.

————. *Utopian Vistas: The Mabel Dodge Luhan House and the American Counterculture*. Albuquerque: University of New Mexico Press, 1996.

Rushing, W. Jackson. "Modern by Tradition: The 'Studio Style' of Native American Painting." In Bruce Bernstein and W. Jackson Rushing, *Modern by Tradition: American Indian Painting in the Studio Style*, 27–73. Santa Fe: Museum of New Mexico Press, 1995.

————. *Native American Art and the New York Avant Garde: A History of Cultural Primitivism*. Austin: University of Texas Press, 1995.

Sánchez, George I. *Forgotten People: A Study of New Mexicans*. 1940; Albuquerque: Calvin Horn, Publisher, 1967.

Schackel, Sandra. *Social Housekeepers: Women Shaping Public Policy in New Mexico, 1920–1940*. Albuquerque: University of New Mexico Press, 1992.

Scharff, Virginia. "'So Many Miles to a Person': Fabiola Cabeza de Baca Makes New Mexico." In *Twenty Thousand Roads: Women, Movement, and the West*. Berkeley: University of California Press, 2003.

Scott, Jay. *Changing Woman: The Life and Art of Helen Hardin*. Flagstaff, AZ: Northland Publishing, 1989.

Sekaquaptewa, Helen. *Me and Mine: The Life Story of Helen Sekaquaptewa*. Edited by Louise Udall. Tucson: University of Arizona Press, 1969.

Shepardson, Mary. "The Gender Status of Navajo Women." In *Women and Power in Native North America*, ed. Lara F. Klein and Lillian A. Ackerman, 159–176. Norman: University of Oklahoma Press, 1995.

————. "The Status of Navajo Women." *American Indian Quarterly* 6.1, 6.2 (Spring/Summer 1982): 149–69.

Simmons, Marc, Fray Angélico Chávez, D. W. Meinig, and Thomas D. Hall. "Rejoinders." *Annals of the Association of American Geographers* 74.1 (March 1984): 169–71.

Sklar, Kathryn Kish. "Hull House in the 1890s: A Community of Women Reformers." *Signs: Journal of Women in Culture and Society* 10.4 (Summer 1985): 658–77.

Szabo, Joyce M. Introduction to Marcella Ruch, *Pablita Velarde: Painting Her People*. Albuquerque: *New Mexico Magazine*, 2001.

Szasz, Margaret. *Education and the American Indian: The Road to Self-Determination,* 1928–1973. Albuquerque: University of New Mexico Press.

Trimberger, Ellen Kay. "The New Woman and the New Sexuality: Conflict and Contradiction in the Writings and Lives of Mabel Dodge and Neith Boyce." In 1915, *The Cultural Moment: The New Politics, the New Woman, the New Psychology, the New Art, and the New Theatre in America,* ed. Adele Heller and Lois Rudnick, 98–115. New Brunswick, NJ: Rutgers University Press, 1991.

Twitchell, Ralph Emerson. *The History of the Military Occupation of the Territory of New Mexico From 1846 to 1851, By the Government of the United States.* Denver: Smith-Brooks, 1909.

U.S. Census Bureau. *Profiles of General Demographic Characteristics,* 2000 *Census of Population and Housing: New Mexico.* May 2001.

U.S. Dept. of the Interior. *The Navajo: A Long Range Program for Navajo Rehabilitation.* Report of J. A. Krug, Secretary of the Interior. Washington, D.C.: Government Printing Office, 1948.

Underhill, Ruth M. *The Navajos.* Norman: University of Oklahoma Press, 1956.

Waltrip, Lela. "Kay Bennett: A Versatile Navajo Woman." *Southwest Heritage* 11.4 (Winter 1981–1982): 10–13, 28.

Waltrip, Lela, and Rufus Waltrip. *Indian Women: Thirteen Who Played a Part in the History of America from Earliest Days to Now.* New York: David McKay, 1964.

Waters, Frank. *Of Time and Change: A Memoir.* Denver: MacMurray and Beck, 1998.

Weber, David J. "'Scarce More Than Apes': Historical Roots of Anglo American Stereotypes of Mexicans in the Border Region." In *New Spain's Far Northern Frontier,* ed. David J. Weber, 293–307. Albuquerque: University of New Mexico Press, 1979.

Weigle, Marta, and Kyle Fiore. *Santa Fe and Taos: The Writer's Era,* 1916–1941. Santa Fe: Ancient City Press, 1984.

Whaley, Charlotte. *Nina Otero-Warren of Santa Fe.* Albuquerque: University of New Mexico Press, 1994.

White, Richard. *"It's Your Misfortune and None of My Own": A History of the American West.* Norman: University of Oklahoma Press, 1991.

Wilson, Chris. *The Myth of Santa Fe: Creating a Modern Regional Tradition.* Albuquerque: University of New Mexico Press, 1997.

Wright, James E., and Sarah A. Rosenberg. *The Great Plains Experience: Readings in the History of a Region.* Lincoln, NE: University of Mid-America Press, 1978.

Young, Robert W. *A Political History of the Navajo Tribe.* Tsaile, AZ: Navajo Community College Press, 1978.

INDEX

Page numbers in italics indicate illustrations.

☙ INDEX ☙

◄ INDEX ►

◈ INDEX ◈